Roots and Routes of
Displacement and Trauma

# ROOTS AND ROUTES
# OF DISPLACEMENT
# AND TRAUMA

## *From Analysis to Advocacy and Policy to Practice*

EDITED BY

Soheila Pashang and Sheila Gruner

**Rock's Mills Press**

Oakville, Ontario

PUBLISHED BY

**Rock's Mills Press**

www.rocksmillspress.com

Copyright © 2015 by Soheila Pashang and Sheila Gruner
ALL RIGHTS RESERVED
*Copyright in individual chapters is held by the authors.*

Library and Archives Canada Cataloguing in Publication is available from the
publisher. Email Rock's Mills Press at customer.service@rocksmillspress.com.

Cover artwork by Fery Pashang

First Edition
ISBN-13: 978-0-9881293-4-4

# Contents

# Contents

# Preface

This book *Roots and Routes of Displacement and Trauma: From Analysis to Advocacy and Policy to Practice* is one of the first peer-reviewed Canadian scholarly edited collections to interrogate the social, political and economic contexts of forced displacement in relation to its traumatic outcomes. It explores the lived conditions and experiences of trauma among the forcibly displaced, refugees and migrants, those who are uprooted from their places of origin, tracing journeys of transition to sites of arrival. This collection brings together scholars, activists, professionals and practitioners from interdisciplinary fields and backgrounds, who are concerned with critical, decolonizing and social justice approaches, and committed to addressing issues of displacement and trauma affecting Indigenous people, refugees, displaced persons, migrants, and asylum-seekers in Canada. The collection commits to transformative praxis, challenging colonial, capitalist and globalized oppressive systems and practices that underpin displacement, and stressing the expressions of resistance, resilience and solidarity in the face of dispossession. These include people exposed to racism, war, armed conflict, gender violence, health and economic disparities, stigma against people living with HIV/AIDS, homophobia, violation of sexual rights and poverty, among many other forms of oppression and violence.

The goal of the collection is to foster a critical analysis of the determinants and contexts of displacement as readers consider, strategize and advocate alongside people and communities to address the lasting health and development effects of forced displacement. Emphasis is placed on the resilience and strengths of migrants and the displaced, and the necessity of a social justice framing among students, allies and practitioners in organizations that work with affected groups. The collection encourages learning about what it means for people to adapt in the face of their new lived realities while challenging oppression, and being inspired to embrace the possibilities encountered as people work to move on with their lives. We are convinced that this meaningful and unique contribution will enhance the fields of social work, health, community development, community and refugee health, Indigenous studies, migration studies, international development and equity studies, among other disciplines.

SOHEILA PASHANG AND SHEILA GRUNER

# Introduction

## Soheila Pashang and Sheila Gruner

In his book the *Wretched of the Earth,* Frantz Fanon describes the world as being divided into two opposing zones: a white colonizer/settler zone — the developed nations or global north, highly protected and securitized; and the colonized/native zone — the developing nations or global south, exploited by means of violence, genocide and subjugation. Colonizers, Fanon argues, owe their power, indeed their very existence, to the colonial system. Colonization is achieved and maintained by the destruction of local communities' power, self-determination and economic independence, as well as the dispossession of their natural resources.

The process of colonization is marked by Europeans' "discovery" of the world, that is, through the slavery and exploitation of indigenous peoples and the extraction of their natural resources, processes which have led to these peoples' systematic displacement, to health and economic disparities, to the destruction of diverse ways of life, and to the degradation of the environment. This, along with continued violence and discrimination, has made a deep impact on indigenous peoples and has been the source of intergenerational trauma. Nonetheless, communities and their allies have resisted colonization, have strived to maintain ways of life, forms of nationhood and governance, and avidly worked to strengthen autonomy and self-determination.

Fanon views decolonization as an ahistorical process, a meeting of two forces in contradiction by their very nature. Those forces may no longer exist in their original form; the slave trade, once integral to the colonial system, has given way to a new system — globalized, neo-liberal capitalism — but the intention and strategies remain the same: to exploit indigenous labour power and extract those people's resources. Theories of decolonization therefore must situate displaced people and migrants in relation to historical forces and socially and politically constructed policies, laws and practices that continue to displace people worldwide. Such exploitation, historically grounded but continuing today, is made possible through trade agreements, restrictive border control policies, immigration reform and, more importantly, through the imperialist militarization of the world.

Meanwhile, racialization, sexual and gender discrimination, underdevelopment, poverty, inequity, vulnerability as a result of both intrastate and interstate armed conflicts, gender violence and poor health have increased tension, levels of displacement, and forced migration in developing nations. The result is to further increase economic dependency and the influence of capitalist forces through such initiatives as trade agreements and development projects. This vicious cycle of oppression means there are now 51 million "Forcibly Displaced Individuals," the highest number since World War II (UNHCR Global Trends Reports, 2013). Forcibly displaced individuals are those who, because of persecution, conflict, generalized violence or human rights violations, are forced to leave their homes.

Furthermore, the United States is known to host over 12 million "illegalized" persons who live and work without legal immigration visas. Unofficial reports estimate that nearly one million "illegalized" persons live and work in Canada. According to the United Nations (2013), there are also an estimated 10 million "stateless" people worldwide — people with no legal citizenship to bind them to any state. Stateless peoples are denied their human rights and opportunity to realize their full potential. Multiple generations may spend many years in refugee camps or detention centres, or live with precarious immigration status in various countries across the globe.

Despite the general misconception that assumes refugees and displaced persons are a burden on the economies of western nations such as Canada, it is poor and developing nations that host 86% of the world's refugees and displaced persons. Western states use anti-immigrant rhetoric in order to avoid fulfilling their international obligations to protect people in need of asylum. Canada, for example, has adopted discriminatory immigration policies that prevent individual refugees in need of protection from entering the country. Instead, Canada has taken measures to increase its use of what amounts to "disposable" labour power through the issuing of temporary visas and programs such as the Temporary Migrant Workers Program, even though participants in these programs often face precarious and dehumanizing working conditions, living and working under deplorable conditions in farms, factories and within the isolated bounds of people's homes.

The present volume, a collection of chapters by experts in the field, takes the reader beyond seeing migrants or those who have been displaced solely as "victims" or "survivors," and further challenges conditions that perpetuate such vulnerability, such as large-scale capitalist development, globalized trade, restrictive immigration and border control policies, neo-liberal and discriminatory programming, and individualistic and diagnostic frameworks in professional practice. The book challenges the tendency to dismiss the resilience of those who remain in their home countries or decide (or are forced) to move. In an era of global tensions with violence on the rise and human rights responses to such violence all too scarce, such perspectives are necessary.

Our aim in editing *Roots and Routes of Displacement and Trauma: From Analysis to Advocacy and Policy to Practice* is to contribute to the fostering of a theoretical and practice-oriented approach — one that links analysis of the political and economic contexts and determinants of human displacement, to the experiences of (and approaches to addressing) trauma among those affected directly by displacement. We want to encourage students to think about the conditions that allow for the continued systematic displacement of the world's most marginalized people, and let such an understanding inform their professional practice.

A critical theoretical approach encourages students and practitioners to grapple with the historical determinants of displacement; to address the ethical, political, material, psychological, and related challenges facing Indigenous and immigrant/refugee communities who have experienced both individual and collective trauma related to their systematic displacement while living within the present-day national borders of Canada; and to recognize the agency of displaced peoples, rather than focusing only on their victimization. This perspective requires students and practitioners to see displacement and trauma as affecting individuals, collectivities and the broader society, as well as being reflective of, and rooted in, structural inequities. This perspective also most certainly requires disciplined study and determined political commitment to transforming dominant power relations.

An important consideration relates to the cultural, linguistic, political-territorial and economic realities of First Nation communities. This subject should be examined in parallel with the experiences of those arriving from elsewhere around the world who also face systematic attempts at erasure and dispossession, stemming from similar histories of colonialism and capitalist social relations. We also examine ongoing forms of displacement inherited by new generations of First Nations peoples, who live with, contest and reshape the outcomes of the colonial legacy on their own terms.

The diverse topics covered in this book will first be grounded in a theoretical approach and exploration of the root causes of displacement and migration. The book consists of seventeen chapters organized in three sections.

The first section, *Roots and Routes: Contexts of Displacement,* establishes the contexts of, and relationships among, colonialism, globalization and imperialism, including the ways in which they perpetuate violence and vulnerability, and attempt to subvert Indigenous and other forms of being on the planet.

In Chapter One, Sheila Gruner offers an introduction to terms, concepts and theoretical approaches to the problem of displacement, grounded in a critique of colonialism and capitalist development. Gruner encourages readers to grapple with literature on decolonization and "decolonizing" thought and practice, with the goal of envisioning historically informed, alternative forms of development, as a means of addressing displacement and the diverse forms of violence and displacement experienced by Indigenous people, refugees, migrants, stateless people and others.

Chapter Two by Rebecca Beaulne-Stuebing first considers the enduring story of this continent long before it was colonized, exploring essential components of the Indigenous worldview and history. Colonialism, Eurocentrism, and cognitive and cultural imperialism are examined in the Canadian context of forced displacement and removal of Indigenous communities, the history of treaty-making, the *Indian Act*, and the residential school system. The lasting intergenerational traumas imposed by physical and cultural displacement continue to affect Indigenous nations. Profound social, political and educational movements for healing and change have sought to restore and renew, proposing meaningful alternatives rooted in Indigenous worldview and life ways.

The third chapter, by Sepehr Pashang, examines the impact of environmental disasters and climate change on human displacement and migration. Pashang shows that nations in the global north, such as Canada, are not only major emitters of greenhouse gases into the atmosphere, but are also enablers of anti-asylum and xenophobic policies, when considering applications from migrants and refugees impacted by environmental events. In order to effectively legitimize the field and to address environmentally induced migration, Pashang argues that agreed-upon definitions, constructive policies, and international commitments are imperative to accommodate the needs of impacted individuals and communities.

The fourth chapter, by Neil Cruickshank, is animated by a political-sociological framework. It examines issues of import to European Roma (and non-Roma), and to Roma seeking asylum in Canada. The issues discussed include statelessness, nationhood (and nationalism), transnationalism and migration, and the overarching condition experienced by nearly all European Roma, marginalization. This chapter also looks at the reasons for continuing and endemic rates of social exclusion, political disenfranchisement and poverty among Roma. Focusing on Canada's new Immigration and Refugee Protection Act, which includes a controversial "safe country" clause, the discussion turns to how the ongoing and widespread stereotyping of Roma may be behind the decision by Canadian lawmakers to deny Roma entry and subsequently deport those already in Canada seeking refuge.

In the fifth chapter, Jennifer Clarke and Soheila Pashang draw upon the critical perspectives of anti-oppression, anti-colonialism, and critical race feminism to address the issue of HIV/AIDS in Africa. The authors argue that HIV/AIDS is rooted in colonialism and oppressive patriarchal and racist structures that impose violence, war, armed conflicts and displacement upon Africans, as well as laws, policies and practices that criminalize and discriminate against Indigenous and racialized women and children, MSM, LGBTQ and Transgendered individuals. HIV/AIDS trauma is exacerbated by a socially and morally constructed discourse of stigma, which subjects HIV-positive individuals and their families to violence, abuse, discrimination, exclusion and the denial of protection and human rights. The authors also examine the impact and manifestation of "that thing" — the stigma of HIV/AIDS — on women and children who are disproportionately affected by the disease, and the grandmothers who care for them.

Chapter Six, by Edgar Godoy, examines resistance by the Mayan community in Guatemala to large-scale mining projects carried out by Canadian firms such as the former Inco and by Goldcorp. Such projects threaten both the environment and traditional ways of life. Godoy shows how Mayan leaders have secured support from international allies, including environmental and labour groups, in their opposition to a development agenda being forced upon them not only by foreign mining companies but by the Guatemalan government itself.

Chapter Seven, by Ezat Mossallanejad, examines the prevalence of war and internal conflicts as well as the authoritarian nature of modern states that has led to the mass exodus of millions of refugees and displaced people – 80% of them women and children. These survivors of war live a protracted, sub-human life in camps and urban areas with inadequate protection. Aside from deplorable living conditions and violence, bipolarization of society, and depopulation, war and displacement also cause individual and collective trauma. Survivors of war suffer from what is known as post-traumatic stress disorder (PTSD) in western psychology. It is important to understand both the symptoms of PTSD, and its limitation as a diagnosis, as a starting point for the treatment of survivors. Mossallanejad draws on his professional experiences working at the Canadian Centre for Victims of Torture (CCVT) and endorses the effectiveness of the holistic method of rehabilitation with the direct involvement of the community as well as survivors themselves.

The second section of the book, *Politics of Displacement and Migration*, traces the "routes" of displacement and migration, and the experiences of people who take these challenging journeys.

Chapter Eight, by Sajedeh Zahraei, uses the lens of gender to highlight some of the experiences of Iraqi refugee women displaced within the context of the "war on terror." Zahraei provides a theoretical framework for understanding refugee women's trauma that builds on models of structural violence, historical trauma and multi-level colonial trauma response theory. The discourse of medical pathology is critiqued along with de-politicized and de-historicized conceptualizations of refugee women's trauma. Instead, the focus should be on the interconnections between these women's historical and contemporary experiences of trauma. Zahraei illustrates the complex and multi-layered aspects of trauma that are shaped by social and political contexts, recognizing the strength, resilience and agency of refugee women.

In Chapter Nine, Sharifa Sharif talks about foreign military and imperialist invasions of Afghanistan that have provoked military nationalism and fostered patriarchal gender inequality, domesticized gender roles, and various forms of displacement. For decades, Afghan women have experienced violence through oppressive family and social practices in the name of nationalism and religion. Violence against Afghan women has affected them individually and collectively, both in war and peace. Their trauma is multilayered and their responses complex, shaped by their struggles for their own survival and that of their communities. Coping strategies for women are shaped collectively and in solidarity with other women-victims in the context of sacrifice, resilience, and survival, most of this occurring in the absence of support by governments and other authorities.

In the tenth chapter, Soheila Pashang examines the politics of death in relation to immigrants, refugees and asylum seekers, and challenges practitioners to move away from multicultural and cultural competency approaches to professional practice in working with bereaved immigrant families, both in the diaspora and in their country of origin. This underexplored topic must be understood within the context of the expansion of global inequities brought about by colonization and globalized capitalism, which has perpetuated armed conflicts, poverty, violence and health disparities. The death of migrants in the host country precipitates a set of complex and discursive struggles between Canadian institutions, international law, and the law of the immigrant's homeland. This complexity is exacerbated by the lack of appropriate support to overcome the trauma of bereavement in exile. Pashang emphasizes the role of professionals in assisting immigrants, refugees and asylum-seekers, drawing on equity, social justice and anti-oppressive theoretical approaches.

Chapter Eleven, by Angie Arora, Ezat Mossallanejad and Rubaiyat Karim, uses an anti-oppression framework to situate people's lived experiences of trauma in the context of larger systemic barriers and inequities. More specifically, the authors use the term "life in limbo" to explore the ways in which immigrants and refugees are victimized through pre-migratory traumas such as war and armed conflict, again during flight and transition, as well as being re-victimized through post-migratory trauma caused by Canada's immigration policies. The authors consider "limbo" a form of modern-day torture. To contextualize this reality, they critique the existing medical frameworks that characterize the experience of trauma as an individual inability to cope in the context of pathology or as culturalized discourse. As an alternative, the authors explore an anti-oppression framework in order to help practitioners and organizations to situate their clients' lived experiences in the context of oppression and marginalization.

Tania Das Gupta examines the experience and meaning of paid work for migrants and immigrants in Chapter Twelve. Precarious work includes work carried out by migrant and immigrant women and undocumented workers, within a framework of capitalist globalization. Das Gupta argues that an insecure relationship with the state as exemplified through one's migration and/or (lack of) citizenship status, and the resultant racialization as the "other," contribute to "employment trauma" and "job trauma," concepts that can help explain how one's precarious place in the labour market (such as uncertainty around the relationship with one's employer) can cause trauma and lack of well-being.

The third section of the book, *Action, Policy and Practice,* examines activism, policy and practice, as approaches to addressing the needs of as well as the barriers and challenges facing those affected by displacement. Included are issues in the post-migration lives of immigrants and refugees, or, in the case of Indigenous people, of ongoing or "post-displacement" within Canada, with an emphasis on activists' and professionals' resistance, advocacy efforts, and creative initiatives to address the unjust and discriminatory conditions people have experienced, through public awareness and consciousness-raising, arts-informed and archival work.

In Chapter Thirteen, Donald Payne addresses ethical issues related to working with refugees. Payne argues that ethical issues repeatedly intersect with the lives of refugees. International ethical conventions and declarations provide some protection, but they are open to interpretation by governments, often in a way that detracts from the standards' intent to provide protection. Governments all too often regard accepting refugees as an act of charity rather than an obligation under international law. The 2012 changes in Canada's immigration policy have raised serious ethical concerns, as do new approaches to provision of health care to refugees. Practitioners need to be aware of ethical issues in dealing with refugee clients, including issues of culture, confidentiality, use of interpreters, pathologizing normal responses to stress, maintaining appropriate boundaries and being aware of their own emotional responses to clients.

In Chapter Fourteen, Doug Gruner, Janet Cleveland, Laïla Demirdache and Kevin Pottie examine issues of access to health care in Canada by refugees, and outline advocacy efforts by health care practitioners across Canada in the face of recent program cuts, which put the lives of refugees at risk, cost taxpayers more money and threaten public health. In response to the cuts, the organization Canadian Doctors for Refugee Care (CDRC) was formed in order to document cases where refugees are being adversely affected, and to inform the public about these cases. CDRC argues that refugees, especially in their first years in Canada, require timely access to quality health care. It is imperative that refugees be able to access primary and preventative health care to ensure that health conditions are identified early and treated, protecting public health as well as the health of the refugee. This chapter traces key moments, gains, policy changes and remaining challenges in the ongoing advocacy efforts to secure adequate health care access for refugees.

Chapter Fifteen by Annette Bailey, Jennifer Clarke, and Bukola Salami interrogates the contexts of colonization, neo-colonial relations, and forced migration, which continue to structure Black mothers' exposure to gun-violence loss and shape their access to valuable grief and trauma supports. Race-based stigma, which is rooted in colonial discourses, dominates Black mothers' surviving experiences, creating social and psychological complexities that implicate their access to services and supports. Their resulting trauma is debilitating and persisting. Their psychological trauma is made more complex by denial of victim compensation, multiple job losses, negative social interactions, and witnessing the devastating social, educational and economic impact of gun-violence loss on their remaining children. The authors advocate that policy-makers and service providers endeavour to make decisions and shape policies and practices that make grief and trauma support equitable and accessible for Black mothers and other survivors of gun violence.

In Chapter Sixteen, Jonathan Dewar explores the history of Indian Residential Schools in relation to the cultural and physical displacement of First Nation and

Métis people, as well as the efforts of Survivors to respond to the trauma they experienced. Dewar places emphasis on the important role the collection and sharing of Residential School photographs, records, and artefacts has played within the healing movement. He examines concepts such as the "profound silences" around Residential School history, and considers recent efforts to reveal the truth of both the policy of assimilation and the experiences of former students, through the role of art and literature, particularly the "Survivor memoir."

Chapter Seventeen, by Bethany Osborne, explores arts-based approaches to working with people who have experienced violence. In particular, Osborne focuses on the impact of violence on the individual and on the broader communities that they belong to. Drawing on work being done around the world, with a particular focus on Canada and Aboriginal people, this chapter examines how art can be used to support people who have experienced violence, with the goal of recovery from trauma. This chapter also examines various coping and healing strategies, including arts-based approaches to empowering individuals and communities who have been impacted by violence. The chapter concludes by providing ideas and practical resources for facilitating creative empowerment support groups.

We are convinced that this unique collection will enhance the fields of social work, health, community development, community and refugee health, Indigenous studies, migration studies, and international development, among other disciplines.

## References

Fanon, F. (1963). *The wretched of the earth*. New York: Grove Press.

UNHCR Global Trends (2013). Retrieved from https://www.documentcloud.org/documents/1201940-unhcr-global-trends-report-2013.html.

# Acknowledgements

The idea behind this edited collection was conceived a few years ago while struggling to locate Canadian scholarly works on the topic of displacement, migration and trauma for college and university students. We found a major gap in the existing literature where politics, theory and policy interact, challenge and inform professional practice when working with immigrants, refugees and asylum seekers experiencing trauma.

Both of the editors have had extensive fieldwork experience, academic background in the thematic area, and share a passion for critical education and social justice. This allowed us to envision and readily collaborate to put together this much needed edited collection. Our journey was not without its challenges and delays.

The title reflects lengthy discussions about the breadth and depth of the topic, exploring some of the nuances between displacement and migration. Pondering a title for the book allowed us to reflect on the lived realities of individuals and communities affected by displacement and trauma, as well as the diverse intellectual, professional and activist commitments of the seasoned contributors who work with them.

We approached a number of colleagues, among them academics, activists and front-line practitioners, who kindly agreed to contribute a chapter despite workload pressures and tight deadlines. We are entirely grateful for their efforts. We are also thankful for the efforts of the anonymous peer reviewers whose thoughtful comments and important feedback provided each author with critical and in-depth insights to help strengthen their work. There are many scholars and practitioners that we wish to recognize for providing feedback and editing support on the initial manuscripts, individual chapters and the completed product of this edited collection. Among them are Emmanuel E. Rozental, Sharry Aiken, Jos Nolle, Dr. Grace-Edward Galabuzi, Dr. Rainey Gaywish, Dr. Michele Green, Dr. Sheila Cote-Meeks, Catherine (Kit) Martin, Mulugeta Abai, Peter Showler, Dr. Margrit Eichler, Valerie Packota, Dr. Vivian Jimenez-Estrada, Dr. Philip Berger, Matt H. B. Smith, Dr. Behrang Ajam, Dr. Rosemary Meier, Dr. Wendell Block, Dr. Meb Rashid, Tasha Beeds, Philip Ackerman, and Jesson V. Reyes. We wish to also thank Camilo Vasquez Rodriguez and Elsa Oliveira for their contributions, and to express our sincere appreciation to the Shingwauk Residential School Centre for the offer of support. Lastly, we would like to express our thanks to Jim Rozsa and David Stover for their efforts and unwavering support for this project.

SOHEILA PASHANG AND SHEILA GRUNER

# Roots and Routes of Displacement and Trauma

# Part One

# Roots and Routes: Contexts of Displacement

CHAPTER ONE

# Bridging Theory: A Critical and Decolonizing Approach to Displacement and Trauma

*Sheila Gruner*

T he number of people displaced in the world as of 2013 totaled 51.2 million, according to the United Nations (2014). This is roughly equivalent to the combined populations of Canada, Greece and the Netherlands. "The number of refugees, asylum-seekers and internally displaced people worldwide has, for the first time in the post-World War II era, exceeded 50 million people. . . . Among these, refugee numbers amounted to 16.7 million people worldwide . . . [which] does not include the 3.5 million stateless people reported by UN offices, an estimated third of the total worldwide population of stateless people" (United Nations, 2014).

In the face of such overwhelming statistics, how can we create an engaging, anti-oppressive, praxis-oriented theoretical framework for addressing this growing problem? How can students, practitioners, scholars and activists grapple with the complex roots of forced displacement (theory), while learning what it means to work with, advocate for, and support those directly affected by it (practice), in the process using more than "Band-Aid" approaches to the problem?

This chapter will set out to address these questions by drawing on critical and decolonizing theoretical approaches, and offering points of a critique of development and conflict-induced displacement theory. The aim is to contribute to a more

1

comprehensive understanding of the linkages between the determinants of human displacement and the commitments to address it. The chapter will thus consider theory and methods that support the transformation of social and structural forces that lead to human displacement, especially those which target identifiable groups of people based on race, gender, class, and other systematically marginalized identities. Practitioners working with those suffering from post-displacement trauma are encouraged to research the complexities related to the broader systemic political, economic and historical contexts of displacement. Doing so is important in order to fully appreciate the experiences of those they work with, as well as to adequately explore means of addressing such trauma. In later sections of the book, trauma related to displacement and migration is theorized in depth.

**Reflective Questions**

1. What are some important parallels and differences in the experiences of Indigenous people and refugees in Canada, related to forced displacement?
2. How can critical and decolonization theoretical approaches aid in understanding issues of displacement?
3. Identify some critical perspectives of terms and definitions related to refugees, internally displaced people, migrants, non-status and stateless people.
4. What does development and conflict-induced displacement theory offer and/or leave out?

A complementary theme relates to the ultimate goal of prevention of, and reparations for, displacement through a commitment to "decolonizing," the protection of the "commons" and the collective cultural, territorial and political rights of people where they live and in their sites of origin, including the rights of Indigenous people in Canada as expressed by the *Royal Commission on Aboriginal People*, and set out in the *UN Declaration on the Rights of Indigenous People*. It also means protecting the basic human rights of people to remain in, or return to, their places of origin without fear of violence or the imposition of unwanted large-scale development. Furthermore, it means supporting those who cannot return home through adequate protection, as outlined in the United Nations *Convention Relating to the Status of Refugees* and the *Guiding Principles on Internal Displacement*, and also through engagement and participation in meaningful projects and initiatives in receiving countries.

This chapter is primarily concerned with theorizing experiences of displacement among people, including refugees, migrants, travelers, Indigenous people and diverse "others" who have come to reside within the contemporary borders of Canada. Such theorizing requires that we examine displacement as an expression and outcome of capitalism, colonialism, violence and conflict; that we critique not only national and global political and economic policies and projects that lead to violence and displacement, but, also, broader racializing and gendered hegemonic processes that shape contemporary society and allow this problem to persist and increase. Decolonizing theory allows us to tie together critiques of colonialism and capitalism in order to envision the world differently, recognizing that other "non-capitalist," "de-colonial" forms of being in the world have existed and continue to

2

exist, in tension with capitalist social relations. While it is impossible in this opening chapter to explore the many-sided, intersecting experiences of the poor and working class, women, racialized groups, migrant labourers, youth, LGBTQIA+ (lesbian, gay, bi-sexual, transgender and queer, intersex and asexual) and others systematically affected by societal and state repression, violence and forced displacement — much will be said about these experiences in later chapters of this volume — theorizing these experiences through the lens of anti-oppression is crucial for those who work as allies in the fields of social work, community development, community health and related areas. Indeed, theory is necessary for informing advocacy efforts by those who seek to become allies in broader societal struggles to eliminate oppressive structural forces in society.

Colonial and neo-colonial policies and practices continue to shape what happens to people within globalization, most negatively those from "peripheral," "non-western" economies and societies. There are parallels then, as well as important differences, in the experiences of those who arrive in Canada and the original people of this land. An important ethical, political and conceptual concern is the recognition of parallel colonial impositions and experiences that shape contexts of displacement. As Kirmayer et al. (2011) note:

> In Canada, the overriding social realities of indigenous peoples include their historical rootedness to a specific place (with traditional lands, communities, and transactions with the environment) and the profound displacements caused by colonization and subsequent loss of autonomy, political oppression, and bureaucratic control.

It is through critical and decolonizing approaches that changes can be envisioned through mutual recognition of the histories and cultural, political and territorial rights of Indigenous people, refugees, migrants, stateless people and others. It is the absence of this recognition in the dominant political discourse in Canada that prevents reparations, reconciliation and adequate attention to the needs of those affected by displacement. Such considerations, of multiple and intersecting histories of displacement, should inform a more integral decolonizing theoretical analysis for students and practitioners. As Harsha Walia (2008) notes in her article "Resisting Displacement, North and South":

> Despite the distinct realities and claims to "home" of immigrant/refugee and indigenous communities, the pieces reveal how the denial of indigenous history and self-determination is closely linked with the exclusion and detention of migrants within Kanada [sic] (p. 21).

Evidently more needs to be done to support changes to the societal mechanisms that continue to marginalize and deny these important histories.

This chapter aims at building a theoretical-methodological approach that attempts to integrate a critical analysis of the global/historical determinants of displacement and concepts related to decolonization in order to support commitments to building alternatives, including grassroots mobilization, resistance and collective political-territorial and community development efforts. Ultimately the aim is the contesting of the systematic forced uprooting of people that has been instigated and exacerbated through neoliberal globalization.

First, I will outline some key related definitions and terms, both "official" and "unofficial," reflecting on critical and structural implications. In the second section, I will provide points of critique of development, conflict and displacement-specific theory, followed by an exploration of a theoretical framework that draws on critical and decolonization theory. Conceptual considerations related to Indigenous and refugee groups in Canada will also be a point of emphasis, given the dearth of scholarly material available. The final section will provide conclusions and a summary of key points of consideration.

## Critical Considerations:
## Terms and Definitions of Displacement and Migration

The terms and definitions related to displacement are many, varied and confusing, and often erroneously used interchangeably (Muggah, 2003). *Displacement* and *migration*, for example, may be terms used to refer to the same concept, related to the general movement of people, yet they have been interpreted in vastly different ways by scholars, activists, global institutions and policymakers. It is important to grapple with these terms without becoming too fixated on "textbook definitions," yet being aware of how they are utilized at official/institutional levels, by practitioners and by grassroots movements. The fact that these terms have acquired specific meanings has meant significant repercussions for those assigned them. Indeed, millions of people have been displaced within the contemporary period of neoliberal globalization, and these terms have shaped their lives following the experience of violent uprooting.

According to the UN Refugee Agency, the UNHCR, **internally displaced people (IDPs)** "are among the world's most vulnerable people. Unlike refugees, IDPs have not crossed an international border to find sanctuary but have remained inside their home countries. Even if they have fled for similar reasons as refugees (armed conflict, generalized violence, human rights violations), IDPs legally remain under the protection of their own government — even though that government might be the cause of their flight" (UNHCR, 2011).

The Canadian Council for Refugees (CCR) outlines a few important differences in the terms associated with the broader category of *refugee*. The general definition of **refugee** is "a person who is forced to flee from persecution and who is located outside of their home country" (CCR, 2010), while a **Convention refugee** refers to

> a person who meets the refugee definition in the 1951 Geneva Convention relating to the Status of Refugees. This definition is used in Canadian law and is widely accepted internationally. To meet the

definition, a person must be outside their country of origin and have a well-founded fear of being persecuted for reasons of race, religion, nationality, membership of a particular social group or political opinion (CCR, 2010).

Also important are **refugee claimant** or **asylum seeker,** terms which refer to a person who has fled their country and is asking for protection in another country although, until their case has been decided, they have not yet been legally identified as a refugee (CCR, 2010). For both IDPs and refugees, there is injustice implicit in their experience, in that it is "involuntary and involves some form of de-territorialization" (Hyndman, 2000, in Muggah, 2003, p. 7).

The term **migrant** differs in that it implies the possibility of a "voluntary" nature to the movements of people, either within or beyond borders, which may or may not be the case. There are many different categories of migrants, differentiated based on their status as **temporary** or **permanent migrants**, or based on the purpose for which they have migrated (e.g., **migrant workers**). The term migrant is sometimes used to refer to anyone not in their home country; "more often, it is used to refer to people currently on the move, for people with temporary status or those without status in the country where they live" (CCR, 2010) — frequently, especially in the case of **precarious migrants**, for reasons beyond their own control. Often, migrants do not meet the narrow definition of refugee in the Canadian context, and may be pursuing permanent status by another means.

Many of the above definitions related to internally displaced people, refugees and migrants are important, both because practitioners must become familiar with the institutional language used by national and global agencies, and also as a potential site of critique. From a critical and structural perspective, it is important to recognize that any legal term is developed by specific people in specific contexts, within prevailing political power relations, in response to specific needs and situations. For example, the 1951 *Convention on Refugees* contains legal definitions to address the refugee crisis of World War II. Such definitions were aimed at protecting European refugees as a result of the war (any refugees identified as pre-1951). There were efforts, however, to expand the geographical (and time-restricted) coverage, which led to the 1967 *Protocol Relating to the Status of Refugees*. This later document broadened the definitions and scope to include all countries, without being restricted to a specific war or time period.

Meant to support people fleeing actual and threatened violence, these terms subsequently underwent policy interpretation at many levels. The way these terms have been interpreted (and re-interpreted) has had very real effects on people, in both their sites of origin and arrival. Each of these terms involves inclusions and exclusions of people as their status is considered, and ultimately how such terms are defined will have material consequences in relation to people's access to services, legal processes, protections, and other resources.

The ethical, political and legal debates over who can be identified as a convention refugee or IDP, for example, reflect institutional missions of agencies as well as national and broader global politics in any given period, and may imply deeply entrenched biases that can effectively re-victimize displaced people. For example, Roma may have sought asylum in Canada to escape violence based on racist stereotyping in a home country. In previous years, Roma under threat of violence would have been accepted as refugee claimants and had their cases heard, but under the 2012 *Designated Countries of Origin* policy regime of the Conservative government in Canada, they now face legislation that may deem them to be from a country that "does not produce refugees," making it more difficult to be accepted as an asylum seeker in Canada.

Equally problematic is the related ideological stance of the Harper government towards those who do manage to arrive in Canada but have not yet entered the legal process — those who have in the news media irresponsibly been dubbed potential "bogus refugee[s]" by government officials (Baluja, 2012). Broadly assigning such problematic labels implies that everyone escaping violence is potentially taking advantage of the social service system in Canada, or "draining the system." Rather than allowing legal processes to identify illegitimate claims, the federal government has engaged in an ideological strategy, promoting in the media a highly biased label that stigmatizes first, rather than beginning in a place of support and assumption of legitimacy.

## Some Other Typologies of Displacement and Migration

- Environmental Refugee
- Conservation Refugee
- Political Refugee
- Migrant Worker
- Traveller
- Development-Induced Displacement
- Conflict-Induced Displacement
- Disaster-Induced Displacement
- Forced Migration and Resettlement

This practice serves to label people who have likely faced deeply difficult situations, often because of their principled commitment to progressive change. Included in this group might be those who denounce environmental, development and human rights abuses, those who contest military aggressions, those who defend the rights of gay, lesbian, bisexual, transgendered people, or those who publicly expose injustices of a given state regime through news reporting, blogging, legal advocacy or other forms of activism. The stigma of "bogus refugee" is subsequently tacitly assigned to all asylum seekers, who may then be regarded with mistrust, despite the important contributions they will make in the receiving societies.

Also confusing matters are other problematic terms such as *illegal migrant* or *illegal refugee*, misleading terms for which there is, of course, no legal foundation, as they simply refer to those who have not completed the legal process and have not yet been assigned an official status. The fact that people have arrived in a host country, such as Canada, without a specific legal status, as victims of violence, disaster or forced displacement, does not make them "illegal," but, rather, people who are legitimately seeking safety. Through use of such misleading terms, they have become what theorists recently term **illegalized**. The word "illegalized" draws attention to the institutional and political processes that present people as illegal, processes which can orient policies, legal decisions, as well as relations between affected migrants and broader civil society (Bauder, 2014). In other words, people are "made illegal" not by their act of arriving in Canada, but by the treatment they receive there, whether it be the host country's government policies, media representation, or other, related processes that shape their experiences. Activists, including church-based and other human rights groups as well as activist networks such as No One Is Illegal, have driven home the fact that we are all human first.

There are diverse fields of study that grapple with issues and theories of migration, displacement and resettlement. In the following section, I will explore some of the intersections and differences in the fields of development and refugee studies, with the intention of fostering better understanding of the roots of displacement, a principal task of this chapter.

## Capitalism, Colonialism, Development and Displacement

Capitalism is the economic system that has fuelled colonialism and imperialism. Since the beginnings of capitalism in England, the forcible uprooting of land-based people has been systematic and ongoing, with particularly negative effects on women and racialized groups (Mies and Shiva, 1993; Federici, 2004). Capitalism allowed for the accumulation of resources and wealth, utilizing wage- or slave-labour, and was the driving economic force of European expansion and colonialism around the world during the period from the fifteenth through the twenty-first centuries. Early capitalism primarily served the interests of European elites at the expense of peasants, workers, and Indigenous peoples, forcibly and systematically uprooting them both in European countries through the "enclosures" of commonly held lands and forests, as well as in newly colonized lands beyond Europe. Elites relied on the development of legal rationales, which became governing policy, in order to justify the forcible uprooting of people from collective forms of living on and managing land (Meiksins-Wood, 1999).

Two key legal concepts arising in the colonial period that co-related to the systematic displacement of people, through the transformation of collective to private land ownership regimes, are the Doctrine of Discovery and *terra nullius*. In the fifteenth century, Christian explorers were granted the right to claim, exploit and govern lands they "discovered," that is, lands not inhabited by other Christians. This doctrine provided the justification for the mass displacement, enslavement and even killing of people in the Americas, Africa and elsewhere. The United States adopted the legal character of this doctrine in the nineteenth century, and it has continued to provide legal rationale for the displacement of Indigenous people in that country as recently as 2005 (Kades, 2000). Accompanying the Doctrine of Discovery is the colonial concept *terra nullius*, which also served as a rationale to physically and culturally displace Indigenous people, while imposing foreign governing systems (Borrows, 2002). According to Mackey (2011):

7

> *Terra nullius* . . . meaning 'empty land' . . . is a framework for thinking about property that was influential in . . . colonization . . . which depended, to a great extent, upon the appropriation and redefinition of indigenous people's territories. It was important for establishing so-called frontiers for exploration, and then for transforming those indigenous lands into private or public property (p. 152).

These concepts created the foundations, including the development policies, laws and other institutional texts, such as the *Indian Act* in Canada, for the systematic physical and cultural displacement of Indigenous people (RCAP, 1996). They also set the stage for such displacements, and the policies that accompanied them, throughout the Americas, and in Africa and Asia. Such early colonial policy entrenched biases, which were then inherent in subsequent policies, based on racialized, gendered, and class identities, and established oppressive boundaries and disparities that continue to be expressed today in material form, including lesser access to services, continued dispossession of resources and assets, direct and indirect displacement, and so forth.

## Critique of Conflict- and Development-Induced Displacement

The ongoing pressure to privatize land is inherent to the capitalist aims of commodification and accumulation, which underpin global development logic and practice. These in turn continue to instigate or exacerbate situations of war, and necessitate the forced displacement and dispossession of people both historically and in the contemporary period. Indeed, this is one of the reasons why development-induced displacement (DID) and conflict-induced displacement constitute a growing scholarship. While DID scholarship provides important documentation and analysis of the scope, depth, and breadth of displacement generated through capitalist development, the field overall lacks historical analysis of colonialism and imperialism as foundational to the logic and policies of capitalist development and its displacing outcomes. Moreover, and perhaps indicative of this lack of analysis, development- and conflict-induced displacement were until recently theorized largely as separate processes (Muggah, 2003).

**Reflective Questions**

1. Why is development-induced displacement not necessarily considered a violation of human rights? Is this problematic in your opinion? Why or why not?
2. What are the links and differences between development and conflict induced displacement?

**Development-induced displacement (DID)** is defined as what happens when people are compelled or forced to move due to economic forces or large-scale development and infrastructure projects of diverse types. Development-induced displacement uproots people from the environments they live in, from their homes, jobs, and cultures (Vandergeest et al., 2007). While DID literature considers development causing displacement as a violation of human rights, it is often believed by states and global financial institutions that "the overall advantages tend to outweigh the rights and entitlements of the minority . . . [based on an assumption of] the state's right to expropriate property in certain circumstances" (Muggah, 2003, p. 8). This belief provides a rationale for global development policies that lead to displacement, supported by the World Bank and other international institutions that finance large-scale development projects worldwide. Because these development policies and projects are supported by global institutions, the incentive to police potential displacements is low, despite numerous protocols and policies that attempt to prevent, monitor and address situations of development-induced displacement. The literature on development-induced displacement is outlined by Bogoumil Terminski (2013), who notes the many consequences of development leading to the immediate or eventual displacement of people, including health risks and the long-term threat of poverty, implying the general deterioration of living conditions. Michael Cernea (2000) developed the Impoverishment Risks and Reconstruction model, which sets out the risks faced by those who are displaced by development, "including landlessness, joblessness, homelessness, marginalization, food insecurity, loss of access to common property resources, increased morbidity and mortality, and community disarticulation" (Terminski, 2013, p. 7).

**Conflict-induced displacement**, when people are forced from their homes as the result of conflict, is "considered to be an unquestionable violation of international humanitarian law and human rights" (Muggah, 2003, p. 8), but this fact does not necessarily mean that those responsible will be held to account, or that development projects that instigate or exacerbate conflict leading to displacement will be cancelled. The problem, according to Muggah (2003), is that there is "no legally binding mechanism [for nation-states or developers] to respond to those internally displaced as a result of development or war" (p. 8).

In both literatures, "development" is not systematically interrogated, monitored and assessed by global regulatory institutions for its capitalist and colonialist underpinnings. Rather, it is still accepted — despite the overwhelming evidence that accumulation-centred development is linked to violence, conflict, and increasing levels of human displacement worldwide — that displacement is an unfortunate but inevitable outcome of the global economic paradigm. The World Bank does indeed provide a great deal of funding to support research towards reducing the displacement effects of development. Yet the underlying assumptions prevail. The discourses of development and displacement indeed "neutralize" and "depoliticize" development itself.

In the academic literature on development and displacement, the terms **migration** and **resettlement**, for example, have been used in ways that allow for displacement as a result of development to appear benign, referring to the simple movement of people from one place to another. This is not to be confused with resettlement as a necessary and positive step for refugees *already displaced* to refugee camps and in other uncertain living conditions following forced migration, as discussed further below. Resettlement in development planning can be problematic, and serve to de-politicize the underlying historical and political contexts within which people are forced to move from their homes. These are nearly always reasons beyond their making or control, and reflect hegemonic, capitalist development interests and arrangements that build on colonial logics and legacies. The terms migration and resettlement seem to imply that processes of development planning are both inevitable and non-coercive. This is misleading, however, as the concentration of decision-making power about resettlement lies in the hands of governments and planners, and rarely in those of the people who are forced to move. The displaced are thus at the mercy of institutionally-driven processes. As Muggah (2003) notes, resettlement is "designed to transfer population from one area to another on a planned basis" (p. 10). Development-related resettlement, sometimes "voluntary" and sometimes "involuntary," is often justified as necessary for the benefit of the broader society at the expense of those being displaced (Terminski, 2013).

At the same time, resettlement may be deemed a far better option for refugees forced to live in refugee camps or in other precarious living situations. The management of refugee crises caused by environmental disasters, famine, conflicts and wars, and so forth, requires that refugees be "resettled" and thus the term is used in this more "positive" sense as a necessary and obligatory support to refugees *after* the fact of displacement. In this sense, the fields of study and practice define how terminologies are used. The point is not whether resettlement is "good" or "bad," but that it is an institutionally-defined and managed process, sometimes necessary and supportive to refugees, and, at other times, highly problematic, especially when it is the result of development policies and processes about which the affected people have had little say. Both, however, speak to contexts of displacement as reflective of broader hegemonic processes rooted in capitalism, colonialism, imperialism that underwrite the systematic forced migrations of people worldwide.

The terms **forced migration** as well as **forced** or **involuntary resettlement** more appropriately qualify undesired migration as coercive and violent and are utilized in academic and professional organizations dedicated to the study of displacement. These terms move beyond development-induced and conflict-induced displacement, implying in the concept itself that there are victims and perpetrators of displacement and migration.

WHAT DOES DEVELOPMENT THAT CAUSES DISPLACEMENT LOOK LIKE? Large-scale hydroelectric dams supported by national governments, in Canada, China, India and elsewhere, are among the most significant examples worldwide of development projects internally displacing large numbers of people (Leslie, 2006). China's Three Gorges Dam is one of the most striking examples of the relationship between development and displacement. According to International Rivers:

The Three Gorges Dam is the world's largest hydropower project and most notorious dam. The massive project sets records for number of people displaced (more than 1.2 million), number of cities and towns flooded (13 cities, 140 towns, 1,350 villages), and length of reservoir (more than 600 kilometers). The project has been plagued by corruption, spiraling costs, environmental impacts, human rights violations and resettlement difficulties (International Rivers, n.d.).

Large-scale oil, mining and industrial forestry projects are other well-known causes of development-induced displacement, development that not only uproots people, but has, in many cases, been documented as destroying local economies and cultures, adversely affecting human health, and leaving significant scars upon the environment (Vandergeest et al., 2007). Organizations such as Mining Watch, Human Rights Watch, the Indigenous Environmental Network, among many others, monitor specific projects, Canadian and other transnational companies, and their displacing effects on individuals, families, communities and their organizations. In Canada, there are numerous examples, historically and in the contemporary period, of racist and gendered processes of displacement caused by capitalist development. Indigenous people, including First Nation, Metis, and Inuit communities, have been systematically displaced throughout Canadian history by development imperatives and interests, from the construction of the Canadian Pacific Railway to the establishment of key sites of resource, tourist and other forms of economic development and geostrategic (military) interest. Indigenous women and men bore the outcomes of displacement differently, as they became immersed in wage economies and new property ownership regimes. Small-scale farmers, mining communities and small- and medium-size rural populations have been consistently affected by the "boom and bust" cycles imposed through global market imperatives and the effects of larger scale industrial and corporate development, particularly throughout the nineteenth and twentieth centuries. Africkville, in Nova Scotia, is another significant historical example of development, displacement and racism, where African descendants were forcibly removed by decree from their homes in the mid-1960s, because those homes were located on the site of planned bridge and industrial development. In 2010, an official apology was issued by the Halifax council to the descendants of the inhabitants of Africkville, establishing a heritage fund towards recognizing the historical significance and effects of the displacement (CBC, 2010). There are many examples in Canadian history of forcible displacement of groups of people largely based on racialized stigmas of those who were deemed to not fit into the national identity and thus considered expendable.

**DEVELOPMENT AS HEGEMONY.** Development projects are the expression but not the ultimate source of displacement. Rather, the broader global hegemonic ideologies and processes of capitalism, colonialism and imperialism underpin development projects, related conflicts and resulting displacements of people. Indeed, to "decolonize" is to recognize the thought processes that permit and justify acts of colonialism and displacement. The act of decolonizing thought patterns is crucial to the process of re-orienting the practices and policies of development that lead to the displacement of people.

Ideological discourses and policies of powerful global interests set the stage for conflict, war and forced migration. For example, the globalizing discourses of the "War on Drugs" and later the "War on Terror" can be traced directly to the instigation or exacerbation of internal conflicts and wars, as well as the production of capitalist development policy that supports dominant global interests, particularly military interests. Broader "national security" policies of Western countries, such as the United States, with Canada's tacit and sometimes direct support over the past decade, have supported military interventions in countries such as Iraq, Iran, Haiti, Afghanistan and elsewhere. These interventions have had the intention, or result, of opening the way for foreign transnational corporate development, including post-war or post-disaster reconstruction projects that serve the interests of dominant military-industrial powers (Klein, 2007).

As such, "development" as a concept needs to be critically examined. Within an anti-oppressive framing, the effects of development on particular groups – women, racialized people, minority religious groups and other marginalized and under-represented groups — must be examined in detail. Development, in pre- and post-conflict and displacement contexts, can be theorized as hegemonic, and demonstrative of a direct or indirect relationship to violence and conflict, producing displacement globally, and targeting already vulnerable groups. Vast numbers of women and racialized groups are displaced due to wars that are directly or indirectly related to resource conflicts, or neoliberal development plans, projects, and policies (Klare, 2001; Geddicks, 2001). Indeed, proposed or implemented development can instigate or exacerbate conflicts through the use of paramilitary and other forms of official and unofficial state-sanctioned violence (Collier, 2003), including targeted violence against women, whose bodies are used as weapons of war (Bannerji et al., 2001; El Jack, 2007).

In the case of disasters that are the result of extreme weather events, displacement is often also theorized as a direct or indirect outcome of large-scale industrial capitalist development. The terms **environmental refugee**, **environmental migrant** and **climate refugee** may be misleading in the sense that they appear to "blame the environment" for displacement and deflect our attention from the problems created by aggressive, advanced accumulation-centered development. Studies show that large-scale industrial development has had significant effects on climate change, which in turns exacerbates the precarious conditions within which many people, but particularly those already marginalized, live (Klein, 2014). In other words, climate "events" instigated by the activities of large-scale oil, hydro, and mining developments that perhaps took place years earlier, place populations living in fragile ecosystems under greater threat of displacement, while at the same time having fewer resources to deal with such events. Further, the application of global economic and conservation policies and projects in vulnerable and coveted regions have in many instances also led to the displacement of people, who have become known as **conservation refugees**, displaced from their historical places of origin, places that have since become national and provincial parks. The justification has been that wildlife, or other sensitive or endangered ecological resources, need to be preserved, even if the reasons for species depletion and related problems are more directly related to global market imperatives than to the practices of people living in these areas (Peet and Watts, 1996).

The conflicts over natural resources are perhaps the most explicit indicators of the inherent relationship among large-scale development, conflict and displacement (Klare, 2001). There are numerous cases of resource conflicts, both overt and covert, that have shaped and exacerbated political, tribal, religious and other types of internal conflicts leading to, in some cases, war and mass-scale displacement with horrendous human rights abuses. While Canada is a key driver and beneficiary of neoliberal globalization through free trade, mining, oil, forestry, hydroelectricity and other large-scale development projects, it is at the same time accepting fewer people into Canada as refugees. This is in large part due to current national governance rooted in a neoliberal ideological stance, including economic development and foreign policies aimed at supporting specific sides in various conflicts, and trade policies meant to promote large-scale energy and mining projects. Most Canadians likely have little awareness of these issues. In 2013, for example, the federal government's budget decision to fold the Canadian International Development Agency (CIDA) into the Department of Foreign Affairs, Trade and Development reflected a shift in focus from foreign aid, human rights, poverty reduction, and community development, to a concentration on Canada's commercial and trade interests around the world. This change in focus is a major concern to a number of agencies, including the Canadian Council for International Cooperation (CCIC), which publicly expressed concern over the watering down of Canada's commitment to poverty reduction in the developing world (CCIC, 2013).

While it is impossible to list all the scholarly and institutional typologies developed to describe categories of displacement and migration, it is important to recognize the multiple "entry points" towards understanding more complex formulations of the problem of displacement. Some of the other "unofficial" typologies can be found in the box on page 6; they draw on concepts from critical geography, political studies, sociological and refugee and migration studies.

## Towards a Critical and Decolonizing Approach to Displacement

Moving beyond theories of development-induced displacement, proposed here is a critical and decolonizing theoretical framing for understanding and addressing displacement. This is intended to contribute to and foster commitment to more ethically informed responses to the political-economic determinants and related social, psychological and other health effects of forced migration. Crucial to critical theory are questions of race, class and gender, which should inform analysis of both the determinants of displacement and policies of attention to displaced people. An emphasis of "decolonizing" development must be to advance the legal rights of those most affected by displacement — Indigenous peoples, ethnic groups, women, and so on — so they are better able to make decisions and shape the types of development that will take place in communities where they live or plan to return.

Further, practitioners who better understand the diverse contexts within which people have been displaced are better prepared to attend to those people's needs and advocate for necessary changes to the systemic barriers they face. Through understanding the social, political and economic nexus of power, practitioners see themselves not as "heroes" or "victims" of displacement, but as allies and protagonists in broader struggles to reshape society in order to contest the ongoing, unjust and often violent uprooting of people, and the colonial legacies that continue to shape society in the contemporary world. As Kirmayer et al. (2011) suggest, we should be working towards

> . . . revisioning collective history in ways that valorize collective identity; revitalizing language and culture as resources for narrative self-fashioning, social positioning, and healing; and renewing individual and collective agency through political activism, empowerment, and reconciliation (Kirmayer et al., 2011 abstract).

The following sections will provide a brief overview of key concepts in critical and decolonizing approaches to displacement, as an entry point for deepened historical reflection on displacement, colonialism and capitalism. Together these theoretical bodies of work bridge interdisciplinary approaches and foster commitment to further conceptual exploration of displacement and trauma for structural social workers, critical community development practitioners, critical health care workers, community psychologists, political theorists, activists and other allies.

CRITICAL SOCIAL THEORY. Critical social theory is embedded within an anti-oppressive, structural approach. **Critical social theory** asserts that the roots of social problems lie in unaddressed systemic issues. As Lather (1991) states, "Knowledge is grounded in politics with the insistence that social phenomena be related to the historical whole, and to the structural context in which they are situated" (in Berman et al., 1991, p. 421). The systematic displacement of people and production of IDPs and refugees around the world finds its roots in often-identifiable political, economic and social processes of capitalist development, as the dominant paradigm that shapes social relations globally. Broadly speaking, from a critical perspective, accumulation and dispossession processes have acute ramifications for people in relation to the exacerbation of violence and conflict leading to human displacement within the world economy (Harvey, 2004).

Critical social theory helps us understand that already marginalized and racialized groups are more directly affected by displacement (Bullard, 1993, 1994; Shiva, 2008). The marginalization of specific groups based on racialized, class, gendered and other identities is systematically organized within the social relations of capitalism, relations which historically established lines between the "haves" and "have-nots" at a global level and within nation-states (Mullaly, 2010). As explored earlier, these relations are an outcome of the imperialist logics and goals of European elites throughout early colonialism, and of the "global north" and corporate elites in the contemporary period (Federici, 2004; Harvey, 2004).

Inequitable relations continue to shape social realities around the globe, between "white" and racialized groups, between women and men, and between "heterosexuals" and people with other underrepresented expressions of sexuality. Ultimately, vast and increasing disparities exist between "privileged" and "oppressed" groups, and the latter continually find themselves at the losing end. These groups comprise the most often uprooted, displaced, and exiled, and are most often without adequate access to essential services. They are the most likely to be re-victimized and re-traumatized in their territories and countries of origin, as well as in the countries that receive them.

---

**Resilience-Centered Research**

An example of a critical, participatory and resilience-centered project is *Volume 44*, a collaborative research study with migrant sex workers in South Africa. The project focused on the underrepresented voices of migrant men, women and transgender sex workers, utilizing multimodal visual and narrative approaches, such as mapping, narrative writing, storytelling and group image review/critique. Moree information is available at www.migration.org.za/page/about-vol44/move.

---

For example, Indigenous people in Canada have experienced multiple forms of displacement over the course of colonial history, and despite the treaties, policies and agreements that have been put in place, in theory to offset some of the unjust losses since the arrival of Europeans, services and supports have often been sub-standard (such as in the areas of health, education and housing), and the political autonomy of First Nation communities and organizations continues to be undermined (Blaser, de Costa, McGregor and Coleman, 2010). The end result is, effectively, the systematic re-victimization of people, and the entrenching of biases throughout the Canadian body politic.

Critical social theory sheds light on the tendencies and patterns of displacement as it affects specific groups in particular, complex and intersecting ways. Critical social theory also enables us to analyze and address the layered and regressive societal attitudes that permit the re-victimization of people who have experienced displacement.

Critical race and gender theory allows us to assert that people living in fragile environments (Indigenous, rural and other racialized, female and "non-Western" groups) are more directly affected by climate change disasters (Shiva, 2008), more often affected by polluting industries (LaDuke, 2005; Bullard, 1993) and more often caught in the proverbial or actual crossfire of political conflicts with little or no protection from nation-state governments. Those who are the marginalized poor, working class, economically dependent or excluded altogether are effectively those most vulnerable to displacement. They face more stigmas, and are more likely to be considered "dissident," illegal, or undesirable, based on their politics, social location, gender, race, religious or other identities. People from any of these social locations can become refugees at any moment — largely because they challenge or simply do not "fit" into the dominant power arrangements that build on historical legacies of colonization and contemporary neoliberal expressions of capitalism.

DECOLONIZATION AND "DECOLONIZING" IN THE FACE OF DISPLACEMENT. Moving beyond the critique of power and development relations, decolonization and decolonizing theoretical work emphasizes the importance of understanding the dominant logic and history of colonization and making visible the histories of multiple "others" rendered invisible through colonialism and capitalism. A key concern of decolonizing theory and practice is to de-centre colonialism and capitalism as dominant narrative, to "decolonize the mind" in order to identify, value and put into practice other forms of being in the world. This process of consciousness development must be carried out in parallel with actual, material changes to people's lives. In brief, decolonization involves political, cultural, economic and cultural transformation, and relies on a praxis-oriented approach to theory, bringing theory together with practice for the reshaping of society. "Decolonizing" is the active commitment to reorient consciousness towards the emancipation, autonomy and the protection of ways of being that have been historically uprooted and disavowed by colonialism.

As such, "decolonizing" thought and practice emphasizes that displaced people are active agents of their own histories and societal transformations, and also emphasizes the roles of allies and grassroots movements that contest the multiple roots and expressions of colonial and capitalist displacement. These movements are crucial to advance the basic rights of disenfranchised people and to commit to addressing the broader determinants of displacement, however difficult that may appear. Such movements are at the forefront of contesting the dissolution of collective property rights, and of proposing productive alternatives to the sort of large-scale, accumulation-centred development that lies at the heart of increasing conflicts worldwide leading to displacement (Shiva, 2008; Coleman, 2011; Mander, 2002).

**Decolonization** focuses on "undoing" colonialism at the political, economic, cultural, physical and intellectual levels (Alfred and Corntassel, 2005) and asserts that we do not yet live in a "post-colonial" world. This is despite the fact that colonial political regimes were transformed through wars of independence as well as legal agreements, at which point the direct political rule by European countries over colonies in the Americas, Africa and Asia came, for the most part, to an end. The hegemonic power of European, and later American, capitalist elites, however, continued to be asserted in the former colonies, through economic, cultural, military and global policy arrangements. **Theories of decolonization** are diverse and varied but centre on a critique of colonization and neo-colonization as disruptive, displacing and dispossessing historical processes.

The Caribbean-French psycholologist Frantz Fanon (1925–1961), who was born in Martinique, theorized the role of violence, class and race and the psychopathology of colonization. He is seen as one of the foundational anti-colonial theorists of the twentieth century. His books include *The Wretched of the Earth* (1961), which examines in detail the plight of people systematically and violently displaced under colonialism in multiply intersecting ways, psychologically, physically, culturally, and economically. His work inspired many other theorists and movements for liberation. Albert Memmi, a contemporary of Fanon born in Tunisia, wrote *The Colonizer and the Colonized*, also about the psychological effects of colonization; the book appeared in French in 1957, with an English translation published in 1965.

Indigenous theorists in Canada and elsewhere have developed an important body of theoretical work related to decolonization (Maracle, 2002; Vine Deloria, 1988; Alfred, 2005). Linda T. Smith's (1999) "Decolonization: Research and Indigenous Peoples," serves as a critique of the Eurocentric research that has played a decisive role in the ongoing dispossession and cultural displacement of Indigenous people, while at the same time proposing ways to actively reconstruct Indigenous communities. Andrea Smith (2005), another important Indigenous theorist, provides a gender analysis of the violent impacts of colonization on Indigenous women, both historically and in the contemporary period. Canadian and North American Indigenous theorists of decolonization emphasize the importance of a commitment to "decolonizing practice" to the resurgence of Indigenous cultures, languages, worldviews and economies, both as resistance and an alternative in the face of ongoing threats of displacement, capitalism and colonialism (Deloria, 1988; Manuel, 2006; Simpson, 2010).

Decolonizing theory is of particular importance both to critique colonialism, neo-colonialism and capitalism, and to move beyond critique, through a re-centering on alternative or non-capitalist, "decolonializing" forms of viewing the world. A plethora of Indigenous scholars have taken up the project of researching the longstanding, diverse and rich Indigenous ontologies that underpin pre-colonial and contemporary non-colonial forms of governance, ecological management systems, and Indigenous economic practices.

There are important parallels here in relation to the experiences of Indigenous people and newcomers to Canada, beginning with recognition of the rich political-territorial histories and cultural and governance practices of Indigenous peoples, established long before European encroachment.

Decolonization theory informs how activists, allies and practitioners in Canada approach and examine the ways in which both newcomers and Indigenous peoples can be better understood and valued for the ways they contribute to and shape Canadian society, ethically, culturally, economically, and in many other ways, as well as in relation to other forms altogether of envisioning societies and lifeways. A "colonial mindset" permits non-Western histories to be discounted and subverted by stigmas and stereotypes that are often perpetuated in media accounts and policies geared towards submission to elitist and unexamined concepts of what it means to be "Canadian."

To theorize the topic of displacement requires that we acknowledge the history of Canada as one of immigration, a history that is deeply rooted in capitalist and colonial drives that led to the physical and cultural displacement of the original peoples, as well as the displacement of many of the early settlers themselves, who found themselves encouraged or even forced to leave their homes in Europe. These settlers originally came as indentured workers, who worked in mining, fisheries, forestry or railroads; as escaped or "purchased" slaves; or as small-scale farmers, working the land in often harsh conditions. They were also to be displaced, sometimes multiple times, based on development, military or other strategic imperatives of the new nation, both historically as well as in the contemporary period.

Currently, grassroots movements that contest and propose alternatives to neo-colonization, capitalism and displacement are many and varied. Resistance to the displacing outcomes of capitalism has occurred since its onset. In England, from the sixteenth century onward, people contested the "enclosures," a process which saw land-oriented people forcibly removed from the collectively owned "commons," for the benefit of private ownership (Colemen, 2011; Snyder, 1990). These earlier movements to protect the commons have in turn influenced contemporary efforts to protect other varied expressions of common or shared resources and property, including common land holdings, water, air, collective intellectual property and so forth (Shiva, 2005; Cavanaugh and Mander, 2004).

Also important are broader political and territorial movements to reclaim land rights in the face of displacement, including Indigenous, ethnic and rural movements in Canada and elsewhere in the Americas, such as the Via Campesina (Desmarais, 2007), the Landless Movement in Brazil (Branford and Rocha, 2002), and many other movements across the Americas. These movements put forward cultural, economic and political alternatives to the displacing economic policies of globalization imposed through the World Bank, the International Monetary Fund and the World Trade Organization (Ruether, 2005). Alternatives to globalization are varied and diverse (Cavanaugh and Mander, 2002) and include initiatives in solidarity economics (Migliaro, n.d.), community food production (Coscione, 2014), local ownership of energy and transportation (Hopkins, 2008), Indigenous economic development (Newhouse et al., 2013), and initiatives for prior consultation and free, prior, and informed consent regarding development projects in Indigenous and Afro-descendent communities, among many others.

Theories of decolonization and resistance must be understood in relation to historical forces of capitalism and ongoing neoliberal imperatives, but must also be seen as fostering possibilities of non-capitalist, non-colonial forms of thinking and being in the world. A decolonizing approach commits to not only a critique of capitalist and colonial policies and how they play out today, but a recognition that there are other forms of governance, other ontologies and epistemological forms of understanding the world, that were in existence before the onset of capitalism and colonialism, and that should inform routes forward, including the shaping of new policy and development practices.

## Conclusion

In sum, a historically rooted and contemporary global problem — forced migration — must be understood as the outcome of complex hegemonic and historical processes and events that are deeply entrenched in economic, political, and subsequently socially normative relations, systems and institutions. These shape people's attitudes, ideological beliefs and political positions, including the positions of those working with refugees, Indigenous people and others affected by the actual and inherited traumas related to displacement. They further inform practical approaches to intervention, to address trauma as well as deepen commitment to understanding and addressing the origins of violence and displacement.

The goal of this chapter has been to foster the development of an interdisciplinary theoretical approach to displacement that provides a critique of the determinants of displacement, and encourages a commitment to decolonization as part of an approach to addressing this growing problem.

Displacement can be understood as the systematic outcome of the dominant and hegemonic social, political and economic paradigm rooted in colonialism and capitalism. Displacement occurred in earlier historical periods before the onset of capitalism — for instance, because of wars and famines — but these factors do not account for the systematic processes of displacement we are theorizing here. Put another way, displaced people from all over the world are "produced" systematically within capitalist globalization, as an outcome of colonialism, neo-colonialism, and related political repression, conflict and violence, processes which affect some groups more than others.

Development- and conflict-induced displacement theories offer insights into the depth, breadth and scope of the roots of the problem of displacement as instigated or exacerbated by development and violence. Yet these theoretical bodies tend to lack historical analysis of colonialism or a critique of the capitalist model of development itself, which, at times, justifies displacement as an inevitable but necessary outcome of development. Therefore we need a theory that is farther reaching. Critical social and decolonization theories are important, then, because they provide a more comprehensive approach to understanding and addressing displacement — an approach that should inform global and national policies on development, displacement, attention to refugees and recognition of the territorial and cultural rights of Indigenous people.

Critical theory examines the determinants of displacement or exile faced by displaced people, understood as reflecting the politics of accumulative development as well as the policies of regressive political regimes that concentrate power for their own gain. This analysis must extend to include race, gender and class in sites of origin as well as of arrival. For example, host countries, which may gain from development projects in sites of displacement, receive refugees from those same places. Efforts are made by host countries to protect displaced persons and provide them with adequate services, yet structural barriers continue to exist and include the lack of meaningful employment and political participation, as well as the lack of sufficient access to social welfare, housing or health care, among other services.

Decolonization theory supports the analysis of displacement, and places development in a historical context of colonialism and capitalism. Indigenous people in particular face daunting legacies of colonialism, expressed as the undermining of territorial and political autonomy and the persistent and chronic underfunding of cultural programs, both of which have contributed to the ongoing threat of cultural and physical displacement. Refugees arrive from places with often similar hegemonic histories of colonialism and capitalism, displacement and violence, expressed through war, state repression, imposed large-scale development projects, or the discourses of national security and the "War on Terror."

Decolonization also places emphasis on the conceptualizing of alternatives to colonialist logics and framings, including Indigenous and other non-capitalist, "decolonial" ways of being, knowing and existing materially in the world. Allies and others who commit to decolonizing become aware of their privilege, and work alongside those affected by displacement to shape a more equitable world. Those practicing decolonization are involved in critical research initiatives; campaigning, activism and solidarity efforts; direct action and more radical social mobilization and resistance movements; policy development and advocacy; and other forms of critical and transformative front-line work.

There is indeed a need for comprehensive global and national refugee policies and programs that support community practitioners involved in development efforts in Canada, particularly those working with Indigenous people, refugees, migrant workers, non-status people, and others affected by displacement. Displacement affects particular groups based on race, gender, sexuality and class, among other marginalized and targeted identities.

Ultimately, analysis and action, as well as policy and practice, must reorient the marginalizing and displacing effects of neoliberal globalization and its politics of accumulation, whether in sites of origin or arrival. That reorientation must be towards a reclamation of political and territorial autonomy for Indigenous people and other "stateless" nations, as well as the right to the integrity of the person and freedom from violence and oppression for all people.

## References

Baluja, T. (2012, Feb. 16). Tories unveil bill to thwart "bogus" refugees. *Globe and Mail*. Retrieved from www.theglobeandmail.com/news/politics/toriesunveilbilltothwartbogusrefugees/article546604/.

Bauder, H. (2014). Why we should use the term "illegalized" refugee or immigrant: A commentary. *International Journal of Refugee Law, 26*(3), 327–332.

# Roots and Routes of Displacement and Trauma

Berman, H., Mulcahy, G., Forchuk, C., Edmunds, K., Haldenby, A., & Lopez, R. (2009). Uprooted and displaced: A critical narrative study of homeless, aboriginal and newcomer girls in Canada. *Issues in Mental Health Nursing, 30*, 418–430.

Blaser, M., de Costa, R., McGregor, D., & Coleman, W. (Eds.) (2010). *Indigenous peoples and autonomy: Insights for a global age.* Vancouver: UBC Press.

Branford, S., & Rocha, J. (2002). *Cutting the wire: The story of the landless movement in Brazil.* London: Latin American Bureau.

Bullard, R. (1993). *Confronting environmental racism: Voices from the grassroots* (pp. 15–24). Boston: South End Press.

Canadian Council for International Cooperation (CCIC) (2013, March 21). CIDA being folded into DFAIT: The Canadian Council for International Cooperation concerned about CIDA's mandate being watered down. Retrieved from http://www.ccic.ca/_files/en/what_we_do/2013-03-22_news_release_Budget_2013.pdf.

Cavanaugh, J., & Mander, J. (Eds.). (2004). *Alternatives to economic globalization.* San Francisco: Berrett-Koehler Publishers.

Coleman, W. (2011). *Property, territory, globalization: Struggles over autonomy.* Vancouver: UBC Press.

Collier, P. (2003). *Breaking the conflict trap: Civil war and development policy.* Washington: World Bank and Oxford University Press. Retrieved from http://www.unhcr.org/53a155bc6.html.

Coscione, M. (2014). *In defense of small producers.* Halifax: Fernwood Publishing.

Desmarais, A. (2007). *Globalization and the power of peasants: La via campesina.* Halifax: Fernwood Publishing.

Dowie, M. (2005, November/December). Conservation refugees: When protecting nature means kicking people out. *Orion Magazine,* 16–27.

El Jack, A. (2007). Gendered implications: Development induced displacement in Sudan. In Vandergeest, P., Idahosa, P., & Bose, P. (Eds.). *Development's displacements: Ecologies, economies and cultures at risk* (p. 61). Vancouver: UBC Press.

Federici, S. (2004). *Caliban and the witch: Women, the body and primitive accumulation.* New York: Autonomedia.

Gedicks, A. (2001). *Resource rebels: Native challenges to mining and oil corporations.* Boston: South End Press.

Harvey, D. (2006). *Spaces of global capitalism.* London: Verso.

Harvey, D. (2004). *The new imperialism.* Oxford: Oxford University Press.

Hoefer, R. (2012). *Advocacy practice for social justice* (2nd ed.). Chicago: Lyceum Books.

Hyndman, J. (2011). *Research summary on resettled refugee integration in Canada.* Report prepared for the UNHCR. Retrieved from http://www.unhcr.org/4e4123d19.pdf.

Kirmayer, L., Dandeneau, S., Marshall, E., Phillips, M., & Williamson, K. (2011). Rethinking resilience from indigenous perspectives. *La Revue Canadienne de Psychiatrie, 56*(2), 84–91.

Klare, M. (2001). The new geography of conflict. *Foreign Affairs, 80*(3), 49–61. Retrieved from http://www.relooney.info/SI_Oil-Politics/China-Resource-War_39.pdf.

Laduke, W. (2005). *Recovering the sacred: The power of naming and claiming.* Boston: South End Press.

Mander, J., & Tauli-Corpuz, V. (2006). *Paradigm wars: Indigenous people's resistance to globalization.* San Francisco: Sierra Club Books.

Mies, M., & Shiva, V. (1993). *Ecofeminism.* New York: Zed Press.

Migliaro, L. (n.d.). *What is solidarity economics?* Retrieved from http://www.luisrazeto.net/content-/what-solidarity-economics.

Muggah, R. (2003). A tale of two solitudes: Comparing conflict and development-induced internal displacement and involuntary resettlement. *International Migration, 41*(5), 5–31.

Mullaly, B. (2010). *Challenging oppression and confronting privilege* (2nd ed.). Don Mills, ON: Oxford University Press.

Newhouse, D., & Orr, J. (2013). *Aboriginal knowledge for economic development.* Halifax: Fernwood.

Peet, R., & Watts, M. (2004). *Liberation ecologies: Environment, development, social movements.* London: Routledge.

Smith, A., Stenning, A., & Willis, K. (eds.) (2008). *Social justice and neoliberalism: Global perspectives.* London: Zed Books.

Shiva, V. (2008). *Soil not oil.* Boston: South End Press.

Terminski, B. (n.d.). Development-induced displacement and human security: A very short introduction.

Retrieved from http://dlc.dlib.indiana.edu/dlc/bitstream/handle/10535/8960/SSRN-id2182302 (15).pdf?sequence=1.

Three Gorges Dam (n.d.). Retrieved July 16, 2014, from http://www.internationalrivers.org/-campaigns/three-gorges-dam.

United Nations. (2014, June 20). *World refugee day: Global forced displacement tops 50 million for first time in post-World War II era* . Retrieved from http://www.unhcr.org/53a155bc6.html.

United Nations. (2011). Internally displaced people. Retrieved from http://www.unhcr.org/pages-/49c3646c146.html.

Vandergeest, P., Idahosa, P., & Bose, P. (eds.) (2007). *Development's displacements: Ecologies, economies and cultures at risk.* Vancouver: UBC Press.

Walia, H. (2008, Summer). Resisting displacement, north and south. *West Coast Line* (42), 21–26.

Wingrove, J. (2014, January 22). Refugee claims hit "historic low" as Ottawa's policy faces fresh criticism. *Globe and Mail.* Retrieved from http://www.theglobeandmail.com/news/politics/refugee-claims-hit-historic-low-as-ottawas-policy-faces-fresh-criticism/article16461486/.

Young, M. (2010). Five faces of oppression. In Adams, M., et al. (Eds.). *Readings for diversity and social justice* (2nd ed.) . New York: Routledge.

CHAPTER TWO

# Restoring Ourselves as Indigenous Nations: An Anishinabe Kwe's Perspective

*Rebecca Beaulne-Stuebing*

Waynaboozhoo nindiniwaymawgunnidoog. Naawakwe giizhigookwe
niindizhinikawz. Migizi niindodaym. Bawating ndoonjibaw. Weesawkoday
Anishinabe kwe niindow.

*(Greetings, all of my relatives. My name is Noon Day Woman. My clan is the
eagle. I live in Sault Ste. Marie. I am a Métis Anishinabe woman.)*

When speaking or writing, I have been taught to first introduce myself. In this
way I centre my voice and commit to being accountable for my words. I take
responsibility for my interpretation of what I have learned from others, my elders,
teachers, and mentors. I acknowledge my distinct voice in relation to how I am
connected in the world. This introduction is an affirmation, an expression of self.
My name, my clan and the land are part of my identity. I firmly root myself in
place as my ancestors also have done.

In what is now known as North America, a grounding of self and community in
the land is vital to being Indigenous. Our history here reaches back thousands of
years. In this depth of time we acknowledge the well-developed systems of
thought, education, economy, governance, and law within and between nations.
The diverse Indigenous peoples in this part of the world thrived for countless
generations with advanced ways of knowing and being.

The last 500 years, then, are only recent history. In this relatively brief time, a
lot has happened to us. Through the course of generations, European colonialism
took hold and choked this continent. Colonial powers employed multiple strategies
for controlling the lives of Indigenous peoples to exercise dominance, expropriate

lands and exploit resources. Indigenous communities were brutally displaced from the ways of living that had nourished us since time immemorial.

In this chapter I will explore how, through law and education, colonialism has displaced Indigenous peoples physically, denying the freedom of movement and connection to land inherent to Indigenous life; and culturally, in relation to Indigenous worldview, thought and identity. This has marked a profound disruption of the land-based systems of knowing which are critical to the survival of Indigenous nations. Considering the legal and educational structures still in place in Canada today, it is clear that we continue to experience the institutions and impacts of colonialism. We do not live in a "post-colonial" world.

I begin with an illustration of Indigenous worldview and lifeways, the basis of which are connections to earth and spirit. Diverse nations flourished across the continent in peaceful coexistence through Indigenous laws. Families and communities moved with a freedom of choice contained in our laws. The depth of our knowing and being as Indigenous nations endures in a complex history; this history puts colonialism in context.

I then look at the concepts of colonialism and imperialism as they have been realized in this part of the world, first with the extermination and displacement of Indigenous communities that was integral to the development of Canada. I will consider the significance of the Eurocentric worldview in shaping these practices of colonialism. Such concepts provide a foundation for understanding the history of an imbalanced relationship between the Crown/Canada and Indigenous nations. This relationship has been carried out through law in treaty-making and the *Indian Act*. Education — namely, Canada's Residential Schools Policy and system — has served as a significant strategy to further, through assimilation, the termination of Indigenous communities and appropriation of remaining Indigenous lands. This strategy has exacerbated physical and cultural displacement of Indigenous nations, imposing lasting intergenerational traumas that are lived and felt daily.

I will also share some important responses in Indigenous education that comprise a broader movement of decolonization, working to replace what was forcibly silenced, taken away or destroyed. The emergence of resistance movements has coincided with the development of community-driven alternatives in education. These movements demonstrate resilience in the reclamation and revitalization of Indigenous values, knowledge and practices, through education as healing.

The art of piecing together my traditional introduction — sharing my name, my clan, my nation and place in the world — is an expression of my identity growth as Anishinabe kwe (Anishinabe woman). It is an act of replacing what had been denied of me, displaced from my lineage for generations. All Indigenous peoples have experienced profound loss. Yet there are evident possibilities in Indigenous education to heal intergenerational wounds, to open doorways for transformation and renewal.

## A Note on Language

When I introduce myself, I have been taught to identify with particular nations as part of the broader Anishinabe nation: *Weesawkoday Anishinabe kwe niindow*. I am a Métis Anishinabe woman. If I so chose, I could lengthen my introduction to acknowledge the many nations I am gifted with in my lineage: *Weesawkoday meenawah Ojibwe meenawah Omushkego meenawah Wemitigoji meenawah Austrian kwe niindow*. I am a Métis, and also Ojibwe, and also Cree, and also French, and also Austrian woman (I have yet to determine a translation in Ojibwemowin for one who comes from Austria).

I introduce myself in the language of the land on which I live. I introduce myself in the language of my teachers and elders, the language that I seek to learn in its fullness. It has been explained to me that Anishinabe refers to "the Original Peoples of this part of the world" in the Ojibwemowin language (Benton-Banai, personal communication). In this way, I understand the English word "Indigenous" to be a rough, but close, translation. I therefore use the term Indigenous to refer to the many diverse Original Peoples of this part of the world. While this chapter primarily focuses on a Canadian context, a consideration of time-depth acknowledges how recently in the history of this continent borders were imposed to establish and distinguish between Canada and the United States.

The term **Anishinabe** is often used to refer to the Ojibwe, as well as the Odawa and Potawatami nations that comprise the Three Fires Confederacy. There are also many closely related nations that together make up the wider Algonquian language family. There is great geographic and linguistic diversity within and among these nations. In the way that I have been taught, each of these peoples could identify themselves as part of the broader Anishinabe nation. If I were to travel to another territory, I would introduce myself in my language. I would also seek to learn how the people of that territory introduce themselves. I would try to honour their traditions and their language while in that place, and I would carry that learning with me through life.

Other terms such as **Aboriginal** or **Indian** are legal constructions in Canada. The words do not come from Indigenous nations. Aboriginal applies to Indian, Métis and Inuit peoples recognized in Section 35(2) of the Canadian Constitution (1982). This term is often used in a Canadian context in attempts to be inclusive of multiple Indigenous nations. Where I use the term Indian it is in specific reference to the legal status enshrined in the *Indian Act* of 1876. As I will explain further in this chapter, there are many Indigenous people in Canada not recognized as status Indians, which is further indicative of ongoing forms of displacement experienced in the contemporary period.

I reference the work of many scholars in this chapter, all of whom have made decisions around the language they use to refer to the Original Peoples of this part of the world. I respect their choices. There is no "one size fits all" term or set of terms that will be agreeable to all Indigenous individuals and nations. I have, however, offered an explanation of my choice around language to promote better understanding of what can be confusing or contentious terms.

## *Mewizhaa* (A Long Time Ago): Indigenous Worldview and Lifeways

An analysis of colonization and its ongoing impacts must first consider the deep historical ways of Indigenous knowing and existence. History in this part of the world did not begin in 1492. In other words: "Columbus did not *discover* the 'New World'. It was already old when he came to it" (Thornton, 1987, p. xv). In the dominant historical narrative, Indigenous peoples have been "relegated to historical footnotes" (Dion, 2009, p. 73). This means that the diversity and complexity of Indigenous societies is eclipsed by the "heroic journey" of the colonizers as they "discovered" and conquered the "New World."

Long before this continent was colonized, many nations prospered here. Indigenous ways of living have always had roots in the land. Values guide these lifeways and flow from Indigenous worldview. There is great diversity within and among nations in our languages, cultural practices, laws and thought. This diversity is reflected in the land. Nations situated in the mountains, by the ocean, throughout the Great Lakes, or in the desert hold songs, stories, ceremonies, and philosophies that honour their physical reality. They are nourished by different foods and they know different medicines. The environment is inexorably tied to Indigenous knowledge, practices and values.

Many Indigenous scholars have contributed to a profound, meaningful and growing body of written work on worldviews and lifeways. These prominent thinkers have reached back into the depth of history with an analysis of our present context and relations, at the same time looking ahead to envision a strong future for all peoples and the earth. It is important to acknowledge the work of Vine Deloria, Jr. (1973, 1988, 2006), Winona Laduke (1999), Gregory Cajete (1994, 2000a, 2000b), Leroy Little Bear (2000), Daniel Wildcat (2009), and Leanne Simpson (2012). I am forever grateful to the leadership of the Three Fires Mide-wiwin lodge, specifically Edward Benton-Banai, Jim Dumont and Pauline Shirt, who have in both their writing and life work deeply influenced my thinking and learning as an Anishinabe kwe.

With all of our differences, there is consistency in worldviews shared by Indigenous peoples. Anishinabe worldview philosophy has two main facets: all of life has spirit, and we come from the earth (Benton-Banai, 1988). This assertion expresses an essential duality and balance in our knowing. Leroy Little Bear (2000) thoroughly explains key philosophies found across Indigenous worldviews:

> Tribal territory is important because the Earth is our Mother (and this is not a metaphor: it is real). The Earth cannot be separated from the actual being of Indians. The Earth is where the continuous and/or repetitive process of creation occurs. . . . Creation is a continuity. If creation is to continue, then it must be renewed. Renewal ceremonies, the telling and retelling of creation stories, the singing and resinging of the songs, are all

humans' part in the maintenance of creation. Hence the Sundance, societal ceremonies, the unbundling of medicine bundles at certain phases
of the year – all of which are interrelated aspects of happenings that take
place on and within Mother Earth. All of the above leads one to articulate
Aboriginal philosophy as being holistic and cyclical or repetitive, generalist, process-oriented, and firmly grounded in a particular place (Little
Bear, 2000, p. 78).

Being firmly grounded in place does not mean that we did not move. There was
a freedom of movement to support the varied lifeways of many nations. International laws were developed among Indigenous nations prior to colonization to
respect and protect land and territory, ensuring that all of life would be taken care
of (Royal Commission on Aboriginal Peoples [RCAP], 1996a, p. 112). The Dish with
One Spoon treaty is one such law. This agreement between the Anishinabe and
Haudenosaunee set out a mutual commitment to look after shared territory in
peace and friendship. Both parties were to use only what they needed, ensuring
families and communities lived well without compromising the land, waters, and
all other living beings. This treaty is one among many laws within and between Indigenous nations that supported unrestricted movement within a context of peace
(Lytwyn, 1997; Borrows, 2010a, 2010b; Simpson, 2012).

Respect for the independence of distinct nations was upheld. As explained by
Johnson (2007), "None of these families [nations] either exercised or expected to
exercise authority over the others" (Johnson, 2007, p. 20). Coexistence meant a
lived policy of non-interference in governance or other practices that supported
the diversity of Indigenous nations.

A significant period in Anishinabe history is known as the great migration, or
Chibimoodaywin. This migration demonstrated the free movement of Anishinabe
people, long before forced displacement was imposed through colonialism. The
enduring oral history of the great migration has been translated and written into
English by Edward Benton-Banai (1988). Simpson (2012) also writes about this
movement.

Chibimoodaywin is said to have lasted 500 years and took place well over a
thousand years ago. Knowledge of this time has been passed down through oral
tradition, painted and carved onto rock, and written on birch bark scrolls. The
great migration was a massive physical movement of Anishinabe people from the
east coast to the western shores of the Great Lakes. There were seven known major
stopping places along the migration, forming Anishinabe communities that still
exist today. When the prophecies came and word travelled, families and communities discussed their meaning and ultimately moved at their own pace, in their
own time. The seven major stopping places became permanent settlements but
many families journeyed north or south along the way. Some people, too, chose to
stay in the east.

The migration was a physical movement but it was also social, political and
spiritual. It is said that the Anishinabe population was abundant and life was good

in the east (Benton-Banai, 1988, p. 94). Prophecies came to the people warning them about the coming of colonization. They were urged to move westward in order to protect the nation.

It is important to note that there was no authoritarian government or leader dictating the movement of the people. An advanced clan governance system provided processes for dialogue and decision-making. The steps taken by the people were of their own free will: "Debate, respect for dissenting voices, consensus, and the respect for the sovereignty of individuals, families, and clans, allowed the spread of Nishnaabeg [Anishinabe] people as a movement of energy over the land" (Simpson, 2012, p. 67).

The Dish with One Spoon treaty and the great migration of Anishinabe people are significant happenings in the history of this continent. These events still only begin to uncover the depth and complexity of Indigenous history in this part of the world. The Dish with One Spoon treaty and the great migration were envisioned and carried out through the values, knowledge and practices embedded in Indigenous worldviews. Colonialism was an unwanted and unwarranted disruption of these ways of being.

## Colonialism in Context

While colonization is a relatively recent occurrence in the history of this continent, it has aggressively altered the lifeways of Indigenous nations. In this section I consider the concepts of colonialism, imperialism, and Eurocentrism as they have been central to displacement of Indigenous communities. Colonizers came to the "New World" to expand the wealth and power of European countries. Colonialism — the establishment of colonies in the Americas — required the conquest of lands and effective clearing of perceived obstacles to settlement and industry. This was a practice of imperialism, wherein one country sought to broaden its scope of power by overtaking territories. Imperialism is the ideological foundation from which colonialism spread.

The expropriation of Indigenous lands was fundamental to colonialism and the establishment of European dominance in this part of the world. To secure control over lands and resources, Indigenous nations were displaced by colonizers. The final report of the RCAP (1996a) outlines the history of forced removal and relocation of Indigenous nations prior to and following the establishment of Canada in 1867. Initial displacement occurred as nations moved to avoid the arrival of European populations in their Indigenous territories.

To make way for settlement and development, colonialism required mass extermination and displacement of Indigenous nations. Indigenous populations were decimated through the spread of disease, warfare and genocide, forced removal and relocation to small, isolated reserves, and the destruction of ways of life (Thornton, 1987). In the lands that now comprise Canada, a population of approximately 500,000 Indigenous people before contact was reduced to 102,000 by 1871 (RCAP, 1996a, p. 21). These numbers constitute a "conservative estimate" based on first "extensive" contact between Europeans and Indigenous nations; some approximations of pre-contact Indigenous populations amount to over 2 million people (RCAP, 1996a, p. 20-21).

Forced displacement of Indigenous nations was fundamental to the establishment of Canada and took the form of administrative and development relocations (RCAP, 1996a, p. 395). Administrative displacements consolidated remote, widely dispersed communities to cut government costs and to make service delivery more "convenient." Administrative displacements documented by the RCAP (1996a) include the "centralization" of Mi'kmaq communities in Nova Scotia in the 1940s (p. 401), relocation of Inuit of Hebron and Nutak, Labrador in the 1950s (p. 405), and the removal of Sayisi Dene of northern Manitoba in 1956 (p. 413). Communities were displaced without consent or consultation and often at short notice (RCAP, 1996a, p. 396).

Transportation, agriculture and energy projects have also forced the relocation of Indigenous communities for the purposes of "development." Canada's first Prime Minister, John A. Macdonald, spearheaded the transnational railway, a project instrumental to the country's economic and political expansion. Daschuk (2013) accounts the brutal treatment of Indigenous communities during this period of development under the direction of Macdonald. The railway expanded westward, stirring up conflict over territories. Macdonald directed the relocation of communities and withholding of food rations to suppress Indigenous resistance to the railway project.

The RCAP (1996a) details further examples of displacement brought on by development projects. The Saugeen Ojibwe in Ontario faced multiple land surrenders and relocations from the early 1830s, pushed "onto smaller and smaller parcels of land" to clear lands for agricultural development (p. 446). The Manitoba Chemawmawin Cree were displaced in the 1950s to make way for development of the Grand Rapids hydroelectric dam (p. 460). In 1910 the Songhees were forced off their land so that the city of Victoria, British Columbia could grow (p. 448). Indigenous nations continue to face development induced displacement, as forestry, mining and energy developments pose ongoing threats to communities and territories.

A Eurocentric worldview has been essential to the colonial project. **Eurocentrism** refers to the privileging of one culture, the dominant White European culture, over all others. This has been recognized as "cultural imperialism" by a number of theorists (Bishop, 2002; Mullaly, 2010). Systems of thought, governance, economy, and law must fit the dominant model to be considered civilized and of value. According to Henderson (2000), Eurocentric thought "serve[s] colonial domination by universalizing negative caricatures of Indigenous peoples to justify aggression, control, and domination" (Henderson, 2000, p. 57). A Eurocentric worldview underpins the values and practices necessary for colonial violence. Battiste (2000) identifies the Eurocentric worldview as **cognitive imperialism** (Battiste, 2000, p. 198).

Indigenous nations that survived colonial assaults on their territories were forced to assimilate into dominant society, to adopt one "legitimate" language, culture, and frame of reference. Imposed through law and education, assimilation has been a profound strategy for the ongoing suppression of Indigenous nations. Assimilative policies disconnect communities from their ways of life. By rejecting Indigenous knowledge, languages, values, and practices and taking up those of the dominant culture, the "uncivilized" can ostensibly become "civilized." Assimilation serves the colonizing governments' long-term goal of eliminating treaty obligations (Truth and Reconciliation Commission [TRC], 2012, p. 12). With no distinct Indigenous identity or legal standing, there can be no distinct Indigenous communities or territories. The empire can then lay claim to all lands.

## Treaty-making Before and After Canada

To understand the historical and present context of Indigenous nations in what is now Canada, a thorough consideration of treaties is necessary. This section offers a brief overview of treaty-making between colonizers and Indigenous nations. The history of treaties before and after the establishment of Canada has been widely studied, but the dominant historical narrative neglects power imbalances involved. Particularly valuable to understanding the complexities of this history are works by Johnson (2007), Long (2010), Venne (1997), Borrows (1997, 2010a, 2010b), Miller (2009), and Asch (2014). The RCAP (1996a, 1996b) final report also provides thorough research and recommendations on the history and future of treaty relations in Canada and is a valuable resource for further research.

Treaties are significant nation-to-nation agreements. A total of 123 treaties and land surrenders had taken place at Confederation in 1867; today the number amounts to over 500 (Dickason 2002, p. 253). It is important to note that many communities in Canada never surrendered their lands in treaty but the lands were still taken (Johnson, 2007, p. 25). In addition to pre-Confederation treaties, a substantial land base was secured for the development of Canada between 1871 and 1921 through what are known as the Numbered Treaties. Treaty-making was at a standstill from the early 1920s into the 1970s, primarily due to provisions in the Indian Act that prevented Indigenous communities from pursuing land claims (Miller, 2009, p. 5). Fifteen modern day treaties, also known as comprehensive land claim settlements, have been agreed to since 1975 (Aboriginal Affairs and Northern Development Canada, 2010).

The nation-to-nation relationship essential to treaties was formally recognized in the Royal Proclamation of 1763. The Proclamation set out parameters for the acquisition of Indigenous lands, including requirements that only the Crown (and not individual settlers) could negotiate with Indigenous nations for land (Miller, 2009, p. 70). This was a meaningful development in the legal recognition of Indigenous nationhood and rights and the protection of Indigenous lands (Venne, 1997, p. 173).

Inalienable rights are also referred to as inherent rights, concepts central to the historical and present context of treaties. These rights are understood as grounded in the land and the very being of Indigenous nations (RCAP, 1996a, p. 605). "Aboriginal title" to lands is considered an untransferable, inherent right: "Aboriginal and treaty rights" are enshrined in Section 35 of the Constitution (1982). From an Indigenous perspective, inherent right to land is a foundation of the treaty relationship. Johnson (2007) articulates this perspective as one family (Indigenous nations) choosing to share its territory and gifts with another family (European nations), out of kindness and respect (p. 25).

This perspective on treaty-making has not been shared by the colonizer. Long (2010) identifies an essential contradiction in the treaty-making process set out in the Royal Proclamation, wherein the Crown "acknowledged aboriginal title, on the one hand, while authorizing its orderly, state-sanctioned extinguishment, on the other" (p. 24). Moreover, Borrows (1997) contends that treaties were "the British [and Canadian] government's attempt to exercise sovereignty over First Nations while simultaneously trying to convince First Nations that they would remain separate from European settlers and have their jurisdiction preserved" (p. 169).

This contradiction exposes a crucial imbalance in understandings of and approaches to treaty-making, a result of distinct worldviews and the colonizing, assimilative imperatives driving Canada's development. From the colonizer's point of view, treaties were about abolishing Indigenous rights to land as these rights were seen as barriers to settlement and industry (Miller, 2009, p. 102). Treaty negotiations were a less expensive means to acquire lands than all-out war, as evidenced in the United States, and were meant to constitute "the final, once-and-for-all means of opening up Indian lands for settlement and development" (Dickason, 2002, p. 255). So despite the nation-to-nation relationship outlined in the Royal Proclamation of 1763, treaty-making has been built on unlevel ground.

In treaty negotiations, lands were surrendered in exchange for various benefits that were guaranteed to ostensibly ensure the well-being of Indigenous nations (RCAP, 1996a, p. 605). These promises included education, health care, food, tools, blankets and financial compensation. The government lived up to these promises minimally, if at all.

Venne (1997) emphasizes the conflict between the written text of treaties and the agreement that was negotiated: the written document expresses only the colonizer's view (Venne, 1997, p. 173). The RCAP (1996b) confirms that what was orally agreed to at the time of treaty signing is part of a treaty's "spirit and intent" (RCAP, 1996b, p. 19). Indeed, misleading treaty negotiations wherein commissioners gave their word to Indigenous nations, to include only some of these words in the treaties, are being uncovered and contended with in Canadian courts (Long, 2010, p. 5).

Johnson (2007) illustrates the linguistic and conceptual misunderstandings at the heart of imbalanced treaty relationships. He documents the discrepancy between the oral history carried within his family and community around the signing of Treaty Six, and the written text of the treaty. Treaty commissioner Alexander

Morris did not accurately explain the written conditions, wherein the Cree people were agreeing to "cede, release, surrender and yield up . . . all rights, titles and privileges" (Treaty No. 6, 1964). These contentions are established in oral history and verified by Morris' journals and letters (Johnson, 2007, p. 41).

Treaties were understood by Indigenous nations as sacred and lasting (RCAP, 1996b, p. 17). Treaties were to endure for generations into the future, "as long as the Sun shines, the Grass grows, and the River flows" (Johnson, 2007, p. 29). However, a persistent Eurocentric worldview and its accompanying values and practices prevented treaty-making "in good faith." Former Prime Minister Pierre Trudeau exemplified this way of thinking, purporting that treaties were "anachronistic 'contracts' with 'historical might-have-beens' which 'shouldn't go on forever'" (Long, 2010, p. 4). This view negates the nation-to-nation relationship so fundamental to treaties. This relationship is further undermined by the legacy of forced assimilation and enfranchisement through law.

## Forced Assimilation through Law: Enfranchisement and the Indian Act

Assimilation and "enfranchisement" have been integral to the cultural displacement of Indigenous nations, the disruption and attempted erasure of lifeways and identity. The concept of enfranchisement in Canada was established in the 1876 *Indian Act* and earlier versions of the Act. The 1857 *Act to Encourage the Gradual Civilization of Indian Tribes* and the 1869 *Act for the Gradual Enfranchisement of Indians* set out a system of control through which the colonizing government — specifically, the Department of Indian Affairs — exercised total authority over the lives of Indigenous peoples. Enfranchisement meant the full legal assimilation of an Indigenous person, giving up all rights as an Indian to become Canadian. Enfranchisement meant rejecting one's identity, leaving one's family and community, and losing all claim to treaty rights and lands. Cultural imperialism is explicitly built into this legislation: "Euro-Canadians confidently expected that Indians would eventually be assimilated, as there was nothing in their way of life that was worth preserving" (Dickason, 2002, p. 239).

Legal assimilation was first attempted through voluntary enfranchisement. It was hoped that Indigenous people would simply "opt out" of being Indian and "opt in" to being Canadian. This exercise failed, as only one person voluntarily enfranchised between 1859-1876 (TRC, 2012, p. 12). Later, involuntary enfranchisement was legislated into the *Indian Act*. A person would be forcibly enfranchised if they wanted to vote, join the military or pursue post-secondary education (Stonechild, 2006, p. 21).

The *Indian Act* has been revised many times over, but for generations has imposed brutal restrictions on the lives of Indigenous peoples. Indian women who married non-Indian men lost their status, as did their children (RCAP, 1996a, p. 254). Indians had no right to vote (RCAP, 1996a, p. 236). The *Indian Act* denied freedom of movement: a pass system required permission from an Indian agent to leave the reservation (Stonechild, 2006, p. 19). A judge could issue a court order to forcibly relocate a reserve, without the community's consent (RCAP, 1996a, 261). Indians could not gather in groups of three or more, for the offence of "incitement of Indians to riot" (Dickason, 2002, p. 268), and they could not raise funds for legal counsel (RCAP, 1996a, p. 272). Cultural practices and ceremonies, so fundamental to Indigenous ways of life, were outlawed (Dickason, 2002, 266). It was mandatory for Indian children to attend residential schools (TRC, 2012, p. 12). The Indian Act imposed a band council governance structure, dictated election processes, and ultimately allowed for the Superintendent of Indian Affairs to overturn any community decision (RCAP, 1996a, 263). Some of these restrictions were removed in 1951 amendments to the Act, but it was not until 1960 that all Indians achieved the right to vote in Canada (RCAP, 1996a, p. 236).

The enduring effects of these restrictions on the lives of Indigenous people and nations cannot be understated. In effect, the Canadian government legislated Eurocentrism and imposed cognitive imperialism in an attempt to suffocate Indigenous lifeways. Johnson (2007) details the crippling dependency created and perpetuated through this legislation, affecting lived physical and cultural realities: "Our dependence is more than psychological. We have become dependent on you [the government] for our very survival" (Johnson, 2007, p. 60). By legislating control over so many aspects of people's lives for the explicit purposes of assimilation, the colonizing government inflicted a lasting trauma that continues to be carried through generations. British Columbia Provincial Court Judge Alfred Scow of the Kwakiutl nation explained to the RCAP (1996a):

> The Indian Act did a very destructive thing in outlawing the ceremonials. This provision of the Indian Act was in place for close to 75 years and what that did was it prevented the passing down of our oral history. It prevented the passing down of our values. It meant an interruption of the respected forms of government that we used to have, and we did have forms of government. . . . We had a system that worked for us (RCAP, 1996a, p. 268–269).

The "gradual enfranchisement and civilization" of Indigenous peoples was further attempted through "blood quantum." A blood quantum system was implemented in the 1869 Act, requiring "at least one-quarter Indian blood" for one to be considered a legal Indian (Dickason, 2002, p. 238). Government imposition and regulation of Indian status through the Indian Act seized any degree of self-determination over Indigenous identity and community membership. It guaranteed that intermarriage with "non-Indians" would lead to "non-Indian" children. This effectively displaced individuals and families from communities. The Act ensures that after so many generations of intermarriage, all that will remain are non-Indian Canadians. The *Indian Act* continues to advance the eventual, but inevitable enfranchisement of all Indians. This system of status regulation is still in place today.

**Displacement through Education: A Solution to the "Indian Problem"**

Education has been used as a tool for assimilation since before the confederation of Canada. Churches and governments colluded to accelerate assimilation through an extensive, legally entrenched system of residential schools that lasted over 100 years. Eurocentric education in residential schools solidified and intensified the physical and cultural displacement of Indigenous nations. Residential schools forcibly removed Indigenous children from their communities and pushed languages and cultures to near extinction.

The first residential school project was established in New France in 1620 (Miller, 1996, p. 39). Early initiatives were considered generally unsuccessful until the idea of residential schools was revived in the 1830s, led by churches and funded by government grants. Prime Minister John A. Macdonald formalized the residential school system in 1883 (TRC, 2012, p. 6). Though operated by various churches, the Canadian government selected principals, covered operating expenses and built the schools. Demonstrating the Eurocentric justification for residential schools, Macdonald stated in 1883:

> When the school is on the reserve, the child lives with his parents who are savages; he is surrounded by savages, and though he may learn to read and write, his habits and training and mode of thought are Indian. He is simply a savage who can read and write. It has been strongly pressed upon myself, as head of the Department [of Indian Affairs], that Indian children should be withdrawn as much as possible from the parental influence . . . where they will acquire the habits and modes of thought of white men (cited in Stonechild, 2006, p . 9).

The TRC (2012) has comprehensively documented the realities of the residential school system in Canada. Over 150,000 First Nation, Métis and Inuit children attended over 150 schools. Children were removed from their communities by force, without their parent's knowledge or consent. Children suffered from poor nutrition and inadequate health care. They were forced to speak English and punished for speaking their Indigenous languages. Students were renamed and assigned numbers. They did not receive quality education; in fact, most staff had no teaching qualifications or experience (RCAP, 1996a, p. 333). There is extensive documentation of physical, emotional and sexual trauma inflicted upon Indigenous students attending residential schools (Haig-Brown, 1988; Miller, 1996; RCAP, 1996a; Fournier & Grey, 1998; Milloy, 1999; Agnes, 2006; TRC, 2012). Moreover, the system imposed a lasting cognitive imperialism:

> Residential schools disrupted families and communities. They prevented elders from teaching children long-valued cultural and spiritual traditions and practices. They helped kill languages. These were not the side effects of a well-intentioned system: the purpose of the residential school system was to separate children from the influences of their parents and their community, so as to destroy their culture (TRC, 2012, p. 1).

This purpose was made clear by Duncan Campbell Scott, one of the most aggressive proponents of residential schools in Canada. Scott headed the Department of Indian Affairs from 1913 until 1932. In 1920, Scott described the system's ultimate goal of assimilation:

> I want to get rid of the Indian problem. I do not think as a matter of fact, that this country ought to continually protect a class of people who are able to stand alone. That is my whole point. Our objective is to continue until there is not a single Indian in Canada that has not been absorbed into the body politic, and there is no Indian question, and no Indian department (cited in Stonechild, 2006, p. 9).

Scott was referring to the objective of the *Indian Act*: to extinguish the "Indian problem." Indians and Indian lands were considered to be in the way of progress. Canada was founded and grew as a nation on this fundamental Eurocentric belief. The supposed salvation of Indians was legislated through the *Indian Act* and the residential school system. Stonechild (2006) explains that students forced into this "radical experiment in social engineering . . . were expected to be grateful to have been given the opportunity to receive such an education" (Stonechild, 2006, p. 19).

While the last residential school closed in 1996, the legacy of this system is a lived reality for many. The residential school system inflicted a collective trauma on Indigenous nations. This trauma is intergenerational. The TRC (2012) has confirmed that this system "was an obvious assault on children, families, communities and generations to come. . . . The effects continue to be inherited by the children, grandchildren and great-grandchildren of survivors" (TRC, 2012, p. 86). These inherited effects are amplified by the Eurocentric curriculum that is maintained in Canada's schools. Battiste (2000) contends that Indigenous students are still invisible in education (Battiste, 2000, p. 198). Illustrating the impact of this curriculum on Indigenous students, Henderson (2000) writes:

> . . . the realization of their invisibility is similar to looking into a still lake and not seeing their images. They become alien in their own eyes, unable to recognize themselves in the reflections and shadows of the world. As their grandparents and parents were stripped of their wealth and dignity, this realization strips Aboriginal students of their heritage and identity. It gives them an awareness of their annihilation (Henderson, 2000, p. 59).

The experience of cultural displacement is exacerbated through education. For Indigenous students, mainstream education is confusing and alienating. There is a constructed sense of belonging nowhere, isolated from one's Indigenousness and ostracized from the mainstream. Indigenous knowledge and worldviews have not been completely destroyed, but are instead left jagged and fragmentary (Little Bear, 2000). As a result of colonial and imperial imposition, many Indigenous peoples walk through this world with what Cajete (2000a) calls a split mind: "We lead lives of paradoxical conflict and contrast... the lack of knowing where we are, where we are going, and where we are coming from" (Cajete, 2000a, p. 187).

## A Decolonization Movement

Though education has been a powerful tool to feed colonization, it can also be used to "heal the split." Indigenous nations in Canada and throughout the world have actively engaged in reclaiming education. This reclamation has been central to the broader movement of decolonization, a rejection and undoing of the colonial project. Decolonization involves restoration of what was denied to Indigenous nations through physical and cultural displacement. It involves multifaceted strategies for rebuilding identities, laws, and territories. A renewal of values and worldviews is made possible through revitalization of languages, ceremonies and lifeways.

In North America, Indigenous movements grew in the 1960s and 70s, the "first stirrings" taking place as World War II veterans attempted to return to their communities and were forced to enter low-wage jobs in cities (Deloria, 1973, p. 3). The "Indian movement," as it is often referred to, began in cities, in prisons, in makeshift community centres and around kitchen tables. It took hold across North America. Those who had kept spiritual and cultural practices underground reemerged in this time (Anderson, 2011, p. 31). Maria Campbell (2011) reflects:

> . . . times were changing in the 1960s, especially in Indian country. The old people had become 'radicals', or so they were called by some officials. They traveled the country holding cultural and spiritual teaching sessions wherever they could find a space, and young people came from everywhere, hungry for their knowledge. It was their stories that brought us back and launched what we now know as the Aboriginal healing movement. Their stories taught us to decolonize ourselves and reclaim our communities (p. xvii).

Protests began taking place across the continent. Deloria (1973) writes of the first significant blockade that took place in December 1968 at the Cornwall bridge. By 1970 the protests had spread far and wide:

> There was no sense [yet] of national coordination and the issues appeared to be a conglomerate of local complaints. . . . It was apparent, however, that beneath all of these local protests there was the important issue of restoring the old ways and raising the question of people and their right to a homeland (Deloria, 1973, p. 7).

The American Indian Movement (AIM) and the National Indian Brotherhood (NIB) are recognized in Canada and the United States as the heart of the Indigenous political movement of this time. Many social, economic and political issues were discussed and acted upon as part of this movement. Education was at the centre. It was woven into the reclaiming and revitalizing of "the old ways."

In 1972 the NIB released *Indian Control of Indian Education*. This policy paper marked "a major turning point in Native education in Canada" (Haig-Brown, 1988, p. 131). A statement on self-determination and the importance of education for Indigenous nations, this paper named the ongoing crisis in Indigenous education rooted in the assimilationist policies and practices of the Canadian government. The NIB emphasized local control and the responsibility of governments to follow through on treaty obligations:

> We must, therefore reclaim our right to direct the education of our children. . . . Indian parents seek participation and partnership with the Federal Government, whose legal responsibility for Indian education is set by the treaties and the Indian Act. . . . [W]e assert that only Indian people can develop a suitable philosophy of education based on Indian values adopted to modern living (p. 3).

In 1973, the recommendations of the policy paper *Indian Control of Indian Education* were adopted by the Canadian government. It inspired and supported language programs and community schools. It drew attention to the widespread crisis and called for action. However, while the federal government symbolically took this paper as a policy directive, their limited actions more accurately reflected their unwillingness to change. The residential school era had not yet ended. The *Indian Act* was still in place with the essential objective of assimilation, the eradication of the "Indian problem" and expropriation of remaining Indian lands.

The broader change movement across Indigenous nations was maintained. Education continued to be central to this movement. *Indian Control over Indian Education* corresponded with monumental legal and political struggles, achieved through the dedication and resilience of Indigenous people. "Aboriginal and treaty rights" were legally recognized in the Constitution (1982). Numerous amendments were made to the Indian Act, notably in 1985 Bill C-31, which reinstated Indian status for women and children who had married non-Indians. Residential school survivors were speaking up about their experiences, leading to numerous apologies from churches and eventually from the Canadian government (TRC, 2012).

While these changes do not undo the physical and cultural displacement imposed over the course of generations, they are significant steps toward a restoration of well-being across Indigenous nations and a better relationship with Canada. These achievements tell important stories of resistance that emerge from incredible resilience. Vital to this resistance has been reclamation of Indigenous worldview and lifeways: languages, ceremonies, knowledge of and connection to the land. Communities have understood that taking back their systems of education means a stronger nation.

Powerful examples of education as reclamation took place in the 1970s. The Red School House in St. Paul, Minnesota, and other culture-based community schools reestablished Indigenous knowledge and worldviews in environments that prepared children to succeed in the contemporary world (Davis, 2013). Elementary and secondary programs inspired higher learning programs and the development of Indigenous-controlled colleges and universities. Control over curriculum meant that families and communities could effectively take back what had been forcibly removed through the residential schools system, policies of termination and assimilation. It also meant that Indigenous people, in their pursuit of higher education, could acquire the tools necessary to challenge the dominant colonial narrative.

The success of community- and culture-based programs has to do with the work of education as decolonizing and as healing. We are repairing severed links to the past, piecing together our history that began long, long before the arrival of colonizers. We are confronting the colonial practices and imperialist narratives that have sought to displace our truths.

A decolonizing and healing education is a pathway for the relearning, rewriting and retelling of our own stories as Indigenous nations. These stories are real and can be restored within the fullness of our knowledge systems and worldview. Education involves an analysis of colonization, its strategies and impacts, but we are no longer forced to know ourselves only as victims of that system. We are not the problem.

Vine Deloria Jr. and Daniel Wildcat (2001) identify that the real "Indian problem" lies in the colonial legacy of Indian education in the Americas. This problem and indeed any solutions affect all peoples living on these lands: "The problem of Indian education in America is really the problem of education in America, regardless of whether the recipients of the education are, figuratively speaking, red, yellow, black, or white" (Deloria and Wildcat, 2001, p. 9).

Eurocentric education has largely silenced and devalued all those who do not fit the dominant culture's way of thinking and relating to the world. This system of education has erased the complex histories and identities of many nations. It has glorified the colonial violence inflicted on peoples across the world through the dominant historical narrative of the "heroic" colonizer. Cognitive imperialism constricts the potential in education to nourish whole-person learning in connection to one's community, history and the world. All people can benefit from a decolonizing education that restores Indigenous worldviews, values and practices.

---

**Reflective Questions**

1. What are some of the key differences between migration of Indigenous people before and after European arrival to present day North America?
2. Name some of the key policies that have played a role in the physical and cultural displacement of Indigenous people.
3. What role does education place in the displacement, as well as the resistance and resilience, of Indigenous peoples?
4. How does the decolonization movement offset the damage done by colonization and displacement experienced by Indigenous people?

---

## Conclusion

The deep and complex history of Indigenous nations across this continent is rooted in the land, our worldview and lifeways. I have offered a piece of the story of colonialism, a relatively recent occurrence in the history of this part of the world. Colonialism and imperialism imposed cultural displacement through law and education, attempting to erase all traces of our deep history and identity. Physical displacement of Indigenous peoples has and continues to be fundamental for the establishment and growth of Canada. The aggressive attack on Indigenous families and communities has been felt at the centre of our being as nations. Even with these wounds, Indigenous nations have proven their resilience through many approaches to a broad decolonization movement. We continue to heal.

Decolonizing is about undoing colonialism. First, we come to understand it. Then we reject it. Our resistance is grounded in our commitment to restore and renew: the dismantling of colonialism means that we envision another world. This world is possible because we know how our ancestors lived. We know they cherished all of life in a full way.

Colonialism displaced us from these ways of living, but it did not destroy them. Our ancestors carried our worldviews, values and practices with such care. They held on to languages, songs, ceremonies, and stories. What they could, they passed on. Some things were hidden for safekeeping.

The coming generations will inherit our wounds. But they will also inherit our commitment to the revitalization of our lifeways as Indigenous nations. It was told in Anishinabe prophecy that we would, in this time, have a choice to make. We can choose to look back, to search, and "to pick up what was left by the trail" (Benton-Banai, 1988, p. 93). What we pick up we can carry into the future.

> When I hear people say 'We've lost this; we've lost that', I do not believe that. We have not lost anything, we have just forgotten . . . [W]e are coming out of a big sleep. . . . We are waking up, and it's a beautiful thing, to wake up and see we are alive, we are still here (Elder Vern Harper, cited in RCAP 1996a, p. 632).

## References

Aboriginal Affairs and Northern Development Canada. (2010, August 15). *Treaties with Aboriginal people in Canada*. Retrieved from https://www.aadnc-aandc.gc.ca

Agnes, J. (Ed.). (2006). *Behind closed doors: Stories from the Kamloops Indian Residential School*. Kamloops, BC: Secwepemc Cultural Education Society.

Anderson, K. (2011). *Life stages and Native women: Memory, teachings and story medicine*. Winnipeg, MB: University of Manitoba Press.

Asch, M. (2014). *On being here to stay: Treaties and Aboriginal rights in Canada*. Toronto, ON: University of Toronto Press.

Battiste, M. (2000). Maintaining Aboriginal identity, language, and culture in modern society. In M. Battiste (Ed.), *Reclaiming Indigenous voice and vision* (pp. 192–208). Vancouver, BC: UBC Press.

Benton-Banai, E. (1988). *The Mishomis book: The voice of the Ojibway*. Hayward, WI: Indian Country Communications.

Bishop, A. (2002). *Becoming an ally: Breaking the cycle of oppression* (2nd ed.). Zed Books.

Borrows, J. (1992). A genealogy of law: Inherent sovereignty and First Nations self-government. *Osgoode Hall Law Journal, 30*(2), 291–353.

Borrows, John. (1997). Wampum at Niagara: Canadian legal history, self-government, and the Royal Proclamation. In M. Asch (Ed.), *Aboriginal and treaty rights in Canada: Essays on law, equality, and respect for difference* (pp. 155–172). Vancouver, BC: UBC Press.

Borrows, J. (2010a). *Canada's Indigenous constitution*. Toronto, ON: University of Toronto Press.

Borrows, J. (2010b). *Drawing out law: A spirit's guide*. Toronto, ON: University of Toronto Press.

Cajete, G. (1994). *Look to the mountain: An ecology of Indigenous education*. Durango, CO: Kivaki Press.

Cajete, G. (2000a). Indigenous knowledge: the Pueblo metaphor of Indigenous education. In M. Battiste (Ed.), *Reclaiming Indigenous voice and vision* (pp. 181–191). Vancouver, BC: UBC Press.

Cajete, G. (2000b). *Native science: Natural laws of interdependence*. Santa Fe, NM: Clear Light Books.

Campbell, M. (2011). Foreword. In K. Anderson, *Life stages and Native women: Memory, teachings, and story medicine* (pp. i–xix). Winnipeg, MB: University of Manitoba Press.

Daschuk, J. (2013). *Clearing the plains: disease, politics of starvation, and the loss of Aboriginal life*. Regina, SK: University of Regina Press.

Davis, J. (2013). *Survival schools: The American Indian Movement and community education in the Twin Cities*. Minneapolis, MN: University of Minnesota Press.

Deloria, V. (1973). *God is red: A Native view of religion*. Golden, CO: Fulcrum Publishing.

Deloria, V. (1988). *Custer died for your sins: An Indian manifesto*. Norman, OK: University of Oklahoma Press.

Deloria, V. (2006). *The world we used to live in: Remembering the powers of the medicine men*. Golden, CO: Fulcrum Publishing.

Deloria, V. & Wildcat, D. (2001). *Power and place: Indian education in America*. Golden, CO: Fulcrum Publishing.

Dickason, O. (2002). *Canada's First Nations: A history of founding peoples from earliest times* (3rd ed.). Toronto, ON: Oxford University Press.

Dion, S. (2009). *Braiding histories: Learning from Aboriginal peoples' experiences and perspectives*. Vancouver: UBC Press.

Fournier, S. & Grey, E. 1997. *Stolen from our embrace: The abduction of First Nations children and the restoration of Aboriginal communities*. Vancouver, BC: Douglas & MacIntyre.

Haig-Brown, C. (1988). *Resistance and renewal: Surviving the Indian residential school*. Vancouver, BC: Arsenal Pulp Press.

Henderson, J. Y. (2000). Postcolonial ghost dancing: Diagnosing European colonialism. In M. Battiste (Ed.), *Reclaiming Indigenous voice and vision* (pp. 57–76). Vancouver, BC: UBC Press.

Johnson, H. (2007). *Two Families: Treaties and government*. Saskatoon, SK: Purich.

Laduke, W. (1999). *All our relations: Native struggles for land and life*. Cambridge, MA: South End Press.

Laduke, W. (2005). *Recovering the sacred: The power of naming and claiming*. Toronto, ON: Between the Lines.

Little Bear, L. (2000). Jagged worldviews colliding. In M. Battiste (Ed.), *Reclaiming Indigenous voice and vision* (pp. 77–85). Vancouver, BC: UBC Press.

Long, J. (2010). *Treaty No. 9: Making the agreement to share the land in far northern Ontario in 1905*. Montreal, QC: McGill-Queens University Press.

Lytwyn, V. (1997). A dish with one spoon: The shared hunting grounds agreement in the Great Lakes and Lawrence Valley region. In D. H. Pendland (Ed.), *Papers of the 28th Algonquian Conference* (pp. 210–227). Winnipeg, MB: University of Manitoba Press.

Miller, J.R. (1996). *Shingwauk's vision: A history of Native residential schools*. Toronto, ON: University of Toronto Press.

Miller, J.R. (2009). *Compact, contract, covenant: Aboriginal treaty-making in Canada*. Toronto, ON: University of Toronto Press.

Milloy, J. (1999). *A national crime: The Canadian government and the residential school system, 1879-1986*. Winnipeg, MB: University of Manitoba Press.

Mullaly, B. (2010). *Challenging oppression and confronting privilege* (2nd ed.). Oxford University Press.

National Indian Brotherhood. (1972). *Indian Control of Indian Education*. Ottawa: National Indian Brotherhood.

Royal Commission on Aboriginal Peoples (RCAP). (1996a). *Report of the Royal Commission on Aboriginal Peoples: Looking forward, looking back*. Vol. 1. Ottawa.

RCAP. (1996b). *Report of the Royal Commission on Aboriginal Peoples: Restructuring the relationship*. Vol. 2. Ottawa.

Simpson, L. (2011). *Dancing on our turtle's back: Stories of Nishinaabeg re-creation, resurgence, and a new emergence*. Winnipeg, MB: Arbeiter Ring Publishing.

Smith, L.T. (1999). *Decolonizing methodologies: Research and Indigenous peoples*. New York, NY: Zed Books.

Stonechild, B. (2006). *The new buffalo: The struggle for Aboriginal post-secondary education in Canada*. Winnipeg, MB: University of Manitoba Press.

Thornton, R. 1987. *American Indian holocaust and survival: A population history since 1492*. Norman, OK: University of Oklahoma Press.

Treaty No. 6 between her Majesty the Queen and the Plain and Wood Cree Indians at Fort Carlton, Fort Pitt and Battle River with Adhesions, 1964. Retrieved from http://www.aadnc-aandc.gc.ca.

Truth and Reconciliation Commission of Canada. (2012). *They came for the children: Canada, Aboriginal peoples and residential schools*. Winnipeg, MB: Truth and Reconciliation Commission of Canada.

Venne, S. (1997). Understanding Treaty 6: An Indigenous perspective. In M. Asch (Ed.), *Aboriginal and Treaty Rights in Canada* (pp. 173–207). Vancouver, BC: UBC Press.

Wildcat, D. (2009). *Red alert! Saving the planet with Indigenous knowledge*. Golden, CO: Fulcrum.

## CHAPTER THREE

# Environmental Migration: A Critical Review of Concepts, Policy and Literature

*Sepehr Pashang*

O ver the past few decades, we have witnessed countless environmental disasters and crises such as flooding, drought, ice storms, mud slides, and rises in sea level that have led to poverty, resource depletion, habitat destruction, and to increased levels of human movement and immobility. While disasters are terrible events everywhere, for populations living in the global south, these events result in more calamitous consequences. This is partly due to the effects of colonization and globalized capitalist economies with the resultant global disparities, such as underdevelopment, overpopulation and poor infrastructure, as well as conflict, war, violence, poverty, and political and economic repression. There continue to be increasing pressures placed on the biosphere by the neoliberal capitalist and consumer classes, especially in the global north. For instance, multinational mining, oil/energy and lumber firms for decades have been extracting natural resources from the earth, and specifically, from the global south. Similarly, the oil sands in Canada, a multi-billion dollar industry, have contributed in a major way to negative environmental and health consequences. The impacts of such activities may include loss of biodiversity, contamination (land, water and air), human illness and death, as well as permanent environmental degradation. Over time, these activities have and will continue to severely shift environmental behavior and patterns, and contribute to climate change.

While the global south and north may face similar impacts, the consequences in the south are much more pronounced due to greater population density, weaker infrastructure, and lack of resources. As a result, there is an increased role for NGOs, governments, and international relief agencies to not only help reduce detrimental environmental consequences, but also to address the effects on people impacted by those environmental disasters. There are several ways social and environmental scientists examine the relationship between environmental changes and disasters, induced migration and displacement. Traditionally, studies examined changes/disasters and human movement independently of each other, without capturing an explicit cause and effect relationship. Over time, and with scientific and technological advances, this relationship was made more apparent and scientists were able to recommend policy changes and promote awareness about the impacts of greenhouse gases and other human-induced factors on migration, displacement, and immobility. Despite these advances, we still lack sufficient international policy, statistical data, or even adequate definitions of the effects of environmental change and disasters on human movement.

This chapter is organized in the following way. First, it will introduce and define environmental disasters, and provide context to understand their past and present relationship with human movement. Second, the chapter will illustrate the intersections, linkages, and associated variables pertaining to migration caused by environmental disasters. Despite earlier comprehensive works, publications, and predictions on environmentally induced migration (by researchers, agencies, and governments), there exists an absence of robust evidence regarding linked variables and relationships between environmental disasters and human migration. For instance, the World Bank (2010, pp. 108–109), in its 2010 *World Development Report*, noted that predictions are founded on "broad assessments of people exposed to increasing risks rather than analyses of whether exposure will lead them to migrate." Third, the chapter will emphasize the need for a universally accepted definition of environmentally induced migration, provide a review of policy, and discuss the gaps in research and literature. Limitations in recent literature are quite surprising as environmental change, migration, displacement, and immobility are at the forefront of international debate. Next, the politicization of terms, anti-asylum lobbying, as well as Canada's role in dealing with environmentally induced migration are discussed. Fifth, adaptation and resilience due to climate change and environmental disasters are discussed, through both a global and community lens. Last, policy recommendations and concluding thoughts are provided.

## Background on Environmental Disasters and Human Migration

In 1990, the Intergovernmental Panel on Climate Change (IPCC) predicted that the most severe consequences of climate change would be those affecting human migration and displacement, as a result of flooding, drought and shoreline erosion (Boano et al., 2008). In the pages that follow, it will be argued that our biosphere has entered a new era, the Anthropocene, where **anthropogenic pressures** (environmental impacts caused by humans) have become the dominant drivers of change. Since the Industrial Revolution and the expansion of human enterprise, our earth's ability to maintain the resiliency of the Holocene epoch (which began 11,700 years ago) has been undermined. In the IPCC's *Fifth Assessment Report* (Stocker et al., 2013), scientific experts determined that, since the 1800s, humans have been responsible for the warming of our planet. The findings undoubtedly support the notion that drastic expansion of **advanced capitalism** and the negative consequences of industrialization, globalization and urbanization have brought about environmental pressures that could destabilize our earth system, and trigger irreversible damage.

Since the 1800s, humans have contributed to the expansion of the **greenhouse effect** by raising the concentration of carbon dioxide ($CO_2$) in the atmosphere by 40%, to 391 parts per million (ppm) in 2011 (Stocker et al., 2013), through burning fossil fuels (primarily coal and oil), land-use changes, and deforestation. Levels of other greenhouse gases have also been increased by human activity: methane is produced by agriculture, the decomposition of wastes in landfills, and livestock manure; and nitrous oxide has been released in increasing quantities through the use of commercial fertilizers, fossil fuels, and biomass combustion. The ozone layer has been depleted through the creation and release of industrial chemicals such as chlorofluorocarbons (CFCs) (NASA, n.d.). Alarmingly, we have already surpassed the "safe level" (350 ppm) of atmospheric carbon dioxide, and continue to increase $CO_2$ levels by 2 ppm annually (Hansen et al., 2008). As a consequence, we have witnessed the environmental events mentioned above. In this chapter, I will use the general term **pollution** to describe the various emissions noted above.

In spite of much new knowledge about environmental problems, little progress has been made in slowing economic production or consumption, along with the effects on the environment that are associated with them. This raises questions about how corporations and governments, particularly Canadian, contribute to environmental events and forced migration, and particularly how their agendas often impede positive outcomes.

Climate change and environmental disasters will also engender political destabilization, human insecurity and economic turmoil, as can be witnessed in many slums and refugee camps around the world. For instance, in Bangladesh, environmental changes provoked employment and income disparities, which in turn, spawned internal and external migration (Alam, 2003). Most people unable to cross borders will search for refuge within their own countries (**internal displacement**) because they can't afford to travel, are refused entry or exit across borders, or fear insecurity in host countries. Consequently, this can lead to overcrowding, sanitation and health risks, and many other hindrances to communities.

## What Is an Environmental Disaster?

Many of us have heard of or have lived through environmental disasters, yet it is necessary to clarify exactly what is meant by the term. According to the Centre for Research on the Epidemiology of Disasters (CRED), **disasters** consist of a variety of natural events; categories include biological, climatological, geophysical, hydrological, and meteorological disasters. For a disaster to be entered into CRED's International Disaster Database (EM-DAT), the following criteria must be met:

(1) Ten or more people are reported killed;

(2) One hundred or more people are reported affected;

(3) There is a declaration of a state of emergency; and

(4) There is a call for international assistance (EM-DAT: OFDA/CRED).

CRED's definition of disasters includes occurrences such as earthquake, drought, epidemic, extreme temperature, flood, insect infestation, storms, volcanoes, and wildfire (EM-DAT: OFDA/CRED).[1] Despite the robustness of CRED's database and classifications, two questions need to be raised. First, why does it omit environmental impacts on other living beings (plants, trees, and animals) that we depend on? Second, why are gradual and less visible disasters, and those with less immediate or identified risks, excluded? Perhaps the most serious implication of this limitation is that such risks may eventually lead to illness or death, yet may not be counted as a consequence of the disaster. Difficulties may arise when attempts are made to raise awareness or implement prevention and intervention policies.

The IPCC's definition differs from CRED's in a number of important ways. Rightfully avoiding the number of deaths and injuries as criteria, the IPCC offers a comprehensive definition of **disasters** by describing them as "[s]evere alterations in the normal functioning of a community or a society due to hazardous physical events interacting with vulnerable social conditions, leading to widespread adverse human, material, economic, or environmental effects that require immediate emergency response to satisfy critical human needs and that may require external support for recovery" (Field et al., 2012, p. 4). The IPCC's definition also addresses gradual and non-visible impacts by observing that "social vulnerability and exposure are key determinants of disaster risk and help explain why non-extreme physical events and chronic hazards can also lead to extreme impacts and disasters, while some extreme events do not" (Field et al., 2012, p. 27). This holistic definition further supports the notion of interconnectedness and interdependence of humans and other living things in our biosphere.

> **Reflective Questions**
>
> 1. In your opinion, how can these definitions be strengthened?
> 2. Why are robust and holistic definitions important in fields such as migration and environmental studies?

### Environmental Migration: Myth or Reality?

Throughout history, some have used religious or philosophical perspectives to justify or explain environmental events as acts of punishment, while others have used political or economic agendas to deny or disregard the linkages between pollution and climate change. Advances in science and technology as well as

---

[1] A detailed list of disaster types, groups, and sub-groups can be found at http://www.emdat.be/classification.

environmental consciousness, activism and education have enabled us to strive for evidence-based determinations. While there is still much debate among the religious, political, and scientific communities pertaining to environmental change and disasters, we can be certain that our biosphere and our livelihoods have never been more at risk of flux and volatility.

In 2010, it was estimated that 214 million people were living in host countries as refugees or immigrants, while it is projected that by 2050 this figure will increase to 405 million (Davis et al., 2013). This, however, is an underestimation of total displacement and migration, as it only takes legalized international migration into account. For instance, the U.S. alone is known to host over 12 million illegal migrants. (A **host country** can be defined as the country that people migrate *to*, in relation to the country they are leaving *from*.)

The majority of the world's projected population in 2050 of nine billion people will reside in urban areas, some of which are vulnerable to rising sea levels, intense storms and droughts, as well as flooding. There is no doubt that these environmental disasters will promote even higher levels of migration and displacement throughout both rural and urban regions. The findings seem to be consistent with other research conducted by the UN Refugee Agency (UNHCR), which states that migration due to environmental and climatic change is evident today, and could in the course of the twenty-first century reach unprecedented levels. Those living in developing nations and in island states will be impacted first and with the greatest severity, as they lack access to adaptive, resilient, and sustainable systems and conditions (Warner et al., 2009). Despite these observations, the causes and impacts of migration are challenging to differentiate when taking into account environmental, socioeconomic and political push and pull factors (Davis et al., 2013).

Even with adaptation measures put in place to reduce migration, poorer nations will be less able to maintain and support such measures and policies. As a result, migration from less developed nations will continue, creating conflict between migrants and those already living in migrants' destination communities (Reuveny, 2007). To confront migratory influx, host nations implement restrictive border control and immigration policies that prevent the movement of unwanted migrants into their territories. The consequences can be dire, as disenfranchised communities impacted by environmental disasters will face a rise in severe uncertainties and consequences such as environmental degradation, illness and death, violence and economic disparity, to name a few.

Although economic and socio-political constituents are key forces of migration and displacement, analysts are more frequently labelling environmental change and disasters as major contributing drivers (Warner et al., 2009). For instance, drought, water shortages, ocean acidification, and decline in fish stocks are said to cause great insecurity and instability in politically destabilized regions. The data are rather controversial, and there is no general agreement. A recent U.S. report, "The Arab Spring and Climate Change," claims that along with the socio-political and economic stressors that led to uprisings in Syria and Egypt, climate change and human mobility, prices of commodities and food insecurity also were driving forces (Werrell, 2013). These findings, while preliminary, suggest that environmental disasters may soon dictate global socio-economic, political and military events. The result would be a vicious circle, since these events also contribute to environmental disasters.

Having defined environmental disasters, it is important to briefly provide an overview of some concepts related to migration. In migration studies, elements of human population such as size, structure, distribution, and behaviour can change across space and over time. **Population change** is quantifiable as a result of births, deaths, and migration. While births and deaths are for the most part comparatively stable over time if we ignore wars and disasters, migration can be unstable, dynamic, and spontaneous. This is certainly true when considering environmental change and disaster-induced migration (Filho et al., 2011). Environmental changes intensify existing development obstacles that reside in affected areas, perpetuating social inequality and poverty. Therefore, it is not surprising that migration becomes top of mind for those who are already facing the impacts of environmental devastation. Some research has indicated that human

> ## Case Study 3.1
>
> Recently, New Zealand's Immigration Protection Tribunal twice rejected a family from Kiribati after the family's claim that rising sea levels made their home nation too dangerous to return to. The tribunal denied the claim on the grounds that no evidence indicated the family faced probable danger such as persecution.
>
> ## Reflective Questions
>
> 1. Why was the tribunal is reluctant to acknowledge this family as environmental refugees?
> 2. What steps must be taken to protect people affected by environmental disasters?

movement and displacement as a result of environmental change may surpass all past movements (Assan & Rosenfeld, 2012). One question that emerges from these findings is how prepared nations and agencies are to accommodate the influx of migrants, and whether they are even willing to make accommodations. It is concerning that many governments, including the one mentioned in Case Study 3.1, are not willing to include environmentally-induced migration as a valid claim. Without systematic immigration policy changes, more families will continue to face rejection, and ultimately **immobility**.

Despite incomplete data illustrating trends in environmentally induced migration, there are countless cases of internal displacement due to hydrometeorological events. For instance, between 2001 and 2008, roughly 465,000 people in Mozambique were displaced due to floods, while about one million people were displaced when Hurricane Katrina devastated New Orleans. In addition to displacement, added levels of vulnerability may be experienced by migrant groups because of language problems, distrust of authorities and lack of priority in seeking employment and housing. For those who are affected by environmental disasters, the complex challenges of displacement and resettlement can serve as yet another layer of disaster in their lives (Field et al., 2012).

**Displacement** can subject people to eight types of risks: landlessness, joblessness, homelessness, marginalization, food insecurity, increased morbidity, loss of access to common property resources, and social disarticulation (Field et al., 2012). Further, when environmental events drive people away from their customary environments, they distance them from the material and cultural resources that they depend on, such as family and community networks, cultural identity, familiar types of housing and other resources (Field et al. 2012). For Indigenous communities, displacement can have greater consequences and disruptions since their ties to the environment and land are essential to their survival, social relationships and networks, and their identities (Field et al., 2012). Other interconnected variables that play a role in pushing people to migrate will be explored in the following section.

> **Reflective Questions**
>
> 1. Should governments change their immigration policies in order to accommodate 'environmental migrants'? And if so, why and how?
> 2. How can migration policies be inclusive of indigenous communities when faced with environmental migration?

## Linked Variables and the Multi-causal Nature of Migration

Today, there is growing concern in the international community about the greater frequency and severity of environmental disasters, such as floods, hurricanes, earthquakes and droughts, and the impact of such disasters on human livelihoods. In order to gain a meaningful understanding of this phenomenon, the linkages and intersections among the above variables must be explored (Black et al., 2012). The link between environmental changes and human migration can be traced back to the earliest days of humanity. Historically, humans resorted to migration when environmental occurrences presented challenges to survival and advancement.

Black et al. (2012) fittingly propose a conceptual framework that offers insight on the linkages between environmental disasters and three related outcomes: migration, displacement and trapped populations (immobility). **Migration** can be segmented into short-term (three months to one year) and long-term (more than one year) movement, while **displacement** is considered to last less than three months. The authors note that the concept of **trapped populations** is more involved, as it is difficult to distinguish between those who voluntarily remain in disaster zones as opposed to those who involuntarily remain. The ability to move depends on social identity (age, gender, nationality and sexual orientation to name a few), health, wealth and social networks, as well as fear and uncertainty of destination location(s). People from underdeveloped nations face far greater stresses and vulnerabilities as they are impacted not only by the disasters themselves, but also by their lack of resources and inability to move as easily or quickly. Therefore it can be said that there is an inverse correlation between vulnerability and wealth.

There are two "major competing paradigms of vulnerability to hazards" (Black et al., 2012, S35). First, the **behaviouralist** paradigm states that natural disasters occur as a result of gaps in planning, preparation and response. The **structuralist** view suggests that deep-rooted societal constructions determine the "people and things" that are vulnerable to disasters (Black et al., 2012). Both paradigms take account of wealth and power inequalities and other local and global economic dependencies. Therefore, vulnerabilities to environmental events are created by human decision-making, which results in the events being disastrous to humans (Black et al., 2012). It is encouraging to compare these findings with those of O'Keefe et al. (1976), who relate disasters not just to environmental events, but also to **human vulnerability**. The contesting impressions of vulnerability to environmental disasters are reflected similarly in migration studies "with behaviour and agency of migrants or deep economic structures" (Black et al., 2012, S35) vying to rationalize migration outcomes. The main emphasis in disaster studies has been on displacement, with both paradigms acknowledging a causal link between disaster and human movement. Post-disaster, migration and displacement can be viewed as the last resort when **resiliency** is no longer possible (Black et al., 2012). Hammond et al. (2005) are more specific, defining displacement as a **survival tactic** when humans are faced with disasters, and migration as a strategy when humans are faced with uncertainty. In a study by Hertel and Rosch (2010), the impacts of environmental disasters (from 1970 to 2000 in 15 countries) showed significant consequences on urban poverty in Bangladesh, Mexico, and southern Africa. These findings were surprising, as urban poor populations are typically made up of rural migrants, leading one to conclude that while environmental disasters affect specific locations, their economic, social or political impacts can influence migrants' destination locations (Hertel & Rosch, 2010).

From a health standpoint, very little research has been conducted on those impacted by environmentally induced migration. There are two major factors that relate to health, migration and environmental events: (1) the health hazards that environmental migrants are faced with, and (2) how these hazards can affect population movement as a whole (McMichael et al., 2012). Extreme environmental changes also have the potential to impact the seasonality, incidence rate and range of infectious diseases such as dengue, malaria, and diarrheal diseases. The lack of access to safe drinking water further adds to this dilemma and is a major cause of illness and death. Therefore, environmental events alone will not necessarily determine human movement, but, rather, these changes will aggravate existing vulnerabilities – making it challenging to endure and survive. This is especially true of developing nations as stressors such as high population density, economic disparity, resource distribution inequality and political conflict will affect migration decisions (McMichael et al., 2012).

It may be helpful to visualize the many linked variables and sub-variables associated with environmentally induced migration. Figure 1 illustrates how occurrences of environmental events, either sudden or gradual, affect the variables and vulnerabilities experienced by people. It also shows that humans are faced with a particular decision or outcome – whether they are able to migrate (internally or abroad), are forced into displacement or remain trapped and therefore immobile.

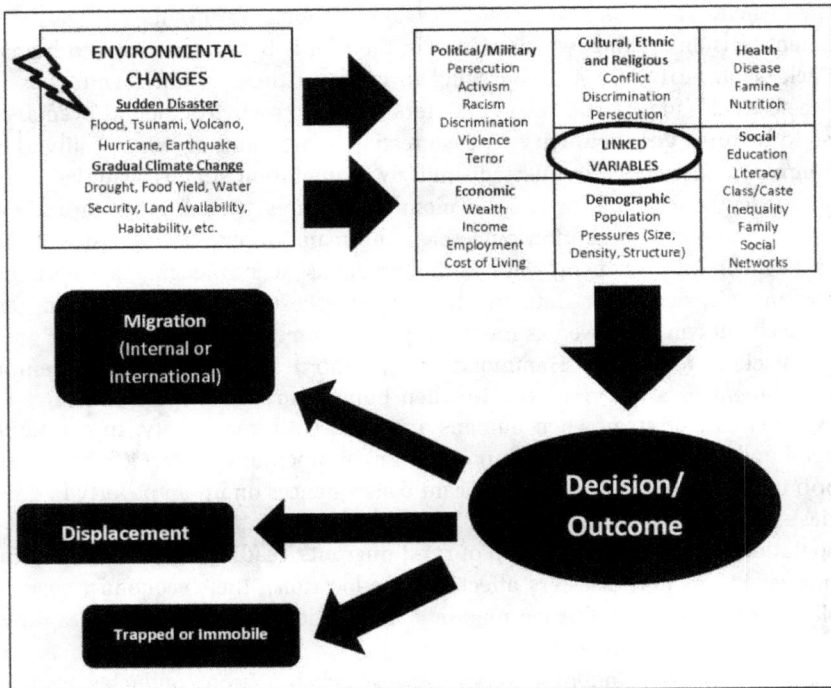

*Figure 1. Linked Variables: Environmental Disasters and Human Mobility/Immobility (adapted from* Foresight: Migration and Global Environmental Change, *2011).*

## Problematizing Definition and Policy Discourses

Having defined environmental disaster and various concepts in migration, it is necessary here to clarify the meaning of **environmentally induced migrants**. Discussion over the past few decades around the linkages between environmental changes and human migration has led to an array of disputed terms, namely "*environmental refugee,* but also *environmental migrant, forced environmental migrant, environmentally motivated migrant, climate refugee, climate change refugee, environmentally displaced person, disaster refugee, environmental displace, eco-refugee, ecological displaced person and environmental refugee-to-be*" (Boano et al., 2008, p. 6). In this chapter, I will use the above terms interchangeably. Despite the acknowledgment and use of these terms by international bodies, they are merely descriptive words with no recognized place in international refugee law or grounds for providing protection. Complexity and debate is added by (1) the lack of effective dialogue between governments, policy-makers and scholars; (2) the lack of agreed upon definitions; and (3) socio-economic and political resistance by governments to accept "undesirable" migrants into their territories (Boano et al., 2008).

The concept of **environmental refugees** was first brought into the spotlight in the 1970s by Lester Brown of the Worldwatch Institute, and later made widely known in a paper written for the United Nations Environment Programme (UNEP) by Essam El-Hinnawi (Assan and Rosenfeld, 2012). El-Hinnawi (1985) used this term to describe "people who have been forced to leave their traditional habitat, temporarily or permanently, because of a marked environmental disruption (natural and/or triggered by people) that jeopardized their existence and/or seriously affected the quality of their life." A habitat, according to the author, would be considered temporarily or permanently unsuitable to support life if its environment was disrupted by physical, chemical or biological changes. El-Hinnawi differentiated between three types of environmental refugees: "those who are temporarily dislocated due to disasters, natural or man-made; those permanently displaced due to drastic environmental changes, such as the construction of dams; and those who migrate as a result of gradual deterioration of environmental conditions."

El-Hinnawi's definition is important in the field, yet fails to distinguish environmental refugees from other types of migrants. More specifically, it fails to differentiate between those who flee immediately after disasters and those who abandon their homes as a result of gradual environmental degradation (Assan and Rosenfeld, 2012). In contrast, Myers (2001) defines environmental migrants as those "who can no longer gain a secure livelihood in their homelands because of drought, soil erosion, desertification, deforestation and other environmental problems" (p. 609). It is due to desperation and lack of alternatives that migrants abandon their homes in search of safety and better lives, often never looking back (Myers, 2001).

To better understand environmental migration from a policy and legal standpoint, Assan and Rosenfeld (2012) discuss three core issues: (1) that an agreed-upon definition of this phenomenon is non-existent; (2) discrepancies in the reported number of environmentally induced migrants by the international community; and (3) the lack of a legal framework. Without doubt, these three interdependent issues must be addressed in order to strengthen advocacy and policy change. However, there are perils in disseminating figures on the number of environmental migrants, as this may cause non-welcoming host communities and/or governments to fear migrants or view them as a threat, thus jeopardizing the flow of movement and allowing opposition groups to create stricter migration policies. In many disaster stricken areas, such policies have been driven by religious, ethnic, class/caste, economic and/or political intentions (Assan and Rosenfeld, 2012).

**Politicization of Terms and Anti-Asylum Lobbying**

Having in previous sections briefly discussed systematic anti-immigration policies that limit the movement of environmental migrants, here I will address anti-asylum lobbying efforts by the global north, and, specifically, Canada's handling of environmental migration. Despite the lack of solid empirical evidence about environmental migration, the publication of growing amounts of scientific evidence of environmental change over recent years has been seminal in highlighting the accounts of environmental migrants. Specifically, evidence illustrating anthropogenic causes of climate change and the consequences of actions initiated by the global north have resulted in the proliferation of discourse and political criticism on issues of asylum and migration (Morrissey, 2009).

Over the past several decades, conservative governments in the global north have both instigated and responded to anti-asylum lobbying to limit the number of asylum seekers and migrants entering from the global south. Governments have managed to instill in their citizens a sense of fear and hatred towards migrants by using indirect and direct xenophobic rhetoric, referring to "overwhelming numbers of foreigners, compromised sovereignty, and welfare cheats" (Morrissey, 2009, p. 9). Anti-asylum lobbyists have pushed for greater restrictionism by embracing the terms "environmental refugee" and "environmental collapse" (Morrissey, 2009). Lobbyists argued that the influx of refugees fleeing environmental collapse in the global south would inevitability lead to a similar collapse in the global north. This discourse places blame on migrants as contributors and carriers of environmental change and collapse, rather than those in the global north, who, as shown by evidence (Olivier et al., 2013), are major contributors. These views are in agreement with Black's (2001) argument that anti-asylum lobbyists use this logic to strengthen rhetoric about "bogus asylum seekers."

The proponents of this discourse claim that asylum seekers arriving in the north would be classified as environmental refugees, and, as per the 1951 United Nations Refugee Convention, would not qualify for a claim to asylum (Morrissey, 2009). Consequently, such sentiment is being used by "both anti-asylum lobbyists to increase border restrictions, and by national governments to shirk their international responsibilities to asylum seekers" (Morrissey, 2009, p. 9). This is consistent with the responses given by governments around the world, including that given by New Zealand's Immigration Protection Tribunal to the family from Kiribati, as discussed in Case Study 3.1. Contrary to extensive evidence given by international agencies and claims made by growing numbers of migrants, governments continue to bar environmental migrants, citing a convention created nearly 65 years ago. Thus, it is imperative to evolve policies and definitions, such as the 1951 Refugee Convention, that capture the struggles faced by migrants today.

**Canada's Role**

Regrettably, climate migration policies have not been a priority for the international community, especially nations such as Canada that are major contributors of carbon emissions. Currently, Citizenship and Immigration Canada does not recognize climate migrants through its humanitarian immigration program, a refugee stream for humanitarian and compassionate cases as well as for people who are admitted temporarily (Becklumb, 2010).

Generally, Canada has responded with temporary and ad hoc policies to severe environmental incidences in other countries that result in forced migration. While these special measures have benefited some individuals in the recent past (for instance, earthquake victims in Haiti), case-by-case directives are considered to follow the "wait-and-see" approach, and are not comprehensive or part of a broader strategy to address or accommodate environmental migration as a whole (Omeziri and Gore, 2014).

Canada's inclusion of climate migrants in its immigration policy would not require legislative change, but, rather, regulatory changes or policy direction (Becklumb, 2010). The nation's withdrawal from the Kyoto Protocol and its poor ranking in two measures of efforts to address greenhouse-gas emissions — the 2013 Climate Change Performance Index (55th of 58 nations) and the Centre for Global Development report (27th of 27 nations) (Burck, Hermwille, & Krings, 2013; Roodman and Clark, 2012) — suggest that Canada will not be taking a leadership role to address environmentally induced migration. Canada's political parties, with the exception of the Green Party, have not addressed or debated environmental migration, let alone informed Canadians that Canada is a major contributor to climate change.

While Canada does very little to address environmentally induced migration, Norway and Switzerland launched a state-led, bottom-up initiative in 2012, the Nansen Initiative (http://www.nanseninitiative.org/), which seeks to address the needs of people impacted by environmental events. Other nations such as Kenya, Germany, Australia, Philippines, Costa Rica and Mexico have agreed to participate in this program, and to produce a joint report in 2015. In addition to running a sustainability deficit and failing to meet countless international climate change commitments, Canada's inaction and plummeting standing as a tolerant and socially conscious nation have been criticized by various international stakeholders. Policy priorities should therefore be to encourage interdisciplinary approaches that generate solution-based results, and ultimately positive action.

**Adaptation and Resilience**

This chapter has so far described environmentally induced migration, displacement and immobility, arguing that the linked variables associated with them add layers of complexity. Despite greater frequency and severity of environmental events, and the impacts they have on our biosphere, the international community has yet to develop protection agendas to address affected populations. In this section I will explore adaptation and resiliency when considering sudden disasters and gradual climate events, and share several approaches proposed by scholars and international agencies.

The term **adaptation** refers to "the ability of a system to adjust to climate change (including variability and extremes) to moderate potential damages, take advantage of opportunities, or cope with the consequences" (Fussell and Klein 2006, p. 319). **Resiliency,** on the other hand, is "the ability of a system and its component parts to anticipate, absorb, accommodate, or recover from the effects of a hazardous event in a timely and efficient manner, including through ensuring the preservation, restoration, or improvement of its essential basic structures and functions" (Field et al., 2012, p. 34).

As previously discussed, environmental disasters and climate change are triggering forced migration, displacement and resettlement. Consequently, it is critical to understand where environmentally induced human migration and immobility fit along the adaptation spectrum. This raises the question whether institutions should support and facilitate migration as an adaptive response to environmental change (Warner, 2010).

---

**Reflective Questions**

1. Do you believe environmental migration is a form of adaptation?
2. If you have faced/were faced with a sudden disaster, how have/would you adapt or react? What steps would you take?
3. If you have faced/were faced with a gradual climate events, how have/would you adapt or react? What steps would you take?

---

This question has gained prominence due to the introduction of migration and displacement in the 2008 UNFCC climate conference. Still, there are sharply contrasting opinions on whether environmentally induced migration can be considered as adaptation. For instance, academics and organizations such as the International Organization for Migration (IOM) suggest that remittances from environmental migrants may lead to adaptation in their home countries (IOM, 2007; Barnett and Jones, 2009). In contrast, others view migration as a "maladaptive response," as it may affect the safety and livelihoods of both migrants and populations in host countries (Warner, 2009; Oliver-Smith, 2009). As has been shown, anti-asylum perspectives sensationalize and place blame on migrants. Alternatively, migration may simply be viewed as abandonment when adaptation is not possible, or migration as a failure of adaptation. Discourse on resiliency and adaptation should challenge the presumption that vulnerable groups are passive, and instead seek to acknowledge agency, skill and collaborative strength (Boano et al., 2008).

Regrettably, governing bodies and agencies have not yet taken systematic approaches to implement adaptation strategies and policies for populations impacted by environmental disasters and climate change. Warner (2009, p. 403) argues that such events are much more complex in nature, and alludes to previous studies describing migration as a "proactive **risk diversification** strategy" for people managing and mitigating a series of simultaneous risks. Since different types of environmentally induced movement (forced vs. voluntary migration, internal vs. external displacement, temporary vs. permanent resettlement, immobility vs. mobility) can occur, some may be adaptive while others may reveal the "failure of the social-ecological system to adapt" (Warner, 2009, p. 403). In addition to materializing progressive changes to governance and policy, the international community must make efforts to mitigate the impacts of environmental changes on communities by reducing vulnerability and allocating resources that strengthen sustainability, adaptation, and resilience (Boano et al., 2008).

What follows is an outline of both global/macro (Adaptation and Disaster Risk Management Approach) and local/micro (Community Based Adaptation) adaptation and resilience approaches.

### Global Perspectives

Exposure and vulnerability to disasters are key determinants of disaster risks and of impacts when risk is realized. As communities around the world differ in social and cultural characteristics, as shown by inequalities in health, wealth, education, gender, age, class and disability, their exposure and vulnerabilities also are dynamic, making strategies for adaptation and transformation complex (Field et al., 2012). However, several approaches can be combined to effectively manage changing risks of climate extremes and disasters, as well as to complement broader sustainable development. Effective risk management is most impactful when used as integrated or combined actions, rather than a singular action (Field et al., 2012). Multidisciplinary perspectives and stakeholders are integral in solution-based approaches when considering the linked variables associated with environmental migration.

As shown in Figure 2, these approaches include (Field et al., 2012):

1. **Reducing Exposure** (mainstream risk management into development processes, building codes and retrofitting, defensive infrastructure and environmental buffers, land use planning, catchment and other ecosystem management, incentive mechanisms for individual actions to reduce exposure).
2. **Increasing Resilience to Changing Risks** (flexibility in decision-making, adaptive learning and management, improved knowledge and skills, systems transformation over time).
3. **Transformation** (increased emphasis on adaptive management, learning, innovation and leadership).
4. **Reducing Vulnerability** (poverty reduction, health improvements, access to services and productive assets enhanced, livelihood diversification, access to decision-making increased, community security improved).
5. **Preparing, Responding, and Recovering** (early warning and communication, evacuation plan, humanitarian: relief supplies, post-disaster livelihood support and recovery).
6. **Transferring and Sharing Risks** (mutual and reserve funds, financial insurance, social networks and capital, alternative forms of risk transfer).

The IPCC considers these to be "low-regret measures," and notes that these approaches are ideal starting points for addressing exposure, vulnerability and climate extremes (Field et al., 2012). **Low-regret measures** can be defined as actions that are low in cost, while generating desirable benefits. These low-regret measures can generate improvements to well-being, environmental conservation, and people's livelihoods. More specifically, they include communication between decision-makers and citizens, early warning systems, sustainable land management, ecosystem management and restoration (Field et al., 2012). Other low-regret measures can include enhancing health surveillance, water supply, sanitation, climate-proofing infrastructure, irrigation and drainage systems, education and awareness (Field et al., 2012). In order for these approaches to be fruitful, cultural and indigenous considerations, among other dynamics, must also be integrated. Applying western doctrines in other regions without such considerations may impede or even prevent positive outcomes.

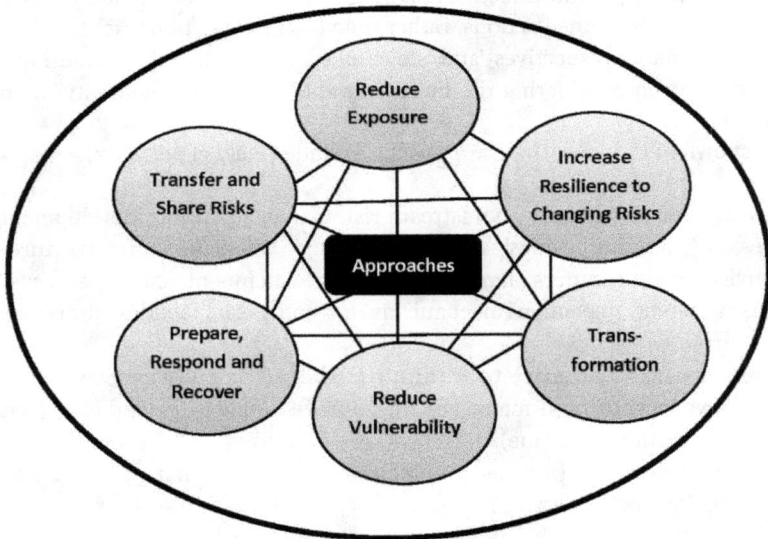

*Figure 2. Adaptation and Disaster Risk Management Approaches for a Changing Climate (Field et al., 2012)*

## Community Perspectives

Now we will turn to adaptation at the **community level**, as vulnerability and the challenges to human livelihood can be illustrated effectively when considering environmental pressures at a micro level.

Three variables are essential for adaptation to environmental events at the community level: (1) accessibility to resources; (2) research and technology; and (3) the level of development (Boano et al., 2008). Specifically, **community-based adaptation (CBA)** can be in the form of education and awareness (impacts of area-specific environmental change), training and preparation (alternative energy, water sanitation, roof water catchment), natural resource management (rehabilitation of land and prevention of land overexploitation) and diversification of livelihood options (Boano et al., 2008).

CBA is an essential way to promote "appropriate development activities, practices, research and policies" (Boano et al., 2008, p. 18). The realization of CBA depends on an approach that challenges existing action-based adaptation strategies and reductionist vulnerability perspectives, and recognizes livelihood resilience, well-being, social capital, access to resources, gender, race, ethnicity and institutional networks (Boano et al., 2008). This would allow adaptation strategies to reduce human vulnerability and exposure to environmental stressors, and acknowledges the role of coping mechanisms and assistance when people are faced with decision-making scenarios. This is particularly important when communities are faced with gradual and less visible changes associated with slow-onset events. Nonetheless, these examples demonstrate the complexity of multi-causal environmental change, and the need for both long-term development policies and short-term mitigation strategies (Boano et al., 2008).

As pointed out above, not every climate adaptation strategy is appropriate, and we must recognize the need for sustainable climate adaptation strategies that address social and ecological justice and integrity (Eriksen et al., 2011). We must also challenge existing hierarchical donor-beneficiary relations by considering power dynamics, decision-making control, the role of community members in innovation and social value creation and the accommodation of informal structures. Social value creation and innovation in multi-level partnerships (local community groups and global institutions), in the context of climate adaptation, involve the exchange and sharing of knowledge, technology, and the creation of social value. This concept is ideal when considering marginalized populations living in labour intensive and resource-dependent communities. In the context of community-based adaptation, **action research** is relevant in addressing collaboration between multi-level institutions and actors.

The *Dictionary of Human Geography* defines action research as being a combination of social change, active participation, and involvement in development and change (Gregory, 2000). CBA incorporates the principles of action research by promoting mutual education and awareness, training and preparation, natural resource management, and diversification of livelihood options (Boano et al., 2008). The implementation of sustainable adaptation strategies at the local level is critical to providing long-term solutions for populations to cope with climate risk. Action researchers would argue that the success of sustainable climate adaptation and resilience depends on multi-level partnerships between formal administrative institutions, local authorities, and informal community groups. Upton (2011) similarly discusses the risks when global donors do not seek to fully understand local power differences and relations. Specifically, Upton's article identifies how donors have a lack of appreciation for "local mechanisms of institutional access" (cited in Rodima-Taylor, Olwig, and Chhetri, 2012, p. 4), something which ultimately excludes the wealthiest and the poorest groups. In order to respect local agency and actors, investments must be made in multi-level partnerships and collaboration in adaptation and innovation (Rodima-Taylor, Olwig, and Chhetri, 2012).

## Policy Development

Due to the multi-causal and interconnected nature of environmental migration, it can be challenging for governments and agencies to move from reactive to pro-active approaches to policy development. Major gaps exist in both economic and environmental literature, making it difficult to make predictions about migration drivers and patterns. After identifying the main economic drivers of migration, Lilleor and Van den Broeck (2011) argue that environmental change on its own does not stimulate migration, but, instead, that individuals will migrate if these changes impact their drivers of migration.

The impacts of environmental events on human migration lead to four conclusions with regards to **policy development** (Boano et al., 2008). First, as King states (2006, p. 545), the severity and speed of movement, resulting either from rapid-onset or slow-onset events, and the likelihood of returning to location of origin, uniquely affect migratory flows and patterns. These variables, in addition to the complexities of multi-causal drivers, reinforce the importance of technology for forecasting, monitoring and mapping migration and environmental trends (Boano et al., 2008). Second, rapid-onset or slow-onset events do not only affect the under-resourced and disenfranchised people; poorer communities as a whole are more exposed and vulnerable to such events, experience greater impacts to livelihoods and to assets, and are less able to cope and recover (Boano et al., 2008). Moreover, "disasters can induce poverty, making better-off people poorer and the poor destitute despite programmes aimed at fighting poverty" (DFID 2005, p. 3). Reducing global disparities, poverty, and the impacts of environmentally induced migration on impoverished communities should be at the forefront of the development agenda (Boano et al., 2008). Alongside these goals, the rights, security and dignity of people should also be protected. Third, due to the multi-causal nature of environmentally-induced migration, national governments, development agencies and donors need to assimilate and embrace environmental factors into projects and poverty reduction strategies (Boano et al., 2008). Finally, the international community must be challenged and held accountable for implementing proactive policies and responses to environmental change and the impact it has on human migration (Boano et al., 2008).

## Conclusions

The detrimental effects of environmental disasters and changes on human well-being, economies and migration flows have been widely reported by the media (World Bank, 2010). Events such as Hurricane Katrina and "Superstorm" Sandy, earthquakes in Haiti, Iran, and Japan, flooding in Pakistan, the Philippines, and Bangladesh, as well as drought, deforestation and water scarcity in much of Africa and Asia illustrate that action must be taken to reduce the pressures we place on our biosphere, and provide assistance to those affected by such environmental events. Despite the greater severity and frequency of disasters in the recent past, very little academic research has been conducted on how environmental disasters and changes influence decision-making by those impacted by such occurrences.

This chapter has reviewed several topics pertaining to environmental disasters and their impact on migration. It was noted that agreed-upon definitions, policies and commitments are imperative to address and legitimize the field of environmental migration. Failure by the international community to realize this fact will reduce adaptation alternatives for those facing disasters, and relegate them to perpetual states of survival. As noted in a UNCHR report (Warner et al., 2009), it is imperative to reduce climate change, expedite policies that focus on human security and resilience, prioritize populations that are most vulnerable and at risk, create more international awareness and recognize and facilitate migration's inevitable role in adaptation strategies. Moreover, specific references to linked variables, such as socioeconomic, political, demographic, and health variables, were made in order to discuss the intersections between the mentioned variables.

In order for the international community to move forward with tangible climate change action, the nations of the global north, especially Canada, must make commitments to significantly reduce their exploitative resource-extraction activities, harmful greenhouse gas emissions and neo-liberal capitalist and industrial agendas. Canada must not only reduce such impacts on the environment and Indigenous communities, but also eliminate its anti-asylum lobbying and xenophobic policies. This begins by taking initiative in defining "environmental migration" and developing comprehensive policies within its immigration program to accommodate impacted communities. As discussion of the topics in this chapter shows, it is clear that gaps and limitations in our understanding of these matters persist, and that further research contributions must be made to advance the field. In addition to this, awareness and activism must connect global citizens and encourage them to advocate for both human rights and environmental rights.

## References

Alam, S. (2003). Environmentally-induced migration from Bangladesh to India. *Strategic Analysis 27*(3): 422–438.

Assan, J.K., and Rosenfeld, T. (2012). Environmentally-induced migration, vulnerability and human security: Consensus, controversies and conceptual gaps for policy analysis. *Journal of International Development 24*: 146–157.

Barnett, J., and Jones, R. (2002). Forced migration: the influence of environmental security. *Global Change 7*(4): 3.

Becklumb, P. (2010). *Climate change and forced migration: Canada's role.* Parliamentary Information and Research Service, Library of Parliament.

Berkes, F. and Jolly, D. (2001). Adapting to climate change: Social-ecological resilience in a Canadian western Arctic community. *Conservation Ecology 5*(2).

Berkes, F., Colding, J., and Folke, C. (eds.) (2003). *Navigating social–ecological systems: Building resilience for complexity and change.* Cambridge: Cambridge University Press.

Black, R., Adger, W.N., Arnell, N.W., Geddes, A., & Thomas, D. (2012). Migration, immobility, and displacement outcomes following extreme events. *Environmental Science and Policy 27S*: S32-S43.

Boano, C., Zetter, R., & Morris, T. (2008). Environmentally displaced people: Understanding the linkages between environmental change, livelihoods and forced migration. In *Forced Migration Policy Briefing 1*, Refugee Studies Centre, Oxford Department of International Development, University of Oxford.

Bogardi, J., and Warner, K. (2008). Here comes the flood. *Nature: Nature reports climate change.* Published online 11 December 2008.

Burck, J., Hermwille, L., & Krings, L. (2013). *The climate change performance index 2013.* Cambridge: Cambridge University Press.

Castles S. (2002). *Environmental change and forced migration: Making sense of the debate. New issues in refugee research, working paper 70.* Geneva: UNHCR.

Davis, K.F., D'Odorico, P., Liao, F., & Ridolfi, L. (2013). Global spatio-temporal patterns in human migration: A complex network perspective. *PLOS ONE*, 1–8.

El-Hinnawi, E. (1985). *Environmental refugees.* Nairobi, Kenya: United Nations Environmental Programme.

Eriksen, S., Aldunce, P., Bahinipati, C. S., Martins, R. D. A., Molefe, J. I., Nhemachena, C., ... & Ulsrud, K. (2011). When not every response to climate change is a good one: Identifying principles for sustainable adaptation. *Climate and Development, 3*(1), 7–20.

*EM-DAT: The OFDA/CRED International Disaster Database.* www.emdat.be, Université Catholique de Louvain, Brussels.

Filho, H.S.B., de Lima Neto, F.B. & Fusco, W. (2011). Migration and social networks: An explanatory multi-evolutionary agent-based model. IEEE Computer Society, 1-7.

*Foresight: Migration and global environmental change* (2011). Final Project Report. London: The Government Office for Science.

Füssel, H. M., & Klein, R. J. (2006). Climate change vulnerability assessments: An evolution of conceptual thinking. *Climatic Change, 75*(3), 301–329.

Hammond, L., Bush, J., Savage, K., & Harvey, P. (2005). The effects of food aid on household migration patterns and implications for emergency food assessments. London: Overseas Development Institute (ODI)/Strengthening Emergency Needs Assessment Capacity (SENEC).

Gregory, D. (2000). Discourse. In Johnston, R.J., Gregory, D., Pratt, G. & Watts, M. (eds.). *The dictionary of human geography.* Oxford: Blackwell.

Hansen, J., Sato, M., Kharecha, P., Beerling, D., Berner, R., Masson-Delmotte, V., Pagani, M., Raymo, M., Royer, D.L., & Zachos, J. C. (2008). Target atmospheric $CO_2$: Where should humanity aim? arXiv preprint. arXiv:0804.1126.

Hertel, T.W., & Rosch, S.D. (2010). Climate change agriculture, and poverty. *Applied Economic Perspectives and Policy 32*(3): 355–385

Hussein, K., Nelson, J., 1998. *Sustainable livelihoods and livelihood desertification. Working paper 69.* Brighton: Institute of Development Studies. Retrieved from www.ids.ac.uk/ids/bookshop/wp/wp 69.pdf.

IPCC (2012). *Managing the risks of extreme events and disasters to advance climate change adaptation. A special report of Working Groups I and II of the Intergovernmental Panel on Climate Change.* [Field, C.B., et al., eds.] Cambridge: Cambridge University Press.

IPCC (2013). Summary for policymakers. In *Climate change 2013: The physical science basis. Contribution of Working Group I to the fifth assessment report of the Intergovernmental Panel on Climate Change* [Stocker, T.F., et al., eds.].

King. T. (2006). Environmental displacement: Coordinating efforts to find solutions. *Georgetown International Environmental Law Review 18*(3): 543–565.

Laczko, F., & Aghazarm, C. (eds.) (2009). *Migration, environment and climate change: Assessing the evidence*. Geneva: International Organization for Migration.

Lilleør, H. B., & Van den Broeck, K. (2011). Economic drivers of migration and climate change in LDCs. *Global Environmental Change 21*: S70–S81.

Lonergan S. (1998). *The role of environmental degradation in population displacement: Environmental change and security project report.*

Marchiori, L., Maystadt, J. F., & Schumacher, I. (2011). The impact of climate variations on migration in sub-Saharan Africa. In *Presentation at the conference on adaptation to climate change* (pp. 18–19).

Marlow, C. (2005). *Research methods for generalist social work* (4th ed.). Toronto: Thomson Brooks/Cole.

McMichael, C., Barnett, J., & McMichael, A.J. (2012). An ill wind? Climate change, migration, and health. *Environmental Health Perspectives 120*(5): 646–654.

Mendola, M. 2008. Migration and technological change in rural households: Complements or substitutes? *Journal of Development Economics 85*(1–2): 150–175.

Morrissey, J. (2009). *Environmental change and forced migration: A state of the art review*. Refugee Studies Centre, Department of International Development, University of Oxford.

Murray, S. (2010). Environmental migrants and Canada's refugee policy. *Refuge: Canada's Journal on Refugees, 27*(1).

Myers, N. (2001). Environmental refugees: A growing phenomenon of the 21st century. *Philosophical Transactions of the Royal Society of London*. Series B 357: 609–613.

NASA. (n.d.) Global Climate Change: Causes. Retrieved from http://climate.nasa.gov/causes/.

O'Keefe, P., Westgate, K., & Wisner, B. (1976). Taking the naturalness out of natural disasters. *Nature 260*: 566–567.

Oliver-Smith, A. (2009). Sea level rise and the vulnerability of coastal peoples: Responding to the local challenges of global climate change in the 21st century. In *InterSections* No. 7. Bonn: United Nations University Institute for Environment and Human Security.

Olivier, J. G., Janssens-Maenhout, G., Muntean, M., & Peters, J.A. (2013). *Trends in global $CO_2$ emissions: 2013 report*. PBL Netherlands Environmental Assessment Agency.

Olwig, M. F. (2012). Multi-sited resilience: The mutual construction of "local" and "global" understandings and practices of adaptation and innovation. *Applied Geography 33*: 112–118.

Omeziri, E., & Gore, C. (2014). Temporary measures: Canadian refugee policy and environmental migration. *Refuge: Canada's Journal on Refugees 29*(2).

Reuveny, R. (2007). Climate change-induced migration and violent conflict. *Political Geography 26*(6): 656–673.

Rockström, J., et al. (2009). Planetary boundaries: Exploring the safe operating space for humanity. *Ecology and Society 14*(2): 32.

Rodima-Taylor, D., Olwig, M. F., & Chhetri, N. (2012). Adaptation as innovation, innovation as adaptation: An institutional approach to climate change. *Applied Geography 33*: 107–111.

Roodman. D, & Clark. J. (2012). *Commitment to development index country report: Canada*. Center for Global Development.

Upton, C. (2012). Adaptive capacity and institutional evolution in contemporary pastoral societies. *Applied Geography 33*: 135–141.

Warner, K. (2010). Global environmental change and migration: Governance challenges. *Global Environmental Change, 20*(3): 402–413.

Warner, K., Ehrhart, C., de Sherbinin, A., Adamo, S., & Chai-Onn, T. (2009). *In search of shelter: Mapping the effects of climate change on human migration and displacement*. Cooperative for Assistance and Relief Everywhere, Inc. (CARE): 1–26.

Werrell, C.E, Femia, F. & Slaughter, A. (2013). *The Arab Spring and climate change: A climate and security correlations series*. Center for American Progress, Stimson, The Center for Climate and Security, 1–58.

## CHAPTER FOUR

# Problems of Territory, Nationhood and the "Stateless": The Situation facing Roma

## Neil Cruickshank

T his chapter, animated by a political-sociological framework, examines issues and concrete examples relating to the displacement, and subsequent movement, relocation and migration, of European Roma. Separately, though relatedly, this chapter will also explore Canada's "new" asylum/refugee regime to ascertain (1) how the changes impact Roma refugees, and (2) what the new system says about Canada's willingness to accommodate Roma migrants — a group unlike any other.

This chapter will begin to answer these and related questions in the hope of showing, in a correlative way, how statelessness has contributed to the Roma predicament — that is, of being a discernible group (such as a nation), but without recourse to self-determination and political power — and remains *still* the underlying cause of the subjection they encounter. Several concrete examples of maltreatment will be outlined and discussed to, again, show what statelessness can lead to in terms of marginalization, social exclusion and political disenfranchisement. Part of the discussion will involve an appraisal of current policy aimed at integrating Roma. It should be noted that, unlike other nations or delimited populations/ethnic groups, like Scots or Basques, Romani political elite are not pursuing statehood or political independence. There is no irredentist rhetoric

## Guiding Questions

1. What is preventing Roma from realizing a place among Europe's established and recognized ethnonations?
2. How have centuries of cruel and unusual treatment, punctuated by the Holocaust (the "*Porrajmos*") affected Roma identity and their interactions with majority populations?
3. Why do Roma remain scapegoats, objects of ire, and the focus of populist rhetoric despite having lived in Europe for nearly eight centuries?
4. Why did Canada recently change its immigration policy to, in effect, dissuade and/or prevent Roma from applying for refuge?

to cite; no quarrel over territory to point to; no recognizable movement for independence. In fact, the emphasis placed on transterritoriality and/or non-territoriality would seem to make them unique among European nations and other substate actors.

With this in mind, the goal of the chapter is three-fold: (1) to identify "who" the Roma are, advancing our understanding of "what" the principal characteristics of the population are; (2) to underscore problems associated with "space" and "place," paying particular attention to maltreatment and conditions of marginality; and (3) to explain why European Roma are seeking refuge in Canada, and what Canada's response has been (historically and contemporarily) to Roma asylum seekers. First and foremost, this chapter is concerned with how statelessness impacts Roma, and secondarily how statelessness (or the idea of it) complicates the attainment of rights, citizenship and self-determination.

In considering the impact of Canada's *Immigration and Refugee Protection Act* on the Roma, I will critique popular stereotypes that have come to define Roma, especially the belief that they are "all criminals," "engage in anti-social behaviour" and are "itinerant" (i.e., nomadic). It may well be that the Canadian government accepted these popular mythologies as truth, and changed the existing system to ensure Roma could not take "advantage" of Canada's "generous" refugee system. When it comes to Roma, misconceptions, falsehoods and enduring misconceptions abound, and while inaccurate, it is not surprising such stereotypes have managed to influence lawmakers and their decision-making calculus, given just how pervasive they are.

## Who Are "the" Roma?

Roma are a heterogeneous and diverse population of approximately 14 million, living throughout Europe and the Americas, and elsewhere, with a territorial attachment to nearly all European states, and all states between India and Norway. They constitute something akin to a national diaspora without having a titular nation, and while possessing similarities, do not exhibit commonalities. This is a very diverse population spread across an entire continent. Among academics, primarily, debates about origin, ethnicity, history and language persist. One thing is for certain, however: Roma remain disadvantaged and politically marginalized.

Despite structural impediments and institutionalized forms of racism, Roma have developed into a coherent political community, with their own anthem, flag and national discourse. The International Romani Union (IRU) began in the 1970s, in London, England, and in 2001 declared:

> Individuals belonging to the Roma Nation call for a representation of their Nation, which does not want to become a State. . . . We, a Nation of which over half a million persons were exterminated in a forgotten Holocaust, a Nation of individuals too often discriminated, marginalized, victim of intolerance and persecutions, we have a dream, and we are engaged in fulfilling it. We are a Nation, we share the same tradition, the

same culture, the same origin, the same language; we are a Nation. We have never looked for creating a Roma State. And we do not want a State today, when the new society and the new economy are concretely and progressively crossing-over the importance and the adequacy of the State as the way how individuals organize themselves (IRU, 2001).

There are other political organizations, and other perspectives, but this idea of *a non-state nation* (or of a *transterritorial community*) is a fairly common one among Roma actors and activists. For example, the late Nicolae Gheorghe self-identified both as Roma and cosmopolitan. His description of cosmopolitanism is telling as it links diaspora, the physical dispersal around the world of a coherent population, with universalism, a commitment to overarching rights, international norms and a common rights discourse. He writes: "I learnt to consider the Roma as people who form a genuinely world-wide diaspora. After the fall of Communism, I started to argue for a cosmopolitan – or at least European – perspective in Roma activism" (Gheorghe, 2013, p. 50).

In Europe, Roma have been living beside and amongst *gadje* or *gadže* (i.e., non-Roma) without interruption for centuries. While the Roma are diverse, there appears to be near uniformity in how they are treated and in the fact they lack political power and political representation. It is difficult (and in a sense wrong) to generalize to such an extent, as generalizations obscure differences among and between Roma, and ultimately contribute to the sort of stereotyping this chapter is trying to undo or mitigate. However, it would be irresponsible to ignore or downplay the common experience of Roma and the ill-treatment they experience everywhere they live — from segregated schooling in the Czech Republic, forced eviction and deportation in France and physical assault and intimidation in Hungary, to forced segregation and separation (in the form of a concrete wall) in Slovakia, pogroms in Bulgaria and "special" identity cards in Italy. Goldston (2002) writes:

> [Roma] are routinely denied access to housing, jobs, restaurants, bars, and even health care simply because of their ethnicity. And such discrimination is an equal opportunity phenomenon; no Roma are too important to merit exemption. Thus, on the eve of the annual human rights meeting of the Organization for Security and Cooperation in Europe (OSCE) in Warsaw in September 2000, three Roma — including the OSCE's highest-ranking official on Roma issues — were forcibly removed from a downtown cafe after refusing to leave when denied service (pp. 157–58).

Such treatment is all too common and all too accepted in Europe. With public opinion showing less tolerance and more animosity toward Roma, and right-wing political parties campaigning *against* integrationist policy, there is every chance things will get worse before they get better.

Roma (also known as Sinti, Manouches, Travellers, Gypsies, and so on) constitute Europe's single largest minority group. Furthermore, and unlike other ethnic/cultural groups, they live in (and are citizens of) every European Union state. They are, in many respects, a stateless nation, though, unlike other European nations, they have no interest in statehood *per se*, only the achievement of greater autonomy and self-governance. The Council of Europe recently urged its membership of 47 countries to "treat the Roma issue not only from the perspective of a socially disadvantaged group, but from the perspective of a *national minority* entitled to enjoy the rights enshrined in the Framework Convention for the Protection of National Minorities (ETS No. 157) and in the European Convention on Human Rights, as interpreted by the European Court of Human Rights (ECtHR)" (Parliamentary Assembly, Council of Europe, Resolution 1740 [February 26, 2010]). These institutions and instruments are just a few of the many supranational and international agreements and organizations that now criss-cross Europe and have afforded Roma new political opportunity structures. Roma can appeal directly to the EU, for instance, and can utilise the ECtHR in Strasbourg to further pressure national state lawmakers, so long as they have exhausted all judicial remedies in their home state. One should not confuse political opportunity with social advancement, however. The first appears to be happening while the second — social advancement — is occurring only marginally if at all.

WHAT'S IN A NAME? "Gypsy" (or plural, "Gypsies") is considered pejorative and offensive. The popularity of the television show *My Big Fat Gypsy Wedding* (on the TLC network) might suggest otherwise, but generally speaking the term "Gypsy" is out of favour among non-Roma and used sparingly among Roma themselves — and usually as a way of identifying themselves to non-Roma. However, some Roma still prefer the moniker "Gypsy" or "Traveller" or some other derivative (e.g., "Roma Gypsy" or "Gypsy Traveller") rather than referring to themselves as Roma. As you might imagine, the process of labelling, identifying and counting any marginalized group — but especially Roma, a group that has been and continues to be targeted based on ethnicity — is problematic. This whole process of naming and classifying has been, and continues to be, controversial and divisive among academics, activists and Roma. Jean-Pierre Liégeois (1994), a leading expert on Roma and Travellers, argues:

> As for the term *Rom* or *Roma*, which is increasingly used in political contexts by Gypsy organizations: it does not cover, even politically, all the groups in question, particularly those who call themselves *Travellers*. It does, however, have the advantage of being clearly distinct from the stereotypes attached to designations attributed by outsiders to "Gypsy" groups, of being a term of self-designation for a significant number of these groups, and of more accurately correspondingly to both the socio-cultural reality and the political will of groups in Central and Eastern Europe, who make up 70% of the Gypsy communities in Europe (pp. 37–38).

Since 1994, gradually and near uniformly, the term "Roma" has become an accepted umbrella term for what amounts to an incredibly diverse group of people, sometimes sharing cultural, linguistic and ethnic commonalities, but sometimes not. Use of the term, as imprecise as it is, is akin to using the term "First Nations" to identify the 600-plus groups that constitute Canada's Aboriginal population. Without delving any further into the controversy, it should be understood (and this is in fact illustrated by my unwillingness to delve any further into the "name game") that not all Roma, Gypsies, Travellers, Manouches, Sinti, etc. agree on what "they" themselves should be called, and many still disagree that there is a "we" at all.

WHY ARE WE STILL TALKING ABOUT THE "ROMA PROBLEM"? Despite well-intentioned policy and a host of programs at both the state and European levels, such as the *Decade of Roma Inclusion 2005 – 15* and *EU Framework for National Roma Integration Strategies*, Roma continue to experience social marginalization, political disenfranchisement and economic exclusion, and, in some (well-documented) instances, physical violence, forced eviction, displacement and targeted harassment. For this reason, many European lawmakers (and academics) see Roma as a litmus test for Europeanization and European integration, and for the whole "European project" insofar as it is seeking to create a singular European demos. Also, as a dispersed population prone to movement and migration, Roma are a bellwether for Europe's nascent human rights regime and the new — some might call it "liquid" — form of citizenship that European integration purportedly promotes and underscores.[1] European integration, i.e., the further political and legal enmeshment of the existing 28 European Union member-states, is ushering in a new era of non-territorially based notions of rights, democracy and political participation. It offers Europeans "free movement" within the Union, and presents to business a European continent bereft of tariffs and trade barriers. This fits well with Roma, as they are not geographically delimited, as such, and — hypothetically — could move to areas showing increased or improving economic opportunity.

However, this so-called Europeanization has presented some European lawmakers the opportunity to "pass the buck," or transfer responsibility for Roma to the European Union government. While it is convenient to consider Roma a transterritorial or transnational population, such thinking could work to absolve states of any responsibility for Roma. This would be a colossal blunder given the fact Roma *have* citizenship rights, and *have* a right to fair treatment in their national-states. Even so, many Roma are leaving Europe for North America in the hope of a better life. This latter development will be explored in more detail below. In a way, Roma are an example of what is wrong with the existing state system, a system based on territoriality and exclusion, utterly incompatible with dispersed populations, diasporic ethno-nations, and non-territorial groups. Our rigidly de-

---

[1] George Ritzer (2011) uses terms like liquidity, solidity and gas to explain processes of globalization.

limited and delineated world makes things very hard for stateless people. At the very same time, however, Roma sensibilities — that is, notions of non-territoriality, cosmopolitanism and transnationalism — are remarkably well-situated in a globalized and regionalized world in which new forms of belonging (or old forms of belonging, rediscovered) are finding footing. Open borders, the growth in international non-governmental organizations (INGOs), international courts (e.g., the European Court of Human Rights [ECtHR] and International Criminal Court [ICC]) and a growing appreciation for diversity would seem, at the theoretical level at least, to work in favour of Roma and other non-territorially-based groups. As Soysal (1996) argues:

> The model of national citizenship, anchored in territorialized notions of cultural belonging, was dominant during the period of massive migration at the turn of the century, when immigrants were expected to be moulded into national citizens. . . . Nation citizenship is losing ground to a more universal model of membership, anchored in deterritorialized notions of persons' rights (p. 3).

European integration and Europeanization, especially the latter, with its insistence on governance, input legitimacy and informal decision-making, has opened the door to new forms of contentious politics and lobbying, which involve both supranational institutions (i.e., the European Commission) and actors and other non-state organizations and networks. Non-state actors, including intergovernmental organizations (IGOs) like the Council of Europe and European Union, have taken a particular interest in Roma and Roma rights. The *Council of Europe Recommendations 1203 (1993) on Gypsies in Europe* states:

1. One of the aims of the Council of Europe is to promote the emergence of a genuine European cultural identity. Europe harbours many different cultures, all of them, including the many minority cultures, enriching and contributing to the cultural diversity of Europe.
2. A special place among the minorities is reserved for Gypsies. Living scattered all over Europe, not having a country to call their own, they are a true European minority, but one that does not fit into the definitions of national or linguistic minorities.
3. As a non-territorial minority, Gypsies greatly contribute to the cultural diversity of Europe. In different parts of Europe they contribute in different ways, be it by language and music or by their trades and crafts (p. 172).

We are still talking about Roma because: (1) Despite seemingly favourable institutional developments at the European level, Roma remain marginalized and subjects of ire; and (2) they are being deported and/or removed from countries like France, which by virtue of EU law they have a legal right to work and live in, and countries like Canada, which seemingly changed its refugee regime to expedite their return to Europe. Even with recommendations like those above, Roma continue to experience poverty and overt racism, and appear unwelcome in any state.

## Core Ideas and Concepts

Before proceeding, I will very briefly go over some of the core ideas and concepts foundational to this chapter. First, a **state** is a territorial unit. They are principal actors in the international system, and by virtue of their juridical personality, that is, the fact they are considered "legal persons" under international law, have considerable power relative to non-state actors and nations (and sub-state ethnic communities). Of course states were/are constituted by and among human beings, for decidedly human reasons, i.e., safety and security. States are **delimited**, meaning they have borders, administered by a government or similar-type of authority, populated by a more or less sedentary population, and are able to engage in international relations. People, nations, ethnic groups seek statehood for sake of self-determination and self-governance; statehood is in many respects the ultimate expression of political belonging and ultimate safeguard against genocide and ethnic cleansing.

A **nation**, on the other hand, is a culturally, ethnically, historically, linguistically, religiously (or any combination thereof) bound group of people who have not attained statehood, but share enough characteristics (real or perceived) to warrant a group name or title. Nations do not populate a territory they claim exclusively for themselves. Hence nations frequently and routinely practice **nationalism**, which is a political doctrine aimed at attaining sovereign statehood. Ernest Gellner (1983) argues that nationalism is "primarily a political principle, which holds that the political and national unit should be congruent." A student of Gellner, Anthony D. Smith, uses the term *ethnie* to denote a population or group that exhibits commonalities. He suggests *ethnies* are "named human populations with shared ancestry myths, histories and cultures, having an association with a specific territory, and a sense of solidarity" (Smith, 1986, 32).

Smith (1996) defines nation as "a named human population sharing an historic territory, common myths and memories, a mass, public culture, a single economy and common rights and duties for all members" (p. 359). Here, the *modern* national state is the product of the *modern* nation, or *modern* nationalism. Through a process of cultural, political and economic entrenchment, the nation forms in a geographically delimited area in which other nations are either pushed out or usurped – or some combination thereof. As Smith (2009) argues, "it was nationalism that invented nations where they did not exist . . . whereas nations had no place in earlier 'agro-literate' societies" (p. 5). This is similar to Gellner's view. He argues "it is nationalism which engenders nations, and not the other way round" (2006, p. 54). Roma constitute a nation, but without concern for statehood stop short of practicing nationalism, as Gellner would understand it.

The terms **transnational**, **transterritorial** and **non-territorial** are used throughout this chapter, but not interchangeably. One is not the same as the other, but together the terms are suggestive of fluidity or movement between, around and through states. The buzzwords of "community" and "network" are applied to policy, social movements, contentious politics and interest groups, and the resultant pastiche of actors challenge state preponderance, especially in the realm of public policy, in effect replacing government with "governance".

**Non-territorial** is self-explanatory, for the most, but the term is being used here to suggest an identity separate to, yet entirely consistent with, state identity or national citizenship. To suggest Roma are non-territorial or transterritorial is *not to suggest* they are without territorial roots or citizenship, as this would be wrongheaded. To suggest Roma are non-territorial or transterritorial is to emphasize the part of their identity that transcends (even predates) the European state system.

### Space and Place

It is easy to forget that Roma are now, in the twenty-first century, a sedentary population. Roma are not a nomadic "tribe" wandering Europe, as it has been portrayed in popular media. During the communist period, in particular from about 1948 to 1989, central and eastern European lawmakers forced Roma into factory towns, urban ghettos and thus into a sedentary lifestyle consistent with that of majority populations across Central and Eastern Europe. Driven by socialist ideology, governments were intent on assimilating Roma, ridding them of cultural idiosyncrasies, their Romani language, nomadic lifestyle and cultural practices – including the skills that, at one point, had made them indispensable as workers. As Dena Ringold (2000) points out, in "Czechoslovakia in 1958, the government issued a decree proclaiming that Roma were not a separate ethnic group and embarked upon a violent campaign against nomadism" (p. 5).

Roma have been depicted in the popular media as travellers, nomads and itinerates for so long that it has become difficult to see them as anything else. They migrate, move and travel, certainly, but no more or less than any other identifiable population. While they live in every European state, are contiguous, dispersed and at the same time incredibly heterogeneous, they have become very much a marginalized and socially excluded people. Barany (1994) posits that "the Roma's marginal condition is the result of exclusionary dynamics in several dimensions . . . [and] since their arrival in eastern Europe some 700 years ago, they have been politically, socially, culturally, and economically marginalised by the dominant populations in the region" (p. 323). A report by the Council of Europe (CoE) captures what is going on today, with Eastern Europe's Roma population. "They are sedentarised Roma who have turned nomadic in a search for a better life. They settle on land outside main cities and are constantly hounded by the local authorities and the local population" (CoE, 11 Oct. 2006).

The history of Roma is wrapped up with the history of Europe itself. They have contributed greatly to European culture, commerce and society, having been instrumental in Europe's industrial transformation. *The Guardian* newspaper recently reported (December 2012) that "a genetic analysis of 13 Gypsy groups around Europe . . . has revealed that the arrival on the continent of their forebears from northern India happened far earlier than was thought, about 1,500 years ago" (Tremlett, 2012). Therein lays the ultimate irony. Roma predate the European state system by hundreds of years yet are treated by the majority population (in any given state) as outsiders, nomads and/or "others." Right-wing groups demonstrating against Roma, usually to intimidate and sow fear, have been known to chant "go home" or "go back to where you came from" (in the corresponding European language, of course). This is a remarkable request, for some obvious reasons, but mainly because Europe *is* their home, and has been for as long as anyone can remember.

**Citizenship**, then, becomes an important part of this discussion, and really of all discussions relating to the place of Roma in an ever expanding EU. After all, citizenship is how states distinguish "their" people from others and why government (some would argue) can legitimately exercise physical violence within a delimited territory. It is also a way in which persons acquire rights, civil and otherwise, and benefits – social, economic and political. When on January 1, 1992 Czechoslovakia split along its federal lines into the Czech Republic and Slovakia, respectively, Roma living in the Czech lands found themselves internally displaced, without citizenship, in communities in which they had lived for decades.

When Czechoslovakia adopted a federal constitution in 1969, citizens of the new Czechoslovak federation effectively acquired dual citizenship: the citizenship of their respective "home" community (Slovak or Czech), and the citizenship of their juridical state, Czechoslovakia. Thus, upon dissolution, Czechoslovaks were being asked, literally, to choose between the two citizenships — not particularly difficult if you were ethnically Czech or ethnically Slovak. Roma, regardless of which side of Czechoslovakia they hailed from, were being told by Czech authorities to relocate to Slovakia. For Czech Roma, staying put in the newly created Czech Republic, where they had lived for many decades, proved difficult. One hurdle (but by no means the only one) was that Roma had to prove residency, difficult given they were relocated by Czechoslovak authorities on a whim in the 1940s and 1950s, or before. As the European Roma Rights Centre (ERRC) contends, "there were approximately 100,000 Roma on Czech territory in 1994 who had previously been Czechoslovak citizens and long-term residents of the Czech half of the federation, but who had not become Czech citizens" (1996, October 12). Moreover, the 1993 citizenship forbade any person with a criminal record from attaining citizenship. O'Nions (2007) notes that "the so-called "Gypsy-clause" also had to be satisfied in any application for permanent residence. It stated that a person "should not have been sentenced for an intentional criminal offence in the previous five years" (p. 119). As Czech human rights lawyer Ina Zoon observed, "It is somewhat of a paradox that in ignoring the severity of the offence and focusing exclusively on when the sentence is pronounced, the citizenship law would allow a person convicted of crimes against humanity after the Second World War to obtain citizenship while at the time barring a person convicted of a minor offense from obtaining citizenship" (2007, p. 119).

The law was ultimately amended, but for a period thousands of Roma were effectively "internally displaced." There is no telling how many Roma live in the Czech half of the former Czechoslovakia without holding Czech citizenship. Statistics relating to Roma, population and otherwise, are notoriously unreliable, inaccurate and, frankly, incomplete. In some European countries, numbers generated by the official census (reported by government) and the actual Roma population (reported by Roma and/or Roma NGOs) can differ by as much as 700,000 – approximately the population of the city of Mississauga, Ontario (CoE 2010). Looking at a Council of Europe report from 2010, one can see the "official" number of Roma living in Hungary is 190,046 (2001), while the minimum and maximum estimates, prepared by Roma NGOs, are 400,000 and 1,000,000 respectively. The average estimate, then, is 700,000. [1]

Such statistical anomalies and/or discrepancies make any discussion about Roma difficult, to put it mildly, and the development of coherent integration policies even more difficult. Without knowing how many Roma live in any given state, one cannot begin to assess the suitability of public infrastructure, policy and services. While most agree attainment of reliable statistics should be a priority for European lawmakers, the EU has been unable to "force" member-states to deal with the many population anomalies. One thing is for certain, however: most European governments under-report the number of Roma living within their borders and thus far have demonstrated little interest in obtaining reliable and accurate demographic statistics.

A recent change worth noting, in brief, is the advent of European Union citizenship. When the Czech Republic, Poland, Hungary, Slovakia and Slovenia joined the EU in 2004, and Romania and Bulgaria in 2007, the Roma in each acquired a new juridical status: European Union citizen. All European passports are explicit in this regard, and all EU institutions are open to Roma – by virtue of their national-state citizenship. Therefore, Roma groups and individual Rom can utilize the EU Ombudsman, the European Commission, Parliament and ancillary institutions like the European Union Agency for Fundamental Rights. A new opportunity structure exists to facilitate lobbying and contentious politics. Advancements have been made *in spite* of national lawmakers, utilizing the ECtHR, European Parliament and European Commission. The ECtHR has ruled against governments, most notably the Czech Republic (see *D. H. and Others v Czech Republic*), for continued discrimination in the sphere of education.

Life chances positively correlate with *education*. That is, the level of education attained is a fairly accurate predictor of the socio-economic position attainable. In most circumstances gender and ethnicity also form part of this calculus. This means, in most instances, that if you come from a wealthy family and belong to the

---

[1] All population statistics are derived from a document (an Excel spreadsheet) prepared by the Council of Europe Roma and Travellers Division. It can be found online at www.coe.int/t/dg3/romatravellers/Source/documents/stats.xls. Last accessed Aug. 1, 2014.

majority population you will, in all likelihood, attain a decent level of affluence yourself, comparatively speaking. Education is therefore vitally important and a key indicator of affluence:

> Max Weber's term *life chances* refers to the extent to which individuals have access to important societal resources such as food, clothing, shelter, education and healthcare. . . . [M]ore-affluent people typically have better life chances than the less affluent because they have greater access to quality education, [etc.] (Kendall, 2013, p. 216).

In the Czech Republic, but also elsewhere in Europe, Romani children end-up segregated, placed in so-called "special schools" (in Czech, *zvláštní školy*) away from non-Roma children. Very few progress beyond elementary school; fewer still attend post-secondary institutions. The *zvláštní školy* are remedial in nature, teaching only basics, and are geared toward pupils with learning or cognitive impairments. This controversial practice was ruled "illegal" by the ECtHR (in 2007) and condemned by a host of NGOs and governments, but persists. A major obstacle to integration and real change, among Roma and between Roma and non-Roma, has been education, or lack thereof, and the difficulties in developing a Roma elite. Progress has been made and universities like Central European University in Budapest, backed by billionaire philanthropist George Soros, are making Roma education (and education of Roma) a priority, but the education gap, unfortunately looks more like a chasm. Little wonder Roma from the Czech Republic, Slovakia and most recently Hungary, are keen to leave Europe behind for the security and safety of Canada.

## Oh Canada!

In the summer of 2012 I had the chance to visit Sajókaza, a small Hungarian village northeast of Budapest. Four Roma, knowing that I lived and worked in Canada, thought I would be able to help them understand legislative changes that were under consideration at that time to Canada's *Immigration and Refugee Protection Act*. There was talk then, before the bill was tabled, of a list of so-called "safe countries" that would be identified and listed in the new legislation. There was real concern this new law would, effectively, permit the government to deport all Roma originating from Hungary and other EU states, as EU states would be deemed "safe". The Roma I spoke with in Sajókaza were worried their family members living in southern Ontario would be returned to Hungary without having had opportunity to plead their case before the Refugee Protection Division (RPD). This was particularly disconcerting to Roma in Sajókaza, as in 2008, not far from their village, a gang of right-wing extremists began a year-long terror campaign against Hungarian Roma, killing at least six, and injuring many others (see Dunai, 2013).

On December 15, 2012, the *Balanced Refugee Reform Act* and the *Protecting Canada's Immigration System Act* came into force. The Act accomplished three things: (1) introduction of Designated Countries of Origin (DCOs) — the so-called "safe countries" list; (2) expedited review process for claimants from DCOs and a limited appeal process; and (3) "replacement of the current Personal Information Form with the Basis of Claim from" (IRBC, 2014). An appeal from a DCO refugee claimant will not be heard by the Refugee Appeal Division. According to the government of Canada, DCOs are "countries that do not normally produce refugees, but do respect human rights and offer state protection" (Citizenship and Immigration Canada, 2012). The federal government is the sole determinant of this list and can seemingly add or remove states at will. Of the listed countries, three — Hungary, Slovak Republic and the Czech Republic — have noted, and notable, human rights violations with respect to Roma. Also, the new DCO regime provides "[the federal] government with a tool to respond to spikes in claims from countries that do not normally produce refugees." In terms of timing, this law was introduced immediately after a spike in claims from Hungarian Roma.

The fall of communism in 1989 promised democracy, rule of law and human rights. And for many Czechs, Poles, Hungarians, and others, matters did improve markedly. But for European Roma, life actually worsened with regime change and transition, pushing Roma further to the margins of society and further below the poverty line. Even the promise of EU membership did not help raise the standard of living nor in the amelioration of anti-Roma policy and sentiment.

Canada is often portrayed as a willing recipient of the world's poor, down-trodden, persecuted and marginalized. Canada's commitment to multiculturalism, democracy and rule of law make it attractive to those fleeing authoritarian states, despotism and intolerance. A news release from February 2013 reveals, in rather stark contrast, the government's concern with the number of refugee claimants from Hungary. Though not mentioned, the vast majority of these refugee claim-ants were and are European Roma. As reported on a government website, "asylum claims from Hungary, Canada's top source country for claimants in 2011 and 2012, have dropped 98 percent compared to the average between 2009 and 2012." There are now hundreds fewer Hungarian Roma seeking refuge in Canada and the government claims the new refugee scheme has already saved taxpayers an estimated $ 2 billion (CIC News Release, 22 Feb. 2013).

One refugee claimant, Viktória Mohácsi, a former Member of European Parliament (MEP) from Hungary, activist, human rights campaigner, and "ambassador of the Roma" (Donath, 2013), will have the opportunity to explain why Hungary should be removed from the DCO list. She is in Canada awaiting her hearing. Having fled Hungary a few years ago fearing for her life, she is adamant her physical safety would be at risk should she be deported back to Hungary. Mohácsi made many enemies when she complained, publicly and directly, about the less than thorough investigation into the murder of six Roma mentioned above. When the police finally responded to the murders in northeast Hungary, they did so with little urgency. Keno Verseck of *Spiegel Online* offers this account:

On the night of Nov. 3, 2008, Éva Nagy, a 40-year-old mother of four, was shot dead in Nagycsécs, a village in northeastern Hungary. Attackers first set the family's house on fire with petrol bombs. As the family fled, they were fired on with shotguns. Éva and her brother-in-law were killed. Tibor was severely wounded. . . . On that same night, Nagycsécs was just the first place to be afflicted by a series of gruesome murders directed at Roma. . . . In 2008 and 2009, right-wing extremist terrorists in Hungary killed six Roma, including a 4-year-old boy, and wounded 55 people, almost all of them Roma. Some of the wounds were life-threatening. These were followed by a long series of botched investigations, and Hungarian authorities only arrested the suspects in August 2009 (Verseck, 2013).

As of 2014, Mohácsi is living in a small apartment in Toronto with her two adopted children — safe and sound, but with an uncertain future. Her refugee application was likely to be reviewed in fall 2014. Should her application prove successful, it could offer other Roma a glimmer of hope, and might well pave the way for a more nuanced DCO system that takes systemic discrimination and marginalization into consideration. An unfortunate reality is that European Roma engaging in contentious politics, working for human rights NGOs, and advocating for rights and economic improvement are placing themselves at risk. This is especially true for those living and working in central Europe, insofar as politics has moved decidedly to the right, with populist rhetoric now all too common in counties like Hungary. The Mohácsi case highlights this new reality.

Canada's new refugee regime, i.e., the DCO system, is working to dissuade Roma from seeking asylum in Canada. Fewer Roma are applying for refugee status in Canada, and instead are looking for "safe" counties within the EU – considering they are legally entitled to move and relocate within the EU. And though Roma are entitled to "freely move" within the EU, states like France and the UK are deporting Roma back to central Europe. This practice has been condemned by EU lawmakers, but persists. It's also worth noting that the numbers of Roma are declining in cities and towns across Canada, but especially in Hamilton, Toronto and St. Catharines, Ontario (CBC, 2012). Suffice it to say that Roma are no longer welcome refugees to Canada.

## Conclusion

This chapter sought to elucidate some of the problems encountered by Roma, in Europe and Canada, through an examination of the historically rooted marginalization and social exclusion they have experienced. Their position (and reality), as described above, is one of statelessness, and corollary circumstances of political disenfranchisement and poverty. The argument is a simple one: lacking a state of their own, Roma have been at the mercy of majority populations that, generally speaking, have demonstrated little to no interest in mitigating the many structural impediments to their emancipation. People are certainly paying attention to Roma now — their plight, the xenophobia and racism they often encounter, and the scope and character of countless policies implemented in the last decade or so to help integrate and ultimately empower them. Published research is helping "us" make sense of the whole situation and appraising the efforts of both European (including EU) and Canadian lawmakers. Unfortunately, the cycle of poverty and marginalization, punctuated by repressive policies and programs, appears to be continuing despite the best of intentions.

This chapter began with four questions meant to orient the reader to the ongoing plight of European Roma, and of Roma seeking refuge in Canada. While the questions were answered in a roundabout way above, it is probably useful to conclude this chapter with definitive, and more succinct, answers to each question in succession, and so the questions are repeated — with answers — below.

## Guiding Questions — and Answers

**1. What is preventing Roma from realizing a place among Europe's established and recognized ethno-nations?**

Persistent racism, ire and stereotyping, at all levels, in all forms and in all contexts, conspire to keep Roma at the bottom rung of Europe's recognised etho-nations. Unlike the Welsh, Scots and Catalans, Roma lack a delimited territory and have never really pursued an irredentist programme. Lacking delimited territory and any political will to acquire one, Roma remain a minority population in every European state they live, despite having lived in Europe from before the advent of the state system (which can be dated, approximately, to the Peace of Westphalia in 1648). Until national governments either integrate Roma, fully and completely, or establish a parallel decision-making body for Roma, with real power, Roma will remain peripheral and marginal.

**2. How have centuries of cruel and unusual treatment, punctuated by the Holocaust, affected Roma identity and their interactions with majority populations?**

Fear and mistrust (and distrust) pervade interactions, both formal and informal, between Roma and non-Roma. A cursory examination of European newspapers and newswires will show just how entrenched and pervasive anti-Roma attitudes are. Democracy, European integration, etc., have had little effect on anti-Roma sentiment. For example, as reported in *Special Eurobarometer 296* (2008): *"When it comes to the Roma, who collectively form the largest ethnic minority in the enlarged EU, the average 'comfort score' drops to 6.0 when respondents are asked how they would feel if their neighbour was a Roma. Around a quarter (24%) of Europeans would feel uncomfortable having a Roma neighbour: a striking difference to the level of comfort with a person from a different ethnic origin in general (where only 6% would feel uncomfortable)"* (p. 8).

**3. Why do Roma remain scapegoats, objects of ire, and the focus of populist rhetoric despite having lived in Europe for nearly eight centuries?**

This is a difficult question to answer, though surprisingly easy to comprehend. Roma lack power — political, economic and social. There are very few Roma politicians, lawyers, judges, doctors, teachers, professors, and so on. And Roma that do attain such occupational status choose not to self-identity as Roma. Ian Hancock (2010) argues that, "lacking military and political strength and a geographic homeland, and being forced to travel in small groups for self-preservation" (p. 39), Roma have remained peripheral actors. This being said, Roma have managed to survive all kinds of maltreatment. Some of the blatant and obvious forms have been mentioned above. In a way Roma are a remarkable people, resurgent in many respects, asserting their cultural, linguistic and artistic identity, in an atmosphere often hostile to their very existence. Hancock suggests that "we [Roma] were one people when we left India, and one people when we arrived in Europe a thousand years after that. An increasing number of Rom seek to restore that lost unity; many *gadže* ridicule our desire to do so" (p. 39). As the economy in Europe has worsened, populist rhetoric has intensified. Again, without power Roma are an easy target.

**4. Why did Canada recently change its immigration policy to, in effect, dissuade and/or prevent Roma from applying for refuge?**

It would seem the Canadian government has accepted the all-too-common stereotypes, misconceptions and popular mythologies, which together portray Roma as itinerant swindlers, born criminals and at best, exotic travellers. These are, indeed, stereotypes. Canada is not immune to racism and ignorance, and government is certainly not beyond populist sentiment. A glaring example of this bigotry comes from Ezra Levant, a media personality on Sun Television: *"These are gypsies . . . a culture synonymous with swindlers. The phrase gypsy and cheater have been so interchangeable historically that the word has entered the English language as a verb: he gypped me. Well, the gypsies have gypped us. Too many have come here as false refugees. And they come here to gyp us again and rob us blind as they have done in Europe for centuries. . . . They're gypsies. And one of the central characteristics of that culture is that their chief economy is theft and begging"* (Berger and Rehaag, 2012).

In the final analysis, given ongoing and widespread hostility toward Roma, statelessness is a significant hindrance to emancipation and/or self-determination. This is something Aboriginal peoples in Canada and elsewhere have also become painfully aware of. While the EU does not identify Roma as a nation, it does refer to Roma as a European minority, a community experiencing marginalization and social exclusion, and a group trapped in a cycle of poverty, disenfranchisement and unemployment. The formula reads: "exclusion from education leads to exclusion from employment. This leads to increased poverty, which forces people to live in poor or segregated housing. This in turn, affects their educational and employment opportunities, as well as their health. And the circle starts again" (European Union Agency for Fundamental Rights, n.d.). Despite the efforts of the EU, Council of Europe and OSCE to integrate Roma, many of the EU's 27 member-states continue to ignore calls for substantive policy change. And as described above, safe(er) countries, like Canada, seem unwilling to entertain the idea of accepting Roma as refugees.

## Online Resources

*The European Roma Rights Centre:* http://www.errc.org/
*European Roma Policy Coalition:* http://romapolicy.eu/
*Roma Community Centre (Toronto, Ontario):* http://www.romatoronto.org/
*European Roma and Travellers Forum:* http://www.ertf.org/

## References

Barany, Z. (1994). Living on the edge: The East European Roma in postcommunist politics and societies. Slavic Review, *53* (2), 321 – 344.

Berger, B. & Rehaag, S. (2012, Sept. 15). Stop vilifying Roma refugees. Toronto Star. Retrieved from http://www.thestar.com/opinion/editorialopinion/2012/09/15/stop_vilifying_roma_refugees.html.

Citizenship and Immigration Canada (2012). Backgrounder: Designated countries of origin. Retrieved from http://www.cic.gc.ca/english/department/media/backgrounders/2012/2012-06-29a.asp.

Council of Europe (2006, October 11). HDIM.IO/477/06. Retrieved from http://www.osce.org/odihr/21645.

Dunai, M. (2013, August 6). Four jailed for neo-Nazi killing spree that terrified Hungary's Roma. Reuters. Retrieved from http://www.reuters.com/article/2013/08/06/us-hungary-roma-killings-ruling-idUSBRE97508920130806.

European Commission (2008). Discrimination in the European Union: Perceptions, experiences and attitudes, p. 8. Retrieved from http://ec.europa.eu/public_opinion/archives/ebs/ebs_296_sum_en.pdf.

European Roma Rights Centre (1996, October 12). Czech government amends anti-Romani citizenship law, but the improvements are cosmetic. Retrieved from http://www.errc.org/article/czech-government-amends-anti-romani-citizenship-law-but-the-improvements-are-cosmetic/1476.

European Union Agency for Fundamental Rights. Retrieved from http://fra.europa.eu/fraWebsite/roma/roma_en.htm.

Gellner, E. (2006). *Nations and nationalism* (2nd ed.). Oxford: Blackwell.

Gheorghe, N. (2013). Choices to be made and prices to be paid: Potential roles and consequences in Roma activism and policy-making. In W. Guy (ed.), *From victimhood to citizenship: A debate*. Budapest: Kossuth Publishing.

Goldston, J. A. (2002). Roma rights, Roma wrongs. *Foreign Affairs, 81,* 146.

Hancock, I. with Karath, D. (2010). *Danger! Educated Gypsy*. Hertfordshire, England: University of Hertfordshire Press.

International Romani Union (2001). "Declaration of a Roma nation." Retrieved from http://www.hartford-hwp.com/archives/60/132.html.

Kendall, D. (2013). *Sociology in our times*. Belmont, CA: Wadsworth.

Liégeois, J. (1994). *Roma, Gypsies, Travellers*. Strasbourg: Council of Europe Press.

O'Mahony, J. (2001, November 3). In the ghetto. *The Guardian*. Retrieved from http://www.theguardian.com/books/2001/nov/03/books.guardianreview.

Organization for Security and Cooperation in Europe (OSCE) (2000). *Report on the situation of Roma and Sinti in the OSCE area.*

Ringold, D. (2000). *Roma and the transition in Central and Eastern Europe: Trends and challenges*. Washington: World Bank.

Ritzer, G. (2011). *Globalization: The essentials*. Singapore: Wiley-Blackwell.

Smith, A. D. (1996). Anthony D. Smith's opening statement: Nations and their pasts. Nations and Nationalism, *2* (3).

Smith, A. D. (2009). *Ethno-symbolism and nationalism: A cultural approach*. New York: Routledge.

Soysal, Y. (1994). *Limits on citizenship: Migrants and postnational membership in Europe*. Chicago: University of Chicago Press.

Tremlett, G. (2012, December 7). Gypsies arrived in Europe 1,500 years ago, genetic study says. The Guardian. Retrieved from http://www.theguardian.com/world/2012/dec/07/gypsies-arrived-europe-1500-genetic.

Verseck, K. (2013, August 6). Justice in Hungary: Neo-Nazis get life for Roma murder spree. *Spiegel Online*. Retrieved from http://www.spiegel.de/international/europe/neo-nazis-in-hungary-receive-life-sentences-for-roma-murder-spree-a-915163.html.

## CHAPTER FIVE

# "That Thing":
# HIV/AIDS Trauma, Stigma and Displacement

## *Jennifer Clarke and Soheila Pashang*

The twentieth century was marked by threats and acts of war and conflict, as well as global attempts at institutionalizing anti-war and peace movements and organizations (Kinney, 2010). These attempts, organizations and groups range from the 1942 Declaration of the United Nations by the Allied Powers of World War II (Hoopes and Brinkley, 1997) to progressive ad hoc and temporary coalitions with links to local and international grassroots movements. Despite these many and varied attempts at peacemaking, from 1990 to 1999 alone, a total of 118 armed conflicts occurred in over 80 states around the globe (10 being interstate[1] and 100 strictly intrastate[2]) (Spiegel, 2004). Sub-Saharan Africa is one region disproportionately affected by both armed conflict (38% of total world incidences) and the HIV/AIDS epidemic (70% of global reported cases). Armed conflict and its aftermath often result in internal displacement, refugee crises across international borders, and, as Hooper (1999) posits, increased HIV/AIDS transmission.

In the case of Africa, this persisting conflict and health inequity is rooted in the history of European capitalist colonialism through the oppression of African peoples and the appropriation of their natural resources. In her book, *Patriarchy and Accumulation on a World Scale: Women in the International Division of Labour,* Maria Meis (1998) provides an in-depth analysis of the subordination of African women whereby their labour power and their bodies were subject to violence, abuse and sexual exploitation. Other scholars argue that the HIV/AIDS virus originated during the colonial era due to harsh treatment of Africans (Hooper, 1999; Chitnis et al., 2000) and sexualization of African women, which exposed them to sexually transmitted infections (STIs) (Susa et al., 2010) and perhaps HIV/AIDS. Over time, with the expansion of capitalism, Africa, like many other post-colonial regions, continued to experience armed conflicts, violence,

---

[1] The term **interstate** refers to conflict between one or more states.
[2] The term **intrastate** refers to conflict among one or more groups representing a state with one or more non-state groups within the same country.

displacement, socioeconomic inequities and political repression. These multiple intersecting factors drive feminized exploitation, stigmatization, discrimination, marginalization and the resultant vulnerability to HIV/AIDS.

Speigel (2004) compares data among populations affected by conflict with those in resource-poor settings, and argues that vulnerability does not necessarily translate into HIV/AIDS epidemics. He suggests that HIV/AIDS transmission depends on various competing and interrelated factors. For instance, pre-conflict-affected populations have lower HIV-prevalence rates, while conflict reduces people's coping mechanisms and resilience, making them more vulnerable to HIV/AIDS. This finding is consistent with high rate of HIV/AIDS prevalence in Africa. Speigel (2004) further proposes two competing discourses: one asserts that conflict increases vulnerability to HIV/AIDS based on such determinants as breakdowns in social structures, secure income and basic needs, sexual violence, increased drug use and lack of health infrastructure and education; and one that conflict decreases HIV transmission because of reduced mobility and accessibility as well as improved protection, health, education and social services in refugee camps. Ultimately these factors must be understood in the context of the pre-conflict prevalence of HIV in the area of origin in relation to the prevalence in the surrounding host population, and the duration of the conflict and time spent at refugee camps. Other related factors include exposure to violence during conflict and flight, as well as the level of interaction between the two communities (those with HIV/AIDs and those not infected) (Speigel, 2004).

While conflict increases displacement, food insecurity, poverty and human vulnerability to HIV/AIDS, there is little evidence that suggests that refugees and displaced persons are threats to or carriers of HIV/AIDS into host countries (Speigel, 2004; Tunstall, 2006). In contrast, refugees tend to migrate from source countries with lower prevalence of HIV/AIDS to countries with higher HIV/AIDS prevalence (Speigel, 2004). Therefore, understanding the statistical distribution of HIV/AIDS is crucial because it defines population vulnerability and risk, and the dynamics of HIV transmission. (See the table on the next page.) The HIV/AIDS rates in Canada are low when compared to the levels in Africa (Amaratunga et al., 2011; Soskolne, 2003). Over the past three decades, the African people have had to cope with a tremendous amount of loss and suffering from HIV/AIDS-related deaths and intergenerational trauma and displacement. While there are some governmental and community services available to help those living with the disease and families coping with the loss of loved ones, the specific needs of women and children are often ignored. In adapting to their new realities and deteriorating health, many also experience the trauma of social stigma attached to their HIV/AIDS status. This stigma is both a leading cause of disease transmission and internal displacement from families and communities.

We begin the chapter with a snapshot of HIV/AIDS in Africa and Canada. We then briefly offer some common understandings of the origins of the disease. Drawing upon HIV/AIDS statistics for the regions, we examine issues of difference, looking specifically at how multiple and intersecting identities of race, gender, class, and sexual orientation contribute to HIV/AIDS vulnerability for certain groups. At the crux of this chapter is the issue of stigma, specifically the stigmatized trauma of HIV/AIDS. We examine the manifestation of stigma at the individual, familial, community and societal levels. We draw upon anti-oppressive, anti-colonial and feminist strategies to highlight community responses to the stigma and discrimination of the HIV/AIDS pandemic. We argue that attention must be paid to the needs of women and children who are disproportionately affected by HIV/AIDS, and the grandmothers who care for them. We conclude the chapter with policy and practice implications and micro, mezzo and macro level recommendations to address the stigmatized trauma of HIV/AIDS.

**HIV/AIDS: A Snapshot**

Acquired Immune Deficiency Syndrome (AIDS) came to the attention of American scientists in 1981 when a large group of homosexual men succumbed to mysterious symptoms (Greene, 2007). Since its discovery, it has claimed over 36 million lives worldwide (Fact Sheet, UNAIDS, 2013), and an estimated 35 million more people are currently living with HIV/AIDS (WHO, 2014; UNAIDS, 2013; amfAR, The Foundation for AIDS Research, 2012). These numbers do not include those who are not tested or aware of their sero-positive status. A UNAIDS Worlds AIDS DAY Report (2012) suggests that 50% of people infected with HIV are unaware of their positive status. HIV/AIDS has a negative impact on the social deter-minants of health[1] and the

| HIV/AIDS Cases by Continent, 2011 | |
|---|---|
| Worldwide | 31.6 million to 35.2 million |
| Sub-Saharan Africa | 21.6 million to 24.1 million |
| South and Southeast Asia | 3.6 million to 4.5 million |
| Eastern Europe and Central Asia | 1.3 million to 1.7 million |
| Latin America | 1.2 million to 1.7 million |
| North America | 1.0 million to 1.9 million |
| East Asia | 0.6 million to 1.1 million |
| Western and Central Europe | 0.8 million to 0.9 million |

*Source: UNAIDS World AIDS Day Report, 2011.*

overall functioning of individuals, families, communities, and the wider society.

The devastating impact of HIV/AIDS on the African continent is widely researched (Amaratunga et al., 2011; Soskolne, 2003). The region is host to 10% of the world population (Sowers & Rowe, 2007), but based on 2012 statistics, over two-thirds (70%) of all people living with HIV (25 million), including 88% of the

---

[1] The World Health Organization (WHO) defines **social determinants of health** as income and social status, education, physical environment, social support networks, genetics, health services and gender.

world's HIV-positive children, live in sub-Saharan Africa (UNAIDS, 2013; amfAR, The Foundation for AIDS Research, 2012).

Although in comparison to Africa's 25 million HIV/AIDS cases (UNIADS, 2013) Canada has a lower rate of HIV/AIDS cases per capita (58,600 to 84,000 cases) (Public Health Agency of Canada, 2012), interlocking issues of race, gender, class and sexual orientation continue to shape the proportion of infected individuals and affected communities (Cloete et al., 2010; de Bruyn, 1998). The impact of colonialism and historical trauma (i.e., colonization of the African continent and Aboriginal peoples in Canada), internalization of oppression (impacts of displacement, racism, sexism, homophobia, precarious immigration status) and exposure to poverty, violence, poor health and sociopolitical and educational inequities significantly increase individuals' and communities' vulnerability to the HIV/AIDS pandemic.

---

**Reflective Questions**

1. Is there any evidence to suggest that HIV/AIDS is a colonial discourse?
2. What are some of the significant historical, social, economic and intergenerational consequences of HIV/AIDS on dispossessed populations?

---

Due to the historical trauma of colonization, displacement, violence and ongoing processes of racialization, Aboriginal people in Canada have higher rates of health challenges (Lavallee, 2009). They are more vulnerable to abuse, violence, poor physical health, early childhood development issues, including childhood sexual and physical abuse, intergenerational interruption through displacement and forced residential school policies, and political, geographical and environmental isolation on reserves. In 2006, Aboriginal people represented only 3.8% of the total Canadian population, and yet they have a 3.6 times higher rate of vulnerability to HIV/AIDS (Public Health Agency of Canada, 2008). Ship and Norton (2001) also noted rapid increase in HIV/AIDS rate among Aboriginal women. Research shows that multifaceted challenges such as access to health care and social services, employment and stable housing (Public Health Agency of Canada, 2008; Statistic Canada, 2008) remain major barriers to the health and well-being of Aboriginal people in Canada.

The HIV/AIDS pandemic also disproportionately affects new immigrants to Canada. This is concerning since the imposition of immigration eligibility criteria, including medical examinations, prohibits applicants with HIV/AIDS from entering Canada. Research shows that new immigrants are much healthier than their Canadian counterparts; however, their health declines within months of their arrival (Beiser, 2005). Studies suggest dramatic increase in new HIV/AIDS cases among new immigrants (Amaratunga et al., 2011).

Racialized immigrant women between the ages of 15 and 29 are particularly vulnerable to HIV/AIDS (Amaratunga et al., 2011). This does not suggest that nationality, gender or race is the cause of HIV/AIDS transmission. Rather, vulnerability is due to systemic barriers and processes of racialization and marginalization that are embedded in the fabric of Canadian society (Amaratunga et al., 2011). One clear example is the lack of available and appropriate services for those with precarious immigration status. Due to anti-refugee and anti-immigrant sentiment, factors of social difference such as race, class, gender, dis/ability, sexual orientation and strict eligibility criteria in the health care system, racialized women with precarious immigration status are at much higher risk of sexual violation, poverty and stress-related mental health conditions. These women have little or no access to sexual health resources, including HIV/AIDS medication and treatment (Pashang, 2011).

## The Origin of "That Thing": HIV/AIDS

There are differing understandings of the history and origin of HIV/AIDS in the literature of medicine and the social sciences. From scholars such as Chitnis et al. (2000), Shilts (1988), Gina (1987), Susa et al. (2010), Yan (2014) and others we learn of moralist, colonial, imperial, scientific and medical explanations about the origin and spread of HIV/AIDS. While we do not engage here in a debate about the origin of HIV/AIDS, it is important to examine current understandings as these help to shape policy and practice responses to HIV/AIDS, as well as how people living with the disease are treated in society. Below we examine the origin of *"that thing"* that some call HIV/AIDS.

Shilts (1988) and Gina (1987) posit that HIV/AIDS came to the centre of North American consciousness in the 1980s following an outbreak among gay men when the "gay culture" was largely illegal and closeted, and underground gay bathhouses and gay bars were ideal social hubs. This provided a moralistic explanation of HIV/AIDS. Scientists later learned that the HIV virus was prevalent in the United States at least a decade earlier. This discovery broadened the scope of research from sexuality to Africanism. Today, many scientists speculate that the virus has been transmitted from African monkeys and apes to humans as early as 1910 to sometime in the 1930s (Korber et al., 2000). Some scholars argue that the virus originated during the colonial era through harsh treatment of African workers (Hooper, 1999), increased practices of bushmeat hunting and exposure to infected Simian Immunodeficiency Virus (SIV) in chimpanzees (Peeters et al., 2002; Vidal et al., 2000), mass medical vaccination malpractices after World War II (Chitnis et al., 2000), and the sexual exploitation of African women.

According to Chitnis et al. (2000), during the late nineteenth and early twentieth century, colonial rulers treated African men harshly and forced many into highly demanding labour camps with poor sanitation. Deplorable living conditions, including poor nutrition and sanitation, could make anything, including sick animals infected with a virus similar to HIV/AIDS — for example, SIV — a source of survival and infection.

Others see a strong relationship between the expansion of African colonial cities where social exchange, sexual promiscuity and prostitution of African women occurred, and the origin and spread of HIV/AIDS. To facilitate the movement of natural resources, colonial states established trade routes. Yan (2014) holds these routes responsible for transporting HIV/AIDS from the forest of Cameroon to the capital of Congo and other trading centers. The rise of labour migration of colonial workers and seasonal workers within the African continent facilitated the spread of the HIV/AIDS through the commercial sex work of African women (Yan, 2014). The British, Dutch and German colonizers also exploited African women as concubines and prostitutes to serve the sexual needs of colonial workers, even though they were prejudiced against the African race (Mies, 1986). Colonizers also engaged in what we now consider human trafficking for sex work, by relocating African women to industrial and trade sites in order to fulfill the sexual desires of male workers. The sexualization and deplorable sexual health conditions of African women are considered sources of sexually transmitted infections (STIs) such as genital ulcer diseases (syphilis) and, possibly, the spread of HIV/AIDS in African colonial cities (Susa et al., 2010).

There is also a "hunter theory" of HIV/AIDS, one which suggests that individuals who engaged in bushmeat activities, as hunters or vendors, were at high risk of contracting SIV, which is transmitted from chimpanzees to humans (Sharp and Hahn, 2011; Greene, 2007). For this reason, some scientists question the role of traditional weapons used by rural populations of Africa during hunting in which the hunters came into direct physical contact with primates. ("Bushmeat" refers to wildlife species including chimpanzees and other primates that are hunted for their meat or for commercial purposes. ) Baldus (2009) points out that, at least in Tanzania, the problem dates back to the expansion of German colonization and the commercial exploitation of wildlife for ivory, skins and feathers.

---

**Reflective Questions**

1. How are processes of colonization responsible for the oppression of African people and the HIV/AIDS pandemic?
2. How do you understand "post-colonial" states' responses to the spread of HIV/AIDS in Africa?
3. What is the relation between stigma and HIV/AIDS pandemic?

---

Several scholars hold colonial and post-colonial medical malpractices as contributing factors in the pandemic of HIV/AIDS. For instance, consider the already existing vulnerability of Africans within colonial societies and the spread of STIs and SIV viruses, then compound that vulnerability through such things as unsafe mass vaccinations for smallpox, where single unsterile syringes were reused. The result might well be an increased risk of mutation of the HIV/AIDS virus (Chitnis et al., 2000; Hooper, 1999). Hooper (1999) posits that another possible source of the HIV/AIDS pandemic was the 1950s oral polio vaccine called "Chat," which was grown in the kidney cells of local chimpanzees. Potentially contaminated by SIV virus, it was given to over a million people in various parts of Africa.

Regardless of its origin, HIV/AIDS is a preventable disease. However, it remains a leading cause of death among women and children, particularly those in developing nations where access to antiretroviral treatment is limited. In 2003, only 7% of the people in these regions had access to appropriate medical care, as pharmaceutical companies refuse to reduce the cost of medication or provide generic brands (Sowers and Rowe, 2007). In addition, women, men, and children living with HIV/AIDS also experience stigma and discrimination, violence, socio-economic-political disparities and abandonment by families, communities and the larger society.

## HIV/AIDS and the "Problem" of Difference

THEORETICAL DETOUR. In this section we take a short theoretical detour to discuss anti-oppression, anti-colonialism and critical race feminism, three critical perspectives that are crucial to any understanding of the "problem" of difference in the HIV/AIDS pandemic in the context of Africa and Canada. **Anti-oppression** is an approach to practice that challenges systemic forms of oppression, power and privilege, as these relate to factors of social difference such as race, class, gender, dis/ability and sexual orientation (Barnoff and Moffatt, 2007; Carniol, 2010; Sakamoto and Pitner, 2005). Anti-oppression emphasis on intersectionality is instructive in getting at the complexities of multiple and intersecting identities and the HIV/AIDS trauma, stigma and discrimination experienced by African women and girls, Aboriginal and racialized women in Canada, and MSM and LGBTQ+ and Transgendered people.

**Anti-colonialism** centres on political struggle and resistance to colonialism by colonized people all over the world (Dei, 2000; Hart, 2009). This perspective emphasizes decolonizing strategies for challenging the history of slavery and colonialism in Africa and Canada, and in this case, to mitigate the trauma, stigma and discrimination of HIV/AIDS on the people of Africa. Anti-colonialism is critical for understanding the current HIV/AIDS pandemic in Africa, especially as this is understood in national and international narratives.

Influenced by Aboriginal and female scholars of colour, **critical race feminism** is crucial for examining the interlocking nature of power and oppression in the lives of Aboriginal and racialized women (Lawrence and Dua, 2005; Razack, 2010), particularly their vulnerability to sexual violence (Razack, 2005) and HIV/AIDS. Critical race feminism helps us understand gender oppression and gender violence, especially as these relate to issues of race, class and the HIV/AIDS pandemic.

We argue that HIV/AIDS is rooted in colonial ideologies and oppressive laws, policies and practices. The perspectives of anti-oppression, anti-colonialism, and critical race feminism allow us to critically examine HIV/AIDS trauma, stigma and discrimination and challenge oppressive structures that exclude and deny people their dignity and human rights.

THE "PROBLEM" OF DIFFERENCE. HIV/AIDS is now considered a leading cause of death among women and girls in their productive years (ages 15 to 49) (WHO, 2012; UNAIDS, 2013; amfAR, The Foundation for AIDS Research, 2012). The research confirms that women constitute more than half of all people living with HIV/AIDS (17.7 million), with 57% of them living in sub-Saharan Africa. This is in large part due to colonial and patriarchal gender roles and the vulnerability of women to sexual violence, food insecurity, poverty and abuse. Armed conflict, environmentally-induced migration and displacement, as well as unequal distribution of material resources, expose women and girls to sexual exploitation, including coercion to transactional sex for survival (Spiegel, 2004). Women are stigmatized for their gender and for having HIV/AIDS.

The stigma of HIV/AIDS shatters families and communities and interrupts traditional protective systems (family and kinship). Stigma also causes feminized displacement, where women are blamed for being carriers of the diseases, pushed out of their homes and excluded from relations with families and friends. This makes women more vulnerable to exploitation, including trafficking for labour and sex work. Even when women and girls reach protective environment such as refugee camps, they continue to be at risk of sexual violence and transmission of HIV/AIDS by armed personnel and UN peacekeepers (Spiegel, 2004). Whether caring for HIV/AIDS infected family or community members or engaged in health and humanitarian aid work, women are at higher personal and occupational risk for HIV/AIDS (Amaratunga et al., 2011; Speigel, 2004; Stephen Lewis Foundation, 2014).

Studies show that the majority of women acquire HIV from their male partners during sexual intercourse (UNAIDS, 2013; amfAR, The Foundation for AIDS Research, 2012). Despite this knowledge, women are stigmatized as the carriers of HIV/AIDS and labeled promiscuous even when they are forced into sex work and prostitution. The feminization of HIV/AIDS stigma dismisses the complexity of colonial, patriarchal and globalized sexist power relations over women's sexuality and sexual activities.

A study by Colete et al. (2010) suggests that HIV/AIDS affects women in three interrelated ways: (1) HIV-positive women are stigmatized as promiscuous; (2) disclosure of infection to family members or partners makes women vulnerable to violence and homelessness; and (3) patriarchal structures and unequal gender relations prevent women from negotiating the use of condoms due to the stigma associated with HIV-positive status. On the other hand, men are reluctant to use condoms, get testing, or attend counselling and support groups (Colete et al., 2010).

The vulnerability of women and girls to HIV/AIDS is intricately linked to the multiple and intersecting oppressions that women experience in society. In 2012, 95% of new HIV infected cases occurred among low and middle-income countries (WHO, 2012), while most infected women were exposed to gender violence and abuse (UNAIDS, 2013; amfAR, The Foundation for AIDS Research, 2012). Gender oppression and gender violence affect women from all walks of life both in the global north and global south. Thus, varying factors such as historic oppression, geographical location, race, class, and age among other factors increase the vulnerability of women to HIV/AIDS.

Sexual orientation and the stigma attached to sexuality and sexual preferences not only violate the rights of LGBQT members to life and safety; they increase their vulnerability to HIV/AIDS infection. Currently, 75 countries criminalize same-sex relationships (Maller, 2013), a fact which places many LGBQT and MSM individuals at risk of prosecution, imprisonment and violence. When criminalization and stigma combine, people living with HIV/AIDS are excluded and denied the necessary supports, services and protections against transmission and discrimination. The socially constructed stigma and fear surrounding HIV/AIDS, and its origins in sexuality and sexual orientation, has created a global dynamic of underground life for LGBQT[1] people. Living with fear and stigma has created a high rate of stress and poor physical and mental health, including depression, anxiety, suicide, substance use, drug and alcohol addictions, smoking, as well as sociopolitical isolation among members of these groups (WHO, 2011).

Men who have sex with men (MSM)[2] and transgendered individuals are also disproportionately affected by HIV/AIDS (WHO, 2011). According to WHO (2011), MSM and transgendered people living in low-and middle-income countries have a 19.3% higher prevalence rate of HIV infection than the general population. The prevalence of HIV is higher among transgendered people (by 68%), because they face additional barriers such as lack of legal recognition and legal protection from state governments and access to appropriate health services (WHO, 2011). This is due in large part to stigma and widespread homophobia, criminalization and discrimination against LGBQT peoples by governments, healthcare providers and the general public. Stigma and discrimination prevent LGBTQ, MSM and transgendered people from accessing HIV/AIDS resources and supports that might be available to the general population. When stigma and discrimination intersect, people living with HIV/AIDS experience what could be termed "triple" jeopardy, which adds to their trauma and displacement from families and communities.

## The Stigmatized Trauma of HIV/AIDS

**Stigma** is a form of trauma that violates the human rights of people living with HIV/AIDS and displaces them internally from families and externally from communities. Stigma can occur at the micro level (individual/family/caregivers), mezzo level (neighbours and community members who stigmatize individuals within public and private spaces such as school, employment, helping profession, faith, or leisure and recreational activities), and macro level (a set of formal systems and institutions such as media, legal, health). According to Parker and Aggleton (2003) stigma is a social process that produces and reproduces relations of power and control. The *UNAIDS Fact Sheet* describes HIV/AIDS stigma this way:

> HIV/AIDS-related stigma can be described as a "process of devaluation" of people either living with or associated with HIV and AIDS. This stigma

---

[1] **LGBQT** refers to Lesbian, Gay, Bisexual, Queer, and Transgender and Transsexual people.
[2] **MSM** refers to men who have sexual encounters only with men, or those who identify themselves as heterosexual but are also engaged in sexual activity with other men.

often stems from the underlying stigmatization of sex and intravenous drug use — two of the primary routes of HIV infection. Discrimination follows stigma and is the unfair and unjust treatment of an individual based on his or her real or perceived HIV status. Discrimination occurs when a distinction is made against a person that results in being treated unfairly and unjustly on the basis of belonging, or being perceived to belong, to a particular group (*UNAIDS Fact Sheet*, December 2003, p. 1).

HIV/AIDS stigma is rooted in colonial ideologies and oppressive structures that construct a hierarchy of difference and unequal relations between and among groups. Parker and Aggleton (2003) posit that dominant groups use stigma as a tool to produce, legitimize and perpetuate social inequalities and to exert social control through the exclusion of stigmatized groups (cited in Ogden and Nyblade, 2005). Stigma also propagates when oppressed individuals and communities internalize their oppression. Internalization of oppression increases people's vulnerability to the stigmatized trauma of HIV/AIDS, particularly those perceived as racialized, homosexuals, transgendered, prostitutes and promiscuous women. When oppression is internalized, people are also more vulnerable to sexual violence, sexual exploitation, discrimination, abandonment, refusal or forceful testing and treatment (UNAIDS, 2006).

MANIFESTATIONS OF HIV/AIDS STIGMA. HIV/AIDS stigma manifests itself in both overt ways, through direct acts of violence and/or discrimination embedded in policies and practices, including lack of protection, and in covert ways, through negative attitudes, behaviours, and stereotypes (de Bruyn, 1998). The emotional consequences of HIV/AIDS stigma can be as traumatizing as living with the physical and social consequences of the disease.

Stigma also leads to fear and anxiety of the physical impact of the disease as well as the emotional and social impact, such as death, hopelessness and change of marital and economic statuses. People living with HIV/AIDS are stigmatized for having the disease and for other characteristics associated with the disease (race, gender and sexual orientation) (de Bruyn, 1998). The discourse of fear paradoxically perpetuates a culture of silence where infected persons are left with no option but to live an "underground" life of HIV/AIDS. As Roberts (2005) notes, stigma aids in the spread of the virus as it prevents seropositive individuals from getting tested and those who are HIV-positive from disclosing it to their partners or medical professionals. (**Seropositive** is a medical term used to refer to a person whose blood test shows that they are producing antibodies for a particular virus, including HIV, indicating the disease is present.)

Therefore, stigma creates a vicious cycle of oppression and contributes to early mortality and the denial of rights to treatment, sexual pleasure and a prosperous life. Stigma is powerful because it displaces individuals from their families, communities, social groups, and society.

**INDIVIDUAL LEVEL: IMPACT AND MANIFESTATION OF STIGMA.** HIV/AIDS stigma results in discrimination and causes deterioration in the health and wellbeing of infected persons, increasing their vulnerability to the disease. Many HIV-infected persons internalize stigma and are further traumatized by the lack of acceptance and rejection they experience from family and community. Deacon et al. (2005) use the terms **internal stigma** and **self-stigmatization** to describe an interconnected form of response to stigma where an individual accepts the existing negative social judgment of one's identity (i.e., HIV-positive), which, as Greeff et al. (2008) note, manifests itself in self-devaluation and negative perception of oneself as well as a diminished sense of personal control. The trauma is often exhibited in anger and self-pity, feelings of guilt, depression, and self-harming behaviours such as drug use, addiction, self-mutilation (Deacon et al., 2005), and loss of self-esteem, all of which exacerbate the illness.

Stigma also creates a sense of guilt when the problem of HIV/AIDS is individualized due to the lack of knowledge about the virus. Stigma challenges individuals to question their sexual activities in relation to moral, cultural or religious belief systems. In some cases, the stigma of particular sexual behaviours is seen as a sin and the illness an act of punishment from God. In societies where certain sexual behaviours are sanctioned, morality stigma can further justify legal discrimination and violence against individuals.

Cloete et al. (2010) reveal that HIV/AIDS-related stigma and fears of rejection create obstacles for individuals to disclose their HIV/AIDS status, or seek medical assistance. HIV/AIDS-related stigma also occurs in the form of "othering," where the "other" is perceived as someone with a different religion or ethnicity, and, if among one's own group, "may intersect with such identities as LGBQT status, lower socio-economic group, and a woman or prostitute" (Cloete et al., 2010). This blaming of the "other" increases personal vulnerability and discrimination against already marginalized groups. More often, denial of vulnerability to HIV virus increases one's own likelihood of infection or decreases the chances of getting help (Colete, et al., 2010). This denial often continues even when symptoms are visible.

In some rural areas with higher prevalence of HIV/AIDS, physical appearance and the overall health or weight loss of an individual can result in their being stigmatized as having HIV/AIDS. For this reason, individuals with poor health conditions are sometimes isolated and discriminated against as carriers of the virus (Cloete, et al., 2010). They may also be excluded from their families and communities and become internally displaced.

**FAMILY LEVEL: IMPACT AND MANIFESTATION OF STIGMA.** HIV/AIDS stigma affects families and caregivers who, on the one hand, witness the impact of stigma trauma on their loved ones and, on the other, face secondary trauma due to their association with stigmatized individuals. Stigmatized trauma occurs through negative attitudes, behaviors and actions towards HIV-infected persons. Stigmatized trauma at the familial level often results in high levels of stress, secrecy, isolation (de Bruyn, 1998) and loss of economic and social status, particularly for those living in smaller communities. These experiences of stigma, when compounded, increase the burden on families and caregivers.

Shame and fear of infection increase stigma within families. HIV/AIDS-infected persons are often isolated from extended family and the larger community, including from education and employment (Fournier et al., 2014). Stigma also subjects infected individuals to potential and ongoing verbal, psychological, emotional, physical and sexual abuse. Other discriminatory treatment includes avoidance and abandonment (Fournier et al., 2014) that may result in poverty and homelessness (Cloete et al., 2010). Therefore, stigma is both a personal and global problem as it never ends with targeting the individual person but extends to a set of social, cultural, and political conditions.

Although men are the main carriers of HIV/AIDS infection, women are blamed for its transmission and face harsh treatment and stigma from their own family members as well as their male partners' families. Gender vulnerability manifests itself in forceful divorce, violence, shaming, abuse and separation from children and families. Gender inequities further expose women to HIV/AIDS (Colete et al., 2010). Gender vulnerability and stigma are key barriers to women accessing testing, treatment, maternal intervention and prevention of mother-to-child transmission, and the voluntary counselling and education needed to control the virus (Colete et al., 2010). Since HIV is transmitted through body fluids, including breast milk, mothers who refuse to breastfeed their children are also stigmatized. To avoid stigmatization and discrimination, some women feel they have no choice but to breastfeed their children even knowing the risk for transmission (Colete et al., 2010). Therefore, stigma works to further the subordination of women and blame them for producing a new generation of HIV/AIDS-infected children.

Constructing female gender identity with HIV/AIDS allows male behaviours and actions for transmitting the virus to women to go unchallenged, and prevents them from accessing health care services including testing (Colete et al., 2010; Amaratunga, 2011). In places where men are expected to act within the patriarchal boundaries of macho culture, they may hide their HIV/AIDS symptoms/illness and/or their sexual orientation. Stigma impedes the behavioural changes required to intervene and prevent the spread of the HIV/AIDS virus (Cloete, 2010). At the same time, the stigmatized trauma of HIV/AIDS does not interrupt the behavioral patterns of infected persons or reduce the spread of the disease. In fact, stigma compounds the problem, making both prevention and intervention more difficult.

COMMUNITY LEVEL: IMPACT AND MANIFESTATION OF STIGMA. Due to the availability of antiretroviral treatment, people living with HIV/AIDS now have a much longer life expectancy and can lead healthier lives (Cloete et al., 2010). However, longer life expectancy does not guarantee a prosperous life. Often, pre-existing stereotypes and judgments about particular groups and HIV/AIDS lead to stigma and discrimination. Stigma forces people to hide the illness from community members to avoid rejection and discrimination (Cloete et al., 2010).

Stigma at the community level can be manifested as forms of occupational and housing discrimination. In communities with limited employment opportunities or where standards and policies are discriminatory, people with HIV/AIDS often suffer job loss, demotion and violation of employment rights (Cloete, 2010; de Bruyn, 1998). They also experience barriers in finding housing, as landlords avoid renting units to HIV-infected persons. Stigma and discrimination in employment and housing can result in homelessness, exploitation and violence as infected persons become dependent on abusive family members or are forced to engage in the sex trade.

Access to health services and attitudes of health care providers are also sources of barriers due to stigma. For example, in Canada, HIV/AIDS medications are very expensive, which makes access a serious concern, whereas in various African nations, medications might be accessible to some communities but fear, stigma, shame and a lack of education prevent people from obtaining them. As Ogen and Nyblade (2005) point out, medical-related stigma is more severe when the virus is linked with deviant behavior or in the context of morally disapproved behaviors such as homosexuality, "improper" sexual encounters, drug addiction and sharing syringes, as these are all considered individual choices.

SOCIETAL LEVEL: IMPACT AND MANIFESTATION OF STIGMA. Stigma at the societal level is manifested in both structural and institutional oppression that marginalizes individuals and groups by failing to protect them and eliminate HIV/AIDS discrimination (de Bruyn, 1998). This lack of protection is particularly acute for Aboriginal and racialized women, immigrants, refugees, members of the LGBQT and transgendered communities, and economically disadvantaged populations living with HIV/AIDS. Stigma and discrimination also lead to a lack of appropriate health care, treatment and social service programs, including prevention strategies to address marginalization, health, employment and housing discrimination as well as the implementation of protective laws and policies (de Bruyn, 1998).

Stigma also changes the context and meaning of the disease and forces people to use different names to refer to HIV/AIDS. In South Africa, for instance, people refer to HIV as "ulwazi" or "that thing" (Colete et al., 2014). Because of stigma, people also refuse to accept the diagnosis of HIV/AIDS, making the work of public health workers and professionals very difficult. If the disease is not acknowledged as existing, the cure also does not exist. This creates a sense of hopelessness, which increases people's vulnerability to the disease and denies them the right to a healthy and fulfilling life.

The stigma associated with HIV/AIDS goes beyond those living with the virus. Since HIV/AIDS is mainly transmitted through heterosexual intercourse during the productive years, many public services (schools, hospitals, and the civil service) are short-staffed and have long-term absenteeism, which affects economic output. The economic burden is also felt by industries as they must continuously recruit and train new workers (Children Orphaned by Aids, n.d.). The discourse of fear and stigma affects attitudes and treatment towards infected persons and groups with many facing ongoing human rights violations, violence, discrimination and inequities at all levels of society.

The high death toll during the reproductive years also means that many children will lose one ("single orphan") or both ("double orphan") parents to HIV/AIDS. After the loss, many children are sent to orphanages and others live with extended families, especially grandmothers (Kuo and Operario, 2010). Therefore, living with HIV/AIDS is an intergenerational trauma. This trauma is exacerbated by the socially and morally constructed discourse of fear and stigma.

## Reflective Questions

1. What knowledge and skills are important in working with individuals living with HIV/AIDS?
2. What theoretical perspectives can practitioners draw upon to engage more critically in their work with marginalized populations such as individuals living with HIV/AIDS, MSM, Transgendered people, LGBTQ, orphaned children, and caregivers?

The growing crisis of orphans due to HIV/AIDS-related death is compounded with societal stigma, and systemic inaction at local and international levels to adequately address or eradicate HIV/AIDS pandemic. Stigma also prevents many children with HIV/AIDS from being accepted into the homes of relatives, forcing them to live in institutionalized settings such as group homes, and residential care facilities known as "Aids Homes" (Fournier et al., 2014).

Stigma also threatens orphaned children's futures as productive members of society and the future economic growth of their countries. In the absence of adequate governmental assistance and social support, many grassroots community organizations, leaders and grandmothers have become the heart of the response to the HIV/AIDS pandemic and caring for orphan children. The involvement of grandmothers in the lives of orphan children models resilience and survival for the next generation. From an Aboriginal perspective, this caring for the next generation is important to "intergenerational connectedness of individuals, families, and communities. It is the way in which Aboriginal languages, spiritual practices and cultural traditions are transmitted and maintained" (De Pauw et al., 2010, p. 85).

We now turn our attention to community responses to HIV/AIDS, trauma and stigma, focusing on direct service level micro responses as well as mezzo and macro level advocacy, activism and structural responses.

## Community Responses to HIV/AIDS, Trauma and Stigma

HIV/AIDS, trauma and stigma require concrete actions to raise awareness about the disease, its transmission, prevention and management, and to eradicate societal stigma. Activists and workers in grassroots and community-based organizations generally respond to HIV/AIDS in two distinct ways. The first is through direct service provision such as grief and trauma counselling, education and prevention, health promotion, peer support, caregiver support, and end-of-life care, to name a few. The second response involves advocacy and activism at the structural and institutional levels to change discriminatory laws and policies and improve the quality of life for people living with HIV/AIDS, and for those caring for them. The significance of these community-based responses was highlighted in Stephen Lewis' January 9, 2003 briefing to the United Nation. As the special envoy on the plight of AIDS in sub-Saharan Africa, Lewis noted:

> . . . there is no question that [the] pandemic can be defeated. No matter how terrible the scourge of AIDS, no matter how limited the capacity to respond, no matter how devastating the human toll, it is absolutely certain that the pandemic can be turned around with a joint and Herculean effort between the African countries themselves and the international community. . . . Africans are engaged in endless numbers of initiatives and projects and programmes and models which, if taken to scale, if generalized throughout the country, would halt the pandemic, and prolong and save millions of lives (Gourevitch, 2010, p. 457).

COMMUNITY PROGRAMS AND SERVICES. Lewis' argument that the "pandemic can be defeated" with community-based programming and initiatives has important implications for social workers, health practitioners and activists who work with people living with HIV/AIDS, particularly those seeking support to cope with the trauma of diagnosis, loss of friends and family members, and to manage the disease. In the absence of national codes and standards of practice to protect individuals from HIV/AIDS stigma and discrimination, professional ethics and codes must guide practice. The critical and transformative approaches discussed earlier inform the current discussion on community responses to HIV/AIDS, trauma and stigma.

Anti-oppression, anti-colonialism and critical race feminism emphasize critical thinking, self-reflexivity, power-sharing, and interrogating privilege, power and oppression as these play a vital role in the prevention, intervention and eradication of the HIV/AIDS pandemic (Sakamoto and Pitner, 2005). Anti-oppressive practice requires social workers, health practitioners and activists to engage in self-reflexivity and unpack their own biases and judgments towards those living with HIV/AIDS before they can interrogate the interlocking power structures that exclude, isolate and discriminate against people living with the disease (Sakamoto and Pitner, 2005). Practitioners must integrate the principle of power-sharing into their decision-making processes if they are to provide effective trauma counselling, grief therapy, health promotion, and harm-reduction services to those infected with HIV/AIDS, and to grieving families (Absolon and Willette, 2005). From an anti-oppression approach, service users must be involved in developing programs and services that are informed by their lived experiences with HIV/AIDS, including the planning, implementation and evaluation of such services.

According to 2012 statistics, over 17 million children were orphaned by AIDS, and nearly 85% of these live in sub-Saharan Africa (UNICEF, 2013). Orphaned

93

children require specialized support because they are more vulnerable to various forms of abuse, mistreatment and exploitation, especially for being perceived as an economic burden on families, communities and society (Fournier et al., 2014). At an interpersonal level, these children are traumatized from observing their parents suffering and must live with the tragedy of loss, often without a chance to grieve. They also face ongoing economic, educational, and caregiving instability and insecurity. They are often displaced from their homes and communities and highly dependent on their aging relatives, especially grandmothers, for support and care. Given the number of people infected with HIV/AIDS, and the stigma associated with the disease, caregiver support is important to those relative and non-family members who care for children and adults living with the disease. Service providers must consider cultural and intergenerational issues in order to effectively support grandmothers and orphaned children.

In Africa, grandmothers fill multifaceted roles, from offering hope to helping children find meaning and move forward with their lives. They also provide safety and support, teach skills to cope with loss, and build resilience to manage the disease and associated HIV/AIDS stigma. Many African grandmothers are caring for grandchildren because their own children have succumbed to HIV/AIDS. The gendered nature of caregiving work is particularly important for social work, which is itself a highly gendered profession (Baines, 2007). The perspectives of anti-oppression and critical race feminism are important in helping practitioners to understand the feminization of HIV/AIDS, both in terms of those infected with the disease and those affected by the gendered nature of women's caregiving responsibilities and stigma. Practitioners and service providers must also be able to develop programs and services to support women, girls and grandmothers, as well as challenge HIV/AIDS stigma and discrimination through anti-oppressive, feminist, anti-racist, anti-colonial lenses.

End-of-life care is important for individuals and families living with HIV/AIDS. The severe physical toll that the disease takes on the body requires practitioners to provide critical end-of-life care and support to those individuals who are fearful of disclosing their HIV/AIDS status and do not seek treatment due to the fear of stigma. HIV/AIDS stigma has a devastating negative impact on individuals, especially those from Aboriginal, racialized, LGBTQ, MSM, Transgendered and low-income families. Community-based organizations must provide grief and bereavement support to help families cope with the loss of their loved ones. Support groups are important in healing and building resilience because they provide a space for children and families to come together and talk about their loss, remember their family members, and to cope with the shame and fear caused by HIV/AIDS stigma. This is especially important for children who have lost both parents and siblings to HIV/AIDS. Service providers must develop the knowledge and skills necessary to work with children and youth who are highly traumatized by their HIV/AIDS diagnosis, or by the loss of parents and family members to the disease and societal stigma. They must also develop creative, age-appropriate, and culturally relevant programs and services to help children and youth cope with loss, and educate them about health promotion, harm reduction, safe sexual health and the importance of seeking regular medical care and taking medications. These education interventions and programs can help to challenge stigma, build coping skills and enhance resilience and community capacity for preventing the spread of HIV/AIDS.

COMMUNITY ADVOCACY AND ACTIVISM. The HIV/AIDS pandemic demands community advocacy and activism at all levels of service provision in organizations and government ministries. At the structural level, practitioners, people living with HIV/AIDS and community activists can lobby government officials to challenge discriminatory legislation and policies, and to advocate for human rights. They must challenge structural racism, colonization, gender inequalities and poverty, as these impact people's vulnerability to HIV/AIDS and their access to medications and other necessary treatments. They must also work together to challenge societal stigma, which creates fear, shame, discrimination and excludes people from society, services and support. Societal stigma also prevents people from sharing their HIV/AIDS status with family members, getting testing and seeking treatment (Gaillard et al., 2002; Rankin et al., 2005).

Advocacy for harm reduction, health promotion and safe-sex education and prevention strategies are very important (Cloete et al., 2010). These strategies include accessible free condom and needle exchange programs that can help to reduce the spread of HIV/AIDS. Unfortunately, fear of stigmatization, particularly in small communities, and biases and discrimination among health care workers, may prevent many people from accessing harm reduction and health promotion resources. Further, some scholars argue that education strategies alone will not change how people behave (Browne et al., 2003; Hayes and Vaughan, 2002). Treatment strategies, according to de Bruyn (1998), must offer protection from discrimination to infected persons and support seropositive people by increasing their access to testing, medical attention and a future life without HIV/AIDS discrimination. These strategies should be used in conjunction with other macro-level strategies, such as challenging power relations, gender inequalities, racism and poverty to improve the overall material living conditions of people with HIV/AIDS.

Community activism and advocacy are crucial to the decriminalization of same-sex relationships, challenging widespread homophobia and discrimination against members of the LGBQT and MSM communities, and breaking the cycle of stigma and fear that prevent many individuals from seeking treatment or receiving appropriate resources and supports from service providers. Practitioners and community activists must also engage in activism to challenge the historic oppression of women, Aboriginal, racialized, LGBTQ, MSM, and Transgendered people, an oppression which increases vulnerability to HIV/AIDS. It is also important that service providers develop critical consciousness around structural forms of oppression, including war and conflict, colonialism, race, class, and gender inequalities, and other factors of social difference, that have a profound impact on people's vulnerability to the HIV/AIDS pandemic.

## Conclusion

HIV/AIDS gained international attention in the early 1980s, and has since claimed over 36 million lives worldwide, including many young women and their children, MSM, LGBTQ and Transgendered individuals (*UNAIDS Fact Sheet*, 2013). Survivors of HIV/AIDS continue to experience stigma and discrimination, along with poor physical, mental and psychological health conditions, such as depression, anxiety, suicide, substance use, drugs and alcohol addictions, to name a few (WHO, 2011). Raising critical awareness through health promotion and education initiatives are important, as approximately 50% of people infected with HIV are unaware of their positive status (UNAIDS Worlds AIDS Day Report, 2012). At the same time, developing laws, policies, programs through anti-oppressive, anti-racist, anti-colonial and gendered lenses will help to address African, Aboriginal and racialized women's and girls' vulnerability to sexual violence and exploitation, displacement and unequal gender relations from colonial, racist and patriarchal structures.

The following policy and practice implications should be considered in order to improve the overall living conditions of people with HIV/AIDS.

## Micro Level

1. HIV/AIDS leaves long-lasting and serious consequences on the livelihood of individuals and their families. Individuals and families require counselling/group support and resources in order to live and to cope with the disease. The first step is to accept the illness and build resiliency for dealing with the trauma of HIV/AIDS stigma.
2. Individuals must take responsibility for behavior change and healthy relationships to diminish the risk of transmission for others.

## Mezzo Level

1. Harm reduction and safe-sex education are important prevention strategies (Cloete et al., 2010) that should be used in conjunction with other anti-stigma and anti-discrimination strategies to improve the life of people with HIV/AIDS. Health promotion and harm reduction strategies including accessible free condom and needle exchange programs can help to reduce the spread of HIV/AIDS. Individuals must understand that substance use and shared needle use are considered risky behaviours. Treatment strategies must offer protection to infected persons as well as support to seropositive people to increase their access to testing, medical attention, and life without HIV discrimination (de Bruyn, 1998).
2. Treatment must be based on the diversity among populations, recognizing that no one program and service fits all (de Bruyn, 1998). Service providers

must recognize the unique and differing needs and challenges of individuals and communities, and develop programs and services to meet those needs. Although cultural sensitivity is important, we must avoid essentializing and culturalizing programs that justify cultural stigma.

## Macro Level

1.  Treatment must acknowledge self-determination, and people's rights to preferred treatment modality (de Bruyn, 1998). Individuals must be able to choose and understand the implications of their choice. Nonetheless, medications must be accessible to anyone wanting to use them.

2.  Canada, along with some 45 other countries, has criminalized non-disclosure of HIV-positive status when intentionally causing the risk of transmission through certain actions including sexual contact (*Globe and Mail*, July 20, 2010). Criminalization is not always positive as it may stigmatize certain individuals or communities, perpetuate racial profiling, or raise fears of testing or reporting. However, when used in conjunction with education, legal protection and other strategies, it may lower the risk of transmission.

## References

Absolon, K., & Willette, C. (2005). Putting ourselves forward: Location in Aboriginal research. In Brown, L. & Strega, S. (Eds.), *Research as resistance: Critical, Indigenous, and anti-oppressive approaches* (pp. 97–126). Toronto: Canadian Scholar's Press.

Amaratunga, C., Bisaillon, L., Farber, A., Kalinda, L., Liyanage, S., Murangira, F., & Rowe, M. (2011). Global Ottawa AIDS Link (GOAL): Story of an "Un-Project." In Spitzer, D. L. (Ed.), *Engendering migrant health: Canadian perspectives* (pp. 213–231). Toronto: University of Toronto Press.

amfAR, The Foundation for AIDS Research (2014). *Making AIDS History*. Retrieved from http://www.amfar.org/About-HIV-and-AIDS/Young-People-and-HIV/Young-People-and-HIV-AIDS/.

amfAR, The Foundation for AIDS Research (2012). *Statistics: Worldwide*. Retrieved from http://www.amfar.org/about-hiv-and-aids/facts-and-stats/statistics--worldwide/.

Auerbach, D.M.; W.W. Darrow, H.W. Jaffe, and J.W. Curran (1984). Cluster of cases of the acquired immune deficiency syndrome. Patients linked by sexual contact. *American Journal of Medicine, 76* (3), 487–92.

Baines, D. (Ed.) (2007). *Doing anti-oppressive practice: Building transformative politicized social work*. Halifax, NS: Fernwood.

Baldus, R. D. (2002). Bushmeat: Some experiences from Tanzania. The bushmeat crisis is nothing new. Bushmeat Training Development Workshop at the College of African Wildlife Management, Mweka, Tanzania, May 7–8, 2002.

Barouch, D.H. (2008). Challenges in the development of an HIV-1 vaccine. *Nature, 455*, 613–619.

Barnoff, L., & Moffatt, K. (2007). Contradictory tensions in anti-oppressive practice in feminist social services. *Affilia: Journal of Women and Social Work, 22*, 56–70.

Beiser, M. (March-April 2005). The Health of Immigrants and Refugees in Canada. *Canadian Journal of Public Health, 96* (2), 31–44.

Browne, A. J. & Smye, V. (2002). A post-colonial analysis of healthcare discourses addressing aboriginal women. *Nurse Researcher, 9* (3), 28–41. Retrieved from http://dx.doi.org/10.7748/nr2002.04. 9.3.28.c6187.

Browne, L., Macintyre, K. and Trujillo, L. (2003). Interventions to Reduce HIV/AIDS Stigma: What have we learnt? *AIDS Education and Prevention, 15*(1), 49–69.

Canadian Aboriginal AIDS Network (CAAN) (no date). *For generations to come: a look at Aboriginal resiliency*. Ottawa: CAAN.

Carniol, B. (2010). *Case critical: Social services and social justice in Canada* (6ᵗʰ ed.). Toronto: Between the Lines.

Children Orphaned by AIDS (no date). Front-line responses from eastern and southern Africa. Retrieved from http://data.unaids.org/Publications/IRC-pub05/orphrept_en.pdf.

Chitnis, A.; Rawls, D.; & Moore, J. (2000). Origin of HIV Type 1 in Colonial French Equatorial Africa? *AIDS Research and Human Retroviruses, 16* (1), 5–8.

Cloete, A.; Strebel, A.; Simbayi, L.; van Wyk, B.; Henda, N.; & Nqeketo, A. (2010). Challenges faced by people living with HIV/AIDS in Cape Town, South Africa: Issues for group risk reduction interventions. *AIDS Research and Treatment*, Vol. 2010, Article ID 420270. Retrieved from http://dx.doi.org/10.1155/2010/420270.

Crosby, S.S., Piwowarczyk, L.A., & Cooper, E. (2007). HIV infection. In P.F. Walker and E.D. Barnett (Eds.), *Immigrant Medicine* (pp. 361–373). Saunders Elsevier.

De Bruyn, T. (1998). HIV/AIDS and discrimination: A discussion paper for the Canadian HIV/AIDS Legal Network and Canadian AIDS Society. Montreal.

Deacon, H., Stepheny, I., & Prosalendis, S. (2005). Understanding HIV/AIDS Stigma: A theoretical and methodological analysis. HSRC Resereach Monograph.

Dei, G.S. (2000). Rethinking the role of Indigenous knowledges in the academy. *International Journal of Inclusive Education, 4*(2), 111–132.

de Sousa, J. D.; Müller, V.; Lemey, P.; & Vandamme, A.M. (2010). High GUD incidence in the early 20th century created a particularly permissive time window for the origin and initial spread of epidemic HIV strains. In Martin, D. P., *PLOS ONE 5* (4), e9936.

Fournier, B.; Bridge, A.; Pritchard Kennedy, A.,; Alibhai, A.,; & Konde-Lule, J. (2014). Hear our voices: A photovoice project with children who are orphaned and living with HIV in a Ugandan group home. *Journal of Children and Youth Services Review* (45), 55-63.

Gaillard, P., Melis, R., Mwanyumba, F., Claeys, P., Muigai, E., Mandaliya, K., Bwayo, J. and Temmerman, M. (2002) Vulnerability of women in an African setting: lessons for mother-to-child HIV transmission prevention programmes. *AIDS*, 16(6), 937–939.

Garland, E. (2008). The elephant in the room: Confronting the colonial character of wildlife conservation in Africa. *African Studies Review, 51* (3), 5.

Gourevitch, P. (2010). We wish to inform you that tomorrow we will be killed with our families. In T. J. Kinney (Ed.), *Conflict & Cooperation: Documents on Modern Global History*. Toronto: Oxford University Press.

Government of Canada (2006). *The human face of mental health and mental illness in Canada*. Ottawa: Minister of Public Works and Government Services Canada. Retrieved from www.phac-aspc.gc.ca.

Greene, W.C. ( 2007). A history of AIDS: Looking back to see ahead. *European Journal of Immunology, 37* (1), S94–S102.

Greeff, M.,; Phetlhu, R.,; Makoae, L.N.,; Dlamini, P.S.; Holzemer, W.L.,; Naidoo, J.R., Kohi, T.W.,; Uys, L.R.,; & Chirwa, M.L. (March 2008). Disclosure of HIV status: Experiences and perceptions of persons living with HIV/AIDS and nurses involved in their care in Africa. *Qualitative Health Research, 18* (3), 311–324.

Hart, M. (2009). Anti-colonial Indigenous social work: Reflections on an Aboriginal approach. In R. Sinclair, M. Hart, & G. Bruyere (Eds.), *Wicihitowin: Aboriginal social work in Canada* (pp. 25-41). Halifax, NS: Fernwood.

Hayes, R. & Vaughan, C. (2002). Stigma directed toward chronic illness is resistant to change through education and exposure. *Psychological Reports, 90*, 1161–1173.

Hooper, E. (1999). *The river.* Boston: Little, Brown.

Hoopes, T., & Brinkley, D. (1997). *FDR and the creation of the U.N.* New Haven: Yale University Press.

Kolata, G. (1987, October 28). Boy's 1969 death suggests AIDS invaded U.S. several times. *The New York Times.*

Kuo, C., & Operario, D. (2010). Caring for AIDS-orphaned children: An exploratory study of challenges faced by carers in KwaZulu-Natal, South Africa. *Vulnerable Child Youth Studies, 5* (4), 344-352.

Lavallée, L. (2009). Practical application of an Indigenous research framework and Indigenous research methods: Sharing circles and Anishnaabe symbol-based reflection. *International Journal of Qualitative Methods, 8*(1), 21–40.

Lawrence, B., & Dua, E. (2005). Decolonizing anti-racism. *Social Justice, 32*(4), 120–143.

Lewis, C. (2013). Case study: Fellow travelers: A co-ed Group for depression and anxiety in a community agency. In D. Maller (Ed.), *Handbook of community mental health practice: Working in the local community*. Santa Barbara, CA: Praeger.

Lubbers, R. (2003, November 28). In the war on AIDS refugees are often excluded. *UNHCR*. Retrieved from http://www.unhcr.org/3fc71f614.html.

Marx P.A., Alcabes, P.G. & Drucker, E. (2001). Serial human passage of simian immunodeficiency virus by unsterile injections and the emergence of epidemic human immunodeficiency virus in Africa. *Philosophical Transactions of the Royal Society* B356 (1410), 911–20.

McNell, Jr., D.G. (2010, Sept. 16). Precursor to H.I.V. was in monkeys for millennia. *The New York Times*.

Mies, M. (1998). Patriarchy and accumulation on a world scale: Women in the international division of labour. London: Zed Books.

Ogden, J., & Nyblade, L. (2005). Common at its core: HIV related stigma across contexts. *International Center for Research on Women*. Retrieved from http://www.kit.nl/-/KIT/9375/(57698)-ILS/ILS-Dossiers.pdf.

Parker, R., & Aggleton, P. (2003). HIV and AIDS-related stigma and discrimination: A conceptual framework and implications for action. *Social Science & Medicine 57*(1), 15–24.

Pashang, S. (2011). *Non-status women: Invisible residents and underground resilience* (Unpublished doctoral dissertation). Ontario Institute for Studies in Education, University of Toronto, Toronto.

Peters, M., Toure-Kane, C., & Nkengasong, J.N. (2003). Genetic diversity of HIV in Africa: Impact on diagnosis, treatment, vaccine development and trials. *AIDS, 17*, 2547–2560

Public Health Agency of Canada (PHAC) (2012). HIV/AIDS surveillance in Canada. At a glance: HIV and AIDS in Canada: surveillance report to December 31, 2012. Retrieved from http://www.phac-aspc.gc.ca/aids-sida/publication/survreport/2012/dec/index-eng.php.

Public Health Agency of Canada (PHAC) (2008). Summary: Estimates of HIV prevalence and incidence in Canada, 2008. Ottawa: Surveillance and Risk Assessment Division, PHAC. Retrieved from http://www.phac-aspc.gc.ca/aids-sida/publication/survreport/estimat08-eng.php.

Public Health Agency of Canada (PHAC). HIV and AIDS in Canada: Surveillance report to December 31, 2008. Ottawa: Surveillance and Risk Assessment Division.

Rankin, W., Brennan, S, Schell, E., Laviwa, J., & Rankin, S.H. (2005). The stigma of being HIV-positive in Africa. *PLoS Med, 2*(8), e247. doi:10.1371/journal.pmed.0020247.

Razack, S., Smith, M., & Thobani, S. (Eds.). (2010). *States of race: Critical race feminism for the 21st Century*. Toronto: Between the Lines.

Razack, S. (2005). How is white supremacy embodied? Sexualized racial violence at Abu Ghraib. *Canadian Journal of Women and the Law, 17*(2), 341-363.

Richman, D.D., Margolis, D.M., Delaney, M., Greene, W.C., Hazuda, D., & Pomerantz, R.J. (2009). The challenge of finding a cure for HIV infection. *Science, 323*, 1304–1307.

Roberts, S. J. (2005). *Resisting stigma: Living positively with HIV/AIDS in South Africa* (Unpublished Master's dissertation). University of Johannesburg, Johannesburg.

Thibault, M., & Blaney, S. (2003). The oil industry as an underlying factor in the bushmeat crisis in Central Africa. *Conservation Biology, 17* (6), 1807–1813.

Tunstall, K.E. (Ed.) (2011). *Displacement, asylum, migration*. Oxford: Oxford University Press.

Sakamoto, I., & Pitner, R. O. (2005). Critical consciousness in anti-oppressive social work practice: Disentangling power dynamics at personal and structural levels. *British Journal of Social Work, 35* (4), 435–452.

Sharp, P.M. & Hahn, B.H. (2011). Origins of HIV and the AIDS pandemic. *Cold Spring Harbor Perspectives in Medicine, 1* (1). Retrieved from http://www.ncbi.nlm.nih.gov/pmc/articles /PMC3234451/.

Shilts, R. (1988). *And the band played on*. New York: Penguin.

Ship, S. J., & Norton, L. (2001). HIV/AIDS and Aboriginal women in Canada. *Canadian Woman Studies, 21* (2), 25–31.

Soskolne, T. (2003). Moving beyond the margins: A narrative analysis of the life stories of women living with HIV/AIDS in Khayelitsha. *Centre for Social Science Research*, AIDS and Society Research Unite, CSSR Working Paper No. 33. Retrieved from http://www.cssr.uct.ac.za/sites/cssr.uct.ac.za/files/pubs/wp33.pdf.

Sowers, K.M., & Rowe, W.S. (2007). *Social work practice and social justice: From local to global perspectives*. Pacific Grove, CA: Thomson Brooks/Cole.

Spiegel, P. B. (2004). HIV/AIDS among conflict-affected and displaced populations: Dispelling myths and taking action. *Disasters 28*(3), 322–339.

Stephen Lewis Foundation (n.d.). *Fact sheet: Children and HIV/AIDS: Key statistics.*

Stephen Lewis Foundation (Spring 2014). *Grassroots.*

UNAIDS (2013). *Report on the global AIDS epidemic.*

UNAIDS (2013). *Fact sheet,* U.S. Centers for Disease Control and Prevention.

UNADIS (December 2003). *Fact sheet.* Retrieved on July 3, 2014, from www.unaids.org.

UNAIDS (2012). *World AIDS Day Report.* Retrieved from http://www.unaids.org/en/media/unaids/contentassets/documents/epidemiology/2012/gr2012/jc2434_worldaidsday_results_en.pdf.

UNAIDS (2006). *The impact of AIDS on people and societies: 2006 report on the global AIDS epidemic.*

UNICEF (2013). *Towards an AIDS-free generation: Children and AIDS: Sixth stocktaking report.* Retrieved from http://www.avert.org/children-orphaned-hiv-and-aids.htm#sthash.tN7A6x5K.dpuf.

United Nations General Assembly (2001). *UNGASS: Declaration of commitment on HIV/AIDS.* UN General Assembly Twenty-Sixth Special Session Doc: A/s-26/L.2.

Vidal, N., Peeters, M., Mulanga-Kabeya, C., Nzilambi, N., Robertson, D., Ilunga, W., Sema, H., Tshimanga, K., Bongo, B., & Delaporte, E. (2000). Unprecedented degree of human immunodeficiency virus type 1 (HIV-1) group M genetic diversity in the Democratic Republic of Congo suggests that the HIV-1 pandemic originated in Central Africa. *Journal of Virology 74,* 10498–10507. Retrieved from http://www.ncbi.nlm.nih.gov/pmc/articles/PMC110924/.

World Health Organization (2014). Global update on HIV treatment 2013: Result, impact and opportunities.

World Health Organization (2011). Prevention and treatment of HIV and other sexually transmitted infections among men who have sex with men and transgender people: Recommendations for a public health approach.

Yan, S. (2014, April 1). How colonialism created the HIV/AIDS pandemic. *Huffington Post.*

## CHAPTER SIX

# Mayan Resistance to Mining Development and Displacement in Guatemala: A New Vision for Life

## Edgar Godoy

T his chapter focuses on how Mayan communities in Guatemala resist dominant forms of development that lead to internal displacement. A central goal of this chapter is to analyze how the dominant development model represented by the Canadian mining company Glamis Gold (now Goldcorp Inc.) generates displacement and, as such, is being challenged by the Mayan communities of Sipacapa and San Miguel Ixthuacán, in the San Marcos province of Guatemala, communities that continue to foster alternative visions of life and development. The chapter draws on Gramsci's conceptions of hegemony and counter-hegemony to demonstrate that Mayan resistance to mining not only represents a counter-hegemonic movement against displacement and the dominant economic model, but also offers routes forward for building community-based development, local autonomy and self-government, and toward preventing future displacement.

> **Reflective Questions**
>
> 1. How does dominant development generate displacement?
> 2. What are the specific effects of displacement and dispossession on Indigenous (Mayan) people in Guatemala?
> 3. What are some key forms of resistance against displacement being advanced by the Mayan people and their allies?
> 4. What is meant by "alternative community development as a strategy to contest displacement"?

In the first section of the chapter, I will provide a brief historical overview of the contested issue of mining development in Guatemala. This will be followed by an analysis of the forms of Mayan resistance to dominant development and displacement, utilizing strategies to foster local, regional, national and international advocacy and solidarity. I will then offer a critique of dominant development followed by an examination of alternative proposals for social and economic community development, based on the distinct Cosmo-vision (or worldview) of the Mayan people, and how these communities deal with the negative impacts of displacement. Finally, I will argue that Mayan resistance to mining in Guatemala is consistent with the historical resistance of Mayans to remain in their territory, preserve their culture, identity, and livelihoods, and ensure their survival in an era of economic globalization.

## A Brief Historical Overview of Mining in Guatemala

> This [Marlin] mining project threatens the well-being of our country, the future of our environment, the preservation of our natural resources and the use of them for the good of all Guatemalans in defense of life and with respect for our ethnic diversity (Ramazzini, Bishop of the Diocese of San Marcos, in a letter to the president of Guatemala, September 2004).

In the letter quoted above that was addressed to Guatemala's President Óscar Berger, Bishop Ramazzini underscores the dangers associated with the Marlin mining project in Guatemala that was spearheaded by Montana Exploradora de Guatemala S.A., a subsidiary of the Canadian corporation Glamis Gold Ltd. This mining project, centered on the extraction of gold and silver, was built in the municipalities of San Miguel Ixtuahuacán and Sipacapa, in the province of San Marcos in the western region of Guatemala, home of the Mam and Sipacapenses Mayan peoples, two of the 26 different Indigenous ethnic, Mayan descendant groups in the country. In his letter, Bishop Ramazzini highlights that it is not only the wellbeing of the country which is at stake, but the future of Guatemala's natural resources, the safeguarding of its water, land and forests for the benefit of all its citizens, as well as the ethnic diversity of the Mayan communities.

> **Reflective Questions**
>
> 1. Why did the Guatemalan government put the interests of businesses before the interests of the country?
> 2. Do you see similar patterns in other parts of the world?

President Berger replied to Bishop Ramazzini: "We have to protect the investors" (*Prensa Libre*, September 2004). This is not the first public expression of disregard by the Guatemalan government for the country's people. Thirty-five years earlier, Piedra Santa Arandi, dean of the Faculty of Economics of San Carlos State University, had sent a message much like Bishop Ramazzini's to the then-president of Guatemala, Méndez Montenegro:

> On behalf of our faculty, I respectfully request your intervention to suspend the economic arrangements between the Guatemalan National Monetary Board and the EXMIBAL Company, a subsidiary of the International Nickel Company (INCO), until all aspects of this financial

transaction are properly clarified. It has to be demonstrated un-equivocally that our country, that is ceding non-renewable resources, will receive an important part of the benefits (May 2, 1969, p. 20).

The reply of the government-backed army at that time was to create a culture of fear and silence by murdering the representatives of the National Commission on Mining, lawyers Adolfo Mijangos López and Camey Herrera (Solano, 2005, p. 38).

Thus, when we compare the experiences of the past with the current conflict in Guatemala between the forces supporting and those opposing mining, we see a historical pattern of clashes between the interests of the Mayan majority and those of business elites, Canadian mining companies and the Guatemalan government. The Inco and Glamis Gold mining projects had, at different points in time, the same result: taking away ancestral lands and displacing the Mayan people from their communities. The only option left for the Mayan people has been to fight back.

## Mayan Resistance to Development and Displacement

Despite the internal struggles within the 26 different Mayan ethnic groups, when their way of life has been threatened, they have united. One of the most recent examples of this unity in resistance was during their massive displacement and exodus to the state of Chiapas in southern Mexico in the late 1970s and early 1980s, which formed the basis for what was to become known as the **Pan-Maya movement**. The Pan-Maya movement of Guatemalan and Mexican Maya brings diverse groups of Mayans together, in response to the history of political violence and marginalization facing Mayan people in Guatemala, culminating in the civil war of 1960–96 (Warren, 2000). Many Mayans have faced historical oppression and discrimination before, during and after the war. Like Indigenous people of Canada, Mayans were segregated, and forced into areas with far less access to land, education, social programs, health and other resources (Jonas, March 27, 2013). The Guatemalan government also accused the Maya of being supportive of the leftist insurgency, in a war largely targeting Mayan people. As evidenced by the 1996 Peace Accords, and two commissions that documented human rights abuses between 1960 and 1996 (the Commission for Historical Clarification [CEH] and the Commission for Recuperation of the Historical Memory Project [REMHI]), Mayan leaders had been displaced, kidnapped, had disappeared and had been killed, not so much because of their involvement with the guerrilla activity, but due to their roles as leaders within their local community organizations.

The civil war resulted in the genocide of Mayan people. Reports show hundreds of villages in the highland area were destroyed. The vast majority of the estimated 140,000 to 200,000 people who were killed or who disappeared during the war were Maya (Briggs, 2007).

During the long and violent civil war in the western Mayan highland, as well as the massive earthquake of 1976, Mayans were forced to leave their villages.

According to reports, over one million Mayan became internally displaced (IDP), with 200,000 fleeing to the southern borders of Mexico (Jonas, 2013). In fact, over 50,000 forcibly displaced Mayans lived in refugee camps in Mexico for ten years. A crucial moment of unity, however, came when these refugees decided to move back to Guatemala to re-establish their homes in the villages. Starting from the bottom up, they worked to organize and re-establish their lives, and, as a united group, negotiated their rights with the United Nations High Commissioner for Refugees (UHNCR) and the Mexican government. The effects of war and challenges to rebuilding life were many.

Another implication of civil war for the Maya in the neighbouring and non-conflict zone communities was the disruption of roads and commercial and trade patterns (Jonas, 2013). The economic crises both at the local and national levels negatively affected the livelihoods of Mayans, as well as Guatemalans generally, causing major unemployment, poverty and instability, which were compounded by international sanctions. Economic crises caused short-term displacement of many people as seasonal workers to neighbouring countries and North America. During the post-war period such trends continued due to a number of environmental disasters such as massive hurricanes and an earthquake.

Despite the effects of the war on infrastructure and labour, perhaps the most significant and longstanding effects on Mayan livelihood have been structural and systemic, shaped by broader globalizing forces. Violations of human rights were allowed, linked to and exacerbated by trade and other international policies that have been embedded into the country's political, social and economic systems. Multinational corporations have caused severe economic, social as well as environmental damage. It is to this we turn our attention.

## The Case Study of Mayan Resistance to Canadian Gold Mining

Mayan resistance to displacement resulting from economic, political and cultural domination is not a new phenomenon in Guatemala. Indeed, since the Spanish conquest, and throughout the colonial and post-colonial periods (1524–1821), Mayan people have resisted and responded to social and political challenges with diverse strategies. Similar to the historical resistance of the original peoples in Canada to defend their territory, livelihood and culture, Mayan resistance has ranged from political negotiations to mass mobilizations and armed struggle in the face of European cultural and political imperialism. However, in the last five decades, that resistance has been against Canadian mining companies and contemporary imperialist policies that support large-scale transnational mining (Solano, 2005).

Opposition to Canadian mining development in the Mayan communities began in the 1960s and 1970s, in the midst of political turmoil, the civil war, persecution, and increased internal displacement of indigenous communities. First, opposition arose against the Canadian mining company Inco, which negotiated a 40-year concession to exploit nickel in the El Estor region of Guatemala in 1966. There was strong public opposition to the mining project (Solano, 2005, p. 38). In 1977, according to Federico (1983, p. 169) a group of 80 mining workers from Minas de Guatemala, located in San Idelfonso Ixtuahacán, Huehuetenango, organized the largest demonstration in the history of Guatemala. Minas de Guatemala was a Guatemalan-owned tungsten and antimony mine, financed by the U.S. Collectively, indigenous miners, men and women tired of the ongoing abuses and discrimination at the mine, marched from their town along the Pan-American Highway to Guatemala City.

What began as a small march turned into a massive demonstration as the days passed, and more people from different communities, including factory workers, sugar and cotton plantation workers and students joined the mining workers. Their courage inspired many more indigenous and non-indigenous people. The movement grew to over 250,000 people, who marched more than 350 kilometres from the mine site to Guatemala City to demand recognition of the workers' rights, including the right to organize a union and negotiate a collective agreement. Their demands also included basic health and safety equipment, decent wages, and death and accident compensation (Infopress, November 11 and 24, 1977). However, Solano (2005) points out that between 1978 and 1981, the leaders of the union were killed or forced into exile.

> **Reflective Question**
>
> In 2006, Juan Tema, a leader from Sipacapa, travelled to Washington for a meeting with the World Bank to request the cancellation of a loan they had provided to Glamis. While he was travelling, rumours circulated that he had travelled to Washington to receive $1 million, a rumour disseminated by Glamis. How do these types of accusations and distortions against Mayan leaders affect the general public and the Mayan resistance movement specifically?

As evident from the above case history, despite the dispossession and the severe and adverse social, cultural and economic consequences of the conquest, the colonization process forced Mayans to unite and resist for the survival of their people. The agency of Mayan people indeed has long historical roots. For instance, during the civil war, thousands of Mayan people individually and collectively opted for armed resistance, which included supporting the guerrilla movement by providing political support, information, food and combatants (Solano, 2005). In the 1960s, after the U.S.-backed coup against the democratically elected President Arbenz and many subsequent years of military rule, oppression, political abuses, and economic disparity between the rich and the poor, the guerrilla movement was organized. It was made up of middle-class intellectuals, workers, poor students and peasants, and non-indigenous peoples who were also oppressed. Nonetheless, in the mid-1970s and '80s the indigenous people made up the majority of the membership of the guerrilla movement.

> This experience of joining forces with the insurgents contributed greatly in shaping the revolutionary movement's platform for the construction of a multicultural and multiethnic nation. Fighting side by side with the

non-indigenous armed insurgency contributed to forging a historical unity between indigenous and non-indigenous progressive movements. Thus, national recognition was given to the specific demands of the Mayan people, such as their cultural rights, their identity, territorial autonomy and land claims. This resistance and the resulting recognition came at a high cost (interview with Felipe, 2005).

Today, a process of denying this long-term agency is underway: the print media and NGOs supporting and created by the Canadian mining company, Glamis Gold, and the Canadian embassy claim that "Mayans are being manipulated into protesting against mining development by the enemies of progress" (Cruz, August 5, 2005). Spreading rumours to discredit local leaders is a tactic used by Glamis, a remnant of the colonial past still alive in the present.

## National and International Advocacy

Resistance to mining in Guatemala is not only supported to some extent by national and international law and the activities of non-governmental organizations. Current resistance to mining also involves active and peaceful resistance, such as citizen participation, education, mass mobilizations, and referendums on mining development projects.

The use of existing national and international statutes has been important. For example, the International Labour Organization's Indigenous and Tribal Peoples Convention (ILOC 169) requires governments to consult with indigenous people when legislative decisions affect these communities directly. Guatemala's Municipal Code spells out the laws, rules and responsibilities pertaining to municipalities and their councils, particularly around municipal autonomy and local development.

A central feature of the resistance to mining by Mayan communities is found in their efforts to forge links with other sectors, including human rights, environmental, labour and other organizations, arguing against mining on a range of grounds, including the environmental consequences of mining, water contamination and health problems. The fight against mining's environmental impacts has been largely advanced through connections between local communities engaged in local mining resistance and the environmental NGO, Madre Selva. Jose Cruz explains how the resistance to mining has become central to the organization's work:

> In 2003, we became aware of the new mining projects and got involved in this new struggle. We understood that mining is an industry of great concern to all of us from an ecological point of view. There was no information on the subject. Therefore, we began our research on mining. Later, we learned that a mining project was underway in Honduras and decided to go on a fact-finding mission there. After our trip to Honduras, we began regular publications on flyers, on our website, press releases, newspaper articles and workshops. Our goal was to make peo-

ple aware of the adverse effects of mining. It quickly sparked a national debate in the printed media (interview with Cruz, 2005).

One of the main criticisms against Glamis is that there has been no discussion about the environmental impact of mining despite the fact that the Mayan communities of Sipacapa and San Miguel Ixtahuacán have experienced significant environmental damage. The effects of mining have also contributed to community conflict in neighbouring Honduras, due to water contamination, displacement and relocation of local farmers (Mining Watch Canada, January 12, 2004, p. 2). Nevertheless, the mine continued to operate "despite strong evidence of skin and respiratory illnesses from mining wastes" (Mining Watch, 2004, p. 5). Contamination also occurred in another Glamis mine, the Marigold Mine in Nevada, where the company admitted in January 2002 that "substantial contaminant plumes under leaking tailing impoundments and waste rock dumps . . . are not being remedied. The plumes are moving toward the Humboldt River and drinking water supplies" (Mining Watch Canada, 2004, p. 2).

> **Reflective Questions**
>
> While there is abundant literature documenting the negative impacts of mining such as Solano, including *Guatemala Petroleo y Mineria* (2005) and Moran's (2006) environmental assessment, Glamis continues undermining its opposition by attacking them as "anti-development forces and enemies of progress"(Mining Watch, 2004, p. 2).
>
> 1. What are some of the conflicting perspectives on development at play?
> 2. What are the environmental effects of Glamis Gold on Mayan communities?
> 3. Do you consider these effects reflective of global pattern of corporate development?
> 4. Are there similar examples in Canada, faced by Indigenous people and/or others?

Mayan resistance to mining in Guatemala has also involved ongoing protests. In February 2004, the first protest against the Glamis Marlin mine was staged in Sipacapa, San Marcos. The national newspaper *Prensa Libre* reported that approximately 500 people from the municipality of Sipacapa participated in the protest against the Marlin mine (*Prensa Libre*, February 21, 2004). This mobilization was organized by the Movement of Peasant Workers, a local peasants' organization in San Marcos, and by the Catholic Church diocese in San Marcos. Their main criticisms of the project concerned the lack of consultation with the local indigenous authorities and population, the possible environmental risks and the violation of municipal autonomy (Infopress, 2004, in Solano, 2005, p. 111).

Solano (2005) notes that on June 19, 2004, various social and environmental organizations and popular leaders from the North Orient region of the country founded the National Front Against Pit Mining of Metals, whose main goal was to stop the authorization of new mining licenses. This initiative was followed by the creation of the Occidental Front Against Mining, signed by the Mayan authorities of eight provinces including Totonicapán, San Marcos, Quetzaltenango, Huehuetenango, Quiché, Sololá, Izabal and Chiquimula. These events clearly showed that the opposition to mining grew quickly, particularly in the indigenous communities. For instance, in November 2004, *Prensa Libre* conducted a survey in San Miguel Ixtahuacán and Sipacapa, the communities affected by the Marlin project; 95.5% of the people surveyed expressed their opposition to the mine (*Prensa Libre*, 2004).

In December 2004, tensions were high in Sololá due to the lack of information and transparency on the part of Glamis and the government. This led to a blockade to prevent passage of a cylinder that was being transported to the mine (*Prensa Libre*, December 3, 2004). A month later, in January 2005, the residents of the province of Sololá organized a peaceful protest in the community of Los Encuentros, approximately 150 kilometres away from the Marlin mining project along the Pan American highway. This protest had two objectives. The first was to oppose dismantling of a footbridge used by the local residents to cross the highway. According to Glamis, the dismantling of the footbridge was temporary to allow the passage of the ball mill (heavy metal cylinder) to the mine site. The second objective of the rally was to support the struggle of the indigenous people from Sipacapa and San Miguel Ixtahuacán, San Marcos against the Marlin mine (Prensa Libre, 2004).

In a memorandum to President Berger from the National Council for the Indigenous and Peasants they stated:

> The concessions and mining exploitations activities constitute a new form of foreign invasion of the Mayan territories. Therefore, we demand from the government the immediate suspension of the exploration and exploitation mining licences, until we discuss and put in place a new mining and resource extraction legislation. This legislation should take into account the principles and values that regulate the indigenous communities (CONIC, 2006).

The memorandum sent to President Berger was part of a larger public document prepared by various organizations during the National Mayan Popular March, which took place on March 30, 2006 to commemorate the eleventh anniversary of the Peace Accord on Identity and the Rights of Indigenous Peoples. Among the organizations that signed the memorandum were the Regional Council of Indigenous Peoples, Defensoría Q'eqchi, Madre Selva Collective, the National Assembly of the Teachers Union, and the National Coordinator of Widows of Guatemala. In addition to calling for the suspension of mining licences, the memorandum demanded the government immediately resolve the ongoing land claims. It called for the government to implement the Peace Accord on Identity and Rights of Indigenous Peoples, assign the necessary financial resources to the judicial system, and, as per the requirements of the accord, comply with the implementation of the C169 as mandated by the ILO and ratify the 1989 International Convention for the Elimination of all Racial Discrimination (Jonas, 2000, p. 75).

These organizations also highlighted the core demands of Mayan peoples, such as recognition of indigenous peoples' rights, transparency, the elimination of corruption and the inclusion of the Mayan communities in decision-making processes.

Contrary to the spirit of the Peace Accords regarding cultural identity, the combatting of racial discrimination, and the defence of Mayan cultural, political, social and economic rights, President Berger consistently demonstrated his lack of political will to assume his necessary obligations as outlined by the Constitution of Guatemala. Instead, powerful local elites and international mining investors are favoured, making invisible the needs and aspirations of the indigenous people, who make up the majority of the population in Guatemala (65%).

Berger's discriminatory approach is further evidenced by his use of violence against the indigenous peoples who had peacefully occupied the Farm Nueva Linda in 2004, an action that resulted in seven persons killed. According to the national coordinator for the National Indigenous Council, the peaceful occupation of an abandoned farm in Nueva Linda is the only option left for thousands of landless Mayan families who were brutally displaced and lost their land during the armed conflict (Araujo in Adital, September 1, 2004).

The Mayan communities were not only active subjects in the civil war, fighting side-by-side with the revolutionary movement, but their representatives were also key players in negotiating and signing the Peace Accords, which ended the 36-year-long civil war. Mayan leaders like Rigoberta Menchú were instrumental in internationally exposing the gross human rights violations, the policies of ethnocide and displacement that indigenous communities were subjected to during the civil war. As a direct result, Mayan leaders built a strong international solidarity movement that supported their struggles in the past and continues to do so today. They were also active in questioning national policies, such as national security and counterinsurgency strategies, that impacted them negatively. A good example of Mayan leadership was their engagement during ten years of national dialogue and negotiations within their own communities, in Guatemala and abroad, sitting at the table with national labour leaders, peasants, women and political organizations, all of whom formed the Assembly of Civil Society (Krznaric, 1999, p. 5)

Currently, Mayan leaders are leading the opposition to mining and questioning corporate notions of development and the neo-liberal policies, such as *Plan Puebla Panama* (PPP) and the Central America Free Trade Agreement (CAFTA). At the same time, they oppose notions of nation-building that have been based on a racist philosophy and policies, which portray the Mayan peoples as "inferior people who should be civilized":

> The racist strategy driven by President Berger to manipulate indigenous peoples by offering direct dialogue with the indigenous peoples, a dialogue that is never carried out. Instead, activities to delegitimize and criminalize the demands of indigenous peoples are implemented (Statement of the I Conference of Mayan Authorities, April 1, 2005).

Ronald Niezen (1998) points out that the goals of the nation-building projects run in the opposite direction of the political goals of the indigenous people. Individual rights and private property are at the heart of Eurocentric nation-building projects, rather than the collective rights, needs and communal property of the indigenous people. The "Liberal Revolution" of 1871, forced labour and the implementation of the policy "to whiten the indigenous population," and more recently the model villages of the 1980s, were not isolated policies. They represent the intrinsic values of the dominant white elites and their systemic policies aimed at assimilating the Mayan people by any means possible (Cambranes, 1996, p. 11).

A central focus of this new political framework advanced by the Mayan leaders has been the goal of strengthening the "Mayan Historical Bloc." This includes accompanying the displaced people and supporting the local community struggles nationally and internationally. Mayan leaders have also promoted legislative changes at all levels of government and questioned the exclusionary and racist orientations of the Guatemalan state. Moen (1997) underscores that the shifting, changing, and ever-growing amalgamation of diverse social forces that have evolved outside the established parliamentary and trade union structures, including the organic farming movement, is an example of what Gramsci referred to as the creation of an historical bloc. This concept directs attention to how people, working together at the grassroots level, create new cultural values and redefine social relations through the building of popular alliances that transcend an exclusive class basis (Moen, 1997, p. 3).

The Mayan leadership has been engaged in open dialogue through national conferences and assemblies of Mayan authorities in the six provinces to advance the indigenous peoples' rights as mandated by the Peace Accords, local autonomy, self-government, and final resolution of their land claims. These gatherings brought together thousands of representatives from the provinces of San Marcos, Totonicapán, Sololá, El Quiche, Huehuetenango and Quetzaltenango (October 2004 and October 2005). The first and second conferences were modelled on the agreement between the communal authorities, the municipal councils of Totonicapán and the representatives of the Guatemalan state authorities. At the Totonicapán meeting, in 2004, the Mayan authorities exerted pressure on the state representatives, justice ministry and the human rights commission on these matters (Statement from the I Conference of Indigenous Authorities, April 5, 2004).

**Forging Solidarity with Indigenous and Non-Indigenous Organizations**

Today, Mayan organizations have recognition and affiliation to networks, such as the Latin Council of Indigenous People of the Americas and the United Nations Permanent Working Group on Indigenous Populations. However, that affiliation, support and recognition did not begin with nor was it limited to the issue of mining; it is the result of decades of hard work. For instance, in the 1990s, Rigoberta Menchú's international work allowed her to share with the rest of world the ongoing human rights violations of the Mayan peoples. These violations included the systemic elimination of their native languages, the destruction of their communities, the confiscation of their lands by the Guatemalan army, their forced displacement, and the harsh living conditions endured by the refugees living in Southern Mexico and in the Guatemalan rainforests. Never before had the collective suffering and dreams of the Mayan people been exposed and fought at this level. As Niezen (2003) suggests, "the mere fact that indigenous leaders gather in international meetings to share experiences and pursue collective strategies suggests a greater degree of global interaction" (Niezen 2003, p.10).

During his Canadian tour, Juan Tema underlined that Glamis was "friendly" at the beginning and its representatives were talking about jobs and "sustainable development." However, he explained,

> As the people in our communities began to raise questions about what kind of development were they offering and at what cost to the environment, the land and water, Glamis got more defensive. Now that we know the facts and have confronted the company, Glamis has changed its approach. Today, we are not only victims of [the] Marlin imposed mine, but the company is also waging a dirty war against the opposition, which include intimidations, death threats and killings (interview with Juan Tema, 2005).

Mayan communities resisting mining have been able to mobilize indigenous and non-indigenous people in great numbers. As a result, a national social movement has been built, with the creation of the National Front Against Mining, the Occidental Front Against Mining and the National Front to Defend Public Services and Natural Resources. Joining with Mayan organizations in these national fronts are environmental organizations like Madre Selva, labour organizations, NGOs and the Catholic Church. Among the alliances that the Mayan resistance movement has made with other groups and organization is their relationship with the Church. Father Jijón from Comitancillo, San Marcos, pointed out in an interview that the local communities are not rejecting mining for the sake of rejecting this industry. "Our communities know what they want in the economic, social and cultural areas," he stated (interview with Father Jijón, August 2005).

The main problem, according to Father Jijón, is that from the very beginning Glamis' representatives were dishonest, failing to pass on accurate information about the mining project. In their talks they focused on the economic advantages, job creation and training (July 2005). Jijón also stressed that there was no mention of the negative impacts such as displacement, environmental and water contamination, rock drainage and the intensive use of water for mining in a region that has scarce water resources.

These other organizations also question mining and how it relates to macroeconomic policies. They correctly identified that mining facilitates international investment, controlled by the new emergent economic elite who support "free trade," rather than benefiting the local communities and Guatemala as a whole.

Within this civil society scenario, Eduardo Canel (1992) underlines the fact that:

> Civil society, as Urry (1981: 31) reminds us, is also the field of interest articulation and social struggles. People's everyday lives are permeated not only by hegemonic practices that legitimate class, gender, sexual and racial inequalities, but also by acts of subversion and adaptation that can be likened to a continuing guerrilla warfare. But by maintaining a sense of oppositional — of the "we" (the subordinates) who are not the same as "them" — popular-cultural resistance no doubt form a necessary pre-condition, if not the necessary cause, of populist radical movements (Fiske, 1989, p. 161, in Canel, 1992).

## A Critique of Dominant Development

The counter-hegemonic movement led by Mayan leaders is not only questioning the practices and discourses of Glamis Gold and the World Bank, particularly regarding economic sustainability, but they are coming to the negotiating table with alternative proposals for development. These are projects that emerge from within Mayan communities and are shaped by local, regional and national debates on development.

For instance, Juan Tema, a leader from Sipacapa, asked the representatives of the World Bank to cancel the $45 million loan for mining and provide his community with $1 million to implement an agro-fruits project that would centre profits in the community. Tema emphasizes that this community project already has been studied, cost-benefit analyses have been conducted, and it has already captured an important share of the local and provincial market with the potential for a significant southern Mexico market (interview with Juan Tema, August 2005). The project consists of peach production and processing, which will create stable jobs and income for the local workers because these products are part of the daily diet.

Central to the opposition to mining is the current national debate about the meaning of development. The dominant theories of development, such as modernization theory, centre on the need for developing countries to improve and increase technologies that will allow them to compete on world markets. Modernization theory, which equated development with industrialization along the same lines as in the global north, was never successfully applied in the case of Guatemala. According to Torres Rivas (1971), there was an important expansion of agricultural exports and import substitution industrialization policies were promoted throughout the Central American Common Market; however, these initiatives failed to industrialize the region or to address social and economic problems. Instead, Guatemala had to settle for garment production through *maquilas* (factories), the promotion of tourism, non-traditional agricultural exports, and the export of cheap labour, particularly to the United States and Canada, as well as remittances from Guatemalans working abroad (Madre Selva, 2004).

Once again, Mayan communities are confronting the development notions advanced by the World Bank, Glamis Gold, and the Canadian and Guatemalan governments. These development approaches promote corporate profits more effectively than the development goals of Mayan communities to address structural poverty and the improvement of the quality of life. On June 15, 2005, 99% of the population voted against mining in Sipacapa (Madre Selva, 2005). Clearly, this signalled rejection of the arguments made by Glamis Gold, the World Bank and the Guatemalan government in support of the mine.

Although Canadian mining investments in Guatemala are facilitated by the Guatemalan government, historically, Canadian mining investments both in Canada and abroad have been closely linked to the expansion of Canadian capitalist interests with the goal of accumulating capital and increasing profits and shareholders' dividends. Those mining investments have always enjoyed the political support and financial backing of the Canadian government. At the political level, the Canadian government has not only created laws that permit mining investment without obstacles, but also promoted the industry as environmentally sustainable. On a financial level, mining corporations enjoy significant tax incentives. Throughout a long history of 150 years of mining production, our country has become one of the most "intelligent" administrators, promoters, users and exporters of natural resources in the world (Lambert, 2004, p. 4). What Ambassador Lambert failed to note is the disregard of Canadian mining companies like Goldcorp for human rights and international law.

In 2005, the Standing Committee on Foreign Affairs and International Trade (SCFAIT) made strong recommendations to the federal government regarding Canadian mining companies operating overseas, including Guatemala. The recognition of the environmental and human rights abuses that implicate Canadian mining companies represent an important political victory not only for the forces opposing mining in Guatemala, but also for the resistance against mining globally.

The SCFAIT's fourteenth report acknowledged these issues and the need for change, including:

> Put in place stronger incentives to encourage Canadian mining companies to conduct their activities outside of Canada in a socially and environmentally responsible manner and in conformity with international human rights standards. Measures in this area must include making Canadian government support — such as export and project financing and services offered by Canadian missions abroad — conditional on companies meeting clearly defined corporate social responsibility and human rights standards, particularly through the mechanism of human rights impact assessments (Fourteenth Report: Mining in Developing Countries, October 2005, p. 2).

The report further advocates new mechanisms for monitoring the activities of Canadian mining companies in developing countries. Ironically, these recommendations were never fully implemented and once again, the Canadian mining companies were left to self-regulate.

## Building a Counter-Hegemonic Movement
## toward Mayan-Defined Development

Drawing on Gramscian theory of hegemony and counter-hegemony (explained briefly below) to understand the resistance movement led by the Mayan leadership and their political allies, one can clearly see they are challenging the legitimacy of the dominant social relations of exploitation and the ideology that justifies them.

**Hegemony** refers to "the dominance of one group over other groups, with or without the threat of force, to the extent that the dominant party can dictate the terms of trade to its advantage; more broadly it is a cultural perspective that becomes skewed to favour the dominant group" (Holsti, 1985, p. 24). The Mayan movement is, in essence, fighting to transform those social relations to construct a new hegemony, a popular hegemony, which would be more representative and inclusive of the Mayan people.

Neo-Gramscian analyses of new social movements maintain the view of **counter-hegemony** "as a unification of class and popular democratic struggles that prefigures a new order, although they emphasize that if it is to be sustained over time a counter-hegemonic movement must do more than construct a collective will; it must also respect the identities and aspirations of its constituents" (Hirsch in Carroll, 1992).

In other words, to sustain the resistance forces, to achieve their political goals of local and territorial autonomy, self-government and respect for their cultural rights, the Mayan leadership must continue to strengthen their unity within the indigenous and non-indigenous organizations that contest the dominant development ideology. These include the women's movement, labour, progressive NGOs, political parties and the Church.

In *Selections from the Prison Notebooks of Antonio Gramsci* (1971), the Italian political theorist and politician (and longtime political prisoner under Mussoni's regime) Antonio Gramsci "attributed much greater importance than had Marx to ideology as a political factor in its own right, and worked out a theory in which ideological factors could be of great importance in affecting social and political relations." Like Marx, Gramsci saw ideology as mainly serving the interests of the ruling class. At the same time, "due to the tension between the ideology and the actual social and material position of the subordinate classes, he saw the possibility for the creation of an ideology representing the interests of the majority in a given society, thus, breaking through the ideological domination of the ruling class." According to Gramsci, "the popular political struggle should thus, in part, be waged on the ideological level, with people rejecting the dominant culture's ideology in which they were immersed and embracing an ideology of social liberation" (Gramsci, 1971, p. 326–327).

The dominant capitalist system and its social relations in Guatemala reinforce values of life that are mediated by the marketplace as the scenario for competition and the realization of people's needs. Those values have been supported by the racist ideology of state institutions, such as education, health care, labour and the judicial system.

As noted by Bianchi et al. (1999), "Racism and discrimination are central part of the hegemonic mentality which permitted the modernization of the Guatemalan state and economy" (p. 15). This is contrary to the community philosophy advocated and defended by Mayan people, where the collective needs of the community take precedence over competition and corporate profits.

Indeed, the United Nations' *National Report on Human Development* (2005) underscores the fact that the Mayan Cosmo-vision provides the basis for the Mayan people's spirituality and religion. This vision is also based on respect for the interrelationships between human beings, man and woman, and nature and the cosmos (UNHDR, 2005, p. 88). Rodolfo Pocop (2005), a CONIC leader, under-lines that the Mayan Cosmo-vision "is not an old religion. Our spirituality is precisely the harmony between humans, Mother Earth, space and nature. When we see the respect for Mother Earth is lost, we feel our roots are being destroyed" (interview with Pocop, 2005). This alternative view to the dominant globalization paradigm is at the centre of the new Mayan theoretical framework, which is com-bined with political action, peaceful mass mobilization, popular education, direct action, lobbying and negotiations with the government.

The dominant discourses on development and free trade have been challenged by local movements. These are real popular movements, proposing an alternative development agenda, a counter-hegemonic movement, which Canel defines as follows:

> [S]ocial movements may be viewed prima facie as agents of counter-hegemony. By mobilising resources and acting outside established structures of state, parties and interest groups, movements create in-dependent organizational bases for advocating alternatives. By contesting the discourses of capital, patriarchy, industrialism, racism and colonialism, and heterosexism, movements destabilise the identities of compliant worker, subservient wife, or closeted queer and create new ways of thinking about ourselves and the world around us (Canel cited in Carroll, 1992, p. 10).

Resistance to mining is also being fought at the educational, cultural and intellectual levels. Fundamental to this debate are the notions of development, who defines and who benefits from it. As mentioned before, the Mayan com-munities have made it very clear that they are advocating, lobbying and fighting for rural community development based on their needs, not on the corporate profit agenda advanced by Glamis and the World Bank. Thus, the Mayan leadership has been working hard toward an education for development that reflects their philo-sophy of life, which is centered on their culture, local and territorial autonomy and community values. Subsequently, they have been securing funds from their own communities, friends and political allies at the national level as well as the inter-national level. These resources have been used to fund the creation of bilingual educational institutions, such as teachers' institutes to educate their future teachers on how to teach their children in their native languages.

They have also created the first Mayan university in order to educate their professional and academics within their own Cosmo-vision. This would better allow the Mayans to promote their values, their history, their languages and cultural identity and forms of local, community development. The Mayan leaders are concerned with rewriting their history, the history of colonization and the civil war. This is evidenced by the significant increase in the number of publications of Mayan literature, books, academic journals, calendars and poetry (Morales, 2002).

In addition, Mayan communities have organized workshops on environmental issues, water purification and the legal aspects of carrying out referendums. The Mayan leaders, in conjunction with the Madre Selva and the Diocese of San Marcos, have organized various international delegations, which have visited their communities and have heard their concerns regarding the negative impacts of the mine (interview with Jose Cruz, August 2005). According to Cruz, Madre Selva obtained the professional services of Robert Moran, an expert on water quality, hydrology and geochemistry with more than 30 years of experience in mining, to review the Environmental and Social Impact Assessment (EIA&S) conducted by Glamis. Moran's report (2004), *New Country, Same Story: Review of the Glamis Gold Marlin Project EIA, Guatemala*, underscores the deficiencies of the EIA carried out by Glamis. Moran emphasizes the fact that "this EIA fails to discuss many of the most fundamental issues that concern the public, issues that must be generally understood by both the citizens and government regulators prior to approving such a project" (Moran, 2004, p. 3).

In today's Guatemala, there are new, dynamic and militant social movements, which are engaged in democratizing the country and advancing economic proposals that go beyond free trade deals and corporate capitalist profits – proposals that are important in the contemporary resistance to dispossession and displacement. These proposals include local, regional and national economic development initiatives based on peoples' needs. The Peace Agreement on Social and Economic Issues is a good example. Moen also agrees with Carroll and Ratner (1994), who assert that, "drawing upon Gramsci, some middle ground is possible wherein the conceptual foci of capital, class, and state remain in the discourse of social theory" (Carroll and Ratner, 1994, p. 5). Carroll and Ratner (1994) further state that:

> A Gramscian viewpoint offers the best prospect for analyzing con-
> temporary movement politics and strategizing about social change. This
> approach retains the insights of historical materialism, avoids the pit-
> falls of radical pluralism, and remains open to ongoing transformations
> in culture, politics, and capitalism (Carroll and Ratner, 1994, p. 3).

Niezen (2000) points out that indigenous groups are participating in international forums fighting to preserve their cultural identity, religion and traditions, but are, at the same time, transforming those forums. For example, the use of information technology, including the Internet, helps indigenous movements connect with their counterparts around the world. In this way, it serves to help preserve traditions, but at the same time, technologies can also change these traditions. Many Mayan organizations, leaders and movements are increasingly using the new communication technologies not only in everyday life but also to advance their struggles. For example, local radio stations are playing an important role in reaching out their communities, promoting their languages and traditions, educating those communities, as well as engaging them in local concerns.

## Conclusion

The dominant paradigm expressed in the Glamis Gold proposals for mining development in Guatemala is flawed and its hegemony is far from complete. In Guatemala, a mining-centered economy has been rejected in local referendums, where Mayan people have overwhelmingly voted against mining. At the same time, the legal framework for mining investment, the Central American Free Trade Agreement (CAFTA), which linked Guatemala and the United States, was ruled unconstitutional by the Guatemalan Supreme Court (2006). On the other hand, the Guatemalan government has increasingly pushed for Canadian investment despite clear violations of national and international law. The use of violence against the Guatemalan people and the Maya in particular resulted in selective and open killings and the military occupation of communities, as well as in the criminalization of social protests.

But through resistance against mining, the Mayan leadership has been able to bring together local communities and build a national political movement opposing mining. They have been educating their communities through workshops, radio, and fact-finding delegations to neighbouring countries in Central America. Their international work has been a key component of this education initiative, particularly tying local activities to international allies who have been touring Mayan communities regularly to find out about the mining projects. As such, indigenous and non-indigenous resistance against mining represents a counter-hegemonic movement, which has contributed to exposing the authoritarian and racist basis of mining development imposed by the Guatemalan government with the complicity of the World Bank and the Canadian government. Mayan communities today are well aware of the environmental, social, economic and cultural impacts of mining.

Alternative development proposals advanced by Mayan communities clearly advocate the benefits of rural community development at the local and regional level, and are based on the Mayan population's actual needs. These proposals challenge the logic and ideology of dominant development, rather than acquiescing in mining projects in Guatemala financed by outside interests, or accepting the inevitability of local peoples having to leave Guatemala for destinations in the global north as temporary and precarious workers. However, for their counter-hegemonic projects to be implemented at the local level, the Mayan leadership must develop a common financing strategy that would foster cooperation and autonomy, rather than competition. The Mayan leadership is also clear that new economic development projects should be created within their communities and take into account the Mayan Cosmo-vision, their culture, community values, and the importance of local and territorial autonomy and self-government. These are consistent with the Mayas' historical resistance and survival in the face of the multiple forms of displacement driven by the political imperatives of imperialism, colonialism, state repression and contemporary neo-liberalism.

# References

Araujo, R. (2004, September 1). Seis Campesinos Muertos Durante el Desalojo de la Finca Nueva Linda. In *Noticias de America Latina y El Caribe*, p. 4.

Arenas Bianchi, C., Hale, C. R., & Murga, G. P. (Eds.) (1999). *Racismo en Guatemala¿ Abriendo el debate sobre un tema tabú*. Guatemala City: AVANCSO.

Estrada, H. M. (2004). *El plan Puebla Panamá: ¿Alternativa o amenaza al desarrollo rural?* Guatemala City: AVANCSO.

Cambranes C., J. (1996). *Café y campesinos: Los origenes de la economia de plantacion moderna en Guatemala, 1853–1897* (2nd Ed.). Madrid: Editorial Catriel.

Canel, E. (1992). New social movements and resource mobilization: The need for integration. In Carroll, W. (Ed.), *Organizing dissent: Contemporary social movements in theory and practice* (pp. 22–51). Toronto: Garamond Press.

Compliance Advisory: Ombudsman/International Financial Corporation (2005, September 7). Assessment of a complaint submitted to CAO in relation to the Marlin Mining Project in Guatemala.

Chun, A. (2003). *Global response newsletter, 2*, p. 6

Collectivo Madre Selva (2004). Retrieved from www.madreselva.org.

Commission for Historical Clarification (CEH) (2004). *Guatemala memory of silence: Report of the Commission*. Retrieved from http://www.aaas.org/sites/default/files/migrate/uploads/mos_en.pdf.

Commission for Historical Clarification (CEH) (1999). *Guatemala memoria del silencio: Mandato y procedimiento de trabajo, causas y orígenes del enfrentamiento armado interno* (1st Ed.).

CONIC (2005, March 30). Memorandum to President Berger.

Defensoria Maya (2003, October). News release.

Frente Nacional en Defensa de los Servicios Públicos y los Recursos Naturales (2004) May 20. *Nueva Linda: Donde no amanece para la justicia*. Guatemala City.

Glamis Gold (2005, Sept. 26). "Glamis announces Marlin start-up — Higher 2005 production expected — Cerro Blanco project updated. News release. Retrieved from www.glamis.com.

Glamis Gold (2005, July 18). Glamis Gold Exercises Chesapeake Gold Corp Warrant. News release. Retrieved from www.glamis.com/properites/guatemala/marlin.html 018/07/2005.

Global Response (2005, February–March). Support indigenous opposition to gold mine in Guatemala. Bishop Alvaro Ramazzini's letter to the President of Guatemala, Berger, September 2004.

Godoy, E. Interview with Juan Tema (2005, August 10). Sipapca, San Marcos, Guatemala.

Godoy, E. Interview with the Mayan Lawyer, Amilcar Pocop (2005, August 7). Forum on the Legal Bases of the Community Referendum, Guatemala City.

Godoy, E. Interview with Jose Cruz, director of the Madre Selva Collective (2005). Guatemala City.

Gramsci, A. (1971). *Selections from the Prison Notebooks of Antonio Gramsci*. Hoare, Q., & Smith, G. N. (Ed. & Trans.). New York: International Publishers.

Guibal, F. (1983). *Gramsci: Filosofia, política y cultura*. Lima, Peru: Centro de Publicaciones Educativas.

House of Commons, Thirty-Eighth Parliament Report (2003). The Standing Committee on Foreign Affairs and International Trade. Retrieved from www.parl.gc.ca/infocomdoc/38/1/parlbus/commbus/house.FAAE/report.

Infopress Centroamericana (2005). National Forum on Mining. February 11. Guatemala City: Infopress.

International Labour Organization (1989). C169 Indigenous and Tribal People's Convention. Retrieved from www.ilo.org/ilolex/cgi-lex/convde.pl?C169.

Jones, S. (2013, March 27). Guatemalan migration in times of civil war and post-war challenges. Migration Policy Institute (MPI). Retrieved from http://www.migrationpolicy.org/article/guatemalan-migration-times-civil-war-and-post-war-challenges.

Lambert, J. (2004, November 4). Mining in Canada. *Prensa Libre*. Retrieved from www.mininwatch.ca /issues/Guatemala/Prensa_Libre.html.

Madre Selva Collective (2004). *"10 añnos de lucha ecológica": Manual de resistencia ecologista*. Guatemala City: Collectivo Ecologista Madre Selva.

Mines & Communities (2004, April). Oil and mineral concessions in Guatemala violate international agreements and Peace Accord. News release. In *Defensoria Q'eqchi*. Retrieved from www.minesand communities.org.

Mines & Communities (2003, Octopber 6). Declaration of the Q'eqchi' communities regarding mining concessions held by INCO. Retrieved from www.minesandcommunities.org/Country/guatemala 2.htm.

Mining Watch Canada (2004, April 21). INCO targeted at annual shareholders' meeting, representatives from communities around the world affected by INCO gather in Toronto. News release. Retrieved from www.miningwatch.ca.

Mining Watch Canada (2004, January 12). Glamis Gold, Canadian government, World Bank implicated as two killed, more injured protesting mine in Guatemala. News release. Retrieved from www.miningwatch.ca/issues/Guatemala/Marlin_ris-12-01-05.html.

Montana Exploradora del Guatemala S.A. (2003). Marlin mining project, Indignous People's development plan, prepared for the International Finance Corporation, February 19, 2004. Retrieved from www.glamisgold.com.

Montana Exploradora del Guatemala S.A. (2004, February 24). Marlin mining project, public consultation and disclosure plan, prepared for the International Finance Corporation. Retrieved from www.glamisgold.com.

Morales, M. R. (2002). *La articulación de las diferencias: El síndrome de maximón*. Guatemala City: Editorial Palo de Hormigo.

North American Congress on Latin America (1974). *EXMIBAL: Take another nickel out*. Jonas, S., & Tobis, D. N.p.: North American Congress On Latin America.

Niezen, R. (2003).*The origins of indigenism: Human rights and the politics of identity*. Los Angeles: University of California Press.

Piedra Santa Arandi, R. (1979). *EXMIBAL contra Guatemala: Comisión de la Facultad de Ciencias Económicas*. (2nd Ed.). Guatemala City: N.p.

Piedra Santa Arandi, R. (1965). *Economía: Las inversciones extranjeras. Instituto de investigaciones económicas y sociales Facultad de Ciencias Económicas*. Guatemala City: Universidad de San Carlos, Editorial Universitaria.

*Prensa Libre* (2005, January 10). Violent incidents in Sololá: One person killed and dozens wounded. *Prensa Libre*, p.1.

REMHI (1999). *Recuperation of the Historical Memory (REMHI): Guatemala, never again*. N.p.: Human Rights Office of the Archdiocese of Guatemala.

Solano, L. (2005). *Guatemala: Petroleo y mineria en las entranas del poder* (Vol. 1, pp. 38–39). Guatemala: Inforpress Centroamericana.

Statement of the I Conference of Mayan Leaders and Authorities (April 1, 2005, April 1). Totonicapan, Guatemala.

Torres Rivas, E. (1971). *Interpretation of the Central American social development: Processes and structures of a dependent society* (2nd Ed.). Costa Rica: Editorial University Centro Americana (EDUCA).

United Nations (2005). Diversidad étnico-cultural y desarrollo humano: La ciudadanía en un Estado plural: Informe nacional de desarrollo humano 2005. Guatemala City: Programa de las Naciones Unidas para el Desarrollo.

United Nations (1969). Office of the High Commissioner for Human Rights: Convention (no. 169) concerning indigenous and tribal peoples in independent countries. ILO, ILOLEX database. Geneva.

United Nations (2005). *Ethno-cultural diversity: Citizenship in a plural state: National report on human development in Guatemala*. Guatemala City: United Nations.

Warren, K. B. (2000). Pan-Mayanism and the Guatemalan peace process. In Chase-Dunn, C., Jonas, S., & Amaro, N. (Eds.). *Globalization on the ground: Postbellum Guatemalan democracy and development* (pp. 145–166). Lanham, MD: Rowman and Littlefield.

## CHAPTER SEVEN

# War, Displacement and Trauma

## *Ezat Mossallanejad*

War, regardless of whether is presented as "just" or "unjust," causes trauma, injury, loss, violence, destruction, displacement and migration. This chapter will begin with an introduction to the concept of war and its relation to capitalism and imperialism. It will then explore the definitions, followed by the impacts, of war, and examine the relationship between war and displacement and the production of refugees. The chapter will then provide an overview of the effects of war on women and children, exploring how war affects people directly and indirectly, individually and collectively leaving long-lasting trauma and mental health challenges. From the western medical perspective, this trauma is framed as post-traumatic stress disorder (PTSD). In recent years, however, many agencies working with the survivors of war and torture have adopted holistic approaches which combine clinical treatments with community-based treatments. These approaches to practice will be examined by relying on the author's professional experiences in working with survivors of war, torture and genocide.

The prospects of living in a world without war are not good. The rich exploit the poor as the countries of the north plunder those of the south. Human greed, combined with nationalism and religious fanaticism, has reduced the earth to an inferno as fully fledged war is waged against our environment. Global warming has already started as a result of capitalist greed and fatal intervention against Mother Nature. In this atmosphere, countries are either preparing for war or are in a constant state of alert, so they will not be invaded by others. The whole planet can be compared to an enormous garrison.

According to the Stockholm International Peace Research Institute's (SIPRI) 2013 report, world military expenditures totaled $1.75 trillion in 2013, with the following three countries in the lead: the United States (39% of the total), China (9.5%) and Russia (5.4%) (SIPRI, 2013). The total number of military personnel in the world serving in governments' regular armies is around 20 million, not counting paramilitary and other armed groups. SIPRI also notes the rising trend in the number of casualties and in the length of conflicts around the world, as a result of the growing internationalization of conflicts with third-party states supporting the direct parties involved in a conflict. The United States spent $685.3 billion on defence in 2012, an increase of 69% from 2001 when the "wars on terror" began. Importantly, this militarization has expanded to non-traditional forms of warfare such as cyberwarfare, something which has necessitated greater cybersecurity military expenditures (SIPRI, 2013).

**Militarism** is defined as "the organization of a society based on the model of an army or the dominance of the military in a society or more broadly in every system of thinking" (Pritchard, 2010, p. 226). Militarism has always been an essential part of the expansionist policies of empires and superpowers, ancient and modern. To hold its empire together, the dominant power uses war as a uniting force and a final solution for conquest and territorial expansionism. History has recorded hundreds of religious and civil wars as well. All these wars have led to the killing, maiming, impoverishment and displacement of millions of people and the outbreak of many diseases.

## Reflective Question

War has been a feature of human existence for thousands of years. History has recorded more than 3,000 wars up to the present time. While some consider war as a permanent feature of history, others approach it as a historical phenomenon arising in specific period of history and vanishing in the future. The omnipresence of war in human society and history leads one to ask about the root cause of war and whether the human race is condemned to living with the evil of war. Will a day come that we all enjoy a durable and meaningful peace?

Wars are associated with the emergence of agriculture, settlements, and formation of exploitative classes that led to social inequality and complex economic and political systems, as a prelude to the advance of state and state power. With the rise of capitalism and the need for the accumulation of capital, the enforced colonization of other nations began. Colonial powers spared no time to plunder, enslave and entomb millions of people in Asia, Africa and the Americas. Aboriginal people in Americas experienced and continue to experience genocide and ethnocide on an ongoing basis. The process of colonization, however, was never smooth, having been combined with wars of plunder and subjugation. Colonial forces suppressed any protest by local people by using violence and massacres. According to the French philosopher Jean-Paul Sartre, colonization is in itself "intrinsically genocidal" because of its destruction of indigenous cultures on the one hand and imposition of the colonial power's culture on the other (Eyoh and Zeleza, 2003).

Following World War II, national liberation movements emerged around the globe as the process of decolonization accelerated. At the same time many colonial wars began, some of which lasted for years. As well, although many nations managed to gain independence, they soon found themselves in wars that were the result of their former colonial status. A glance at the map of Africa reveals that some regions are divided by straight lines where colonial powers have separated one tribe into two nations. Many contemporary conflicts, like the Indo-Pakistani wars, the war between Pakistan and Bangladesh, the Vietnam War, or any number of the ongoing conflicts in sub-Saharan Africa are rooted in such colonial history. In all these wars, millions of people were internally displaced or crossed national borders, in the process being relegated to protracted lives as refugees.

By the start of the twentieth century, capitalism had reached its imperialistic stage. **Imperialism**, in its modern sense, is defined as a stage in the development of capitalism in which the system becomes monopolistic, leading to the overwhelming growth in influence of capital and finance, and the existence of giant corporations. This development is followed by the territorial division of the world by capitalist states, with the consequence being imperialistic wars in which one country or another attempts the "re-division" of the world in order to further its expansionary interests. In this sense, imperialism and war are complementary. Lenin, for example, viewed World War I as an imperialistic war (Lenin, 2010, Chapter VII). Imperialism, in the course of its development, brought into being state monopoly capitalism, a system that combines the power of the state with the power of monopolies to intensify the exploitation of people and the plunder of human and natural resources of poor nations. Today, we live in the age of **globalization** where Western countries have erected many walls against the movement of people, specifically those who are looking for asylum. At the same time, capital has become absolutely free to move anywhere, including to the poorest countries where natural and human resources are cheap. Transnational corporations rule the world and control states.

At the same time, religious fanaticism, mixed with chauvinistic attitudes, has led to ever-increasing global violence; "since 2000, 43 percent of civil wars have been tainted by religious rhetoric" (Micklethwait and Wooldridge, 2009, p. 24). In Bosnia Herzegovina, for example, religion mixed with ethnic chauvinism provided justification for radical Catholic and Orthodox forces to involve themselves in massacres and ethnic cleansing, as a result of which 7,000 Muslims were massacred and 24,000 became internally displaced by the Bosnian Serb army. The Al-Qaeda terrorist attack of September 11, 2001 triggered a violent response, the consequences of which (such as the occupation of Afghanistan and Iraq) continue to result in a high human toll.

It is a fact that wars are caused by many factors including identity, religion, ethnicity, environment, resources, retaliation, territory, ambition, greed, militarism, exploitation, domination and tribalism, to name just a few. To work against war is to address its root causes. Let us not forget that peace is not the absence of war. **Peace** is the state of conscious collaboration and solidarity among groups and nations. It is in peace that all parties would develop into their full potential. Grassroots organizations and peace activists around the world have largely come to this realization. There are scholars and human rights activists who believe that peace has also been a significant feature of our history. According to Robert Hinde:

> A number of countries have abandoned war as a way of settling disputes. Some no longer have armies. Waging war is not envisaged as a possible political tool by, for instance, Sweden or Switzerland. Western European

states used to be in constant conflict but now war is almost unthinkable for them (Hinde, 2008, p. 15).

## Definitions of War

Wars are waged with a wide variety of incentives and intentions. This prompts us to come up with different categories of wars, among which the following are the most significant:

**Defensive war,** in which force is used to resist force. The party to defensive war responded to attack and is not considered the aggressor. A defensive war, however, can, at any time, develop into an offensive one.

**Preventive war,** in which a party strikes the enemy before being attacked by the enemy. This might be prompted by the opponent's preparations for war (e.g., amassing armies on the border).

**Preemptive war,** in which a party strikes at a potential opponent that might pose a threat in the future despite there being no immediate danger.

**Offensive war,** which is waged by an aggressive power by choice without being compelled to do so. Despite its aggression, the offender may justify its war as defensive or preventive. Greed for territory, natural resources, military presence, population, domination (colonial, religious, political), and wealth are some examples of motive forces behind aggressive wars.

**Civil war** that is waged by one segment of a society against another segment of the same society. Examples are wars of segregation or independence.

**War of interdiction,** which is aimed at removing barriers to the interests of the instigating party.

**War of liberation,** with the intention of emancipation from foreign domination or domination of an oppressive or exploitative class in order to usher in a radical change in the society (revolution).

**Globalizing war,** a type of conflict that extends beyond national borders to have direct or indirect impacts on the whole world (e.g., World War II, the Vietnam War or the so-called "Global War on Terror") (James and Friedman, 2006).

The American historian, Howard Zinn, believes human history is a "history not only of cruelty, but also of compassion, sacrifice, courage, kindness." (Zinn, 2011, p. i). In keeping with this view, anti-war movements have been in place for the last hundred years. The establishment of the International Criminal Court in July 2002 represents a serious development in the fight against war crimes. Meanwhile, organizations like the Center for Constitutional Rights in Washington, D.C., and the Stop the War Coalition in the United Kingdom work hard against violence by promoting public awareness of war, organizing meetings and demonstrations, and by challenging their respective governments.

### Definitions of War

Scholars have defined **war** according to their academic discipline and political inclinations. Differences in definitions of war speak to its complexity: "Diachronically and synchronically, within and cross-culturally, war is waged and experienced differently. As times change, the war phenomenon changes along in diverse ways that need to be examined contextually and cross culturally" (Pittaka, 2007, p. 24). Brian Ferguson defines war as an "organized purposeful group action, directed against another group that may or may not be organized for similar action, involving the actual or potential application of lethal force" (Ferguson, 1984, p. 5). In fact, human force and weapons are essential requirements for war. Weapons are manufactured and people are incited to go to war as institutions controlled by the state create hysteria to prepare people to kill and be killed. To achieve this result, states perpetuate a culture of war, encouraging an atmosphere of panic, hate, terror, violence, intimidation, racism, chauvinism and demonization of "others." The culture of war and martyrdom helped Ayatollah Khomeini to recruit thousands of children during the Iran-Iraq war to clear landmines. It was the same culture that enabled George W. Bush to cry havoc and initiate widespread anxiety and mass fear among the American people in preparation for his invasion of Afghanistan and Iraq.

Scholars have considered the grounds on which wars are justified, or, in Latin, *jus in bellum*. Their analysis considers such factors as the motivation for the war and how it is conducted. The right to **self-defence** provides the most common argument for a "just war." But the dilemma of the concept of just war stems from the fact that a war that is just for one group is not necessarily just for others. War, just or unjust, impacts many innocent civilians, leaving long-lasting scars on vulnerable populations.

## The Impacts of War: A General Overview

In wars, many (including large numbers of young people) are killed in the front lines while civilians also die or become displaced. While in wars fought up until the early years of the twentieth century, the majority of casualties occurred among military personnel, the proportion has changed drastically since then. During World War I, 6.6 million civilians lost their lives, whereas over the course of World War II a total of 60 million people were killed, with two-thirds of them — 40 million — being civilians (Kahn, 2008, p. 14). Today, due to advances in war technology, 90% of war casualties occur among civilians. Therefore, it is fair to say that all modern wars are characteristically wars against civilians, particularly women and children.

Also noteworthy as features of modern warfare are **state terrorism** and **non-state terrorism**. These two faces of terror nourish each other and are complementary; both use abhorrent means – including torture — to achieve their main goal of power (Mossallanejad, 2005). For example, the violence associated with the United States' so-called "war on terror" has led to counter-violence that operates in the shadows and justifies the use of any means possible, including suicide bombing.

War robs people of their human potential and material resources. The thirty-fourth president of the United States, Dwight D. Eisenhower, admitted this in his speech of April 16, 1953 before the American Society of Newspaper Editors:

> Every gun that is made, every warship launched, every rocket fired signi-
> fies, in the final sense, a theft from those who hunger and are not fed,
> those who are cold and not clothed. This world in arms is not spending
> money alone. It is spending the sweat of its laborers, the genius of its sci-
> entists, the hopes of its children. . . . We pay for a single destroyer with
> new homes that could have housed more than 8,000 people. This is not a
> way of life at all in any true sense. Under the cloud of threatening war, it

is humanity hanging from a cross of iron (cited in Hodge and Nolan, 2007, p. 279).

In a state of war or ethnic conflict, where certain people are regarded as enemies, the demonization and dehumanization of the enemy is used to sanction such actions as torture, rape, sexual slavery and violence. According to Ignatius Martin-Baro:

> War implies social polarization, the displacement of groups toward opposite extremes. A critical split is produced in the framework of coexistence, leading to a radical differentiation between "them" and "us." . . . People, actions and things are no longer valued in and of themselves. . . . Thus the basis for daily interaction disappears (cited in Aron and Caron, 1994, p. 112).

Ultimately, the sinister by-products of war — abject poverty, deprivation, occupation, humiliation and insecurity — lead to a lack of respect for life itself. When human life loses its value, death emerges as an unquestionable demonstration of honour, courage, loyalty and moral character. War intensifies the circle of violence and leads to the destruction of our human rights and humanitarian system of values. According to Simone Weil, war "destroys moral fiber and engenders despair, cruelty and oppression" (cited in Brenner, 2002, p. 47).

With the passage of time, it may be possible to reconstruct war-ravaged areas or compensate for war's human and material damages. It is, however, impossible to repair the universal values that once united us. The most valuable asset that the human family can lose in war is that system of values that distinguishes between the things that are acceptable and those that are not. This is true for all wars – aggressive or defensive. According to Ernest Hemingway:

> An aggressive war is a great crime against everything good in the world. A defensive war, which must necessarily turn to aggressive at the earliest moment, is the necessary great counter-crime. Never think that war, no matter how necessary, nor how justified, is not a crime (Hemingway, 2003, p. xxvii).

The systematic massacre of vulnerable civilians, women, children and elders alike, and the destruction of houses, crops and livestock are justified by both sides as "collateral damage," or the inevitable price that must be paid for "freedom." The most inhuman and brutal atrocities are sanctioned and justified as necessary evils, with almost no respect for customary international law. War may reach an ominous stage that destroys any kind of compassion and humanitarian emotion on the part of ordinary people. The next section will examine the impact of war in relation to refugee crises as well as its effects on women and children.

**Refugees and Displaced People**

Before, during and even after each war, hundreds of thousands of people cross borders, assuming desperate lives as refugees, or become internally displaced in their countries of origin. War therefore causes significant depopulation of war-ravaged countries due to the destruction of infrastructure, environment and resources, as well as the death and mass exodus of civilian populations. At the same time, it can cause overpopulation in the host countries receiving the refugees. At the start of 2012, the world refugee population was 15.2 million, and the number of internally displaced persons (IDPs) worldwide was estimated to be 29.5 million. Of all refugees, around 50% reside in Asia and about a quarter reside in Africa. Although the number of refugees from the Latin America sub-region remains relatively stable, the 2014 UNHCR regional operations profile on Latin America anticipates an increase due to recent violence as well as criminal activities by non-state actors in the Americas.

Some 55% of refugees come from only five war-ravaged countries: Afghanistan, Somalia, Iraq, Syria and Sudan. António Guterres, UN High Commissioner for Refugees and head of UNHCR, has noted:

> These truly are alarming numbers. They reflect individual suffering on a huge scale and they reflect the difficulties of the international community in preventing conflicts and promoting timely solutions for them (UNHCR website, Global Trends 2012 Report, 2013).

The number of refugees in the Middle East and North Africa has considerably increased over the past two years, mainly due to the Syrian refugee crisis as well as the conflict in Mali. Far from being stable, the region continues to experience dramatic developments which have resulted in more refugee outflows, more internal displacement, and, sadly, more loss of life. As of 2013, there were over one million Syrian refugees, 75% of them women and children. This refugee population is primarily located in Lebanon, Jordan, Iran and Egypt. One of the greatest risks for these refugee populations is their registration. In Jordan, 75% of Syrian refugees are not in camps, and there is a growing discontent in urban areas. Sex and gender crimes in refugee camps are rampant. Refugees suffer as a result of local traditional hostility to foreigners and the absence of a national asylum system in their host countries, as well as from the lack of any legal framework for their protection.

According to the 2014 UNHCR report, over two million Syrian refugees had already been registered or received registration appointments, mainly in the neighbouring countries and beyond. The crisis has had an equally devastating impact inside Syria itself, with more than four million persons internally displaced and over six million people affected. In some cases, Syrians were forcibly displaced more than once as violence spread across the country. It is important to understand that this situation should not simply be classified as a Syrian refugee crisis; it is, rather, a global crisis compounded by inadequate empathy and protection (Mossallanejad, 2013, p. 15).

It is unfortunate that in our era of globalization, the international asylum system is falling apart. As is well known, Article 14 of the UN *Declaration of Human Rights* has categorically stated that every human being has the right to seek asylum. An effective asylum system addresses the issue of refugees' access to territory and protects them from *refoulemen* (forcible return to persecution). It contributes towards their humane and dignified treatment, including protection against arbitrary detention and fair and efficient resolution of their status, and will lead to durable solutions to their plight. But today we observe concerted efforts by western governments to limit this fundamental right, through the introduction of new legislation, policies and practices that undermine it. This has affected new asylum seekers and has kept many recognized refugees in state of "immigration limbo."

The ever-increasing growth of the IDP population is due to the fact that most governments, especially western ones, want to keep refugees within their own national borders. National and global assistance for IDPs is increasingly complex. When national policies and aid are not available to assist IDPs, international governing bodies may have to intervene in national politics. According to the Internal Displacement Monitoring Centre (IDMC), which monitors IDPs globally, over 90% of those who are internally displaced are in a state of protracted displacement (Mossallanejad, 2013, p. 12 ).

It becomes increasingly important to create policies and practices to address the causes and effects of displacement. There is a need for a multi-sectorial approach. In many cases national governments are not capable of providing protection or assistance to their IDPs. This failure warrants international humanitarian action and intervention to alleviate the plight of displaced populations. Unfortunately, such intervention is not always possible due to the lack of resources and political will on the part of national governments. The challenges of the near future for refugees and IDPs include funding, lack of legal frameworks, security concerns, regional stability, and lack of coordination with development processes. At the same time, interlinked problems of food insecurity, water scarcity and natural disasters are becoming more dramatic and more frequent with humanitarian consequences, multiplication of conflicts and unpredictability. Today, even humanitarian workers are under attack and at risk of abuse, abduction and death.

## Impacts of War on Women

War takes a heavy toll on women. They may be war's first casualties, as was shown by the 2014 Israeli air strikes in Gaza; when missiles hit civilian areas, the heaviest death tolls belonged to women and children. Dozens of their wounded or dead bodies were left in the streets (*The Guardian*, July 21, 2014).

For women, the impacts of war go far beyond the immediate casualties of combat. In a state of war or ethnic conflict, where certain people are regarded as enemies, all sorts of war crimes and crimes against humanity are justified and even sanctioned by both the belligerent governments and extremist groups. Women suffer most from gender-based violence when gender becomes a mean of retaliation in order to put shame to the other party.

Before and during World War II, for example, 200,000 "comfort women" or *lanfu* from eastern and southeast Asia were enslaved and forced into sexual servitude to Japanese Imperial Armed forces (Nobe, 2009) . Girls as young as 12 were taken from poor families or from rural areas through coercion, intimidation and deception. As a result of multiple rapes, many of the women suffered from gynecological problems and were unable to marry or bear children (Nobe, 2009, p. 25). Years later, a handful of these women broke silence by organizing the Women's International War Crimes Tribunal that in year 2000 found Emperor Hirohito of Japan guilty of crimes against humanity posthumously (Hawkesworth, 2006, p. 79).

During the Iran-Iraq War (1980–1988), military and paramilitary forces from both sides raped women in occupied zones without compunction, easily finding moral and religious sanctions for their actions. Women were raped or gang-raped during the Rwandan genocide of 1994: "In almost every case, these crimes were inflicted upon women after they had witnessed the torture and killings of their relatives, and the destruction and looting of their houses. Some women were forced to kill their own children before or after being raped" (Nowrojee, 1996, p. 39). Rape was also used as a weapon of war during genocide in the former Yugoslavia. Serbian forces raped women publicly in the

## Torture and Its After-effects

Based on my experience at the Canadian Centre for Victims of Torture, around 31% of refugees and displaced people have experienced torture or other cruel, inhumane or degrading treatment or punishment. Most of them suffer from the after-effects of torture, what is known as Post-Traumatic Stress Disorder (PTSD). Uprooted people, especially in camps, are subject to re-traumatization due to their hard lives, abuses, and lack of protection. This is an issue of less significance to the UNHCR due to the intensity of refugee and IDP crisis.

presence of friends, relatives and family members "in a pattern of intimidation and abuse focused on forcing the Croatian or Bosnian population to flee" (Bames, 2005, p. 300).

Rape, sexual slavery, enforced prostitution, forced pregnancy, enforced sterilization and many other forms of gender and sexual violence have been widespread in many war-torn regions of the world, including Sierra Leone, Uganda and Sudan. In Sudan, for example, large numbers of militia and government forces have killed civilians and abducted and raped women and girls due to their ethnic origin, calling them "slaves" as they "beat them with whips, gun butts or fists." (Human Rights Watch, 2007, p. 38). Rape is one of the least-reported techniques of torture and weapons of war. For a long time it was not even recognized as torture or a war crime. A number of reasons are cited that contribute to denial of and secrecy about rape, including shame, danger of excommunication and lack of a safe environment to speak. Fortunately, in 1994, the International Tribunal for Rwanda and the former Yugoslavia recognized sexual violence against women (rape, sexual enslavement, forced prostitution) as a form of genocide and war crime. Articles 7 and 8 of the Rome Statute for the International Criminal Court have confirmed rape, sexual slavery, enforced prostitution, forced pregnancy, and enforced sterilization as crimes against humanity and war crimes (International Criminal Court, 2011, pp. 3–5).

In war, women are vulnerable to health complications, ranging from fear and anxiety to untreatable diseases to miscarriage, death and mortality during pregnancy. They are forced to live a sub-human life in camps inside and outside their home countries. With husbands gone, women have to deal with everything single-handedly: collecting wood, cooking, washing, taking care of children and the elderly, just to name a few examples. Refugee and displaced women may continue to suffer after the conflict is over. Starvation and destitution may force them to exchange sex for their own and their children's survival. This has often resulted in their being infected with HIV/AIDS and other contagious diseases. Mothers' hopes for the future of their children are shattered as they witness them playing war games using sticks for guns.

> ## Reflective Questions
>
> A survivor of rape at CCVT revealed her tragic experience to me, as her trauma counsellor, 20 years after the initial trauma and five years after becoming my client.
>
> - Why do women rarely speak of their experiences of sexual violence?
> - Why is rape considered a shame for women rather than their perpetrators?

## The Impacts of War on Children

A great human tragedy is the recruitment of children by armed groups and government forces to fight in wars. They use children because they can easily brainwash them to obey orders and engage in fearless killings. The phenomenon of child soldiers is an ever-increasing problem. There are currently 36 countries where it is reported that children under 18 are participating in armed conflicts (Barnitz, 1999, p. 82). The exact number of child soldiers is unknown, but it is likely to run to more than 300,000, despite the Optional Protocol to the *Convention on the Rights of the Child* and the *Rome Statute for the International Criminal Court* that have prohibited the participation of children in armed conflict. Children are conscripted, kidnapped or pressured into joining armed groups. Warlords have converted thousands of innocent children into participants in armed conflicts by providing them with lightweight weapons and making it possible for children, even those under 10 years of age, to become effective killers.

Children are also forced into sexual slavery and to become labourers, cooks or servants, messengers or spies. Girls are particularly vulnerable to sexual exploitation, whether by one commander or a whole troop. They may also join boys on the front line. Girls were part of government, militia, paramilitary and/or armed opposition forces in 55 countries between 1990 and 2003 and were actively involved in armed conflict in 38 of those countries (UNICEF, 2004, p. 42). The abduction of girls is a worldwide phenomenon. In the past 10 years, girls have been kidnapped and forced into wartime service in at least 20 countries (UNICEF, 2004). Since girls are more vulnerable to assault and rape is a common occurrence, they often contract sexually transmitted infections. In Sierra Leone, health workers estimate that 70% to 90% of rape survivors tested positive for sexually transmitted diseases (UNICEF, 2004, p. 43).

Moreover, young women who were girls when they were abducted or forcibly recruited and later return with "war babies" may be stigmatized and rejected by their families and communities because of the shame attached to rape and to giving birth to babies fathered by the girls' captors. In Sierra Leone, for example, "a broader population of children born to young mothers and to single mothers may be given the local 'baby rebel' stigma" (Carpenter, 2007, p. 85). This makes the impact of war and sexual violence intergenerational. For example, in some war-ravaged regions, many of these unwanted and undesirable children were kept captive to form a new generation of warriors, sold to sex/organ traffickers or sold for adoption to Western countries.

Recent efforts to rehabilitate child soldiers, such as programs of demobilization, disarmament and reintegration, are only a Band-aid solution, which, while important, cannot hope to resolve the fundamental problem of child soldiers. A multi-faceted effort at all levels is needed to address the root cause of this evil and alleviate the problem of child soldiers. According to Archbishop Desmond Tutu:

> We must not close our eyes to the fact that child soldiers are both victims and perpetrators. They sometimes carry out the most barbaric acts of violence. But no matter what the child is guilty of, the main responsibility lies with us, the adults. There is simply no excuse, no acceptable argument for arming children (cited in Greenbaum, Veerman and Bacon-Shnoor, 2006, p. 311).

There have been government sponsored programs in some countries to develop best practices for the rehabilitation and reform of child soldiers. In 2005 and 2006, for instance, a special commission was established in Democratic Republic of Congo to address the specific reintegration needs of child soldiers. In or around 1997, the Rwandan government handed over 1,000 child prisoners to UNESCO for reform. They were accused of direct involvement in the 1994 genocide.

Reform programs are comprehensive, holistic and community-based, with special attention given to help children to overcome their fragility, fear and security concerns. Special attention is also paid to child psychology, specifically that of a child warrior. Since child soldiering is grounded in the structural violence of poverty and social inequalities, "developing comprehensive community services" for effective "demobilization and reintegration of child soldiers" is of vital significance (Hartjen and Priyadarsini, 2012, p. 118).

It was in 1996 that Graça Machel proposed the immunity of children from armed conflicts: "Let us claim children as 'zones of peace.' In this way humankind will finally declare that childhood is inviolate and that all children must be spared the pernicious effects of armed conflicts" (Machel, 1996, para. 318). Eighteen years have passed and the plight of war-affected children has worsened beyond imagination.

In every corner of the world, war is taking its toll on children and robbing them of their childhood. In some conflict zones, the fighting is older than the children themselves are. There are children of war who have never experienced any other life. In some areas of heavy bombardment, when the bombs begin to drop, children run to shelters in pairs, one or two with their father and others with their mother. They are never all together: otherwise, if a bomb hits, the whole family might be wiped out.

Disruption of children's education and destruction of schools is another sinister by-product of war. This is being done despite the categorical provisions of the Rome Statute for the International Criminal Court (ICC) that have, among other things, classified deliberate attacks on children and schools as war crimes. The tragic memory of the massacre of the children of Beslan (a city in southern Russia) in their school is still fresh in our minds. In September 2004, the taking of hostages at the school by a Chechen armed group and the counterattack of Russian security forces resulted in the massacre of more than 350 people, 150 of them small children. This tragic event speaks to the outrageous disdain for the most basic principles of human decency by the government and rebel forces.

Children are innocent victims of all wars. Childhood plays a crucial role in building the personality of each and every individual. Traumatic experiences such as torture and war leave negative impacts on the social and emotional development of children. Devastating psychological effects may appear later in their adult lives. Younger children suffer more due to their vulnerability. Children's trauma resulting from torture and war may later develop into a collective trauma at the social level. War-affected children are particularly at risk. By being direct witnesses to the massacre of their families and the destruction of their community, they may constantly blame themselves for not doing enough to protect their loved ones. This feeling of absolute helplessness and guilt of conscience may remain with them throughout their lives.

It is a well-known fact that children have a powerful sense of imitation. In conflict zones, they are at risk of imitating violence committed by belligerent forces. They see a gun as a source of power and therefore the solution to all problems. They internalize the indoctrination that killing is a shortcut to overcome all difficulties. This is a great danger to future hopes for peace. When children of war grow into adults, they may view war and violence as the universal solution to all problems.

Children who are affected by war and torture rarely trust others and are not normally capable of establishing close relationships at the social and individual levels. The trauma may remain with them for many years. They lose the joy of childhood and behave like gloomy old persons with a strong sense of cynicism. It is unfortunate that the world has so far been shortsighted in not giving priority to its children. This unjustifiable negligence, if not addressed, will lead to irreparable harm to humanity's future.

## War and Trauma

Survivors of war, genocide and torture mostly suffer from severe mental health complications. Victims include civilians in the war zones, refugees and displaced people who have escaped war and all those who directly or indirectly affected by war. Western psychiatrists focus on **post-traumatic stress disorder (PTSD)** to explain mental health problems related to war and similar traumas. The American Psychiatric Association introduced the term in the year 1980 and expanded its definition in 1987. PTSD "is a psychiatric condition that can occur in individuals who experience extremely stressful or traumatic life events" (Philip et al., 1999, p. 1). It may develop in people who have experienced a tragedy that is beyond the range of a normal human experience. It is believed that PTSD leaves negative effects on survivors' consciousness, values, feelings and the way they relate to others. The impact of PTSD may go so far as to impair the person's daily life. Symptoms of PTSD may disappear over time or develop into a chronic mental disorder.

Western psychiatrists usually focus on **intrusion**, **avoidance** and **hyperarousal** as three major characteristics of PTSD. By intrusion, they mean unexpected reoccurrences of the trauma through frequent "flashbacks" that intrude into the daily lives of survivors. People with PTSD may become emotionally dead. They may also avoid people and places — even their immediate family members — as well as matters or situations associated with the original traumatic incident. People with PTSD show constant hyper-arousal symptoms, such as sleep disorders, irritability, hyper-vigilance and lack of concentration. They feel persistently threatened by their initial traumatic event. PTSD, according to a report, "is a serious condition with significant morbidity and a high suicide rate" (Azadian et al., 1997, p. 163).

The multi-faceted atrocities of war may traumatize the entire population in a war-ravaged region – a complication known as **collective trauma**. Treatment is scarcely effective when everybody is traumatized. Trauma remains chronic and reproduces itself as long as social causes are not addressed and perpetrators continue to enjoy impunity. The whole society may suffer from an everlasting culture of pain.

Experiences of survivors of the Armenian genocide and the Holocaust show that collective trauma may persist through generations. Unfortunately, there is no magic formula for rehabilitation. Collective trauma can be alleviated through cohesive and collective efforts such as constant community support, recognition, remembrance, solidarity, communal therapy and massive cooperation.

There are hundreds of institutions around the world working to rehabilitate survivors of war, torture, genocide and crimes against humanity. But there is a dilemma in this field. Western mental health professionals have increasingly involved themselves in treatment of survivors who are mainly non-western. They work within the framework of western health care that is critiqued for "the medicalization of life." They treat their underprivileged patient from a privileged position without reflecting on their own competence and the authenticity of their discipline in relation to non-western patients. Survivors must listen to them and follow their prescriptions, while these western caregivers often have little basic knowledge about their patients' cultures or the complex realities of the wars that have affected them.

It should be noted that the impact of war on the mental health of survivors is controversial. Agencies involved in rehabilitation of survivors use two different modes of practice: (1) a **clinical approach**, which draws upon various types of medical and psychological therapies; and (2) a **holistic approach**, which combines clinical treatments with other social needs and services such as befriending, art therapy, appropriate housing, ongoing counselling, legal and immigration services, and employment skills training, just to name some. To respect cultural and linguistic barriers, most of the caregivers are selected from a background similar to that of survivors. Utilization of the services of volunteers also plays a vital role in this approach. The goal of the holistic approach is to enhance the coping capacity of torture survivors and to facilitate their participation in social life. The holistic approach has a strong base in the community. The effectiveness of the community-based holistic approach can be judged by the mental-health experience of survivors of war in Northern Ireland where, "[o]ver this 30-year period there is no evidence of a significant impact on referral rates to mental health services (Loughrey, 1997). Presumably, much of the human pain engendered during this lengthy period has been managed within the family and community" (Summerfield, 2000, p. 421).

## Working with Refugee Women
## at the Canadian Centre for Victims of Torture

Despite their tormenting experiences of torture, inhuman atrocities and irreparable bereavements, I have found war-affected women highly resilient. I have seen them demonstrating astonishing power, courage and life-force in promoting their coping capacities to overcome their traumas. I have witnessed how refugee women in Canada have successfully collected fragments of their shattered lives to build a new home here. Following are some examples from the experiences of refugee women attending the Canadian Centre for Victims of Torture (CCVT):

I.  Pearl has lost her husband and three children as a result of war in Afghanistan. She lived a devastating life in a refugee camp in Pakistan before being resettled in Canada by the government. She has nobody in the world. At the age of 60, she attends our English classes regularly despite not being able to concentrate properly. She cooks delicious Afghan food and sweets and offers them generously to students, teachers and counsellors.

2.   Canchi's husband was murdered following torture during the war in Sri Lanka. She was also detained and experienced torture there. She came to Canada with four small children and applied for asylum. We documented her torture and helped her with her refugee claim, which ended successfully. Two decades of hard work in Canada has brought its fruits. Canchi is a full-time government employee, two sons are working as professional engineers, one daughter is a nurse and the other an artist.

3.   Warda is a Moslem woman from Kosovo. She was gang-raped in the course of the war and became pregnant as a result. She was in the early stages of pregnancy when she was brought to Canada under a special government program for resettlement of Kosovar refugees. We provided her with the holistic services of the CCVT and offered her support while she was deciding about her pregnancy. She chose to keep the baby. Today, she is a prestigious social worker living happily with her child who is going to school.

Throughout my work at CCVT, I have had failures too. A distant relative brought an African war-affected woman to my office for trauma counselling and referral to one of our on-site psychiatrists. I found her highly traumatized. I offered her tea or coffee that she politely refused. I tried my best to build mutual trust. Eventually she shared her story with me while crying, sometimes slowly and at other times loudly. She had lived in a war-ravaged area occupied by government and rebel forces. One gloomy day soldiers raided her house and asked about the whereabouts of her husband and two brothers. She told them that she had no information whatsoever. They kicked her with their boots, hit her with rifle butts, and left. A few hours later, she left the house and, taking tremendous precautions, went to the mountainous areas where her loved ones were hiding in a cave. She told them the story and warned them to be extremely watchful. Next day, soldiers entered her house with her husband and brother tied up. They gang-raped her at gun-point in the presence of her family members. They then killed her husband and brothers one by one, followed by her five children. She begged them to kill her, too. They refused, saying that she should survive and suffer for the rest of her life.

The story was so horrible that I forgot about my role as a caregiver and shed tears in front of the bereaved woman and her relative. I was unable to do anything for her in that moment. I arranged a three-hour appointment for the next day to allow me to do a thorough case assessment and develop a treatment strategy. She never returned.

## Conclusion

Tyrants and plunderers have always glorified war and found virtue in it. At the same time many human rights activists emphasize the importance of peace, harmony, justice, freedom, equality, abundance and wisdom. It is a well-known fact that conflict and displacement increases **gender-based violence** (GBV), especially for women and girls. There is an utmost need for specialized GBV programs at the very beginning of an emergency situation of displacement. The focus should be on the concrete, practical steps that must be taken within the collective responsibilities of UNHCR and NGOs to alleviate the plight of affected populations. There is a long way to go in this area and failure to address this important need will have a disastrous impact. Indeed, positive change can be effected through public awareness and grassroots consciousness. But it will only be achieved through our collective and life-long endeavours. This chapter aimed to raise consciousness about the devastating impact of war on individuals and communities, particularly women and children. The chapter further emphasized the need to work with survivors of war, torture, genocide and crimes against humanity, on the one hand, and, on the other, to strengthen service organizations and anti-war agencies. It has been a trend in modern history that human rights achievements have emerged following catastrophic wars. The United Nations Organization and its Charter were created after World War II. Likewise, the UN *Declaration of Human Rights* was adopted on December 10, 1948. It set the foundation for scores of international human-rights legal instruments and a monitoring system that is in operation today. Almost all human-rights instruments are antiwar by nature. Thus working for peace is, in practice, working towards the implementation of an effective human-rights mechanism during war and peace.

## References

Ardrey, R. (1961). *African genesis: A personal investigation into the animal origins and nature of man.* New York: Dell.

Aron, A., & Caron, S. (Eds.) (1994). *Writings for a liberation psychology.* Cambridge, MA: Harvard University Press.

Asadi, M. (2004). *Living by the sword: The war addiction of America's elite.* N.p.: Lulu.

Azadian, A., Stenn, P. & Gupta, A. (1997). Aftermath of trauma: Posttraumatic stress disorder. *The Canadian Journal of Diagnosis* (February 1997).

Barnes, A. (Ed.) (2005). *Handbook of women, psychology, and the law.* San Francisco: Jossey-Bass.

Barnitz, L.A. (1999). *Child soldiers: Youth who participate in armed conflict.* Booklet No. 1 in a series on international youth issues. N.p.: Youth Advocate Program International.

Brenner, R.F. (2002). *Writing as resistance: Four women confronting the Holocaust: Edith Stein, Simone Weil, Anne Frank, Etty Hillesum.* University Park, PA: Penn State University Press.

Brown M.E., Coté, Jr., O.R, Lynne Jones, S.M. & Miller, S.E. (1998). *Theories of war and peace.* Cambridge, MA: MIT Press.

Carpenter, (2007). *Born of war: Protecting children of sexual violence survivors in conflict zones.* Bloomfield, CT: Kumarian Press.

Casey-Maslen, S. (2013). *The war report 2012.* Oxford: Oxford University Press.

Clausewitz, K.V. (1985). *Two letters on strategy.* (P. Paret & D. Moran, Trans.) Kansas: Army College Foundation, Inc.

Coleman, P. (2006). *Flashback: Posttraumatic stress disorder, suicide, and the lessons of war.* Boston: Beacon Press.

Crook, D.P. (1994). *Darwinism, war and history: The debate over the biology of war from the "Origin of*

*Species"* to the First World War. Cambridge: Cambridge University Press.

Eller, J.D. (2010). *Cruel creeds, virtuous violence: Religious violence across culture.* Buffalo, NY: Prometheus Books.

Erasmus, D. (2008). *The praise of folly.* (J. Wilson, Trans.) Rockville, MD: ARC Manor.

Erikson, K. T. (1995). *A new species of trouble: The human experience of modern disasters.* New York: W.W. Norton.

Eugene, M. (2003). *Colonialism: An international, social, cultural and political encyclopedia.* Vol. I. Santa Barbara, CA: ABC-CLIO.

Eyoh, D. & Zeleza, P.T. (Eds.) (2003). *Encyclopedia of twentieth-century African history.* London: Routledge.

Fahey J. & Armstrong, R. (1992). *A peace reader: Essential reading on war, justice, non-violence and world order.* New Jersey: Populist Press.

Ferguson, B. (1984). *Warfare, culture, and environment.* Waltham, MA: Academic Press.

Frantz, F. (1967). *Toward the African revolution.* New York, 1967. Reprint of *Pour la revolution africaine.* Paris, 1964, p. 53.

Fry, D.F. (Ed.) (2013). *War, peace and human nature: The convergence of evolutionary and cultural views.* Oxford: Oxford University Press.

Golding, W. (2007). *The lord of the flies.* New York: Penguin.

Greenbaum, C.W., Veerman, P.E. & Bacon-Shnoor, N. (2006). *Protection of children during armed political conflict.* Oxford: Hart Publishing.

Hartjen, C.A. & Priyadarsini, S. (2012). *The global victimization of children: Problems and solutions.* New York: Springer Science.

Hawkesworth, M.E. *Globalization and feminist activism.* Lanham, MD: Rowman & Littlefield.

Hedges, C. (2003). *War is a force that gives us meaning.* New York: Anchor.

Hemingway. E. (2003). *Hemingway on war.* New York: Scribner.

Hinde, R. (2008). *Ending war: A recipe.* Nottingham, England: Spokesman.

Hodge, C.C. & Nolan, C.J. (2007). *U.S. presidents and foreign policy: From 1789 to present.* Santa Barbara, CA: ABC-CLIO.

*Human Rights Watch* (2007), 19 (15[A]).

James, P. & Friedman, J. (2006). *Globalization and violence, vol. 3: Globalizing war and intervention.* London: Sage.

International Criminal Court (2011). *Rome statute of the International Criminal Court.* Retrieved from http://www.icccpi.int/iccdocs/PIDS/publications/RomeStatutEng.pdf.

Kahn, P. (2008). *The European Union.* New York: Infobase.

Kapferer, B. & Enge, B. (Eds.). *Crisis of the state: War and social upheaval.* New York: Berghahn Books.

Kegley, C. & Blanton, S. (2014). *World politics: Trend and transformation, 2014–2015.* Boston, MA: Wadsworth, 2015.

Lenin, V. (2010). *Imperialism: The highest stage of capitalism.* New York: Penguin.

Lipold, A. (2013). *The permanent establishment of peace.* N.p.: Xlibris.

Machel, G. (1996). *Report: Impact of armed conflict on children.*

Micklethwait, J. & Wooldridge, A. (2009). *God is back.* New York: Penguin.

Mossallanejad, E. (2013). Participation at the UNHCR–NGOs consultation meeting. *First Light* (Summer 2014).

Mossallanejad, E. *Torture in the age of fear.* Hamilton: Seraphim Editions.

Mueller, D.C. (2003). *Public choice III.* Cambridge: Cambridge University Press.

Nobe, C. (2009). Comfort women: Japan's military sexual slavery. *First Light* (Winter 2009).

Notes From Nowhere (Ed.) (2003). *We are everywhere: The irresistible rise of global anticapitalism.* London: Verso.

Nowrojee, B. (1996). *Shattered lives: Sexual violence during the Rwandan genocide and its aftermath.* New York: Human Rights Watch.

O'Brien, S. (1999). *Things fall apart.* Piscataway, NJ: Research & Education Association.

O'Driscoll, C. (2008). *Recognition of the just war tradition and the right to war in the twenty-first century.* New York: Palgrave Macmillan.

O'Tuathail, G.O. (1996). *Critical geopolitics.* Minneapolis, MN: University of Minnesota Press.

Philip, D., Harvey, P.D., and Yehuda, R. (1999). *Risk factors for posttraumatic stress disorder.* New York: American Psychiatric Pub., Inc.

Pittaka, A.A. (2007). *Culture of peace enabled zoom along Cyprus*. Ann Arbor, MI: ProQuest Information and Learning Company.

Pritchard, D.M. (Ed.) (2010). *War, democracy and culture in classical Athens*. Cambridge: Cambridge University Press.

*Protecting children of sexual violence survivors in conflict zones*. Bloomfield, CT: Kumanian Press.

Rosenberg, E.S. (Ed.) (2012). *A world connecting: 1870-1945*. Cambridge, MA: Harvard University Press.

Spielvogel , J. (2009). *Western civilization: Alternate volume: Since 1300*. Belmont, CA: Thomson.

Stefoff, R. (2004). *Chimpanzees*. Tarrytown, NY: Benchmark Books.

Stockholm International Peace Research Institute (2013). *SIPRI yearbook 2013: Armaments, disarmament and international security*. Oxford: Oxford University Press.

Summerfield, D. (2000). Childhood, war, refugeedom and "trauma": Three core questions for mental health professionals. *Transcultural Psychiatry, 37*, 417–433.

United Nations High Commissioner for Refugees (2014). *Syria inter-agency regional refugee response update 20–26 July 2014*. Retrieved from http://data.unhcr.org/syrianrefugees/regional.php.

United Nations High Commissioner for Refugees (2014). *2014 UNHCR regional operations profile: Latin America*. Retrieved from http://www.unhcr.org/pages/49e45be46.html.

United Nations High Commissioner for Refugees (2013, June 19). *New UNHCR report says global forced displacement at 18 year high*. Retrieved from http://www.unhcr.org/51c071816.html.

United Nations High Commissioner for Refugees (2013). *UNHCR global trends 2012: Displacement: The new 21st century challenge*. Retrieved from http://unhcr.org/globaltrendsjune2013/UNHCR%20GLOBAL% 20TRENDS%202012_V08_web.pdf.

UNICEF (2004). *The state of world's children 2005: Childhood under threat*. New York: UNICEF.

Vasquez, J.A. (1997). *The war puzzle*. Cambridge: Cambridge University Press.

Wilson, E.O. (2013). *The social conquest of earth*. New York: Liveright.

Wright, Q. (1983). *A study of war*. Chicago: University of Chicago Press.

Zinn, H. (2011). *War*. New York: Seven Stories Press.

# Part Two

# Politics of Displacement and Migration

CHAPTER EIGHT
# The Social and Political Context of Iraqi Refugee Women's Trauma

*Sajedeh Zahraei*

T his chapter draws on the author's research to present a theoretical framework
for understanding Iraqi refugee women's trauma that emphasizes the interconnections between the historical and contemporary contexts of their lives.
Drawing on theoretical frameworks of structural violence and historical trauma
enables us to illuminate the unique experiences of Arab Iraqi refugee women living
in Toronto, taking into account their transnational identities and the globalized
nature of the "war on terror." The chapter begins with a brief overview of the social
and political contexts of Iraqi refugee women's lives following the U.S.-led 2003
invasion and occupation of Iraq. It will then provide a conceptual definition of
trauma and present the key theoretical frameworks and concepts of structural
violence, continuum of violence, historical trauma, trauma in a transnational
context, and colonial trauma response. These theoretical concepts will then be
applied in the analysis of the trauma of the "war on terror" drawing on recent
studies of Iraqi refugees. The chapter also examines some of the emerging and
promising holistic approaches to addressing trauma in refugee populations. The
conclusion provides a brief summary of the main content covered in the chapter
and is followed by a specific case example as well as discussion questions to facilitate critical reflection and application of theory to practice.

Despite claims of "liberation," "freedom," and "democracy," used as justifications for the invasion of Iraq, Iraqi women's status has significantly deteriorated following the 2003 occupation. There was a significant decrease in women's labour force participation, particularly for professional women who were targeted for kidnapping and murder due to the rise in sectarian violence, fundamentalism, and more conservative gender ideologies. Illiteracy rates rose exponentially with women and girls being forced to leave schools and universities and stay home for their own safety. Increased poverty rates and unemployment, particularly among the high number of widows and female-headed households with no formal supports, led to increased prostitution and sex trafficking of Iraqi women and girls (Al-Ali, 2007; Zangana, 2007).

General conditions of lack of safety and security, lack of infrastructure, increased gender-based and sectarian violence combined with a rise in social conservatism and religious fundamentalism, poverty and lack of access to basic needs have led to displacement of millions of Iraqis, many of whom are women and children. An estimated 1.2 million to 1.4 million Iraqis fled to Syria following the 2003 occupation, seeking safety and security. Iraqi asylum seekers in Syria were not recognized as refugees by the Syrian government since Syria is not a signatory to the UN convention. These asylum seekers had no permanent residency and no work permits. They were forced to live on their own savings with limited access to health care and education, and faced ongoing threats of deportation and further violence (Al-Ali and Pratt, 2006; Amnesty International, 2008; CCR, 2006; Harper, 2008; Refugees International, 2010).

Canada's response to the Iraqi refugee crisis has been widely critiqued by human rights and refugee advocacy groups as being severely limited, fraught with bureaucratic delays, the inadequate processing of applications, a general attitude of suspicion towards, and inhumane treatment of, applicants, high refusal rates and family separations. Despite its repeated commitment to take in about 20,000 Iraqi refugees, Canada has accepted only about 12,000 Iraqi refugees since 2006, and about half of them have come under the private sponsorship program (CCR, 2006 and 2013; CIC News Release, January 15, 2013; Keung, 2011).

Contrary to the national mythologies of Canada as a multicultural, humanitarian, peacekeeping nation, Canada has been a staunch ally in the U.S. imperialist mission and the invasions of Afghanistan and Iraq. Canada has made explicit commitments to support the U.S. in the war in Afghanistan, providing troops and resources, and being involved in peacekeeping and combat missions. Canada has also been a key player in the invasion and reconstruction efforts in Iraq, supplying war planners, aircrafts, pilots, and soldiers embedded in British forces on the ground supporting the invasion (Engler, 2009; Fawn, 2008).

Since the September 11, 2001 attacks in the United States, Canada has implemented a series of anti-terrorism measures including the *Anti-terrorism Act* of 2001; the enactment of security certificates under the *Immigration and Refugee Protection Act (IRPA)*; Canada's Passenger Protect Program; and the more recent Beyond the Border agreement with the United States in 2011. These measures have had differential and severely detrimental effects on Arabs and Muslims in Canada, including increased racial profiling, unlawful detentions, torture and deportations (Bahdi, 2003; CAF and CAIR-CAN, 2005; CAIR-CAN, 2005; CCLA, 2010; Siddiqui, 2008). Within this backdrop of militarization, securitization and criminalization, the Canadian government has also taken drastic measures that have amounted to a complete overhaul of Canada's immigration, refugee determination, and citizenship policies. Some of these policies and regulations have included the introduction of Bill C-31 (*Protecting Canada's Immigration System Act*); Bill C-43 (*Faster Removal of Foreign Criminals Act*); cuts to the Interim Federal Health Program; cuts to settlement funding and services; and changes to citizenship eligibility criteria and residency requirements (Albiom and Cohl, 2012; Bhuyan et al., 2013; Zahraei et al., forthcoming).

## Definitions

**Structural Violence:** Social injustice and exploitation with unequal power and unequal life chances as its hallmark, embedded within violent structures. It is violence that is exerted systematically (indirectly) by everyone who belongs to a certain social order. Structural violence of oppression and inequalities is embodied as adverse outcomes such as death, injury, and trauma.

**Continuum of Violence:** All forms of controlling processes ranging from everyday micro-aggressions, social exclusion, denial of social support to vulnerable populations, to militarization of everyday life and heightened security.

**Everyday Violence:** Violence that is socially incremental and is often experienced as expected, routine, even justified.

**Trauma:** Shock, wound.

**Historical Trauma:** Concept used to examine historical and social events that have resulted in intergenerational stress responses among individuals and communities. It is conceptualized as a complex collective trauma inflicted on a group of people who share a specific group identity or affiliation. It is cumulative, intergenerational, and is linked to a variety of psychological and social responses and multiple negative health outcomes such as depression, self-destructive behaviour, substance abuse, anxiety, guilt and chronic bereavement.

**Multi-level Trauma Framework:** Explores the impact of historical trauma at three interrelated levels — individuals, families and communities — recognizing that responses to historical trauma are varied and complex.

**Colonial Trauma Response (CTR):** A framework that takes into account the complex interaction of historical and contemporary traumatic events within the context of colonization.

**Transnational Trauma:** Frameworks that examine trauma in a transnational context, take a critical perspective on the increasing traumatization of collective violence, and rethink trauma in a transnational world paying particular attention to the social, cultural, historical and political contexts.

## Conceptualizing Trauma

Canadian studies relating to the "war on terror" seem to be focused primarily on its implications for citizenship, belonging, privacy and human rights. Not enough attention has been paid to the potential social, health, and mental health consequences of the "war on terror" and its impact on the everyday experiences of individuals, families, and communities of Arab and Muslim origins living in Canada. This is the main focus of this chapter since the "war on terror," in its multiple facets, is experienced as "trauma," which could have serious and ongoing consequences for these communities as a whole. In this context the word **trauma** is not meant in terms of its medical/psychiatric definition and diagnostic symptoms, but rather in its broad sense as a "wound" or a "shock." The Oxford dictionary defines trauma as "a deeply distressing or disturbing experience; [mass noun] emotional shock following a stressful event or a physical injury, which may lead to long-term neurosis," and traces the origins of the word to the seventeenth century and a Greek word meaning "wound."

Several scholars have critiqued the inadequacy of post-traumatic stress disorder (PTSD) to describe the intricacies of trauma caused by racism, colonization and wars, structural, political and economic violence, globalization and capitalism, and call for alternative broader definitions of trauma (Burstow, 2003; Evans-Campbell, 2008; Zarowsky and Pederson, 2000). Theoretical frameworks of structural violence and historical trauma have been applied to various populations who have experienced oppression and structural and political violence.

## Structural Violence

Galtung (1990) defines **structural violence** as social injustice and exploitation with unequal power and unequal life chances as its hallmark, embedded within violent structures. In this definition, the threat of violence is also seen as violence. Galtung (1990) further elaborates "that a violent structure leaves marks not only on the body but also on the mind and the spirit." Therefore, the needs deficits created by direct and structural violence can lead to individual trauma or, if experienced by a group, **collective trauma**. This trauma then "can sediment into the collective subconscious and become raw material for major historical processes and events" (Galtung, 1990, p. 295).

Paul Farmer (2004) builds on the structural violence framework introduced by Galtung and approaches it from a critical medical anthropological point of view in studying the modern epidemics of AIDS and tuberculosis (TB) in Haiti. Farmer defines **structural violence** as "violence that is exerted systematically – that is, indirectly – by everyone who belongs to a certain social order" (Farmer, 2004, p. 307). Farmer (2004) further argues that when one studies the experience of people who are subjected to different forms of oppression such as marginalization, racism and gender inequalities, structural violence is embodied as adverse material outcomes such as death, injury, illness, subjugation, stigmatization, psychological terror, epidemic diseases, human rights violations and genocide. In his book *Pathologies of Power: Health, Human Rights, and the New War on the Poor*, Farmer (2005) argues that human rights violations are "symptoms of deeper pathologies of power" and are closely interconnected to social and economic rights violations that determine whose human rights will be violated and who will be protected. In order to better understand the dynamics and distribution of suffering, our analytical model must be geographically broad and historically deep, recognizing the increasingly interconnected world that we live in as well as simultaneously considering the social factors (such as race, gender and class) that render individuals and groups differentially vulnerable to extreme suffering.

Nancy Scheper-Hughes and Philippe Bourgois (2004) offer a critique of Farmer's notion of structural violence, arguing that the concept needs to be further elaborated to avoid being too linear and deterministic, and to relate it to other forms of violence and power in everyday life. Bourgois and Scheper-Hughes extend Farmer's analysis to articulate how "everyday life is shaped by the historical pro-cesses and contemporary politics of global political economy as well as by local discourse and culture" (comment in Farmer, 2004, p. 318). Scheper-Hughes and Bourgois (2004) propose a theory of a violence continuum. The key aspect of the **continuum of violence theory** offered by Scheper-Hughes and Bourgois (2004) is the notion that permitted everyday acts of violence are part of the same dynamic that enables war crimes and genocide. **Everyday violence**, they argue, "is socially incremental and often experienced by perpetrators, collaborators, by-standers – and even by victims themselves — as expected, routine, even justified" (Scheper-Hughes and Bourgois, 2004, p. 22). As the authors indicate, the con-tinuum of violence includes all forms of controlling processes ranging from social exclusion and dehumanizing practices that deny social support and human care to vulnerable populations, to the militarization of everyday life in the form of "super-maximum prisons" and the "heightened technologies of security" practices.

## Historical Trauma and Colonial Trauma Response

For over a decade, the concept of historical trauma has been used to examine historical and social events that have resulted in intergenerational stress responses among individuals and communities. Different terms have been used to describe the concept of historical trauma in the literature, including "survivor guilt," "inter-generational grief and bereavement," "post-traumatic slave syndrome," "collective trauma," "intergenerational trauma" and "multigenerational trauma" (Brave Heart, 1999a, 1999b, 2000; Brave Heart and Debruyn, 1998; Danieli, 1998; Degruy Leary, 2005; Kellerman, 2001; Krieger, 2001). Historical trauma has been used to study several historically oppressed communities including Jewish Holocaust survivors, African Americans dealing with the consequences of slavery, and Japanese Americans after internment. More recently and predominantly, it has been based on the experiences of Native American populations, building on the seminal work of Maria Yellow Horse Brave Heart and her colleagues (Brave Heart, 1999a, 1999b, 2003; Brave Heart and DeBruyn, 1998). **Historical trauma** has been conceptualized as a collective complex trauma inflicted on a group of people who share a specific group identity or affiliation. It is cumulative, intergenerational and is linked to a variety of psychological and social responses

143

and multiple negative health outcomes such as depression, self-destructive behaviour, substance abuse, anxiety, guilt and chronic bereavement (Brave Heart, 1999a, 1999b, 2000; Brave Heart and DeBruyn, 1998; Estrada, 2009; Evans-Campbell, 2008). Several scholars have used models of structural violence and historical trauma in studying trauma in Aboriginal communities in Canada and examining their historical and contemporary contexts (Jacklin, 2008; Pearce et al., 2008; Wesley-Esquimaux and Smolewski, 2004). These studies foreground the history of colonial European contact and the resulting genocide and devastation in explaining the physical, spiritual, emotional and psychological trauma characterized by deep and unresolved grief that has persisted over multiple generations of Aboriginal communities.

Although there are significant historical and contemporary contextual differences between Aboriginal communities and Arab/Muslim communities in Canada, these findings point to potential consequences of the trauma of the "war on terror" experienced by Arab Iraqi women in Canada. Theoretical concepts of historical trauma are relevant to examining the situation of Arab Iraqi women due to histories of colonization and ongoing American and European intervention in the Middle East including the recent U.S.-led occupation of Iraq. However, since the majority of Arab Iraqi women in Canada are recent immigrants with transnational ties and due to the globalized nature of the "war on terror" with its extensive networks of international collaborations and border controls, new analytical models of trauma are needed to reflect the uniqueness of their experiences and their potential consequences. Some relevant analytical models explored below include concepts of **transnational trauma** from the field of transcultural psychiatry (Zarowsky and Pederson, 2000), and the multi-level trauma theory, **colonial trauma response**, developed by Evans-Campbell and Walters (2006).

## Trauma in a Transnational Context

Zarowsky and Pederson (2000) invite academics and practitioners in the field of transcultural psychiatry to "take a critical perspective on the increasing 'traumatisation' of collective violence" and to rethink trauma in a transnational world, paying particular attention to the social, cultural, historical and political contexts. The authors argue that highly individualized models of trauma emphasizing healing of "ethically and politically neutralized emotions and memories" are inadequate, do not recognize individuals as part of multiple overlapping social networks and miss key aspects of collective experiences of trauma (Zarowsky and Pederson 2000, p. 292).

Pederson (2002) explores the health implications of political violence, ethnic conflicts and contemporary wars in Latin America for Amerindian populations, arguing that their poor health status is a clear reflection of the powerful interplay of their colonial past, a history of socio-political and structural violence, trauma, and globalization processes that have contributed to increasing economic and health disparities. Similarly, Antonio Estrada (2009) develops a theoretical perspective for examining the health status of Mexican Americans in the southwestern United States, highlighting the legacy of Spanish colonialism and Anglo–American neo-colonialism and drawing parallels to historical trauma among Native Americans, African Americans, and Pacific Islanders. Estrada argues that the history of colonialism, dispossession and subordination, combined with current anti-Mexican sentiments, the militarization of the U.S.-Mexican border and subordination of Mexican nationals have led to internalization of negative stereotypes, self-hate, alienation, and marginalization which over time have contributed to negative health outcomes, including increased rates of substance abuse, hypertension, metabolic syndrome, anti-social personality disorders and Type 2 diabetes mellitus across generations of Mexican Americans. Estrada emphasizes that the identification and examination of social and historical determinants of health that have influenced the health status of individuals within a particular racial/ethnic group are key components in developing interventions that help address the negative health outcomes of historical trauma (Estrada, 2009, p. 331).

In addition to the necessity of exploring historical and social determinants of mental health, several authors have also emphasized the importance of examining **community strengths and resilience** in the face of historical and collective traumas (Denham, 2008; Jacklin, 2007; Zarowsky and Pederson, 2000). Using person-centered ethnography, Denham (2008) highlights how a four-generation Native American family frames their traumatic past into oral histories and narratives that transmit resilience strategies and family identity. Denham's (2008) research affirms the diverse responses to historical trauma and highlights the importance of examining alternative characteristics or manifestations of historical trauma that are often overlooked in the literature. Therefore, as Denham articulates, it is important to distinguish between historical trauma and historical trauma response (Denham, 2008, p. 393).

Several scholars have discussed the limitations of the concept of historical trauma. Denham (2008) reviews empirical challenges raised in the literature around the validity of historical trauma transmission and questions the extent to which, like PTSD, a diagnosis of historical trauma is being used for political or biomedical agendas. Estrada (2009) raises concerns around the measurement, specificity (i.e., specific causes and effects), and conceptual limitations of historical trauma itself. As Evans-Campbell (2008) articulates, standard diagnostic PTSD models account for some of the symptoms but fail to explain the impact of multiple traumas over generations, account for mechanisms of historical trauma transmission or explain the relationship between historical and contemporary traumatic experiences. Although the concept of historical trauma has been developed to address this gap and has been applied to several communities including holocaust survivors, Japanese Americans, and Aboriginal communities, it has been conceptualized in broad and sometimes conflicting ways (Evans-Campbell, 2008, p. 317).

To address the limitations discussed above, Evans-Campbell (2008) presents a **multi-level framework** for exploring the impact of historical trauma at three interrelated levels, individuals, families and communities — a framework which will be further elaborated on below. The framework recognizes that responses to historical trauma are varied and complex. Most research has focused on the individual-level responses, which encompass physical and mental health issues that could include symptoms of PTSD, anxiety, grief and depression. Previous research has also shown that survivors and their descendants have varying responses to trauma, while some individuals exhibit negative symptomatology; many others show resilience in spite of their histories (Evans-Campbell, 2008). Responses at the family level are less researched, however, and may include loss of traditional culture and values, high rates of physical illness and alcoholism, family violence and internalized racism. Research among diverse communities has also shown that descendants of historic trauma survivors maintain a current interest in ancestral trauma and suggest intergenerational trauma can be an organizing factor in families (Evans-Campbell, 2008). As Evans-Campbell indicates, although the link between traumatic events and community-level responses may be clear intuitively, traditional empirical research has not focused on this aspect. However, emerging historical trauma research recognizes the collective group impacts of traumatic events, particularly with respect to the forced residential schooling of indigenous children and its devastating lasting impacts on individuals, families and entire communities through the imposition of assimilationist strategies and loss of language and cultural traditions. These effects have been manifested through weakened social structures, higher rates of suicide, higher rates of alcoholism and child maltreatment that consequently may make the communities more susceptible to negative second-order effects (Evans-Campbell, 2008, p. 328). The multi-level framework advanced by Evans-Campbell emphasizes the fact that individual and family responses are experienced "within the context of a traumatized community" (Evans-Campbell, 2008, p. 328); thus the three levels are clearly interrelated and may reciprocally influence each other.

Moreover, Evans-Campbell (2008) highlights two key factors that influence the severity of historical trauma. The first factor is the crucial influence of communication around the traumatic events, both at the familial level and the community level. At the familial level, secrecy and parental silence around the traumatic events contributes to feelings of confusion, guilt and resentment which are significantly related to poor mental health outcomes such as paranoia and anxiety for children and grandchildren of survivors. At the community level, societal reactions such as silence, indifference, disbelief, and avoidance may further silence survivors and increase their sense of isolation, loneliness and mistrust. The second key influencing factor is the strong interplay between historical trauma and high rates of contemporary assaults and micro-aggressions experienced by indigenous communities that are themselves traumatic. As Evans-Campbell (2008) suggests, these everyday contemporary traumatic events are, from the perspective of indigenous communities, clearly linked to the historical traumatic events. Hence, they take on additional emotional and cultural significance that makes historical trauma the ongoing context of their daily lives.

*Roots and Routes of Displacement and Trauma*

Evans-Campbell and Walters (2006) build on the historical trauma literature and develop the **colonial trauma response (CTR)** framework that takes into account the complex interaction of historical and contemporary traumatic events within the context of colonization. As Evans-Campbell (2008) elaborates: "CTR reactions may arise as an individual experiences a contemporary discriminatory event or micro-aggression that serves to connect him or her with a collective and often historical sense of injustice and trauma" (Evans-Campbell, 2008, p. 333).

## Trauma of the "War on Terror" for Iraqi Refugees

The following section uses this theoretical framework to analyze studies of Iraqi refugees examining the mental health consequences of the "war on terror" with its accompanying negative media portrayals, racism, discrimination, and the ensuing more restrictive immigration and refugee policies over the past several years. The discussion will then focus on findings from the author's study of Iraqi refugee women in Toronto in order to illustrate the social and political context of their historical and contemporary trauma.

Within the post-9/11 context, several studies have documented the adverse consequences of the negative media coverage on Arabs and Muslims in Canada (Caidi and McDonald, 2008; Hirji, 2006; Rostam and Haverkamp, 2009). Findings from these studies have illustrated the close association between negative portrayal of Iraqis, biased reporting and participants' experiences of discrimination and identity conflicts. The psychological impacts of these experiences ranged from anger, shame and humiliation to lack of trust, changes to their sense of identity and worldviews and a general sense of pessimism, hopelessness and resentment. Individual responses, however, were varied and diverse, including increased reliance on alternative news sources, turning to faith, connecting to families and increased social and political activity. These findings are consistent with other U.S.-based studies demonstrating the relationship between increased anti-Muslim, anti-Arab bias post-9/11 and higher psychological distress, poorer health status and lower levels of happiness among these communities (Amer, 2005; Hassouneh and Kulwicki, 2007; Moradi and Hasan, 2004; Rippy and Newman, 2006; Padela and Heisler, 2010).

In addition to psychological distress related to experiences of discrimination, a number of studies of Iraqi refugees living in the U.S. have reported a higher prevalence of trauma histories and mental health difficulties such as PTSD, depression and anxiety among Iraqi refugees (Hassouneh and Kulwicki, 2007; Jamil et al., 2002, 2006, and 2007). For instance, in a pilot study of mental health in 30 Arab Muslim women, Hassouneh and Kulwicki (2007) found a strikingly high number of the participants (93%) had experienced trauma in their life time with 87% reporting general disaster (the vast majority of which was attributed to war and military occupation related incidents) and 30% reporting physical and sexual abuse as specific types of experienced trauma. Moreover, as Jamil et al. (2007) have shown, recent Iraqi refugees, compared to other Iraqi immigrants, were more likely to have been exposed to war-related trauma as well as higher levels of acculturation stress and discrimination in the post-9/11 U.S. climate.

One major limitation of these studies is the reliance on the use of culturally inappropriate western psychiatric measures taken from studies of U.S. veterans to study the mental health issues of this refugee population. There is a tendency to focus on acculturation stress while failing to examine the impact of the "war on terror," including increased surveillance, scrutiny, discrimination, racial profiling and the ongoing trauma of the 2003 occupation and current violence in Iraq.

Shoeb et al. (2007) present one of the rare studies of mental health issues among Arab Americans that uses ethnographic interviewing to explore narratives of Iraqi refugees and critiques the application of structured clinical interviews and the use of standardized PTSD checklists with this population, favouring the exploration of indigenous idioms of distress. The study involved the analysis of life stories of Iraqi refugees living in Dearborn, Michigan, home to the largest Iraqi refugee population in North America, to examine issues of identity, home, and exile. Participants in this study described their struggles with defining identity and home in exile within the context of historical and contemporary trauma, war and political violence in Iraq. They expressed varied views on belonging in America, reflecting their diverse vantage points based on a variety of factors including their past experiences, immigration history and level of acculturation and social integration. Shoeb et al. (2007) found that despite the varying views and experiences, faith emerged as a central construct in the narratives of study participants, defining their identity, home, and future in the face of exile, political violence and war. Their religious faith enabled them to make sense of their pain, get through their daily struggles, and gave them hope in their future. This finding highlights the need to go beyond traditional ways of conceptualizing trauma and sheds light on the importance of understanding individuals' meaning systems and associated coping strategies to develop possible intervention strategies aimed at strengthening individual and community resilience.

Other studies of Iraqi refugees in Europe and Australia have examined the psychological sequelae of loss and trauma in connection with family influences, ongoing threat of violence for family members living in conflict zones and the availability of social supports (Gorst-Unsworth and Goldenbergh, 1998; Nickerson et al., 2010; Nickerson et al., 2011a). Findings from these studies emphasize the significance of loss, trauma, and ongoing threat of violence for family living in conflict zones, in considerations of the impact of refugee trauma. These studies further indicate that the availability of social support, particularly affective social support, is an important factor in alleviating PTSD and depressive symptoms. Therefore, they underscore the importance of providing integrated rehabilitation programming along with facilitating the availability of social supports and family reunion.

As discussed earlier, the majority of studies of Iraqi refugees in diaspora have primarily relied on psychiatric medical conceptualizations to examine the mental health outcomes of Iraqi refugees. Although some have taken into account pre-

and post-migration experiences and socio-demographic factors, the general tendency has been to neglect the overall historical, political, economic, and exclusionary policy contexts shaping the lives of Iraqi refugees. A number of recent studies have focused their attention on the relationship between more restrictive immigration policies adopted by countries of the global north and the impact on refugees' mental health outcomes and their resettlement experiences in their host countries. There is growing concern about the status of asylum seekers in connection to the adoption of more restrictive immigration and refugee policies. These concerns range from allegations of abuse and untreated medical and psychiatric illnesses to suicidal behaviour, hunger strikes and outbreaks of violence in detention centres (Silove et al., 2000). Mounting evidence shows that post-migration stress faced by asylum seekers complicates the effects of previous trauma, placing them at further risk for ongoing PTSD and other psychiatric symptoms (Mansouri and Cauchi, 2007; Silove et al., 2000; Silove 2002; Steel et al., 2006). Additional studies conducted in Australia, Sweden and the Netherlands provide further evidence linking post-migration resettlement stress, restricted access to rights and services and temporary immigration status to poor mental health outcomes for refugees (Laban et al., 2005; Lindencrona et al., 2008; Nickerson et al., 2011).

Although most of the studies discussed above are based on the Australian and European contexts, they have direct relevance to Canada, which is increasingly adopting similar policies of deterrence, detention and deportation of refugees. Some of the key recent immigration policy changes affecting refugees seeking safety and protection in Canada include the introduction of Bill C-31, which drastically altered Canada's refugee determination system creating different classes of refugees subject to differential treatments, processing timelines, and differential rights; changes to refugee sponsorship regulations; the introduction of regulations facilitating the cessation of refugee protected status and loss of permanent residency; the introduction of the Assisted Voluntary Return Program, which facilitates the deportation of refugees to their country of origin; drastic cuts and changes to services and benefits afforded to refugees and refugee claimants; and cuts to the Interim Federal Health Program, which provides basic health coverage for refugees.

Research interviews conducted with recent Iraqi refugee women in Toronto illustrate the ways in which the structural violence of state policies contributes to their increased precariousness and vulnerability (Zahraei, 2014). Iraqi women's loss of status, poverty, lack of access to basic needs and human rights violations following the 2003 occupation, continue with their displacement into neighbouring countries such as Syria and Jordan, and into their resettlement in Canada. Interviews with Iraqi refugee women have shown that their interactions with social services, health care and educational systems are beset by multiple barriers, lack of trust, and different processes of social exclusion, ranging from lack of access, language and cultural barriers, anti-refugee sentiments, accusations of fraud and abuse of the system and inadequate supports and resources. Along with other Arabs and Muslims, the exclusionary refugee and immigration policies in Canada, securitization, racial profiling, Islamophobia, and everyday micro-aggressions and symbolic acts of violence facilitate Iraqi refugee women's social exclusion, lack of access to social citizenship rights and violations of human rights. In this context of structural violence, racism and social exclusion, Iraqi women's experiences of historical trauma of war, occupation and gender-based violence are further complicated and intensified by their contemporary trauma.

## Emerging Practices in Addressing Refugee Women's Trauma

The following section provides an overview of some of the emerging and promising practices in addressing trauma healing in refugees, as identified by the National Centre of Trauma Informed Care in a comprehensive review conducted by Blanch (2008) entitled *Transcending Violence: Emerging Models for Trauma Healing in Refugee Communities*. Consistent with the multi-level trauma framework presented in this paper, the primary focus of this section is on discussing community-based approaches that address trauma on multiple levels of intervention.

Adopting a **holistic public health framework** in responding to trauma in refugee populations entails a focus on wellness rather than illness and utilizing **strengths-based approaches** that emphasize the natural resilience of refugees. Moreover, embracing a public health approach to refugee trauma necessitates addressing social determinants of health such as housing, income, employment and other essential supports. Further implications of adopting a public health approach as outlined by Blanch (2008) include a move away from pathologizing or overgeneralizing the suffering of refugees; providing **trauma-informed services**; and taking a **population health approach** that promotes prevention and community-level interventions with a human rights focus. This approach is of particular importance in the context of increasing border controls, and the adoption of more restrictive immigration and refugee policies by many countries around the world.

As we have seen in the Canadian context over the past several years, recent changes to Canada's refugee determination policies as well as cuts to refugee health benefits and social entitlements have had adverse consequences for many refugee and asylum seeking women (Albiom and Cohl, 2012; Alaggia et al., 2009; Bhuyan et al., 2013; CCR, OCASI, MTCSALC, COP, 2012). Several refugee advocacy groups, violence-against-women service providers, and health and social service providers have joined forces and established networks to advocate for the reversal of these policies and for the protection of the rights of refugee and non-status women who are among the most vulnerable groups in our society (CCR, 2012; CCR, OCASI, MTCSALC, COP, 2012; Douglas, Go, and Blackstock, 2012; METRAC, 2012). Moreover, multiple levels of government, provincial health authorities, health and social service providers are adopting a population health approach that recognizes the importance of social determinants of health in addressing unjust health disparities affecting immigrants and refugees in Canada. There is widespread acknowledgement and growing evidence to demonstrate the declining physical and mental health of refugees and migrant populations due to racism, social exclusion, poverty, unemployment or under-employment and lack of access to necessary health and social services and supports (Khanlou, 2009; Mental Health Commission of Canada, 2009; Toronto Public Health, 2011 and 2013).

In a recent immigrant mental health policy brief, Khanlou (2009) articulates a **systems approach to mental health promotion** for migrants. This approach uses a multi-layered framework that outlines strategies at the individual (micro level: e.g., age, gender, cultural background), intermediate (mezzo level: e.g., family and social support networks; acculturation), and systems (macro level: e.g., economic barriers, appropriate services, access to healthcare, racism and discrimination) levels. This approach also recognizes the intersecting and interconnected nature of many of these factors that influence and complicate health outcomes for many individuals and communities at risk. The policy brief contains several recommendations aimed at improving migrant wellbeing that have particular relevance to addressing refugee women's trauma, including the need to support integrated community-based mental health services that are gender specific; the need to recognize challenges, strengths and resilience of migrant groups; and the need to address the social determinants of health (Khanlou, 2009, p. 16). Similarly, Vasilevska et al. (2010) propose the following promising practices for promoting refugee mental health at the front-line and agency levels. At the front-line level, Vasilevska et al.'s (2010) findings emphasize the importance of establishing rapport and trust, listening to refugees as experts on their own mental health, providing linguistically and culturally appropriate services, and using flexible case-management approaches that recognize the ongoing and often intertwined nature of larger settlement issues as key components of promoting refugee mental health in direct practice. The authors propose that these front-line practices could further be strengthened by agency-level practices aimed at fostering strategic partnerships, serving clients where they live and adapting services to their needs, and providing intensive, consistent and predictable services that are flexible, holistic and culturally competent (Vasilevska et al., 2010). Similar **psychosocial approaches** seem to be increasingly implemented in developing countries addressing the needs of internally displaced refugees. Psychosocial programs address a full array of physical and mental health needs in addition to clinical treatment, including specialized mental health services, recreational and social support programs, housing and legal assistance, and income and employment programs that emphasize the importance of work and meaningful activity (Blanch, 2008). Several studies in post-conflict countries such as Bosnia, Peru, Namibia and Guatemala have addressed trauma among internally displaced refugees by providing psychosocial support groups, community workshops on personal and interpersonal empowerment, and facilitated community reflection groups. These programs have also tended to focus on rebuilding trust and social support networks through education and discussion at the community level (Fabri, 2011).

Women and girls comprise about half (48% in 2011 and 2012) of refugee populations seeking safety from war, political violence, and sectarian and gender-based violence (UNHCR, 2012; UNHCR Global Trends, 2012). In situations of war, genocide and political violence, women are often victims of systematic rape, torture and other forms of gender-based violence, such as restricted mobility and participation in public life, honour killings and domestic violence. Upon displacement and resettlement, refugee women continue to experience different forms of gender-based violence and social exclusion that render them more vulnerable to developing mental health problems. Gender-based trauma programs recognize women's vulnerability to suffering more traumatic events, including gender-based violence both pre- and post- resettlement, and their higher risk of discrimination and exploitation in their adopted homeland (Blanch, 2008). These vulnerabilities are further exacerbated by the loss of status, loss of family, loss of social support networks, social isolation, and multiple burden of caregiving experienced by many refugee women. Several research studies have shown that women who have experienced violence and trauma are at higher risk of developing PTSD, depression and anxiety disorders. Gender-based trauma programs take these vulnerabilities into account. They aim to create environments of safety and promote advocacy, empowerment and a multi-sectoral approach to abuse prevention. In addition, they address the unique needs of women and build on participants' existing strengths and resilience (Blanch, 2008). Moreover, in a systematic review of mental health and psychosocial support interventions for sexual and gender-based violence in areas of armed conflict, Tol et al. (2013) indicate that counselling and strengthening community-based supports are the most commonly used interventions in humanitarian settings. These interventions include individual and group counselling, cognitive behavioural therapy, and psychosocial interventions such as traditional healing, medical services, skills training and micro-credit loans. However, Tol et al. (2013) emphasize the need for further research and evaluation to identify the most effective strategies to improve the well-being of these populations. To that end, trauma-informed care is an approach that is increasingly being used in mental health and addictions programs for women.

**Trauma-informed practices** are evidence-based approaches that have developed over the past decade in the mental health and substance use systems (Blanch, 2008; Jean Tweed Centre, 2013). Trauma-informed practices are integrated into existing systems in order to facilitate the creation of welcoming, appropriate and effective services for individuals. A trauma-informed approach to services acknowledges the prevalence of trauma and its profound impacts on all individuals involved with organizations, staff and teams. As Blanch (2008) states, although trauma-informed practices were not specifically developed for refugee populations, the "model is based on acknowledging the pervasive impact of violence, building on people's natural strengths and capacities, and empowering individuals to define their own problems" (p. 25). Some key considerations need to be taken into account when applying this model to refugee women, including the recognition of cultural variations in understanding and addressing trauma, the availability of linguistic and culturally competent services, and the establishment of trauma-informed partnerships with relevant services that the women are likely to utilize (Blanch, 2008; Jean Tweed, 2013). As discussed earlier, the provision of effective, culturally competent gender-based trauma interventions necessitates centering refugee women's voices, contextualizing their experiences, and broadening our understanding of trauma beyond individualized pathologizing conceptualizations to include historical, structural analyses of trauma and holistic models of intervention.

## Conclusion

This chapter presented a theoretical framework for understanding refugee women's trauma that builds on theoretical models of structural violence, historical trauma and multi-level colonial trauma response theory. A key aspect of this theoretical framework is its shift away from limited psychiatric conceptualizations of trauma that pathologize refugee women's experiences. This framework resists de-politicized and de-historicized conceptualizations of refugee women's trauma, and instead allows us to examine the interconnections between their past and present experiences of trauma. Through a discussion of Iraqi refugee women's experiences in the context of the "war on terror," the chapter illustrated the complex, multi-layered aspects of trauma that are shaped by the social and political context of refugee women's everyday lives. More restrictive immigration and refugee policies, along with everyday experiences of racism and discrimination, have facilitated the social exclusion of Iraqi refugee women and further complicated their historical traumas. Therefore, it is paramount to recognize and build on refugee women's strength, resilience and agency in the face of the multiple adversities they experience. Additionally, this chapter has emphasized the need to move beyond medically-based individual treatments to incorporate holistic community-based and population-based interventions that promote social determinants of health and advocate for human rights, equity, and social justice.

## Case Study and Reflective Questions

The following case example is taken from the author's research interview conducted in 2012 as part of a research study of Iraqi refugee women in Toronto. The name used is a pseudonym and certain facts are changed or withheld to protect the study participant's anonymity.

Sundus is a 30-year-old Muslim married woman who was trained as a computer scientist and worked for one of the universities in Iraq. She and her three sisters were highly educated and grew up in an upper middle-class family. Both her parents were working professionals and held moderate views with respect to religion and the expectations they held for their daughters. Sundus was used to enjoying a certain level of personal freedom and loved her job. However, all of this changed after the 2003 war and the rise in sectarian violence, as well as the targeting of female professionals by fundamentalist militia groups. She was increasingly under pressure to start wearing the hijab and quit her job and stay at home. She felt threatened on a daily basis when she went to work, and did not know whether she would make it safely there and back. Women working in various professions were threatened and kidnapped on a daily basis. These conditions of violence, harassment and fear forced her and her family to leave Iraq and go to Syria in 2006.

While in Syria, she managed to find part-time employment as an office assistant. This helped her cover her personal expenses while her parents covered living expenses from their savings. Her older sisters had already left Iraq and were living in various countries in Europe. Life in Syria offered a certain level of safety but was still insecure due to their lack of immigration status there. Sundus did not see a future for herself in Syria, even though she had met her Syrian fiancé there and had intended to marry him. She and her parents had applied for asylum through the UN and had been accepted as convention refugees. After a few years of waiting, her file was processed and she was accepted to move to Canada as a Government Assisted Refugee, but her parents were not accepted and had to remain in Syria.

Sundus moved to Canada about three years ago. She went back to Syria to marry her fiancé about two years ago and has been trying to sponsor her husband since then. As is the case for other Government Assisted Refugees, Sundus had received a loan from the Canadian government to help cover her travel expenses to Canada. The agreement was that she would pay off the loan by monthly instalments. During the first year of her arrival, Sundus received financial assistance from the government but the monthly payments she received were barely enough to cover the rent for her small basement apartment. She found part-time employment in customer service within the first three months of her arrival so she could supplement her income. She was also making regular monthly payments to pay back her loan.

By the time she went back to Syria to get married, she had made all the loan payments on time, but missed the last payment because she had gone away and had forgotten to mail it. While she was away, Citizenship and Immigration Canada sent her a letter about the late payment, but it went to her previous address and she never received it. As a result of the missed payment of $104, the sponsorship application for her husband was cancelled. She made the last payment upon her return, but this was not communicated to the Canadian consulate in Syria where her husband was following up on his application. Shortly after, the political situation in Syria had deteriorated and the Canadian consulate was shut down. All Iraqi refugee files were transferred to Jordan for processing. When I met with Sundus, she was desperately trying to find out where her husband's sponsorship application stood. She had faxed proof of the last loan payment to the immigration processing office here in Canada several times and had provided a copy to her husband to show the Canadian consulate in Syria. She had contacted her local MP and engaged a lawyer to see if they could get answers on her behalf, but all her efforts were unsuccessful. Her husband and her parents remained trapped in Syria amid deteriorating political conditions and increasing violence.

By this time, Sundus was working full-time in customer service. About six months ago, she decided to start wearing the hijab as her way of protecting herself. Although she had resisted wearing the hijab in Iraq, she felt this was necessary now. She felt vulnerable as a young woman living alone and working as a waitress in a restaurant. She wanted to avoid any potential problems with men who frequented the restaurant. She thought she would wear the hijab temporarily for a few months until her husband came to Canada. However, once she started wearing the hijab, she began to be treated differently from other people she encountered. She was no longer able to work downtown where she used to work. She felt confined to working in Middle Eastern restaurants, in neighbour-hoods that were predominantly Arab and Muslim. She noticed even the bus driver refused to stop for her when she was running to catch the bus. She had started out wearing the hijab as a means of self-protection, but now it was working to her detriment. She was still weighing whether to keep wearing the hijab or not. She did not want the hijab to turn into another obstacle for her preventing her from moving ahead in her future career goals. Although she had had some positive experiences with some service providers and a few other people she had encountered, overall she felt alone and isolated.

## Reflective Questions

1. In your opinion, what are the different forms of violence Sundus has encountered in Iraq, in Syria and in Canada?
2. What are the consequences of these different types of violence in Sundus' life?
3. In what ways has Sundus responded to the historical and contemporary events in her life?
4. What approaches and strategies would you use in working with Sundus?

## References

Al-Ali, N. (2007). *Iraqi women: Untold stories from 1948 to the present*. London: Zed Books.

Al-Ali, N. & Pratt, N. (2006). Women in Iraq: Beyond the rhetoric. *Middle East Report (MERIP) 239*, 18–23. Retrieved from http://wrap.warwick.ac.uk/1090/1/WRAP_Pratt_0873082-150709-al-ali_pratt 239final.pdf.

Alaggia, R., Regher, C., & Rishchynsk, G. (2009). Intimate partner violence and immigration laws in Canada: How far have we come? *International Journal of Law and Psychiatry, 32*(6), 335–341.

Alboim, N., & Cohl, K. (2012). Shaping the future: Canada's rapidly changing immigration policies. *Maytree Foundation*. Retrieved from http://maytree.com/spotlight/shaping-the-future-canadas-rapidly-changing-immigration-policies.html.

Amer, M. (2005). Arab American mental health in the post September 11th era: Acculturation, stress, and coping. Doctoral dissertation, University of Toledo, *Dissertation Abstracts International, 66*, 1974.

Amnesty International (2008). *Iraq: rhetoric and reality: The Iraqi refugee crisis*. Amnesty International Publications. Retrieved from www.amnesty.org/en/library/asset/MDE14/011/2008/en/2e602733-42da-11dd-9452091b75948109/mde140112008eng.pdf.

Bahdi, R. (2003). No exit: Racial profiling and Canada's war against terrorism. *Osgoode Hall Law Journal, 41*(2–3), 293–316.

Bhuyan, R., Osborn, B.J., & Juanico Cruz, J. F. (2013). Unprotected and unrecognized: The ontological insecurity of migrants who are denied protection from domestic violence in their home countries and as refugee claimants in Canada. *CERIS Working Paper* No. 96. CERIS – The Ontario Metropolis Centre, Toronto. Retrieved from http://www.ceris.metropolis.net/wp-content/uploads/2013/02/CWP_96_Bhuyan_Osborne_Cruz.pdf.

Blanch, A. (2008). *Transcending violence: Emerging models for trauma healing in refugee communities.* National Center of Trauma Informed Care.

Brave Heart, M. (1999a). Oyate ptayela: Rebuilding the Lakota Nation through addressing historical trauma among Lakota parents. *Journal of Human Behavior in the Social Environment, 2,* 109–126.

Brave Heart, M. (1999b). Gender differences in the historical trauma response among the Lakota. *Journal of Health and Social Policy, 10*(4), 1–21.

Brave Heart, M. (2003). The historical trauma response among Natives and its relationship with substance abuse: A Lakota illustration. *Journal of Psychoactive Drugs, 35,* 7–13.

Brave Heart, M. Y. H., & Debruyn, L. M. (1998). The American Indian Holocaust: Healing historical unresolved grief. *American Indian and Alaska Native Mental Health Research, 8*(2), 56–78.

Burstow, B. (2003). Toward a radical understanding of trauma and trauma work. *Violence Against Women, 9*(11), 1293.

Caidi, N., & MacDonald, S. (2008). Information practices of Canadian Muslims post 9/11. *Government Information Quarterly, 25,* 348–378.

Canadian Arab Federation [CAF] & Canadian Council on American Islamic Relations [CAIR-CAN] (2005). *Brief on the review of the Anti-terrorism Act, justice, human rights, public safety and national security.* Retrieved from http://www.caircan.ca/downloads/CCC-RAA.pdf.

Canadian Civil Liberties Association [CCLA] (2010). *Canada's "No Fly List" in need of transparency.* Retrieved from http://ccla.org/wordpress/wp-content/uploads/2009/12/Newsnotes-Spring-2010. pdf.

Canadian Council on American-Islamic Relations [CAIR-CAN] (2005). *Presumption of guilt: A national survey on security visitations of Canadian Muslims.* Retrieved from http://www.caircan.ca/ downloads/POG-08062005.pdf.

Canadian Council for Refugees [CCR] (2006). *Analysis of a small number of Iraqi private sponsorship applications refused at Damascus.* Retrieved from http://ccrweb.ca/IraqiPSRrefusals.pdf.

Canadian Council for Refugees [CCR] (2012). *Comments on the notice published by Citizenship and Immigration in the Canada Gazette, Part I, Vol. 146, No. 10 – March 9, 2012.* Retrieved from https://ccrweb.ca/files/cprcommentsmar2012.pdf.

Canadian Council for Refugees [CCR] (2013). *Important changes in Canada's Private Sponsorship of Refugees Program.* Retrieved from http://ccrweb.ca/files/psr-changes-2013.pdf.

Canadian Council for Refugees [CCR], Ontario Council of Agencies Serving Immigrants [OCASI], Metro Toronto Chinese and Southeast Asian Legal Clinic [MTCSALC], and Colour of Poverty Campaign [COPC] (2012). *State of immigrant and refugee women's status in Canada – 2012: A joint report.* Retrieved from http://www.ocasi.org/downloads/State_of_Immigrant_Refugee_Women_in_Canada_2012.pdf.

Citizenship and Immigration Canada [CIC] (2013, January 15). News Release – Canada to welcome 5,000 refugees now in Turkey. Retrieved from http://www.cic.gc.ca/english/department/media/releases/2013/2013-01-15.asp.

Danieli, Y. (Ed.) (1998). *International handbook of multigenerational legacies of trauma.* New York: Plenum Press.

DeGruy Leary, J. (2005). *Post traumatic slave syndrome: America's legacy of enduring injury and healing.* Baltimore, MD: Uptone Press.

Denham, A. (2008). Rethinking historical trauma: Narratives of resilience. *Transcultural Psychiatry, 45*(3), 391–414.

Douglas, D., Go, A., & Blackstock, S. (2012, December 5). Canadian Immigration changes force women to stay with sponsoring spouse for two years. Retrieved from http://www.thestar.com /opinion/editorialopinion/2012/12/05/canadian_immigration_changes_force_women_to_stay_with_sponsoring_spouse_for_two_years.html.

Engler, Y. (2009). *The black book of Canadian foreign policy.* Halifax, NS: Fernwood Publishing/Red Publishing.

Estrada, A. L. (2009). Mexican Americans and historical trauma theory: A theoretical perspective. *Journal of Ethnicity in Substance Abuse, 8*(3), 330–340.

Evans-Campbell, T. (2008). Historical trauma in American Indian/Native Alaska communities: A multilevel framework for exploring impacts on individuals, families, and communities. *Journal of Interpersonal Violence, 23*(3), 316–338.

Evans-Campbell, T., & Walters, K. L. (2006). Indigenous practice competencies in child welfare practice: A decolonization framework to address family violence and substance abuse among First Nations Peoples. In Fong, R., Mccoy, R., & Ortiz Hendricks, C. (Eds.), *Intersecting child welfare, substance abuse, and family violence: Culturally competent approaches* (pp. 266–290). Washington: CSWE Press.

Fabri, M. (2011). Best, promising and emerging practices in the treatment of trauma: what can we apply in our work with torture survivors? *Torture, 21*(1), 27–38.

Farmer, P. (2004). An anthropology of structural violence. *Current Anthropology, 45*(3), 305–325.

Farmer, P. (2005). *Pathologies of power: Health, human rights, and the new war on the poor.* Berkeley: University of California Press.

Fawn, R. (2008). No consensus with the commonwealth, no consensus with itself? Canada and the Iraq war. *The Round Table, 97*(397), 519–533.

Galtung, J. (1990). Cultural violence. *Journal of Peace Research, 27*(3), 291–305.

Gorst-Unsworth, C. & Goldenbergh, E. (1998). Psychological sequelae of torture and organized violence suffered by refugees from Iraq. Trauma-related factors compared with social factors in exile. *The British Journal of Psychiatry, 172*(1), 90–94.

Harper, A. (2008). Iraq's refugees: Ignored and unwanted. *International Review of the Red Cross 90*(869), 169–190.

Hassouneh, D. M., & Kulwicki, A. (2007). Mental health, discrimination, and trauma in Arab Muslim women living in the US: A pilot study. *Mental Health, Religion & Culture, 10*(3), 257–262.

Herman, J. (1997). *Trauma and recovery. The aftermath of violence — from domestic abuse to political terror.* New York: Basic Books.

Hirji, F. (2006). Common concerns and constructed communities: Muslim Canadians, the internet, and the war in Iraq. *Journal of Communication Inquiry, 30*(2), 125–141.

Hyman, I. (2009). *Racism as a determinant of immigrant health.* Retrieved from http://canada.metropolis.net/pdfs/racism_policy_brief_e.pdf.

Hyman, I. and Wray, R. (2013). *Health inequalities and racialized groups: A review of the evidence.* Prepared in collaboration with Toronto Public Health. Retrieved from http://www.toronto.ca/health.

Jacklin, K. (2008). Strength in adversity: Community health and healing in Wikwemikong. Proquest Information & Learning. *Dissertation Abstracts International, Section A: Humanities and Social Sciences, 69* (1-A), 264–264.

Jamil, H., Hakim-Larson, J., Farrag, M., Kafaji, T., Duqum, I., & Jamil, L. H. (2002). A retrospective study of Arab American mental health clients: Trauma and the Iraqi refugees. *American Journal of Orthopsychiatry, 72*(3), 355–361.

Jamil, H., Nassar-McMillan, S., Lambert, R. G., & Hammad, A. (2006). Health assessment of Iraqi immigrants. *Journal of Immigrant & Refugee Studies, 4*(4), 69–74.

Jamil, H., Nassar-McMillan, S., & Lambert, R. (2007). Immigration and attendant psychological sequelae: A comparison of three waves of Iraqi immigrants. *American Journal of Orthopsychiatry, 77*(2), 199–205.

Jean Tweed Centre (2013). *Trauma matters: Highlights of trauma-informed practices in women's substance use services.* Retrieved from www.jeantweed.com.

Kellerman, N. (2001). Transmission of holocaust trauma: An integrative view. *Psychiatry: Interpersonal & Biological Processes, 64*(3), 256–268.

Keung, N. (2011, June 21). Quality of refugee decisions in question. Toronto Star. Retrieved from http://immlawyer.blogs.com/my_weblog/2011/06/toronto-star-article-on-overseas-refugee-decisions.html.

Khanlou, N. (2009). Immigrant mental health policy brief. Retrieved from http://w.ocasi.org/downloads/Immigrant_Mental_Health_Policy_Brief_Final.pdf.

Krieger, N. (2001). Theories for social epidemiology in the 21st century: An ecosocial perspective. *International Journal of Epidemiology, 30*(4), 668–677.

Laban, C. J., Gernaat, H. B. P. E., Komproe, I. H., van der Tweel, I., & de Jong, J. T. V. M. (2005). Postmigration living problems and common psychiatric disorders in Iraqi asylum seekers in the Netherlands. *The Journal of Nervous and Mental Disease, 193*(12), 825–832.

Lindencrona, F., Ekblad, S., & Hauff, E. (2008). Mental health of recently resettled refugees from the Middle East in Sweden: The impact of pre-resettlement trauma, resettlement stress and capacity to handle stress. *Social Psychiatry and Psychiatric Epidemiology, 43*(2), 121–131.

Mansouri, F. & Cauchi, S. (2007). A psychological perspective on Australia's asylum policies. *International Migration, 45*(1), 123–150.

Mental Health Commission of Canada and Centre for Addiction and Mental Health (2009). *Improving mental health services for immigrant, refugee, ethno-cultural and racialized groups: issues and options for service improvement.*

Metropolitan Action Committee on Violence Against Women and Children [METRAC]. (2012*). Statement on amendment to the immigration and refugee protection regulations: Proposed conditional permanent residence period for sponsored spouses.* Retrieved from http://www. metrac.org/about/press.room/downloads/statement.conditional.permanent.residence.10apr12.pdf.

Moradi, B., & Hasan, N.T. (2004). Arab American persons' reported experiences of discrimination and mental health: The mediating role of personal control. *Journal of Counseling Psychology, 51*(4), 418–428.

Nickerson, A., Brooks, R., Bryant, R., Silove, D., & Steel, Z. (2010). The impact of fear for family on mental health in a resettled Iraqi refugee community. *Journal of Psychiatric Research, 44*(4) 229–235.

Nickerson, A., Brooks, R., Bryant, R., Silove,D., & Steel, Z. (2011). Change in visa status amongst Mandaean refugees: Relationship to psychological symptoms and living difficulties. *Psychiatry Research, 187*(1), 267–274.

Nickerson, A., Bryant, R., Brooks, R., Chen, J., Silove, D., & Steel,Z. (2011a). The familial influence of loss and trauma on refugee mental health: A multilevel path analysis. *Journal of Traumatic Stress, 24*(1), 25-33.

Padela, A. & Heisler, M. (2010). The association of perceived abuse and discrimination after September 11, 2001, with psychological distress, level of happiness, and health status among Arab Americans. *American Journal of Public Health, 100* (2), 284–291.

Pedersen, D. (2002). Political violence, ethnic conflict, and contemporary wars: Broad implications for health and social well-being. *Social Science and Medicine,* 55(2), 175–190.

Pearce, M. E., Christian, W. M., Patterson, K., Norris, K., Moniruzzaman, A., Craib, K. J., Schechter, M.T., & Spittal, P.M. (2008). The cedar project: historical trauma, sexual abuse and HIV risk among young Aboriginal people who use injection and non-injection drugs in two Canadian cities. *Social Science & Medicine, 66*(11), 2185–2194.

Refugees International. (2010). No way home now way to escape: The plight of Iraqi refugees and our Iraqi allies. Retrieved from http://refugeesinternational.org/policy/testimony/no-way-home-no-way-escape-plight-iraqi-refugees-and-our-iraqi-allies.

Rippy, A.E., & Newman, E. (2006). Perceived religious discrimination and its relationship to anxiety and paranoia among Muslim Americans. *Journal of Muslim Mental Health, 1*(1), 5–20.

Rostam, H., & Haverkamp, B. E. (2009). Iraqi expatriates' experience of North American media coverage of the Iraq war. *International Journal for The Advancement Of Counselling, 31*(2), 100–117.

Scheper-Hughes, N., & Bourgois, P. (2004): Introduction. In Scheper-Hughes N., & Bourgois P. (Eds.), *Violence in war and peace.* Malden, MA: Blackwell Publishing.

Siddiqui, H. (2008). Muslims and the rule of law. In N. Bakht (Ed.), *Belonging and banishment being Muslim in Canada* (pp. 1–17). Toronto, Canada: TSAR Publications.

Shoeb, M., Weinstein, H., & Halpern, J. (2007). Living in religious time and space: Iraqi refugees in Dearborn Michigan. *Journal of Refugee Studies,* 20(30), 441–460.

Silove, D., (2002). The asylum debacle in Australia: a challenge for psychiatry. *The Australian and New Zealand Journal of Psychiatry, 36*(3) 290–296.

Silove, D., Steel, Z., and Watters, C. (2000). Policies of deterrence and the mental health of asylum seekers. *JAMA: The journal of the American Medical Association, 28* (5), 604–611.

Steel, Z., Silove, D., Brooks, R., Momartin, S., Alzuhairi, B., & Susljik, I. (2006). Impact of immigration detention and temporary protection on the mental health of refugees. The British Journal of Psychiatry: The Journal of Mental Science, 188 (1), 58–64.

Tol, W.A., Stavrou, V., Greene, M. C., Mergenthaler, C., Ommeren, M., Moreno, C. (2013). Sexual and gender-based violence in areas of armed conflict: a systematic review of mental health and psychosocial support interventions. *Conflict and Health,* 7(13), 7–16.

UNHCR (2012). Displacement: Facts and Figures, 2012. Retrieved from http://www.unhcr.org.uk/fileadmin/user_upload/pdf/Displacement_Facts_and_Figures_Final.pdf.

UNHCR Global Trends (2012). *Displacement: The new 21st Century challenge. UNHCR Global Trends 2012.* Retrieved from http://www.unhcr.org/51bacb0f9.html.

Vasilevska, B., Madan, A., and Simich, L. (2010). Refugee mental health: Promising practices and partnership building resources. Toronto: Centre for Addiction and Mental Health.

# Roots and Routes of Displacement and Trauma

Wesley-Esquimaux, C. & M. Smolewski (2004). *Historic trauma and aboriginal healing*. Aboriginal Healing Foundation: Ottawa. Retrieved from http://www.ahf.ca/publications/research-series.

Zahraei, S. (2014). *Memory, trauma, and citizenship: Arab Iraqi women*. (Unpublished doctoral dissertation). Toronto: University of Toronto.

Zahraei, S., Bhuyan, R., Osborne, B., Villanueva, F., and Quach, V. (forthcoming). A feminist intersectional analysis of Canadian immigration and citizenship policies, 2008-2013.

Zangana, H. (2007). *City of widows: An Iraqi woman's account of war and resistance*. New York: Seven Stories Press.

Zarowky, C. & Pederson, D. (2000). Rethinking trauma in a transnational world. *Transcultural Psychiatry, 37*, 291–293.

CHAPTER NINE

# Gender and Trauma:
# The Case of Afghanistan

## *Sharifa Sharif*

Trauma is inseparable from life and has impacted humans and humanity severely whether it has resulted from direct, power-driven, human-made crises such as war and political tyranny, or from environmental disasters such as tsunamis, hurricanes, and earthquakes. Patriarchal social relations, structural oppression and oppressive political and ideological regimes all subject disadvantaged and vulnerable populations, women in particular, to traumatic experiences throughout their lives.

This chapter explores the social and cultural dynamics that intersect with women's experience of trauma, and the socioeconomic realities which subject them to such victimization. It will analyze the process of traumatic impact on women, particularly Afghan women, and how it creates a different pattern of response and coping strategies for them.

First, this chapter will argue that women are subject to visible and invisible forms of violence — both declared violence in wartime, and the undeclared wars waged on them through their normal life cycles (Sharratt, 1999). Second, I will maintain that while wars, natural disasters, poverty, and political and ideological tyranny are the visible vehicles of violence, torture and abuse against women, patriarchal norms of socioeconomic and cultural relations, family dynamics and constructed gender roles create invisible means for an ongoing war against women in the form of partner abuse, forced marriage, female genital mutilation, rape and incest. Third, this chapter will discuss the impact of trauma on women and will argue that gender and sexuality largely determine the scale and intensity of violence and its impact on women. Although rape and sexual assault are not confined to female victims, women and their bodies are more often and acutely objectified and weaponized during both war and peace (Sharratt, 1999).

The fourth point I would like to make is that while sexuality has become a tool to objectify and weaponize women's bodies, with the most visible and common form of violence being rape and assault, it also empowers women as owners and protectors of this weapon. Finally, this chapter will suggest that patriarchy controls women's sexuality and bodies in order to extend paternal lineage and inheritance. Hence, women in patriarchal societies are mainly defined by their sexuality and roles as mothers, and gain status by having sons who carry on the lineage and inherit property. Mothering, which thus becomes women's social and cultural role, is glorified through social discourse and literature in order to confine women to the domestic domain of home and family. However, I will argue that women's nurturing nature and protective consciousness is not limited to their maternal instinct and protection of their children. Women are socially conscious and responsible individuals whose nurturing nature in times of war and chaos further empowers them with resilience and with responsibility for the protection of others, the social order and their own personal agencies as citizens.

The chapter will conclude with the assertion that while the visible and declared violence and their consequent trauma impact both men and women of the same social and economic strata, women's experience of ongoing war and violence and their responses to (and coping strategies for) trauma are expressed differently. On the one hand, women generally experience violence more intensely through their intimate and private bodies-identities; on the other, their lived experience of various forms of visible and invisible violence means they face a daily trial of defending themselves against potential traumas. The above ideas will be elaborated in the following sections, but I will narrow the scope of discussion to those societies, such as Afghanistan and Pakistan, where my studies have been focused.

## Visible Wartime Violence Against Women

The most common form of violence in wartime is rape, which subjects women to direct forms of traumatic experience as well as socio-political and economic isolation. Rape is used as a "double weapon," against women's physical bodies and their social and cultural identities, as well as against the collective honour of their community-society. In many communities women are perceived as badges of men's honour, their roles limited to private relations confined to the family unit. In war, when the community-society is targeted as a whole, women are associated with collective honour of this male-dominated society.

The loss of loved ones, especially sons, brothers, fathers and husbands, signifies another multilayered traumatic experience for women. In societies where women are financially dependent on and identified by their familial relations, specifically their male relatives, loss of these family members creates an additional social vacuum for them. As well, in Afghanistan, for instance, legalized violence against women (such as that sanctioned by the Taliban) and its traumatic implications have had enormous political and social impact. This issue will be explored in detail.

Violence against women during wartime is the magnified and visible form of the violence that targets them every day, in peace as well as war (Sharratt, 1999).

A visible, much-studied form of such is rape and sexual assault. Sometimes such assaults have been carried out on a large scale and documented widely, while at other times assaults have taken place in smaller numbers and have gone unreported and often unspoken, due to social risks such as cultural shame, loss of honour, isolation and absence of legal protection (Mukherjee, 2014). The rape of millions of women in Rwanda, Somalia and the former Yugoslavia, for example, has been widely studied and reported. According to a UN report (April 2014), "Rape is used as a weapon of war to intimidate local communities, and to punish civilians for their real or perceived collaboration with the armed groups or the national organization." More than 683,000 women are raped every year and 12% to 15% of women experience rape at some point in their lives (Tull, 2012).

In patriarchal societies where military invasions have fostered the growth of social and religious conservatism, such as in Afghanistan and Pakistan during the last decade of U.S. anti-terrorism operations in the region, gender roles and status are defined within the male-dominated family domain. While gender segregation is culturally and socially reinforced, women are secluded from the public and confined to the privacy of the home and family, which are headed by men. Religion further forbids sexual interaction outside marriage and defines women's social, emotional and sexual boundaries within the family unit where the husband, father, or brother is assigned as guardian and provider. A woman is identified as someone's daughter, sister, mother and wife who is culturally responsible for preserving his family privacy-honor. A girl is her brother's and father's honour until she gets married and becomes her husband's possession and honour. In peace time, every family unit, or clan, claims the honour of their female relatives, but when there is a force targeting them from outside their community, women become symbolic of their collective honour, and protecting them from foreigners and invaders becomes a social and cultural responsibility (Kuehnast, 2011; Moqhissi, 1999). Rape of a woman in such societies not only victimizes the woman, but invades the privacy and violates the honour of her male guardians and her entire community (Naili, 2014).

There are few published accounts of rape of women in Afghanistan during the 30 years of war with the Soviet army, civil war and wars involving NATO and the Taliban. However, the alarming number of mentally disturbed women dealing with symptoms of post traumatic stress disorder (PTSD) in Afghanistan clearly indicates the traumatic experiences they have gone through (Cordoz, 2005). The violence during the war has been inflicted on women either directly by the offensive sides (soldiers and fighters), or indirectly through perpetuating a chaotic environment which provokes bullying and intimidation of women and other vulnerable groups. Local women and girls were not raped by the fighting armies alone, but also by local men who took advantage of the period of insecurity to abuse women.

War is traumatic and terrorizes an entire society through death, destruction and loss. Rape and sexual assault inflict terror on women through assault on their bodies and souls, creating a paradoxical mixture of physical, mental, social and cultural pain and shame. Rape and sexual assault invades a woman's private territory and violates all attributed norms and laws of her sexual and social being (Marcus, 2002). Women in many societies do not own their sexual identities and "owe" them to their male guardians. Their sexuality is socially constructed and viewed as much or more an aspect of a man's honour than it is of their own. While a woman doesn't fully own her sexuality-honour, she is held responsible for safeguarding it, so as to avoid shame and dishonour to her male guardians and the community at large. Therefore raping a woman inflicts multifaceted pain and trauma on her by violating both her personal honour and the honour of her socially and culturally shared identity as a wife, daughter or sister. In Afghanistan, during nearly 30 years of conflict, armed factions turned traditional norms of honour and shame into weapons of war, engaging in rape and sexual assault against women of opposing groups as the ultimate means for disgracing entire communities and reducing people's capacity to resist military advance (Jalal, Joya and Koofi, 2011).

Thus a woman's experience of trauma is further complicated with mixed emotions of guilt, shame, pity, pain and powerlessness, as well as sexual diseases, unwanted pregnancy and abortion. This complex and multifaceted infliction of trauma on women leads to different patterns of response and coping strategies that will be discussed in detail later in the chapter.

Another visible traumatic experience caused by declared wars is loss of loved ones, mostly sons, husbands, brothers and fathers. Such losses impact women differently and create different responses. Such loss means a loss of social identity and economic support. The trauma caused by the death of a male protector becomes more complex with the potential loss of respect, economic and social safety. In Afghanistan, a widowed woman is vulnerable to social and cultural stigmas and yet also the holder of her in-laws' honour. While it is beyond the scope of this chapter to discuss the dynamics of a widow's rights and relations, it is important to indicate ways which the impact of visible traumatic experience intensifies, changes, and interacts with culturally and socially defined gender identities.

Although all declared wars are power-driven political manoeuvres for enforcing an imperialistic agenda, ideological supremacy, religious fundamentalism, or extending a dictator's power, and are mostly carried out by powerful men, gender issues and rights have been used in psychological campaigns to gain conservative backing and support the patriarchal, misogynistic norms in conservative societies. (Mojab, 2010; Moghissi, 1999). Afghanistan, Pakistan and Egypt are some of the countries where revolutions and wars have resulted in laws that force women out of the public sphere and marginalize them on the periphery.

In Iraq, proposed legislation to legalize marriages of girls as young as 9 and boys as young as 15 was viewed as a way of attracting conservative support (Naili, 2014). Women under such discriminatory regimes experience legalized trauma. Afghan women were persecuted for their female identity during the governments of the Mujahedeen ("holy warriors") from 1992 to 1996, and under the Taliban

(1996–2001). Women's autonomy and personhood were targeted, as they were forced by law to hide their physical identity and were punished, humiliated and dishonoured if they showed up uncovered. Women feared entering the public social space. That space belonged to men and women were persecuted for trespassing onto it.

Much has been written about the Taliban's misogynist laws and conduct. This chapter, however, more specifically refers to the legitimized violence against Afghan women and the legalized character assassination that has had a traumatic impact on women. The Afghan civil war (1992–1996), with its ethnically divisive power centres, subjected women of different ethnicities to horrifying experiences, such as gang rape, public kidnapping, forced marriage and public torture. Horrific stories of cutting women's breasts, rape and torture both in public and in front of women's families, forcing women in labour to give birth in public for entertainment, and invading homes and snatching away young girls spread widely through Afghan communities, terrifying men and women alike and creating predictable traumas in women's minds (Koofi, 2011). As noted by Azizi (2011):

During the civil war Afghan women were targeted as a military strategy by various factions to humiliate and demoralize opponents. Women and girls were raped in front of their family members as a form of psychological torture. Many were kidnapped and forced into marriage by high-ranking officials in the militia, some of whom had as many wives as they wanted . . . (Aziz, 2011, p. 231).

The Taliban's legalized violence against Afghan women had a multilayered impact on women's gender identities, social agency, bodies, characters, social and intellectual ability, as well as their cultural collective identities. As wives and daughters they had become agents of shame and dishonour. As citizens they were rejected and pushed away from the social sphere.

The traumatic experiences penetrated women's minds and remained permanently in their conscious and subconscious memories. During the Taliban regime (1996–2001) and also the civil war, the fear of prosecution for women became as real and as near to them as their own selves. They were not allowed to be who they were. They were required to hide their physical, psychological and personal identities in order to preserve social and cultural norms and avoid shame, distraction, and sin in the society. With their gender identities under siege, Afghan

## Case Study 9.1

An Afghan-Canadian woman who was a medical doctor during the Taliban regime in Afghanistan spoke about her traumatic experiences:

*"I was beaten by a Talib (singular for Taliban) on the street for having a glimpse of my ankle showing. I was so traumatized and humiliated by the experience that even at home, I could not dare take off my chadari (top to toe cover) for a couple of days."*

### Reflective Questions

1. What social and cultural identities made this Afghan woman a target of persecution by the Taliban?
2. Explain the implications of beating this woman on her and on her community. Is this an individual or collective trauma?

women internalized fear and trauma, and their fears spread regardless of age, status and education, and across space and time. How that internalized fear of persecution could transform itself into resilience and courage will be discussed below.

## Invisible Ongoing Violence and Wars Against Women

Patriarchy and systemic oppression, through cultural, social and family dynamics as well as economic and political laws and relations, not only oppress and marginalize women but also expose them to cruelty and violence against their bodies, minds and sexuality. This section will first discuss how women encounter violence and its consequential trauma in their normal life cycle, and then will explore some forms of harmful and discriminatory cultural and social violence and practices, such as rape by strangers and known friends and relatives, intimate partner violence, forced marriage, child marriage and polygamy. While the forms, intensity and impact of violence against women vary across nations and cultures, the implications of trauma on women's lives have global parallels. Violence against women at home and in public during peace time is driven by patriarchy and its dynamics, just as in wartime. As Mladjenovic puts it, "Violence against women is magnified during armed conflicts, in the process exposing the artificiality of the boundary between 'wartime' and 'peace time' violence" (1999, p. 88).

Rape is further defined in the context of patriarchal oppression and control over women in order to sustain male power and women's subordination. Fear of rape restricts women's economic and political participation (Baron and Straus, 1987). The gang rape and murder of Jyoti Singh Pandey in New Delhi in December 2012 on a public bus can be seen as an example of the manifestation of group masculinity (Mishra, 2014, p. 65). Systemic oppression and gender inequality create societal responses to rape that reinforce subordination and adherence to patriarchal norms (Donat and D'Emilio, 1992). The notion that "women are asking for it" and the subsequent tendency to blame them for their style of dress, pattern of socialization ("Women should not go out at night"; "Women should never go out alone") restrict women's social domain and

---

### Case Study 9.2
### Gang Rape and Strangling of Cousins in India

Bodies of two teenage cousins, ages 14 and 15, both belonging to the Dalit community, also called "Untouchables" in the Indian caste system, were found hanging from a tree hours after they had disappeared from fields near a village in India. After the villagers' silent protest, two police officers and two other men were arrested. Autopsies confirmed the girls had been raped and strangled before being hanged.

### Reflective Questions

1. Discuss the multiple variables of class, gender, age, race in this case.
2. How would this experience affect the villagers' perception of their safety and their coping strategies?

SOURCE: ASSOCIATED PRESS.

---

behaviours, and confine them to the oppressive role patriarchy has defined for them. The definition of rape as an act of forced sexual intercourse should be expanded to include any imposed and unwanted sexual assault or violation toward a woman's body in any context that leads to fear, resentment, anger and contempt. I believe rape has similarly traumatic impact on women's minds and bodies, whether it happens during war or peace, in a developed or an underdeveloped country. It is only the level of vulnerability, including social and legal implications, availability of resources and access to them that may alter the experience. The social and cultural implications and consequences of rape vary according to many variables, such as age, marital status (losing their virginity can be detrimental for unmarried women in some societies), relation of the rapist to the family, mental status of the victim, race, and so on, and consequently can create varied psychological and emotional responses among the victims.

In the absence of choice and voice in making major decisions about her marriage, education, children and appearance, a woman is mostly forced into fearful submission, constantly anticipating the prospect of violence. In conservative, patriarchal societies a woman's sexuality defines her role and status, and obliges her to provide sex and care for her husband. The limits and nature of intimacy depend on the husband, his mood and his temper. Lack of control and uncertainty about their sexual lives as well as other aspects of daily domestic life make trauma and violence a predictable reality for many women. It is in this context that **intimate partner violence** has been studied (Ali, 2012).

## Violence Against Women and Intimate Partner Violence

**Violence against women** (VAW) by their intimate partners is a global reality, widely discussed and studied (Ali, 2012; Shani and Bhandari, 2014). Discussing the forms and nature of VAW and its causes and consequences is beyond the scope of this chapter. However, it is imperative to note that violence in any form creates a terrifying environment, and when it is directed against one's body and/or emotions, it becomes a traumatic experience permanently imprinted in the subconscious memory. The more frequent the experience of violence is, the deeper and wider the scar, but the physical and psychological impact of trauma is immediate. The bodily and psychological response to a first traumatic experience of rape, beating, insults or threats does not necessarily subside or become suppressed prior to a second or third incident occurring. Anticipation and expectation of violence prolongs the impact of traumatic experiences. Women in abusive situations live in ongoing fear and anxiety as they hope to avoid further violent episodes. Any word or action, or not saying or doing the "right" thing, can potentially provoke violence: shopping, visiting friends, coming home late, cooking, cleaning, laundry, children, or just being.

Fear traumatizes and living with fear is akin to living in trauma. Emotional trauma is an inextricable part of many women's lives in most patriarchal and conservative nations. In polygamous societies such as Afghanistan, fear of one's husband marrying another wife is another daily anxiety that women live with (Smith, 2011). The prospect of another wife being brought into the household as well as actually going through the experience can readily traumatize women. Some react hysterically and overtly, others supress the hysteria and live with it ("A Malaysia First Wife Speaks of Polygamy," 2009). The husband's desire for another woman in any form conveys a sense of inadequacy and deficiency to a woman-wife, and impacts her image and confidence. The ongoing "war at home" reflects a situation marked by daily intimidation, threat and trauma. The number of women living in such abusive circumstances is alarming. Even in wealthy western countries like Canada, one of every three women experiences some form of abuse and "[o]n average, every six days a woman is killed by her intimate partner" (Jain, 2014, p. 57).

But violence at home is only one form of the ongoing war against women.

## Forced and Child Marriage

**Forced marriage** is another form of the invisible, ongoing war in women's lives, once again grounded in patriarchal relations. Like all forms of VAW, forced marriage is an expression of a patriarchal system that makes women more vulnerable through ethnic, class, culture and tribal relations (Cross, 2013, p. 95).

Forcing young girls to marry without their consent and despite their resistance, often by (literally) dragging them to hostile new homes, leaves permanent imprints of horrific memories on their minds while their lives and well-being are systematically compromised. This is a daily occurrence (Cross, 2013). According to a UN report:

> The often criminal and hidden nature of forced marriages, combined with the fact that most forced marriages take place in closed families, groups, communities or societies, makes it particularly difficult to compile reliable statistics on how many women and girls are subjected to forced marriages of any kind every year (Huda, 2007, p. 96).

Forced marriage is described slightly differently in various countries by different authorities. In many such situations, the parents or those forcing the marriage claim that there was no expressed lack of consent from their child. These are situations of passive and unconscious consent, where silence is interpreted as consent. Passive consent is not confined to under-age and child brides. In many cases, young adult women 18 years of age or older lack information about their future husband, or their knowledge is limited to what they hear from their parents and others. Nor are they aware of the consequences and expectations of marriage. Apart from parents' physical and psychological pressure on girls to enter unwanted marriages, patriarchal and oppressive systemic social, economic and cultural relations force women to abstain from disagreement and choice. Opposing parents' decisions — even voicing consent, or lack of it, to a marriage — is stigmatized as foul-mouthed and rude. Financial concerns, fear of poverty, cultural stigmatization of unmarried women, the pressure of social norms, religious beliefs, familial norms of parental obedience — all these factors pressure women to submit to their parents' or guardians' decision about their marriage.

This section does not intend to elaborate on the cultural and social contexts of forced marriage; however, in order to illustrate the embedded fear and trauma in entering such contracts, some special situations of women's forced silence will be discussed. Historically, the celibacy of women after what is considered a marriageable age is stigmatized through language, drama, poetry and other cultural expressions. For example, "rotten," "abandoned," "unwanted," "burdensome" and the like are adjectives applied to unmarried women in Afghan culture. Patriarchal gender roles and lack of access to economic resources make women vulnerable to dependency. With patriarchal lineage and residency structures that encourage married sons to remain in their parents' family homes, girls become superfluous family members in those homes after they reach a marriageable age. A woman's financial security lies with her future husband. These social and cultural obligations and restrictions act to narrow women's choices and limit their decision-making power. Entering marriages intimidated and powerless subjects most women to fearful anticipation of the unknown. Fear of poverty, dependency, social rejection and stigmatization, and psychological stress related to meeting the expected standards all pressure many women to enter marriages regardless of the consequences. In most situations, women are faced with only two options — bad and worse.

Since physical attractiveness along with a socially and culturally acceptable character and background make a woman a desirable wife, an unmarried woman is presumed to lack these attributes. Anxiety about potentially being blamed by their families — a blame that can extend to broader social and cultural stigmatization — haunts many young women and drives them into unwanted marriages where the constant fear of abuse and violence by their partners haunts them even more. Many young girls entering marriages, usually to older men, do so with passive and unconscious silence, only to often be surprised by the shocking and horrifying sexual and cultural expectations of their married lives. Their first sexual encounter terrifies them, leaving them with the anxiety of whether they will be visibly virgin, the experience of physical pain and a feeling of shame for sharing their private bodies. Virginity defines a woman's marriageable quality and its absence justifies her rejection by her in-laws and ultimately from society. In some countries, such as Afghanistan and Pakistan, young girls have been rejected for not being virgins because of misunderstanding and lack of education about female anatomy. While bleeding upon first intercourse is considered the most representative natural consequence and indicator of prior virginity, not witnessing blood can sometimes suggest — erroneously — that the bride has had previous sexual encounters when, in fact, she has not. All these factors make women hostage to their sexuality — virginity and other qualities, the lack of which impugns their character, shatters their pride, shames their family, and hence makes trauma inevitable.

The phenomenon of **child marriage** overlaps with that of forced marriage. A child may give consent because of her limited awareness of the implications and consequences of marriage. Every year, hundreds of thousands of girls lose their childhood, dreams, hopes and health to forced marriages. Their parents seek "bids" for them, in exchange for money, honour or even in an exchange for another girl. According to the report by the Girls Not Brides organization, around the world every year about 14 million girls under 18 are married. This equates to more than 25,000 girls every day, or 19 every minute. In developing countries, one in seven girls are married before reaching their fifteenth birthdays. Some are as young as eight or nine (Girls Not Brides, 2014).

All these girls are traumatized by the fear of unknown men and their sexual and behavioral expectations of them. While the health consequences that early marriages incur on girls' bodies remain visible, the psychological pain and the traumatic impact are suppressed, leaving permanent but often subconscious scars. Dragging female children to forced marriages not only traumatizes the girls, but also leaves horrifying memories for their loved ones, particularly their mothers. Many mothers oppose their daughters' early marriages, especially when it is a repetition of their own experiences, but they have no or little voice in confronting their husbands, brothers-in law or other males who are making the legal decisions.

## Political and Cultural Marginalization

Legalized and forced gender segregation, marginalization and invisibility create a hostile environment for women who constantly fear persecution for violating government laws and social and cultural norms. The constant anxiety of observing and obeying these boundaries puts women on trial in their own bodies. Global power dynamics have also given rise to, and perpetuated, many misogynist political regimes and movements. Imperialistic nationalism, capitalism and masculinism have always been integral aspects of wars waged in developing countries and have encouraged the persistence and spread of patriarchal, misogynistic ideologies. As Rosalind Petchesky puts it: "Militarism, nationalism and colonialism as terrains of power have always been in large part contests over meanings of manhood militarism" (Petchesky, 2002). By polarizing nations and cultures — the "free and democratic West" against the "backward and enslaved East," or "civilized Christianity" as opposed to "barbaric Islam" — such wars stimulate and mobilize patriarchally

### Case Study 9.3
### A Bus Trip

A woman was trying to get on a bus after the workday in Kabul during the Soviet occupation of Afghanistan. A group of local men pushed her away and angrily shouted: "Go away! It is you women and your miniskirts that brought the country to this stage." She heard many similar stories from other women.

### Reflective Questions

1. What social and patriarchal norms were the men's attitudes based on?
2. How does the expression of anger and hatred affect the woman's social agency and citizenship?

driven oppressive values, such as nationalistic movements. **Misogyny,** negative and demeaning attitudes towards women, leads to prejudice and the assumption that women are inferior and less deserving (Napikoski, 2014). Foreign invasions justify military nationalism and misogyny as a cultural norm. During the Soviet invasion and occupation of Afghanistan, women, especially liberated urban women, were resented by some freedom fighters (the Mujahedeen) for (in the Mujahedeen's view) perpetuating the invasion of the country by the atheist Soviet army because the women carried out "un-Islamic" acts, such as not covering themselves in public and denying their traditional roles as housewives and mothers.

Since Islam as a religion was perceived as being attacked by the Soviets, whose country, the USSR, was officially atheist, religion became politicized and was used to force women out of the public domain into their patriarchally defined domestic role. Enforcing gender segregation and defining home and domesticity as women's proper and religiously ascribed position was perceived as a national defence strategy against the infidel invaders. Islam was protected by strictly adhering to its rules, and national honour was preserved by guarding women within the private sphere. Redefining women's roles as mothers and housewives was highlighted as Islamic cultural value. Thus, gender inequality and subordination, privatized gender roles and politicized religious beliefs — all rooted in partriarchy — were transformed into fundamental national values and cultural identities and then were used to defy colonial imperialism (Moghissi, 1999).

As Mojab (2014) argues, it is historically and politically evident that U.S. capitalism and Islamic fundamentalism are symbiotic and do not contradict each other. The bold misogynist regime of the Taliban in Afghanistan, whose defeat was politicized as part of the United States' "war on terror," was in fact initially created with the help of the U.S.:

> Masculinism is alive and well, but concealed in its Eurocentric guise of rescuing downtrodden, voiceless Afghan women from the misogynist regime it helped bring to power (Petchesky, 2002, p. 40).

It is beyond the scope of this chapter to elaborate on the reasons for U.S. military and financial support of the Afghan Mujahedeen, despite the Mujahedeen's apparent discriminatory agenda towards women, nor on how such support led to civil war and the formation of the Taliban. Support by the U.S. of notorious warlords who carried out misogynist agendas, as well as its role in the formation of the Taliban, have been widely discussed (Rashid, 2000; Coll, 2004). These policies have had clear and lasting consequences on women's personal and social identities.

The Taliban regime in Afghanistan, and their allies in Pakistan and in some other parts of the world, are examples of regimes that openly declared misogynist policies meant to publicly target and terrorize women. Terrifying stories of state terrorism against women during the Taliban regime have been widely discussed

(Koofi, 2011; Armstrong, 2002 and 2013). However, in order to describe the extent of public traumatizing of women and the persistent social memory of such events, it may suffice to recall the public stoning of women in the national stadium, something which has been extensively publicized. While the stoning of women in the name of honour and religion continue to terrorize women in Afghanistan and the state government turns a blind eye to such events, at least these atrocities are no longer legally sanctioned by the state. One can argue that although the U.S. and its allies defeated the Taliban government in 2001 and installed a government ornamented with western-style democratic policies that is ostensibly in support of women's liberation, the oppressive patriarchal infrastructure still determines the state's decisions and outlook in relation to gender roles and rights. The extreme misogyny fed by politicized religion that was used as a counterbalance to imperialistic interventions has become so deeply rooted in the psychological fabric of male-dominated Afghan society that government authorities have to acknowledge it and acquiesce to its continued existence, in order to remain in power.

Dominated and defined by societal norms of patriarchal conservatism, the Afghan government's policies on women's rights are little more than a dysfunctional body of contradictory laws. State protection of women and their rights exists in the form of laws with language borrowed from the west that may appeal to American voters but is meaningless to the majority of Afghans. Workshops and seminars on the topic of "gender equity" are held by NGOs and the Afghan Ministry of Women's Affairs and sponsored by funds from donors. But the term "gender" is not translated into an equivalent Dari or Pashto concept, as the term does not exist in those languages (Zahedi, 2011, p. 296). While the Taliban government may have been removed and its laws replaced by ones more favourable to women, 12 years later many women still do not feel safe to be visible in public and seek justice. Every day women continue to experience or hear about a brutal murder, a barbaric torture or a terrible abuse — events that resonate in their traumatized memories and will terrorize them for many more years to come.

Such collective traumatization creates a long-term social memory that equates the experience of womanhood with the experience of crime and terror. Such situations are not limited to Afghanistan. Consider, for instance, the fact that about 1200 Aboriginal women went missing and were murdered in Canada over the past 30 years (Jiwani, 2006). The gang rape and murder of Jyoti Singh in Delhi in December 2012 (Bains, 2014, p. 34) was yet another horrifying example of trauma that resulted in public protests by women and a change of policy in India. These are some of the cases where trauma has been recognized by political authorities. You will also likely be familiar with the story of Malala Yousefzai's being targeted by the Taliban, and that of the raping and hanging of the two teenage cousins in India.

Marginalization and segregation that are normalized in cultural beliefs bar women from trespassing into public, or "male," territory. The normative boundaries defined for the male and female spheres, boundaries constructed of expectations about behaviour, appearance, interaction and language, leave women in the precarious situation of being constantly judged by their families and communities. Women live on the edge, always afraid of being accused of an unlawful conduct.

## Trauma and its Gender-Based Impact

In this section, trauma will be explored in relation to gender sexuality. We will consider how the physical and psychological and cultural implications of gender sexuality affect the intensity and depth of traumatic experience for women, and, second, we will analyze how such trauma influences and shapes responses and coping strategies. The section will conclude by suggesting that because the various forms of violence against women have multiple cultural, social and economic implications, they similarly create multilayered and complex physical, psychological and emotional responses in women.

War has a different meaning and impact for men and women on personal, social and historical levels, and hence its impact is inevitably gender-based. In the words of Sabine Scheffler and Agnes Muchele (1999):

> While dominant discourses (including those of the mainstream media and the state) are focused narrowly upon the "organization of war" and issues of concern to men (e.g., battles lost and won; number of personnel injured, missing or dead), the violence experienced by women is targeted and total, and is used as a way of sapping the morale and weakening the resolve of men. Objectified and subjected to torture, humiliation and violence, the destruction of women's dignity undermines and destroys the social bonds and values of the culture in which they live" (1999, p. 124).

Women's experiences of trauma and violence remain largely undocumented and they are not officially recognized as casualties of war by UN sources in this context. It is the number of dead or injured soldiers and (to some degree) civilians that are pronounced as casualties, not the number of women who have been raped or tortured directly or indirectly during a war.

One can argue that publicly recognized violence creates a collective response, which can function as a psychological resource of collective expression and as a healing outlet. While monuments for lost soldiers and civilian casualties, and museums of warfare and even of torture or of genocidal events, can be the visible forms of such collective expression, there is no visible recognition of women's victimization, including their experiences of rape, humiliation, mental and physical torture. The many factors discussed previously — including stigma, shame, fear of potential consequences including threat, death, intimidation and recurrence of violations, among many other socio-political-economic factors — prevent women and their communities from acknowledging or publicizing the fact that rape has occurred. This limits women's experience of war to the personal realm of individual trauma, with no or limited access to collective resources.

The highly gender-specific impact of violence is caused by the ongoing invisible war that patriarchy and systemic oppression wages on women in the form of incest, forced marriage and partner abuse, as explored above. While there are public *male* narrative expressions of pain and fear during wartime, the ongoing war against women, and prevailing patriarchal social relations, do not provide for any social and economic resources for women to either express their pain and fear, to heal, or to escape from them. Blamed for being victims, women's denunciations of and attempts to escape from the violence against them, even in peace time, are labelled as taboo, and deemed shameful and dishonourable. In Nahid Aziz's words, "Women have no protection from domestic violence. Those who flee abusive marriages are frequently imprisoned, prosecuted for running away or for alleged adultery" (Aziz, 2011, p. 233).

Since the violence inflicted on women directly targets their bodies and sexuality, its pain has a more penetrating, long-term effect, leaving permanent scars on their psyches. Women's experience of trauma is also different, as the trauma is mostly blunt and fierce. The normative social and cultural pressures to suppress the pain further deepen and personalize the impact, as women attach guilt, shame and blame to their pain (Garrido, 2014). Women not only carry the physical burden of being tortured, but also the psychological torment of being invaded in their private bodies and losing their personal, social and cultural dignity. After being raped and dishonoured, women not only agonize over the loss of their personal dignity, but also about how their experience has brought dishonour to their families and communities. All this suppressed pain and shame remains an open wound, leaving women vulnerable to further harm, including cultural and social stigmatization and alienation.

## Gendered Response to Trauma and Gender-Specific Coping Strategies

War impacts men and women differently, and stimulates different coping strategies in them. As mentioned earlier, men's experience of violence and trauma is generally public and collectively recognized with open networks for expression and sharing. They are more expressive and extroverted about their experience of trauma, and their post-traumatic behavioural and cognitive patterns differ from women.

The patriarchal norms, social, economic and family relations that shape women's responses to trauma, and their strategies for coping with it, also define the boundaries and forms of expression for those responses. Women's "agency, resistance and critical conscious remained constrained by multi-layered power relations" (Chaudhry, 2009). While trauma for women is mostly blunt and direct, its expression is less overt and visible. Women have learned to suppress their narrative and silence their voice in order to avoid cultural alienation and social rejection. "From childhood a girl is socialized to be silent, patient, and submissive, to become a selfless person who is pleased to keep her husband and her in-laws, especially her mother-in-law happy" (Ali, 2012).

It is a survival strategy and cultural adaptation for women to be more compliant in traumatic and difficult situations. Parveen Ali's study of abused women indicated that victims' responses to trauma was mainly passive and quiet. Their coping mechanism included sharing the pain with their mothers, sisters, female friends, and also praying and crying (Ali, 2012).

Another factor in gender-specific responses to trauma can be women's unique perspectives on their own needs and ways of expressing and achieving them. As mothers and protectors, women's perceptions of their personal wellbeing are formed within the boundaries of communal and collective needs. Their protective instincts toward their children broaden to include family, community and society at large. While the protection and nurturing of children require a woman's physical and emotional presence, maintaining family integrity and social coherence necessitates her compliance to, and compatibility with, the normative relations. Women's coping strategies are thus inclusive of their personal and collective social survival needs. This assumption of collective responsibility enables women to move on with their lives and obligations as keepers of the family and community, and further step out of their victim position to act as healers and agents of social construction. "Women are not only victims, they are also agents of reconstructing, of going ahead and finding answers to the situations" (Garrido, 2014). Carrying the multiple burdens of emotional, physical and cultural responsibilities, women have refused to submit to hardship. Instead they strive to survive, not only as individuals, but as mothers and as protectors of their families. Survival, in most cases, has involved adapting to hardship for the sake of rescuing not only oneself, but larger social or human entities, such as one's children, family, and ultimately the entire community.

Many women have worked towards resolving their daily abuse through securing the future of their children. Women's resilience and resistance against both declared and undeclared wars manifest their selfless and collective response against egoistic, power-driven forces. The underground network of home-based schools run by women in the face of serious threats during the Taliban regime in Afghanistan indicate women's collective determination to support the right of young girls to education (Humanity Denied, 2001; Koofi, 2011). It was women's and girls' solidarity that enabled them to show such bravery. A network of women took turns in providing their homes for students to study, and developed collective strategies to keep their schools secret.

Women's unity at times of conflict and collective threat is not formed on the basis of their shared gender identity alone. The experience of common causes and consequences of conflicts and violence unites them as victims of common oppression (Butler, 1988). War, patriarchal norms, colonialism, capitalism and misogynist cultural discourse create unified patterns of violence against women which lead to common experiences of oppression. These common experiences form a collective identity for women, and unite them in their journey of oppression, struggle and resilience.

By ignoring their self-interest, and at times their social assigned status, women have created coping strategies to preserve collective family and communal entities, and have thus built bridges to change and progress. While patriarchy victimizes women, it also shapes their responses, and through those responses, women are empowered to be consciously selfless and collective (equality-driven as opposed to power-driven) in their survival strategies.

Women find themselves in the paradoxical position of being both victims and healers, survivors and fighters in the face of wars both declared and undeclared. The complex cultural differences and multilayered forms of trauma that Afghan women have experienced during many decades of war have placed them in a unique situation, where they have been both victimized and also empowered with resilience and courage. While there have been many studies in the fields of social science and social work on women's experiences in conflict zones, it will be very important for social workers to recognize the unique realities of Afghan women as a group, and also to understand the diversities that exist within the group. While there are community organizations that render settlement and training services for Afghans in their own languages, such as the Afghan Women's Organization in Toronto, more broad-based organizations are needed, so women can have easy access and can reveal their problems without fear of cultural stigmas and shaming. Since mental illness is mostly stigmatized in Afghan communities, more accessible professional and social services are needed for people with PTSD, to provide them with a safe environment and resources for healing. It will be in that process of sharing traumatic experiences and healing that women's accounts of bravery, solidarity and resilience will be told, and will be transformed into a clear and confident voice for asserting their dignity, standing, and agency as citizens.

## References

A Malaysian first wife speaks of polygamy. (2009, September 12). *Toronto Star*. Retrieved from www.thestar.com.

Ali, P. (2012, March 12). Intimate partner violence in Pakistan: A systemic review. *Trauma, Violence, and Abuse* (Epub ahead of print). doi:10.1177/1524838014526065.

Armstrong, S. ( 2002). *Veiled threat: The hidden power of the women of Afghanistan*. Toronto: Penguin.

Armstrong, S. (2013). *Ascent of women*. Toronto: Random House Canada.

Aziz, N. (2011). Psychological impact of war. In Heath, J., & Zahedi, A. (Eds.). *Land of the unconquerable* (p. 231). Berkeley: University of California Press.

Bains, S. (2014). Living in fear: Violence as a societal scourge. In Ajit, A. (Ed.). *Violence against women all-pervading* (p. 34). Toronto: Elspeth Heyworth Centre for Women.

Baron, L., & Straus, M.A. (1987). Four theories of rape: A macrosociological analysis. *Social Problems, 34* (5).

Butler, J. (1988). Performative act and gender constitution. *Theatre Journal, 40* (4), pp. 519–531).

Chaudhry, L. (2009). Narrating trauma and reconstruction in post conflict Karachi. *Feminist Psychology, 3*, p. 298.

Coll, S. (2001). *Ghost war*. New York: Penguin.

Cordozo, B.L. (2005). Mental health of women in postwar Afghanistan. *Journal of Women's Health, 4* (14). Retrieved from http://www.ncbi.nlm.nih.gov/pubmed/15916500.

Cross, P. (2013). *Violence against women*. Toronto: CCMW.

Donat, P. L.N, & D'Emilio, J. (1992). A feminist redefinition of rape and sexual assault: Historical foundations and change. *Journal of Social Issues, 48* (1), pp. 9–22.

Garrido, M.T. (2014, March 27). Women: victims of conflict or agents of change? *IRIN*. Retrieved from http://www.irinnews.org/report/99847/women-victims-of-conflict-or-agents-of-change.

Girls Not Brides (2014). *Girls not brides*. Retrieved from www.girlsnotbrides.org.

Heath, J. & Zahedi, A. (Eds.). (2014). *The children of Afghanistan: Path to peace*. Austin, TX: University of Texas Press.

Huda, S. (2007, January 27). *Special report on the human rights aspects of the victims of trafficking in persons*. UN Report.

Human Rights Watch (2001), *Humanity denied: Systematic violations of women's rights in Afghanistan, 13* (5).

Jain, A. (2014). *Domestic violence: All pervading*. Toronto: Elspeth Heyworth Centre for Women.

Jalal, M., Joya, M., & Koofi, F. (2011). Voice of parliamentarians: Four women MPs share their thoughts. In Heath, J., & Zahedi, A. (Eds.). *Land of the unconquerable* (pp. 128–134). Berkeley: University of California Press.

Jiwani, Y. (2006). Missing and murdered women: Reproducing marginality in new discourse. *Canadian Journal of Communication , 31*(4).

Koofi, F. (2011). *Letters to my daughters: A memoir*. Vancouver: Douglas & McIntyre.

Kuehnast, K. Jongs, C.Q. & Hernes, H. (Eds.). (2011). *Women and war: Power and protection in the 21st century*. Washington, DC: US Institute of Peace Press.

Marcus, S. (2002). Fighting bodies, fighting words. In Butler, J. (Ed.), *Feminists theorize the political* (pp. 385–403). New York: Routledge, 2002.

Mui, C.L., & Murphy, J.S (Eds.). *Gender struggle: Patriarchal approaches to contemporary feminism*. Lanham, MD: Rowman & Littlefield.

Mladejenovic, L. (1999). Beyond war hierarchies: Belgrade feminists' experience working with female survivors of war. In Sharrat, S., & Kaschak, E. (Eds.). *Assault on the soul: Women in the former Yugoslavia* (p. 83). New York: Haworth Press.

Moghissi, H. (1999). *Feminism and Islamic fundamentalism*. London: Zed Books.

Mojab, S. (2014, Summer). Resistance: A feminist critique. *Solidarity*. Retrieved from http://www.solidarity-us.org.

Mukherjee, A. (2014). Women's bodies as the site of patriarchal violence. In Ajit, A. (Ed.). *Violence against women all pervading* (p. 14). Toronto: Elspeth Heyworth Centre for Women.

Naili, H. (2014, April 17). Iraqi girl-marriage bill called vote-getting ploy. *We News*. Retrieved from www.womensenews.org.

Naili, H. (2014, April 9). Video going viral tells men "the rapist is you." *We News*. Retrieved from www.womensenews.org.

Napikoski, L. (n.d.) Misogyny: Women's history definition. Retrieved from http://womenshistory.about.com/od/glossary/a/misogyny.htm.

Petchesky, P. (2002). Phantom towers: Feminist reflections on the battle between global capitalism and fundamentalist terrorism. *Society, 2*, pp. 40–45.

Pourzand, N. (1999). Female education and citizenship in Afghanistan: A turbulent relationship. In Davis, N., & Werbner, P. (Eds.). *Women, citizenship and difference* (pp. 87–99). New York: Zed Books.

Rashid, A. (2000). *Taliban*. New York: I. B. Tauris.

Saleema, (2000, July, 10). Taliban Assault on Educational Courses in Kabul. Retrieved from www.rawa.org.

Scheffler, S. & Muchele, A. (1999). Women and therapy. In Sharrat, S., & Kaschak, E. (Eds.). *Assault on the soul: Women in the former Yogoslavia* (p. 124). New York: Haworth Press.

Sharrat, S., & Kaschak, E. (Eds.). (1999). *Assault on the soul: Women in the former Yugoslavia*. New York: Haworth Press.

Smith, J.D. (2011). Between choice and force. In Heath, J. & Zahedi, A. (Eds.). *Land of the unconquerable* (p. 163). Berkeley: University of California Press.

Sohani, Z. & Bhandari, M., The reality of intimate partner violence in India. In Jain, A. (Ed.), *Violence Against Women: All Pervading* (pp. 88–91). Toronto: Elspeth Heyworth Centre for Women.

Tull, M. (2012, January 29). Symptoms of PTSD after rape. *IRIN*. Retrieved from http://www.irinnews.org/advancedsearchresults.

Zahedi, A. (2011). When the picture does not fit the frame. In Heath, J. & Zahedi, A. (Eds.). *Land of the unconquerable* (p. 294). Berkeley: University of California Press.

## CHAPTER TEN

# The Politics of Death: Situating Immigrants, Refugees and Asylum Seekers

## Soheila Pashang

I n recent years the fields of gerontology, health and social work have expanded our understanding of death and grief. Despite this, many frontline professionals and community activists continue to face challenges not only in assisting immigrants to process the ceremonies and rituals associated with death, but also in acquiring critical knowledge and expertise to provide bereavement support. The purpose of this chapter is to demonstrate the complexity of death, burial and grief among immigrants, refugees and asylum seekers. This chapter begins with an overview of factors such as armed conflicts, poverty, violence and health disparities that increase the vulnerability of disenfranchised communities to mortality and death. Next, the chapter will situate the death of migrants within the ongoing discursive struggle between Canadian institutions, international law and the law of the immigrant's homeland. These discourses hold the power of imposing institutional policies over the wishes, needs and rights of the deceased immigrant family members, permitting the burial of dead bodies within constrained spatial locations, or authorizing the freedom of movement of the deceased through prolonged and expensive repatriation services. Other central themes covered here include decisions regarding burial in exile as a way of rooting in the host country and a sign of defiance against the immigrant's own system of government at home, or repatriation of the deceased to the homeland to contest against a sense of alienation from, and show solidarity with, that homeland. The chapter will further address complex grief as a systemic factor which may hinder bereavement or interfere in the healing process. Anyone who is bereaved and uprooted needs appropriate support to overcome the trauma of bereavement in exile. Through a review of the existing literature on bereavement, the chapter will illustrate the role of professionals in assisting immigrants, refugees and asylum-seekers by drawing on equity, social justice, and anti-oppressive theoretical approaches.

## Lives That No Longer Count

Death is a universal experience. It "is the permanent disappearance of all evidence of life at any time after live birth has taken place" (United Nations, 2001, para. 57). While everyone's death is an individual experience, the ambiguity of death depends on socialization, psychological discourse (Selket, 2007), political conditions, the law, faith and religious ideologies or lack of thereof. There are many theories pertaining to death; however, this chapter will mainly focus on the notion of death from displacement and migratory related perspectives.

According to the World Health Organization (WHO, 2013), an estimated total of 56 million people died worldwide in the year 2012. This estimate may be flawed, as most births and deaths in the global south or poor countries are not registered. While global life expectancy is projected to be 70 years, mortality is not evenly distributed across populations. For example, in the global north or rich countries, people mainly die of aging-related factors (7 in every 10 deaths) (WHO, 2013). In the case of Canada, for instance, advancements in diagnostic capacities have had a positive impact on longevity and quality of life and have resulted in better care for the elderly, so that people live (on average) well beyond the age of 80 (Statistics Canada, 2012). At the same time, in the global south or poor countries, a disproportionate number of deaths occur among children under the age of 15 (4 in every 10 deaths) (WHO, 2013). Nearly 99% of deaths among children under the age of five in these regions are the result of malnutrition and lack of an effective health care system (WHO, 2013). The HIV/AIDS epidemic is also a leading cause of death in sub-Saharan Africa, resulting in more than 1.1 million deaths in 2012. Fully 80% of those deaths were of persons between the ages of 15 and 59 years (WHO, 2013). Various reports put life expectancy in sub-Saharan Africa at only about 50 years (United Nations Human Development Index, 2006; WHO, 2013), with the figures for Democratic Republic of the Congo (49.5 years), Central Africa (48.4 years) and Sierra Leone (46.5 years) below the 50-year mark (WHO, 2013).

The widening gap between rich and poor countries and the lack of willingness to systemically combat that gap greatly affects population health in the global south. According to a United Nations World Mortality report (2011), 45.4 million people die each year in African and other poor nations around the world. The disproportionately high death rates per capita in these nations are due, in part, to the colonial legacy, and in part to the harsh conditions in post-colonial societies struggling for independence and political rights while being exposed to capitalist and globalized forces. Under conditions of state corruption, human lives are valued far less, and governments often prioritize military spending over development, primary health care, and the safety and wellbeing of the bulk of the populations they purport to represent. In the face of economic, health, and social disparities and political instability, death can occur due to violence, armed conflict, poverty, malnutrition and poor preventive health care practices, as well as forced migration and displacement.

## Roots and Routes of Displacement and Trauma

In recent decades, the right to live with dignity and free from violence has become an issue discussed by international governing bodies. The Universal Declaration of Human Rights of 1948 was created as a response to the Holocaust and the immense destruction of World War II, which claimed 50 million to 80 million lives. The 1989 Convention on the Rights of the Child (CRC) was of particular importance in moving toward greater protection for the sanctity of life. Despite this, over 100 million people, including refugees and asylum seekers, remain unprotected from abuse, genocide, and violence (Helton et al., 2000). For instance, each year, armed conflicts alone claim the lives of 250,000 people. While international legal instruments guarantee the "right to life, liberty and security" (Article 3, UN Declaration of Human Rights), many countries fall short in enforcing that guarantee. The main problem with UN conventions is that their application is left to individual states. Through treaty bodies, periodic review by the UN Human Rights Council and Special Rapporteurs takes place; however, there exists a need for systematic measures to ensure that states that have ratified a given convention live up to their obligations. As well, UN declarations, unlike conventions and covenants, are not legally binding, as they are only meant to provide general guidelines to states party to them. Therefore, it is not surprising that (according to 2006 estimates) over one billion children under the age of 18 lived in areas of conflict, with 300 million of them under age 5, and more than 18 million of them either refugees or internally displaced (United Nations Children's Fund [UNICEF], April 2009). Violence against children is a deliberate act in armed conflict to recruit armed forces or for labour, sexual and/or commercial exploitation. Often children are attacked and killed in schools, hospitals, or when fleeing along roadsides. Regrettably, many of the displaced migrants do not make it to safety and die in the course of their journeys. They drown during perilous sea journeys, freeze to death, or are gunned down by gang members and armed groups along dangerous roads. Others lose their lives in the midst of escaping from war, while imprisoned or under torture. If they die in the course of their journeys, their bodies will remain unidentified.

It is equally important to distinguish between typologies of mortality, including those caused by the immediate actions of other people (violence, war, armed conflict, ethnic cleansing), those that are the result of more generalized human actions (e.g., environmental degradation and pollution), and those that are the result of "natural" causes (tornadoes, volcanic eruptions). Each category differs in the systemic processes of intervention, prevention and allocation of resources. For example, international rescue teams respond more systemically to environmental disasters than armed conflict. These realities reflect societal judgments about whose life is more valuable, whose grievances are addressed, and whose remains are cared for or neglected.

This becomes even more complicated when migrants die trying to cross national borders. Under international law, states are endowed with sovereign rights to protect their territories and citizens (Jimenez, 2009). To respond to the flow of unauthorized migration, many states have now adopted strategies, including border control and surveillance, to prevent unauthorized entry into the country. These strategies, however, have had both intended and unintended consequences that have claimed the lives of many migrants (Cornelius, 2001). For instance, from 2000 through 2008, the number of unauthorized Mexican migrants in the U.S. increased from 8.4 million to 11.9 million, with on average one migrant dying every day while trying to cross the Mexico–U.S. border (Jimenez, 2009). Therefore, while death is generally considered a natural process, associated with an aging body or a deadly disease, the deaths of immigrants, refugees and asylum seekers raise distinct ethical concerns, since the power over their lives is socially and politically constructed.

Even when migrants manage to cross national borders, they are vulnerable to exclusionary immigration processes and may face deportation and the possibility of violent death upon return to their home country. This is particularly concerning as nations such as Canada have adopted "voluntary return" policies in order to manage deportation of undesired immigrants. At the same time, there have been reported cases of asylum seekers' deaths while under custody in the prison system or in detention centres, due to state negligence or because of suicide (either to avoid humiliation while under custody, or out of fear of possible torture and violent death upon deportation). The humiliation of migrants' lives often extends after life itself, to their burial, and specifically, to restrictions placed on burial sites. Many old and new immigrants have endured discrimination both during their lives and when burying their loved ones. As Lunman (2001) notes, their gravesites and tombstones remind us of prevailing racial prejudice against immigrant communities — a prejudice that has now been extended to their dead bodies.

## The Silencing of the Other: Deceased Immigrants in Canada

In most societies, a funeral is a communal event, for it brings communities together to pay respect to the dead and share the grief of the surviving family members. Unfortunately, due to exclusionary and discriminatory practices engrained within the fabric of the Canadian society, the right to burial and respect for the dead has been a challenging process for some groups. Historically, many cemeteries across Canada were reluctant to accept non-Christians, Aboriginals, or those falling within the concept of the "other." According to Edward Said (1978), the concept of the "other" has a social, political and economic implication, with a tendency to subordinate, stigmatize and exclude certain individuals or groups of people from society. These included African Canadians and Chinese Canadians, whose corpses were buried in separate cemeteries. Despite such burials at separate cemeteries, racialized individuals still experienced and feared harassment and abuse while mourning their deceased (Lunman, 2001).

Frantz Fanon stated that the colonized must constantly be conscious of their image to protect their position in a hostile and racially segregated world (Fanon, 1963). There is evidence to suggest that the Chinese buried in Ross Bay Cemetery in Victoria, British Columbia, in 1873 were identified only by number, not by name (for instance, "Chinaman No. 1" and other derogatory labels) (Lunman, 2001). There have also been numerous cases in Canada where Aboriginal children were buried in mass graves or placed in unmarked graves, as if they never existed or had no history attached to their names. One recent case is the genocide and mass graves of children who attended residential school in Brantford, Ontario (Annett, 2001). Since then, political efforts have been made to show respect by issuing public apologies to specific communities. For example, Chinese community members in Victoria, B.C. advocated exhuming Chinese remains and storing their bones or shipping them back to China, or restoring neglected cemeteries and banished tombstones (Lunman, 2001). In March 1998, the government of Canada also issued a Statement of Reconciliation and public apology for its discriminatory treatment of Aboriginal children who died while attending residential schools. Over 3,000 children had died, many being buried in mass or unmarked graves. Cemeteries and funerary practices represent the politics of our time, where indifference or lack of respect to the body of a deceased immigrant or non-western "other" is an extension of racial politics.

With the changes in the social values and composition of Canadian society, the nature of cemeteries has undergone a transformation. Today, most cemeteries are non-denominational and non-sectarian, and open to burials of more recent immigrants from diverse faiths and cultural backgrounds. A respect for diversity has brought Canada to a new stage where immigrant communities are now provided with the option of ethno-cultural and multi-faith cemeteries and a right to preferred burial ceremonies, including repatriation of the body of the deceased to his or her homeland.

## The Repatriation of the Body of the Deceased

Repatriation is the reality of a global divide where, on the one hand, deprived families in the home country desire to reunite with the deceased to pay homage, and, on the other, the deceased is separated from remaining family members in exile. Repatriation is also about protest against spatial imposition, the right to the homeland, and fear of the fluidity or uncertainty of migratory movements. The practice of repatriation of the deceased, as Page et al. (n.d.) note, is rooted in the process of nation building, and in the sense of belonging. While many immigrants and their families, consciously or not, accept the absence of their loved ones in the aftermath of displacement, they still hold to the view that their interment must be in the home country. It is this changing historical pattern and the desire of grieving families to repatriate the body of their loved ones that has given rise to new forms of corporate funeral enterprise in the late twentieth and early twenty-first centuries.

For most people, though perhaps for immigrants in a heightened way, death is imbued with a sense of belonging to a community or a geographic domain. In fact, studies on the first generation of immigrants show that the decision to bury or repatriate their dead is closely linked to kinship ties, past memories and marginalization (Wyndham, 2003; Uehling, 2001). This is what prompts them to bury their dead in the homeland where their cultural identity is rooted. Conversely, attachment to burial sites, forming new nuclear family relations, and ties to a new homeland, play a vital role in helping the second generation of immigrants to take root in the host country. This option is particularly true for those immigrants who consider the burial of their loved one in exile as a sign of defiance against the system of government at home. But whereas immigrants may have convictions and some level of decision-making power related to where and how the bodies of their loved ones should be buried, international political relations, state laws and cemetery regulations often frame, limit and subvert such decisions.

The following case study puts the challenges of transporting a body back to the homeland into perspective.

## Case Study 10.1: Mugaya

Mugaya came to Canada as refugee with her two children in 1986, to escape war and political persecution. After the death of her eldest son Sam to untreatable cancer, she decided to bury him in their family cemetery in Africa. This decision was subsequently shaped by the prevailing political realities: first, her family members would not be able to acquire Canadian visitor visas to attend his funeral; and second, due to their political activities, some of her immediate family members were banned from exiting the country. To repatriate the body, Mugaya was left with no option but to seek assistance from her embassy, something which further complicated and delayed the transport of the body. After an autopsy and, later, sanitization and embalming, Sam's corpse became the hostage of bureaucracy. A long process ensued of sending documents back and forth to the federal government, then to the embassy officials for approval and then back to the hospital and funeral home. Throughout this process, Mugaya had no chance to grieve but had to support her grieving daughter who had lost her loving brother. In the end, the entire process of repatriation cost Mugaya $10,000 and a long delay in burying her son's body. This was culturally and religiously unacceptable for Mugaya and her family members.

As the case study shows, repatriation of a deceased body is a complex and expensive process ruled by a set of socio-political, medical, and legal relations. These relations, along with domestic and international laws and regulations, maintain power over immigrants' options in respect to end of life, death, burial, and the right to mourn for one's beloved in the diaspora. Ironically, the repatriation of the body often contradicts the cultural and religious belief systems of the deceased. For example, when religious doctrines emphasize the importance of burying the body within a limited time, the sense of belonging gained through repatriation takes away from the significance of early burial. Given available options related to burying the dead in the diaspora or in the homeland, the meaning of repatriation entails a sense of alienation from, and solidarity with, a particular place.

Significantly, due to fears of prosecution or a precarious status, an immigrant may be banned from exiting the new country or entering the homeland, whereas the corpse is free to cross international borders (with the exception of transport of an infidel's body to countries whose governments may prohibit arrival and burial). This freedom is conditional and subject to numerous medical procedures, such as embalming, to prevent the spread of disease, given the rapid deterioration of the body. As a result, the corpse becomes an object confined within the ambivalent boundaries of political relations and regulations governing international borders as well as administrative and legal bureaucracy. This includes translating necessary documents, obtaining a death certificate, identifying next of kin, addressing wills and inheritance, and transport approval. In the absence of a direct flight, the condition of the remains must also meet the criteria of the transit country. For example, if transiting via the UK, the coffin would have to be hermetically sealed in order to comply with anti-terrorism legislation, since lead, the preferred lining for coffins, is impervious to x-rays (Satterlee, 2007).

Although a corpse is not property under Canadian law, the executor of the estate does have certain property-like rights over a body (including the right to ensure burial). There may also be other rights of possession that resemble property rights if the body acquires different attributes after death, for instance through the preservation techniques (Whaley, 2012) required to comply with rules regarding the transportation of the remains. Unfortunately, family members in the diaspora (if, for example, some siblings live in Canada while others are located elsewhere) and those in the homeland can end up disagreeing about the process, procedures or place of burial. This assumes, of course, that the deceased has an executor or next of kin with the financial and linguistic abilities to arrange repatriation. In many situations, families have no option but to rely on their embassies, community members, or the Canadian government. This is particularly challenging when the state is to make legal and financial decisions without the input of distant family members. This relationship becomes even more complicated when minor children are involved. In that case, dependent children of the deceased immigrants are placed under the care of the state or child protection agencies (e.g., the Children's Aid Society) and become wards of the Crown. In particular, young children can get caught in a custody battle between state and the remaining family members and divided between two geographies. For instance, the Canadian-born children may remain in Canada, while a child born abroad may be sent back home. In essence, they may or may not be reunited with their siblings or their family members. This gives rise to a trans-border dialogue in which family members, unable to cross highly secured borders due to financial, social and political constraints, seek to overcome barriers of grief in order to compensate for their loss. This has a significant traumatic impact on the friends and relatives of the deceased, impeding the grieving process. In dealing with their grief, immigrants and their family members may guard themselves against expressing pain or grief as a result of hopelessness or a feeling of guilt for not being able to have closure. This is partly due to their inability to attend the funeral as a result of their immigration status and lack of mobility rights, or inability to afford the cost of travel.

**Dealing with the Trauma of Distant Death**

Death at a long distance causes unexpected distress and tension for close relatives and acquaintances. This tension is exacerbated by legal procedures and bureaucratic processes in the host country and by the deceased's executor's (if there is one) unfamiliarity in navigating such systems in order to make informed decisions. These procedures include identification of the body, registration of death and obtaining a death certificate, and locating wills and material possessions.

When death occurs at such a distance, the deceased may be identified or could remain unidentified. This is partly due to the issue of mobility rights, such as the need to obtain a valid visa to travel, or lack of awareness about the whereabouts of the deceased, particularly in a situation of illegal migration. The inability to identify human remains in such cases leaves many family members in limbo about the whereabouts of their missing relatives. This uncertainty affects the grieving process and causes additional psychological suffering, from feeling guilty for one's loss to lack of closure and complex grief. All this takes place despite the fact that international law has established guidelines for dealing with dead bodies in war, peace and in the case of environmental disasters.

Due in part to fear, lack of resources to repatriate bodily remains, or language barriers, family members are unable to approach law enforcement agencies for help. The death of an immigrant therefore can cause an unanticipated sense of hopelessness, unresolved crises and fear and uncertainty over a long period of time. For the family members, distance burials often represent permanent loss and separation caused by factors or conditions over which they have little or no control. They may be informed of the news in vague or insensitive ways by formal or informal sources that lack accurate details of medical or legal investigations or decision-making processes about the time and place of burial. In instances of restricted immigration policies by the host country (lack of legal visas or travel documents), or when mobility rights are lacking (for example, when people are living in refugee camps or "underground"), the separation further inhibits access to the burial ceremony.

Table 10.1 on the next page briefly explores my own professional experience in working with individuals and families dealing with distance grief.

In the case of armed conflicts or major disease outbreaks, deaths can occur in large numbers and collectively. Yet, distanced families and community members displaced across international borders are unable to grieve collectively. Further research is required about collective grief (for example, about the nature of grief experiences during such tragedies as the Armenian genocide, the Holocaust, or genocide in Rwanda). In such cases, the focus should be on restitution, reparation, compensation, recognition and rehabilitation. Finding a way to respect the memory of victims through narratives, poems, books, music, monuments or expressive artwork can be useful. Collective responses depathologize and increase the resilience of the remaining family and community members.

**Table 10.1. *Variations in Grief Response***

| Description | Factors Affecting Variation in Grief Response |
|---|---|
| Conveying the News | **Direct news:** Hearing news of a death of a loved one directly from family members who are living overseas. The direct communication with family members allows individuals to mourn and receive support.<br>**Indirect news:** Hearing news of a death of a loved one indirectly through government officials, news reports, acquaintances and informal sources. The indirect news can create a high level of shock, anxiety and emotional and psychological trauma. |
| Multiple Deaths | Dealing with multiple deaths caused by acts of violence, armed conflict, war and displacement. Immobility to access or to offer emotional and financial support causes additional level of trauma. |
| Types of Deaths | • Sudden and unexpected death by accident, violence, natural disasters or man-made causes, as well as suicide.<br>• Death caused by the process of aging or an illness.<br>• Death as a result of deportation to homeland. In this case, since death occurs outside of the deporting state's jurisdiction, families face additional challenges to pursue legal action against the deportee state or homeland. |
| Final Closure | • Inability to communicate with the deceased prior to death.<br>• Inability to participate in funerary or religious/cultural rituals due to immobility whether as a result of precarious immigration status or financial/resource constraints.<br>• Fear of persecution which prevents one from communicating directly with loved ones.<br>• Feeling guilty or responsible for leaving loved ones behind (or not communicating with the deceased). |
| Relationship to Deceased | • Close ties through emotional connection or family kinship, such as loss of child, partner, parents, comrade. |
| Place of Death | • Death in homeland, transit country, refugee camp, en route.<br>• Death in a host country and within closer proximity, where survivors may or may not be equipped with knowledge about the existing resources and cultural/political/legal procedures. |
| Death under State Custody | • Death under custody in the homeland or flight country.<br>• Death under custody in safe country while crossing the border, or in detention.<br>• Death while under custody (in jail, detention centre) in host country, where family members lack political power, resources or influence to seek accurate information, pursue investigation, engage in legal procedures, access medical records or repatriate the corpse. |

## Theories of Grief: From Pathology to Resilience

Death and life are reflected in two conflicting discourses. While for the most part birth is celebrated, grief over death — the expression of the inner psychological and emotional response to loss — is also considered universal. Mourning, or the social expression of feelings of loss, is often framed in cultural and religious or spiritual contexts. Recently there has been a shift towards theorizing the notion from within mental health and psychological perspectives.

Historically, mourning and grief for the loss of a loved one was seen as a natural process in which the individual experiencing the loss interacted with community and religious or spiritual leaders. With the modern trend toward institutionalization of death and professionalization of grief therapy, our notions of loss and conceptualization of grief have changed. Many professionals agree grief can occur before the loss, can be expressed as an immediate response to loss, or may even surface long after the loss or through the death and loss of others (Kasternbaum, n.d.).

In retrospect, most twentieth-century theories of bereavement have been psychological or situate the discourse within the politics of family system theory (Klass and Goss, 2003). Accordingly, many mental health practitioners label grief as a pathological problem because of its damaging consequences for the mourner, who goes through negative, painful and disruptive experiences (Pomeroy et al., 2009). The western notion of bereavement therefore incorporates a strongly prescriptive approach, which pays more attention to "tasks" and "stages" than to respecting the time and process needed by the grieving person to internalize their lived conditions and socio-economic and political realities.

In their work, Pomeroy et al. (2009) de-pathologize grief and go on to present a strength-based framework by focusing on the mourner's inherent resiliencies, rather than deficits, in navigating the grieving process and adjusting to the absence of the loved one(s). The mourner comes to the situation with both **individual strengths** and **environmental strengths**. The individual strengths include aspirations, competencies and confidence, all of which are dependent on a combination of biological, psychological and social factors. The environmental strengths, on the other hand, include resources, social relations and opportunities. Together they affect one's sense of wellbeing, empowerment and life satisfaction (Pomeroy et al., 2009). The strengths-based approach appropriately considers grief narratives in relation to environment, and further emphasizes resiliency and power relations, but falls short in contextualizing global sources of domination and exploitation of bereaved immigrant family members within legal and structural systems. These systems of power influence, and in part interfere with, the grief of those categorized as immigrants.

The fields of social work and social service work also face contradictions shaped by the process of forced and voluntary migration. This is particularly evident where, because of a radical shift toward justice and inclusion, human rights concerns may emerge. These discursive forces place an expectation on professionals to adopt new approaches to knowledge and skills in order to enhance their competence in working with diverse populations. As a result, many professionals now approach death and grief from perspectives grounded in a understanding of diversity and cultural competency. Such approaches encompass respect for cultural and religious funerary, tradition and grieving rituals. However, whether we appreciate culture as a shared experience or as a factor that divides human beings, concentrating to an overly large degree on issues of culture or religion can result in the stereotyping of an entire group (Choudhuri et al., 2012) and hence disregard for the diversity within and among individuals. An overemphasis on cultural pluralism further neglects the fact that some people migrate as a protest against and escape from discrimination that has been normalized and masked under the guise of cultural practices. The culturalization of a community may also pose a danger of neglecting the intersectionality of race, class, age, gender, sexual orientation, political and ideological stands, and faith (or lack of thereof) between and among people. Jones (2005) criticizes the "cookbook approach" to diversity and to the understanding of ethnic minorities for its risk of perpetuating new myths or stereotypes as well as inaccuracies and misunderstandings.

On the other hand, if we agree that culture is not static and changes over time and place, we may find the wishes of individuals and families in conflict with professional ethics and obligations when it comes to end-of-life and burial decisions. Professionals must understand the ways in which the processes of colonization or forced Christianity, for instance, have impacted Blacks and Aboriginal peoples in viewing end-of-life, death, and grief issues, and the ways in which colonized educational systems have influenced professionals working with marginalized and dispossessed populations. Unfortunately, the discourse of cultural competency (or, to use a term recently coined, "cultural intelligence") is often used as a pretext to mask the broader unjust practices, regulations and hegemonic power over immigrants and racialized persons in dealing with complex grief processes.

Consider the case of Mugaya, mentioned earlier in this chapter. Her struggle is not necessarily due to cultural factors or "a right way to grieve," but is, rather, a political one. The complexity surrounding her son's death intersected with Canadian immigration laws and regulations, as well as diplomatic relations between countries. Mugaya was conflicted about making the right decision and such responsibility placed a tremendous personal, ethical, and psychological pressure on her, hindering her ability to grieve. We are left with the fact that, while Mugaya's resiliency overcame the barriers to repatriation of Sam's body, the multilayered pain of loss compounded with systemic barriers created a sense of alienation from her diasporic home and also left her feeling abandoned by her homeland. She felt guilty for disrespecting Sam's body, which was entangled in bureaucratic processes.

Disenfranchised grief occurs when the loss cannot be acknowledged. For example, in situations where same-sex relationships are illegal, seen as sinful, or carry with them political and/or social consequences, the remaining partner is not able to express grief or follow mourning rituals. In such cases, grief and mourning are individualized in isolation. The same is often true in situations where women are valued based on their reproductive power. Often mothers who undergo abortion or miscarriage fear potential consequences. Similar issues emerge when death is stigmatized as a result of HIV/AIDS. Stigma and shame attached to sexual violence while under state custody, in prison or during armed conflict also prevent family members from openly expressing their sorrow of loss. These factors, among others, push the discourse of grief and the grieving process to the forefront of politics and international relations, where national borders become a political line denying or delaying bereaved family members the right to grieve at home or in the diaspora.

## Grief: Equity, Social Justice and Anti-oppression Perspectives

The loneliness of exile makes death and coping after the death of loved ones difficult, as the individual must deal with the situation within the context of being uprooted from their country of origin. In such cases, extra support from the community is needed. The vacuum should be filled by offering ongoing support and empathy to the bereaved, while acknowledging the resiliency of individuals in dealing with their loss. In recent years, many higher education programs in social work, social service work, education and other disciplines have adopted **anti-oppression (AOP) frameworks**. AOP is a practice framework in which practitioners (including social workers) challenge political adversity and individual, cultural and systemic oppressions of race, gender, class, sexual orientation, immigration status, nationality, culture, and religion, in order to prevent the marginalization of racialized groups and disenfranchised populations.

This section explores experiences of life and death from intersecting approaches rooted in empowerment, equity, and social justice and ingrained in anti-oppression theoretical frameworks. My emphasis is on the strength and resiliency of bereaved family members in dealing with their losses, and on further confronting social injustices and structural barriers hindering one's right to grief.

In reality, immigrants react to and cope with the loss of their loved ones in many different ways. Individual belief systems, type and locality of death, relationship with the deceased, whether one has witnessed the death, the site of burial and participation in rituals all have an impact on the way in which people come to terms with their loss. Drawing on equity, social justice and anti-oppression frameworks, can we situate bereaved family members within their everyday lived experiences and promote an understanding of their internalization of grief within the context of national and global politics? Such a contextualization starts from the barriers set by law, legislation and the Canadian immigration system, and extends to Canadian international relations with other countries. These interlocking systems do not, however, exist in isolation and often interact with a broader world system of politics and economic and trade relations.

Practitioners working from equity, social justice and anti-oppressive approaches must understand the role of western media (including social media), the educational system and organizational practices and approaches to grief and the ways in which they may devalue individuals, groups, and communities' ways of handling death or expressing grief. For example, the mass media continue to showcase the horror of the dead bodies of innocent civilians from developing countries through armed conflict, war and violence. An Afghan or Iraqi child killed by aerial bombardment is considered collateral damage, whereas a fallen soldier or police officer is the cause of national mourning. This is where the contradiction in attitudes towards death and mortal bodies comes into full view. Under such circumstances, the immigrant family must come to terms with death, often mourn from a distance, and do so in the absence of the dead body or community support.

Interruption of the grief process causes trauma and emotional limbo and negatively affects individuals' psychological integrity.

The Toronto District School Board (2008) and the City of Toronto (2006) describe the practice of anti-oppressive framework as "[a]ctively working to acknowledge and shift power towards inclusiveness, accessibility, equity and social justice." In other words, helping professionals must raise social consciousness through education, action and advocacy. They must navigate individual, community and structural injustices to raise awareness of existing barriers confronting bereaved family members, and must promote strategies for further policy change. Hollenbach (2008) notes that effective advocacy must be grounded within the rights of the displaced individual, and further emphasizes these rights by analyzing them in their social and political context (p. 3). When the law neglects the rights and dignity of the deceased immigrant or his/her family members, the law must change. The author insists that advocacy strategies are an integral part of the ethical responsibility of professionals. One of the main hindrances faced by non-governmental organizations in Canada involved in advocacy work involves fear of funding cuts. Under such conditions, practitioners are caught between their professional responsibility to offer meaningful advocacy and support and what they perceived as risk to the ongoing funding of their organizations.

On the next page, Table 10.2, which is based on my professional experience, illustrates the role of social workers acting within an equity, social justice, and anti-oppressive framework in assisting immigrants, refugees and asylum seekers dealing with the challenges of grieving.

In his masterpiece, *Man's Search for Meaning*, Victor Frankl speaks about maintaining meaning in life as a coping mechanism to endure the hardship of concentration camps and to deal with the death of friends. Following the death of his son, Karl Marx wrote to his friend Friedrich Engels: "After the death of Edgar I would have committed suicide if we had not meaningful things to do together." In recent years, some hospitals have gathered bereaved people together and organized a mutual support group called "Compassionate Friends." Unfortunately, participation in such groups is not usually available to refugees because of lack of language interpretation services or sufficiently diverse professional staff. Given that people in exile have already become vulnerable because of multiple losses over the course of their forced displacement, the loss of a family member adds to their sense of vulnerability and experience of trauma. This reality is exacerbated by the impossibility of return for refugees and exiles, something which makes dealing with the deaths of family members back home extremely difficult.

**Table 10.2. A Multilevel Framework: Death, Burial and Grief**

| | |
|---|---|
| **Families and Individuals** | • Gather accurate legal, procedural information by considering type of death, relationship of bereaved family member with the deceased, and place of death.<br>• Compile list of appropriate referral sources.<br>• Follow up and case management.<br>• Legal support through referral or an explanation of the legal system.<br>• Explore economic options, including fundraising efforts, to afford funeral or repatriation services.<br>• Access to translation and interpretation services. |
| **Bureaucracy** | • Assist to create a "to do" list for individual/family to overcome bureaucratic challenges.<br>• Liaise/assist with overcoming bureaucratic obstacles in obtaining death registry, death certificate and other administrative tasks.<br>• Support in dealing with funeral system, embassy, external affairs. |
| **Advocacy** | • Promote and advocate for social justice and human rights strategies.<br>• Raise awareness about the existing barriers to burial and grief.<br>• Assist to create advocacy "to do" list for individual/family and the larger community.<br>• Advocate for individual/family mobility rights.<br>• Empower and mobilize community.<br>• Increase individual/family knowledge about administrative and legal issues.<br>• Advocacy with and on behalf of family to overcome systemic barriers and unjust laws and regulations.<br>• Work with and support family to act as a bridge between local and global system. |
| **Repatriation** | • Ensure all family members are in agreement with repatriating the deceased to homeland and attempt to assist in resolving differences.<br>• Provide accurate information about repatriation process from cost to procedural practices.<br>• Ensure individual/family is in close contact and agreement with deceased's family members in homeland.<br>• Provide information to family and work with them to deal with the processes involved in the Canadian legal and funeral systems as well as transport of the body, international regulations and international law, policies and procedures. |
| **Diaspora Burial** | • Assist individual/family to identify appropriate funeral home and funerary process.<br>• Support in notifying employer/school/family members and acquaintances.<br>• Provide "to do" list to address municipal, provincial, federal requirements.<br>• Assist in dealing with home, car insurance, utilities, landlord/tenants, bank, family doctor, government officials and other agencies/institutions involved.<br>• Assist individual/family to deal with issues of personal belongings, assets, inheritance, estates, credit, loans, tax, will, debts, and other claimed or unclaimed properties/debts and legal contracts.<br>• Work closely with child protection agencies, other remaining family members, or potential caregivers in identifying the best interest of children. |
| **Distance Death** | • Explore the idea of hosting symbolic burial/ritual.<br>• Individual/family support to overcome immediate and long-term needs.<br>• Mental health support.<br>• Advocacy with and on behalf of family to obtain mobility power.<br>• Raise community awareness about the complexity of dealing with distance death. |
| **International Level** | • Assist with obtaining passport and other required documentation.<br>• Support around contacting/informing family members abroad.<br>• Support around individual/family needs and realities and national/international barriers to burial.<br>• Join allies and engage in advocacy work with and on behalf of family members to overcome legal and political barriers<br>• Assist with obtaining documentation including death certificate, and assist family if there is a lack of legal documentation or details about the place and cause of death (such as death under torture). Some governments that use capital punishment as a way of suppressing freedom of movement or terrorizing political prisoners may falsely label their victims as criminals or drug dealers in order to dehumanize family members or justify the individual's death. This causes additional trauma and uncertainty for the family in acquiring information or overcoming their loss. |

## Conclusion

This chapter draws attention to the agony of death among immigrants, refugees and asylum seekers, as well as its emotional, socio-cultural and political implications for the surviving members of the family. Some who escape from the harsh realities of their home countries never make it to their destination, as they vanish in the course of their journey or die in refugee camps. Those who do make it to their host country will have to cope with a different set of problems. They must integrate into a new society, while feeling nostalgic about their own. The death of a family member is an experience that accentuates this sense of nostalgia and the quest for cultural identity. Dealing with the death of loved ones can trigger a high level of stress and anxiety among the families of the deceased, especially when there is a considerable physical distance separating them from the site of death or burial. Under such circumstances, repatriating the body may be the only option, but this also involves its own challenges and traumas. Repatriation is an expensive enterprise and a highly bureaucratic process, one which often conflicts with immigrants' cultural, religious and spiritual belief systems. Some immigrants bury their dead in a local cemetery in the host country. But in that case, the policies of the country of origin in regard to such things as travel visas, and its relations with the Canadian government, may restrict individual family members living abroad from travelling to and participating in burial ceremonies.

This chapter argued that, as a society, we need to move beyond a cultural competency framework and apply social justice, equity and anti-oppression principles. After all, it is our ethical responsibility to remove barriers imposed on us at individual, local and global levels. This includes socially constructed immigration policies, regulations and procedures governing the mortuary practices which, in one way or the other, delay the process of grief. The first step could be achieved by forming a socio-political-legal body with a goal of diminishing the impact of local bureaucratic requirements and regulatory policies and procedures, with linkages to global human rights laws. The second step is to critically examine helping professionals' practices in dealing with grief. While this chapter explored the complexity of death and grief among immigrants, refugees and asylum seekers, further research is required to address issues faced by remaining family members, particularly underage children, as well as issues such as family reunification, wills and possession, unidentified corpses, and corpses whose status is in limbo because of the deceased's suicide or death while under state custody (in detention or prison). Such matters are complicated even further in the absence of political relations between the diaspora and host countries. In Canada, although a radical shift towards institutionalization and regularization of the handling of death has increased life expectancy, we continue to fall short in valuing life on a global scale. This shortfall is reflected in Canada's role in colluding with the exploitation and displacement of people from poor countries through political and trade policies, as well as the enactment of restrictive immigration and border control policies which prevent refugees and displaced persons from reaching safety.

# References

Annette, K. D. (2001). Hidden from history: The Canadian holocaust. *The Truth Commission into Genocide in Canada*. Retrieved from http://www.whale.to/a/annett.html.

Choudhuri, D.D., Santiago-Rivera, A.L., & Garret, M.T. (2012). *Counselling and diversity*. Belmont, CA: Brooks/Cole.

City of Toronto (2006). InvolveYouth 2: A guide to meaningful youth engagement. Retrieved from http://youthcore.ca/download.php?id=114.

Cornelius, W. (2001). Death at the border: Efficacy and unintended consequences of U.S. immigration control policy. *Population and Development Review, 27*(4), 661–685.

Fanon, F. (1963). *The wretched of the earth*. Constance Farrington (trans.). New York: Grove.

Frankl, V. (2006). *Man's Search for Meaning*. Boston: Beacon Press.

Helton, A.C., Schachter, O., Henkin, L., & Bayefsky, A.F. (2000). Protecting the world's exiles: The human rights of non-citizens. *Human Rights Quarterly, 22* (1), 280–297.

Hollenbach, D. (2008). *Refugee rights: ethics, advocacy, and Africa*. Washington, DC: Georgetown University Press.

Jimenez, M. (2009). *Humanitarian Crisis: Migrant Death at the U.S.–Mexico border*. Mexico's National Commission of Human Rights and the American Civil Liberties Union of San Diego and Imperial Counties.

Jones, K. (2005). Diversities in approach to end-of-life: A view from Britain of the qualitative literature. *Journal of Research in Nursing, 10*(4), 431.

Kastenbaum, R. (2008). Grieving in contemporary society. *Handbook of bereavement research and practice: Advances in theory and intervention*. Washington, DC: American Psychological Association, 67–85.

Klass, D., & Goss, R. (2003). The politics of grief and continuing bonds with the dead: The cases of Maoist China and Wahhabi Islam. *Death Studies, 27*(9), 787–811.

Lunman, K. (2001, April 9). Ceremony sweeps decades of dirt from Chinese graves. *The Globe and Mail*. Retrieved from http://oldcem.bc.ca/cem_ch1.htm

Toronto District School Board (March 2008). *Report of the middle & secondary model schools for inner cities "Beyond Elementary" work group: Report and recommendations to the Toronto District School Board*. Retrieved from http://www.tdsb.on.ca/Portals/0/Community/Community%20Advisory%20committees/ICAC/research/Model%20Schools%20Phase%20III%20finalFeb18-2010.pdf.

Page, B., Mercer, C., & Evans, M. (n.d.). *Death and the diaspora: the everyday necropolitics of belonging*. Retrieved from http://www.geog.ucl.ac.uk/about-the-department/people/academics/ben-page/files/Workingpaper1.pdf.

Pomeroy, E. C., Bradford Gracia, R., & Green, D. L. (2009). Bereavement and grief therapy. In Roberts, A. R. (Ed.), *Social workers' reference* (2nd ed.). New York: Oxford University Press.

Said, E. W. (1987). *Orientalism*. New York: Pantheon.

Satterlee, S. (2007, November 28). Dying abroad. *Gaurdian Weekly*. Retrieved from http://www.guardian.co.uk/money/2007/nov/28/expat-finance-health.

Selket, K. (April 2007). *Exiled bodies and funeral homes in Aotearoa New Zealand*. Victoria University of Wellington, New Zealand, Wellington, N.Z.

Statistics Canada (2012). *Life expectancy, at birth and at age 65, by sex, Canada, provinces and territories, annual (years)* (CANSIM Table 102-0512). Ottawa: Statistics Canada, 2012.

Uehling, G. L. (2001). The crimean Tatars in Uzbekitan: Speaking with the dead and living homeland. *Central Asian Survey, 20* (3), 391–404.

United Nations Children's Fund (UNICEF) (April 2009). *Machel study 10-year strategic review: Children and conflict in a changing world*. New York: United Nations and UNICEF. Retrieved from http://www.unicef.org/publications/files/Machel_Study_10_Year_Strategic_Review_EN_030909.pdf.

United Nations (2001). Department of Economic and Social Affairs. Statistics Division. Principle and Recommendations for a Vital Statistics System (Revision 2). Paragraph 57, Section A. Retrieved from http://unstats.un.org/unsd/demographic/sconcerns/mortality/mortmethods.htm#A.

United Nations (2011). *World Mortality 2011*. New York: United Nations.

UNHCR (2012). *Global trends report: Displacement: New 21st century challenges*. UNHCR. Retrieved from http://www.unhcr.org.uk/about-us/key-facts-and-figures.html.

UNICEF (September 2002). *International criminal justice and children*. Florence, Italy: UNICEF Innocenti Research Centre. Retrieved from http://www.unicef.org/emergencies/files/ICJC.pdf.

Whaley, K. (2012, April). Disputes over what remains: Bodies, burial, ashes, and new developments. Paper presented at The Law Society of Upper Canada's Six Minute Estates Lawyer Conference, Toronto, ON. Retrieved from http://whaleyestatelitigation.com/resources/WEL_Disputes_Over_What_Remains May2012.pdf.

World Health Organization (2010). *Injuries and violence: The facts.* Geneva: World Health Organization.

World Health Organization (2013). *Global health observatory: Mortality and global health estimates.* Geneva: World Health Organization. Retrieved from http://www.who.int/gho/mortality _burden_disease/en/.

Maugh II, T.H. (2001, October 4). WHO: 1.6 million die in violence annually. *Los Angeles Times.* Retrieved from http://www.bayarea.com.

Wyndham, M. (2003). Dying in the new country. *Humanities Research, 10*(3), 171–178.

CHAPTER ELEVEN

# Life in Limbo:
# Depathologizing Trauma

## Angie Arora, Ezat Mossallanejad and Rubaiyat Karim

The purpose of this chapter is to use an anti-oppression framework to situate people's lived experiences of trauma in the context of larger systemic barriers and inequities. More specifically, the term **life in limbo** is used to explore the ways in which immigrants and refugees are re-victimized through migratory traumas as well as post-migratory trauma caused by Canada's regressive immigration policies. Limbo, we argue, is a form of modern-day torture (Mossallanejad, 2005). The term **limbo** originates from the Latin *limbus*, meaning hem, edge, margin or border. It is normally used to denote any place or condition of uncertainty, instability or being taken for granted (Capps and Carlin, 2010). To contextualize this reality, the chapter will first broadly define trauma, and then will frame the concept of life in limbo as a form of modern torture. The existing definition of **torture** will be critiqued in the era of increased global armed conflicts, forced displacement and migration, where individual migrants find themselves powerless in the transition between gaining legal immigration status on one hand and facing exclusionary immigration policies on the other. It is then argued that refugees are victimized and re-victimized through post-trauma migration, particularly through the mechanisms built into the refugee determination system, that keep non-citizens in limbo and in an indefinite condition of total uncertainty. This systemic trauma leaves long-lasting impacts on the lived conditions of refugees. The chapter further critiques current frameworks of understanding trauma that individualize and pathologize people's experiences based on medicalization and culturalization of the trauma discourse. The impacts of such frameworks will be explored and an anti-oppression model discussed in order to help practitioners and organizations support survivors of trauma.

**Defining Trauma**

Trauma is generally understood as an emotional response to a deeply disturbing or overwhelming event that is outside the range of "normal" experiences (Briere and Scott, 2012). This can include a vast range of experiences that affect people individually as well as collectively. In other words, while environmentally induced disasters or human-made disasters affect people's individual safety and wellbeing, the wellbeing of the entire community is also affected. This chapter provides a brief overview of the vast range of experiences which contribute to both individual and collective forms of trauma. Briere and Scott (2012) summarize experiences of trauma as belonging to several key categories of environmentally induced disasters, torture, war, mass interpersonal violence, rape and sexual assault, and large-scale transportation accidents.

**Environmentally induced disasters** refer to large-scale events that, due to the lack of preparedness and prevention strategies, impact a significant number of people through injury and/or death (e.g., fires, floods, earthquakes, tornadoes, hurricanes). Such disasters also create internal displacement and migration, and in the absence of aid resources result in poverty, violence and deplorable health conditions. **Torture** refers to intentional physical, mental, spiritual, sexual, and psychological pain or injury inflicted upon a person by or with the consent of state authorities for a specific purpose to gather information, intimidate, terrorize or silence individuals, communities or the entire nation. **War** can be interstate or intrastate armed conflict and encompasses a wide range of violent experiences, including but not limited to immediate threat of death, witnessing the injury and/or death of others, prisoner of war experiences, captivity, rape and mass displacement, among other economic and social factors. **Mass interpersonal violence** includes intentional violence that impacts a high number of people but not in the context of war. Examples can include the actions of totalitarian regimes and such events as mass school shootings. **Rape and sexual assault** can be perpetrated by someone the survivor knows in the context of an intimate or familial relationship, or within a relationship where the perpetrator is in a position of authority. It can also include gang rape and experiences of sexual assault where the survivor does not personally know the perpetrator (e.g., situations of armed conflict, assaults by a stranger). **Large-scale transportation accidents** can include airline crashes, train derailments and shipwrecks and other maritime accidents. All these forms of trauma, including accidents, are human constructs and preventable, regardless of their impacts. As will be discussed later in the chapter, people tend to have adaptive responses to trauma (Pupavac, 2002).

In general, each person's reality and response to trauma is shaped by many individual and systemic factors; however, trauma can place one in a state of limbo. Limbo affects the overall health and wellbeing of traumatized peoples. The following section will explore the impact of life in limbo as a form of modern torture, and will expand on the intersection of individual and systemic factors as it relates more specifically to Canadian immigration policy.

Limbo is a state of contradiction in which individual refugees are uncertain, unstable and confused about things (such as immigration status) that are affecting their journey (Mossallanejad, 2005). In this state of confusion, refugees are unable to evaluate their situation or understand where they are standing. Therefore, being in limbo,

> . . . you feel lost about who you are and what will happen to you. Limbo is a place for people who are forgotten and cast aside for an indefinite term. Thus, people in limbo feel totally out of time, out of place and out of themselves (Mossallanejad, 2005, p. 195).

According to Mossallanejad (2005), exclusionary immigration policies place refugees in a state of limbo, unable to obtain identification documents to prove admissibility and gain legal immigration status.

## Life in Limbo as a Form of Modern Torture

In day-to-day life, people loosely use the term "torture" to describe all sorts of painful but, in the broader context, non-life-threatening experiences. On the other hand, tyrannical regimes and their professional torturers use soft words when they refer to their horrendous acts of torture and human butchery.

Article 1 of the United Nations (UN) *Convention against Torture and Other Cruel, Inhuman or Degrading Treatment or Punishment* defines torture as:

> Any act by which severe pain or suffering, whether physical or mental, is *intentionally inflicted* on a person for such purposes as obtaining from him or a third person information or a confession, punishing him for an act he or a third person has committed or is suspected of having committed, or intimidating or coercing him or a third person, for any reasons based on the instigation of, or with the consent or acquiescence of a public official or other person acting in a public capacity. It does not include pain or suffering arising only from, inherent in or incidental to lawful sanctions.

As the above definition indicates, we cannot refer to *any* act of violence as torture. At the same time, while it is crucial to have a recognized and universal definition of torture, the definition falls short in addressing state- and religiously sanctioned tortures, which are prevalent in many parts of the world. More often than not, governmental policies and practices in countries of both the global north and south lead to unrecognized torture against people, particularly those who are part of marginalized communities, such as non-citizens. This includes implementing exclusionary border control and immigration policies, prolonged detention, and deportation of refugees in need of protection.

Another serious deficiency in the Article 1 definition of torture is the invisibility of women. Not only is masculine language used (the article refers to "he" and "him") but, while women are tortured for the same reasons as men, they are also subject to gender-specific forms of torture, including female genital mutilation, rape, child marriage, forced marriage, domestic violence and many other forms of torture.

It should not be forgotten that torture is not committed only by people in positions of authority. Today, specifically with the end of the Cold War and rise of ethnic conflicts, we see instances of systematic torture with invisible linkages to state or sub-state actors, perpetrated by paramilitary groups and members of death squads. There are also organized gangs and cartels that by definition fall outside of state-specific military and paramilitary forces, even though they may have ties with the state.

Article 1 of the Convention against Torture does not address the lack of government protection for victims at the mercy of non-state parties who are accountable to no one and who therefore can act with impunity.

It is a tragedy that in the twenty-first century, there is no shortage of torturers across the globe. Methods of torture have become increasingly sophisticated and involve a combination of sexual, physical, spiritual and psychological techniques. Torturers are capable of inventing new methods tailored to the physical and psychological make-up of each victim (Mossallanejad, 2005, pp. 29–32).

In an era of increased global armed conflicts, forced displacement and migration, torture can also refer to life in limbo. Limbo is one of the most tormenting states of human life in which victims find themselves powerless and suffer endlessly. This powerlessness stems from the gap in the refugee determination process, a gap which can re-victimize and re-traumatize non-citizens, including refugees. In his book, *Torture in the Age of Fear* (2005), Mossallanejad refers to such a state as "Limbo in Paradise." The following section will discuss the effects of living in limbo on human life in general, and on the lives of torture victims in particular, by using an anti-oppression framework.

## Re-victimization through Post-Migration Trauma

We live in the age of refugees, displaced persons, migrants, undocumented workers, repatriated people and those with precarious immigration statuses. Although all these people are uprooted from their homes, some distinctions should be made between refugees and other categories of migratory people. A refugee's choice between remaining at, or escaping from, home is a choice between life and death. They clutch at any straw to survive. Despite this, mainstream society often forgets that refugees are people who do not want to be displaced or uprooted from their homes. They did not want to be refugees.

It is unfortunate that more than two-thirds of the world's refugee population lives in deplorable conditions, in poor countries' refugee camps and urban communities where there is no peace or security (Edwards and Ferstman, 2010, pp. 137–138). Their tormenting limbo has continued for years or even generations. This is an insult to human dignity and to the global system of human rights. Thus far, the international community has failed to find a durable solution for this abhorrent human problem.

Limbo leaves its most devastating marks on **protracted refugees** — those who are confined in refugee camps for a long time (sometimes for decades) without the right to move, work or involve themselves in any kind of business. There is not a ray of hope for them on the hazy horizon of exile. In the course of time, officials become uninterested in their lives and do not bother to serve their basic needs. They are taken for granted. Protracted situations reduce hundreds of thousands of men, women and children to the rank of "nobodies." The impact is collective trauma with the feeling of being "warehoused."

Refugees in this situation live a life of total uncertainty, not knowing what the future will bring for them. Homelessness and despair eat at their self-worth. Because of living in remote, desolate and dangerous border areas, these refugees are subjected to violence at the hands of local criminals, and, in some cases, uncontrolled militias (UNHCR, 2006).

Following are some of the outcomes of living a protracted life in closed camps: abject poverty, malnutrition, inability to marry and enjoy family life, violence, sexual slavery and forced prostitution. The end result is multiple psychological and mental health conditions at the mass level without possibility of any kind of treatment (Adelman, 2008, pp. 7–8).

## Re-victimization through Immigration Policy

The effects of trauma in one's home country can be exacerbated in the host country during the settlement and integration process. People experience many losses prior to, and after, arrival in Canada. For example, they may have lost a sense of control over their bodies, their homeland, language, family members, social networks, culture and professional identity. These losses can increase the likelihood of isolation and marginalization (Mossallanejad, 2005).

The lack of security people often face after experiencing trauma makes the settlement process even more difficult. For example, the refugee determination system imposes additional stressors on individuals who have fled their home country having experienced violence. Refugees are forced to live in their host country with the possibility of being returned to their home country. They are often separated from family, thereby limiting their social support in the host country. Some live with a precarious immigration status and, lacking the rights of citizens, have difficulty improving their economic and health status. The refugee process requires individuals to relive the trauma by sharing their experiences with lawyers, doctors and social service professionals, not to mention the Immigration and Refugee Board. This reality prevents them from experiencing security and stability, the very factors that are key to healing from trauma.

Of particular concern is Bill C-31, the *Protecting Canada's Immigration System Act*, an amendment to the *Immigration and Refugee Protection Act* that came into force in 2012. A key purpose of this reform was to deal in a timely fashion with the backlog of those seeking asylum. However, many groups, including the Canadian Council for Refugees (CCR) and the Ontario Council of Agencies Serving

Immigrants (OCASI), have openly expressed criticisms and concerns with the changes (for more information refer to the Canadian Council for Refugees website at https://ccrweb.ca/en/comments-amendments-bill-c-31).

The time period for processing refugee claims has been shortened, now ranging from 30 to 45 to 60 days depending on the category of refugees. This is neither feasible nor just, although on the surface the reduced timeline may appear an effective and systemic strategy for preventing life in limbo. But finding and collecting the proper documentation of someone's torture by making use of the services of psychiatrists, psychologists and physical practitioners can take time. Surviving trauma can involve memory loss and dissociation. Claimants may be suffering from deep depression and severe mental health problems associated with their trauma, and may not be able to recall the information required on such tight timelines, especially if the trauma they endured was experienced recently. Not being able to recall key details may diminish their "credibility" and thus reduce the likelihood of success of their claims. Rejected refugee claimants, with a well-founded fear of torture and persecution back home, are trapped between hope and despair for a long time. They have to play a sinister hide-and-seek game of survival in order to escape removal from Canada. If they are lucky enough to stay, they have to wait for one year to be eligible for Pre-Removal Risk Assessment (PRRA).

The second area of concern related to Bill C-31 is the fact that almost everyone in five refugee claimant categories is now denied access to the refugee appeal division, and in some cases claimants are not allowed to present their cases to the Federal Court

Another area of concern is the introduction of a system of designated countries of origin, commonly known as "safe countries of origin." Those who come from these countries, which are considered safe and democratic, are denied protection. It should be acknowledged that we are living in a changing world: the situation in a country can change overnight in a way that no country can be designated as totally safe. There are also some categories of people — for example, people identifying as part of the LGBTTQI community (LGBTTQI is an acronym meaning "lesbian, gay, bisexual, transgendered, transsexual, queer, intersex") — who may have been subjected to torture, but since their country is listed as one of designated countries of origin, they may be denied protection. So far, the government of Canada has deemed more than three dozen countries safe for refugees, some of which are known to have a record of human rights violations. Alternatives for genuine refugees coming from these countries are limited. They will be detained in Canada or, if they manage to leave the detention centre, their refugee cases may be rejected. They may end up living an "underground" life in Canada in order to avoid the risk of torture and persecution if they are sent back to their home countries.

Another area of concern involves "designated foreign nationals," which refers to those who come to Canada in an irregular manner — for instance, in boats, etc. (PRAIDA, 2012). According to the new legislation, they can be arrested upon arrival and be kept in detention for a long period of time, something that causes re-traumatization and all sorts of psychosomatic disorders. They can remain in limbo for many years, because they are denied access to the landing process for five years. They have no opportunity for family reunification. Even if they are accepted as protected persons, they are directed to report to the police, and as such are treated as criminals. Such treatment is against article 16 of the Convention against Torture, which categorically prohibits "other inhumane, cruel, degrading treatment or punishment" (United Nations Treaty Collection). Another area of grave concern in the new legislation is the fact that it imposes limitations on applying for Pre-removal Risk Assessment (PRRA) and Humanitarian and Compassionate Review after one year of a refugee claim's rejection. These two processes served as remedies for survivors of torture in the past. All the above limitations keep non-citizens in limbo and in an indefinite condition of total uncertainty (Abai and Mossallanejad, 2013, pp. 14–17).

## Impacts of Limbo on Non-Citizens: Case Studies of Survivors

While the psychological impacts of living in limbo are difficult for every human being, they can be especially challenging and even fatal for survivors of torture, war, genocide and crimes against humanity.

Consider the following examples from Ezat Mossalnejad's experience working at the Canadian Centre for Victims of Torture (CCVT):

### Reflective Thoughts

As you read each case study, reflect on the following:

- How would the phrase "in limbo" apply to each case?
- What examples of systemic trauma do you see?
- What do you see as the priorities in this situation?
- What are the referrals you would make?
- How would you work collaboratively with others to prevent trauma of life in limbo?

*1. A single mother has been living in limbo for 12 years. The trauma, brought on by her experience of torture in Iran, has been compounded by the uncertainty of her immigration status. She suffers from anxiety and depression and fears for herself and her 11-year-old daughter, who is a Canadian citizen. Her daughter understands the situation very well and it weighs on her heavily.*

*2. A young woman has been living with a psychological condition as a result of vacillating between fear and hope for the last 15 years. She wants to continue her education, but is not able to do so because of the lack of proper immigration status.*

*3. A man was imprisoned in his country of origin and suffered various forms of torture. He opposed the government's violence, but ended up associated with an organization deemed violent by Canada. After escaping through different countries, he sought asylum in Canada but was denied access to the refugee determination system, as he was considered inadmissible upon his arrival. He spent 23 months in a Canadian detention centre before being released from custody after bail has been paid. He was accepted under the Pre-Removal Risk*

*Assessment but has remained a non-status person due to his immigration admissibility. He often wakes in the night and has difficulty falling back asleep, as he experiences nightmares of his torture. Although he works and tries to remain physically active, the condition of tormenting limbo causes him to feel depressed most of the time. With the introduction of new amendments to the Immigration Act, he was denied access to medical care through the Interim Federal Health Plan (IFHP). He suffers from multiple illnesses without receiving any kind of treatment.*

There are thousands of similar cases of non-citizens in Canada who have been languishing in limbo for many years; among them are members of groups who already experience high levels of marginalization, including women, children, youth and older adults. Many things, including lack of identity documents, concerns regarding national security, lack of immigration status and alleged or real criminality can cause such limbo.

In particular, the use of "security certificates" against "inadmissible non-citizens" (IRPA s. 34) has led to people being detained or jailed in appalling conditions of limbo. The security certificate is a legal tool that can be used against foreign nationals if they are considered "a risk to national security." It allows the government to detain non-citizens indefinitely for the purpose of deportation without charges being laid. By allowing individuals to be detained indefinitely on the basis of secret evidence and without any charges being laid, the security certificate process infringes upon the basic rights guaranteed by the *Canadian Charter of Rights and Freedoms*, notably, the right not to be arbitrarily detained and the right to be informed of the reasons for one's detention.

There are also scores of cases of prolonged detention of non-citizens for issues that are solely immigration-related. Living for a long time under detention can be very harmful for vulnerable groups including women and children, as well as for survivors of war and torture. The experience can lead to their re-traumatization and irreparable life-long psychological harm.

One of the most tragic impacts of keeping non-citizens in limbo is the separation of families. Delays in granting permanent residency status to convention refugees and other categories of uprooted people (e.g.. live-in caregivers) lead to further delays in family reunification. Furthermore, non-status people cannot sponsor their family members to immigrate to Canada. It is expected that Canada respect its international obligations towards the protection of family life. Article 10 of the International Covenant on Economic, Social and Cultural Rights calls upon states to provide "the widest possible protection and assistance" to "the family, which is the national and fundamental group unit in society."

Limbo has frequently acted as an implicit psychological torture imposed through the bureaucracy of the immigration system against children who either remain separated from one of their parents or witness the ongoing re-traumatization of their parents. While states are not held accountable for causing such torture, at the same time international law leaves states to decide who they accept as citizens and who they reject as non-citizens. In the case of children, more often than not, their own lack of permanent resident status in Canada prevents them from enjoyment of their rights as minors. This occurs despite Article 37 of the UN Convention on the Rights of the Child, which protects children against torture (United Nations Treaty Collection). It is also against Article 24 of the International Covenant on Civil and Political Rights, which speaks about the child's right to protection "on the part of his family, society and the state" (United Nations Treaty Collection).

Keeping non-citizens in limbo is against Article 14 of the UN Convention against Torture (CAT). This article obligates states to guarantee the rights of torture victims to redress, compensation and rehabilitation. Limbo creates a situation that prevents redress, reparation and rehabilitation of survivors. It cripples the hopes of its victims.

## The Mental Health Impacts of Life in Limbo

The physical and mental health concerns experienced by refugees and victims of torture may be directly linked to ongoing limbo and lack of secure legal status (Across Boundaries, 2009). There is also the loneliness of living in limbo and the feeling of being excluded and rejected, which in turn can lead to feelings of apathy, hostility, isolation and social invisibility. It leaves negative impacts on survivors' efforts to empower themselves.

The main reason non-citizens are kept in limbo is because of the existence of a powerful bureaucracy that works behind closed doors and prolongs the process. Perhaps some of its managers and employees are concerned that a streamlined immigration process might reduce staffing levels (it is an old truism that bureaucracies exist to perpetuate their own existence). There is also the problem of the unjustified discretionary power that immigration and visa officers hold, combined with a lack of accountability on the part of these officials. The absence of face-to-face contact between people in limbo and immigration officials often results in a lack of compassion and absence of attention paid to individual needs and emergency situations. There are also problems in dealing with the lack of correct information and inexperience, inadequate training and sheer ignorance on the part of immigration or visa officials.

> ## Reflective Questions
>
> A number of survivors of torturous limbo arrive in Canada as asylum seekers or refugees.
>
> - Do we understand them?
> - Does our refugee determination system treat them humanely?
> - Do Canadian immigration and refugee policies and practices recognize the post-traumatic experiences they have endured or do we keep them in a kind of indefinite immigration limbo?

Life in limbo creates a continuous experience of trauma. Refugees flee from torture in their home countries, continue to experience trauma through their travels, and often this experience continues even once in a "safe" country like Canada. However, within the Canadian context, the ways in which we have been taught to understand trauma shape how we view and support people who have experienced trauma. For example, because trauma is often presented as an individualized experience, one may not automatically consider precarious immigration status as a form of torture.

As illustrated thus far, life in limbo creates a continuum of trauma. The Western mental health framework holds that if a person is exposed to trauma, they have been **traumatized** (Pupavic, 2002). More specifically, there is an assumption that refugees who have been affected by torture, persecution and war will be traumatized and develop post-traumatic stress disorder (PTSD) (Pupavic, 2002). While this may be the case, the *Diagnostic and Statistical Manual of Mental Disorders* (the DSM) falls short in addressing the root causes of trauma. The following section will explore and critique existing frameworks for understanding trauma, more specifically, the ways in which trauma is pathologized and culturalized.

## Pathologizing Trauma

People tend to have adaptive responses to trauma. Reactions can be physical in nature (e.g., changes in sleep patterns, aches and pains), psychological (e.g., expressions of helplessness, dissociation, etc.) and emotional (e.g., anxiety, denial, shock, hyper-alertness, irritability) (Briere and Scott, 2012). These reactions can help people survive the immediate threat, learn how to cope, and develop skills to overcome the intensity of their pain and suffering. Therefore, physical, psychological and mental reactions to trauma can serve a helpful purpose for survivors. However, as stated by Burstow (2005), "the purposive responses of stressed people are decontextualized and depicted as symptoms of a disease" (p. 433). The purpose of this discussion is not to determine when adaptive responses become maladaptive, but, rather, to understand issues that can arise when these reactions become pathologized and labelled as symptoms of a disease.

According to the *Diagnostic and Statistical Manual of Mental Disorders* (DSM) criteria for post-traumatic stress disorder:

> The person has been exposed to a traumatic event in which he or she: (1) witnesses the traumatic event in person; 2) learns that the traumatic event occurred to a close family member or close friend (with the actual or threatened death being either violent or accidental); or 3) experiences first-hand repeated or extreme exposure to aversive details of the traumatic event (not through media, pictures, television or movies unless work-related) (American Psychiatric Association, 2013).

This definition and diagnosis of PTSD emerged as a result of advocacy for American soldiers returning to the United States after the Vietnam War (Joop, 2005). The introduction of the PTSD diagnosis was meant to formally recognize psychiatric consequences of war and consequently improve supports. Since then, however, the clinical concept has been applied in many other contexts, including natural disasters, rape, and torture, to name only a few. The diagnostic system of PTSD has been highly criticized by feminist scholars, as the DSM works from a deficiency model and consequently individualizes trauma. As noted in the definition above, the criteria for what constitutes PTSD tie trauma to a specific event. They do not, however, account for insidious trauma; that is, the ongoing trauma experienced by marginalized groups in the context of systemic oppression (Bryant-Davis, 2007; Burstow, 2003). An individual's social location may expose them to ongoing and intersecting forms of oppression such as colonialism, racism, sexism, heterosexism, ableism, ageism and classism, forcing people to live with possible and actual threats to their safety and well-being. Because the DSM presents trauma in an individualized context, it thereby minimizes the historical, political, and social contexts in which trauma occurs.

In addition to individualizing trauma, the DSM has institutionalized the field of psychiatry. As Kutchins (2003) argues, the DSM definition "has become the label for identifying the impact of adverse events on ordinary people. This means that normal responses to catastrophic events often have been interpreted as mental disorders. Moreover, people must demonstrate how 'sick' they are in order to get help; that is, assistance is offered to victims only after they demonstrate how mentally ill they have become" (p. 125). Instead of viewing the reactions to trauma as normal reactions to pain, reactions have become labelled as symptoms and these collective symptoms have been diagnosed as a disease.

According to Burstow (2003), through this model stigmatized identities are imposed on individuals and then followed by harmful treatment methods. The DSM regulates and mediates the systemic application of diagnoses and therefore treatments, constructing the notion of mental "illness." This socially constructed notion reduces people's individual power and resiliency and further reinforces the status of the medical field as expert and diagnostic tools as fixed, enhancing medical practitioners' institutionalized power to diagnose and treat patients through their "expertise."

The history of the word **trauma** reveals that it stems from an ancient Greek word meaning "wound" (Eyerman, 2013). While we are not suggesting that medical responses to trauma have no purpose, to automatically work from this framework without question or critique can be harmful when providing support to people who have experienced trauma. For example, working from a medical model tends to position the person who has experienced trauma as weak and lacking the necessary skills to effectively "cope." If we view a group of people as emotionally damaged and fragile, we fail to see their strengths and resiliencies. Furthermore, this supposes that their existing coping mechanism strategies have not served their purpose.

This approach sets the stage for those working with survivors of trauma to know what is best for survivors. Once one is diagnosed with the label of living with mental illness, the stigma associated with such a label can invalidate the survivor's knowledge and strengths (Burstow, 2005). This can create unhealthy power dynamics between those providing support and those receiving support, as individuals' right to self-determination may be jeopardized. For example, when we view someone as solely a victim and stripped of strength, it becomes difficult to engage them in a meaningful relationship based on mutual endeavour and shared learning.

The construct of PTSD has been criticized for its dangerous potential to medicalize human suffering (Hinton and Lewis-Fernandez, 2010). If a person's experience of trauma gets framed as a medical issue, the social contexts in which the trauma occurred become reduced to a set of biological consequences. The root cause of such trauma becomes less a focus, thereby enabling the oppressive systems that cause and perpetuate the trauma to remain intact. This may prevent practitioners from collaborating with those seeking support to challenge and change the systems that cause oppression in their lives. The work we do is more than simply providing direct service; it is about effecting change at a micro level so that people become informed of the systems impacting their lives and become agents of change in shaping these systems to be more accessible and responsive.

**Culturalizing Trauma**

In addition to pathologizing trauma, we must be cautious not to reduce the experience of trauma to culture. This process has been referred to as "culturalizing trauma" (Eyerman, 2013). A cultural approach to trauma first dismisses the fact that some traumas are the result of racist, sexist, patriarchal and homophobic practices justified under the guise of culture; and second, disregards the fact that these practices perpetuate the vulnerability of marginalized peoples, resulting in forced displacement, migration and the trauma of life in limbo. Therefore, culturalizing trauma is in itself a form of trauma and a source of re-traumatization of those perceived as the "other." There are varying definitions of culture that are impacted by contextual nuances; however, for the purpose of this discussion, **culture** is defined as a particular group's shared system of values and beliefs, manifested through things such as language, religion, faith, food and traditions (U.S. Department of Health and Human Services, 2001).

One model that runs the risk of culturalizing trauma is a **cultural competency framework**. A "cultural competency" practitioner is defined by Fong as someone who "knows the cultural values and indigenous interventions of the client system and use them in planning and implementing services" (Fong, 2001, p. 6)

A culturally competent approach to working with immigrants, refugees and racialized communities therefore requires service providers to become knowledgeable and "competent" in specific cultures, in order to be effective. The key problem is the feasibility of "learning" or "knowing" another culture and becoming "competent" in it within the professional context, as well as in offering trauma support. This by itself can be considered an appropriation and misrepresentation of cultural norms and risk stereotypes.

While understanding culture can help in getting to know an individual's experiences of trauma, including his or her specific needs or preferences of mode of treatment, no culture is uniform. The dangers of such a framework are that when clients share certain practices, beliefs and traditions, the practitioner can unintentionally attribute these to all members of people from the same or similar culture. To treat cultures as static assumes homogeneity (Carpenter et al., 2007). Therefore, the assumption that cultural attributes apply to all individuals within that culture is presumptuous and can reinforce stereotypes, racism and other interlocking forms of oppression. Similarly, if we centre culture as the driving force of one's identity, practitioners may miss or ignore other parts of the person's reality that play an important role in how trauma is experienced.

By encouraging practitioners to better understand a culture, that culture is perceived as "different" from the norm. The "western" way of living becomes the ideal and anything that deviates from this becomes understood as "different." Eurocentric norms frame mental health services and this fact can produce a barrier for those seeking support (Shahsiah and Yee, 2006). For example, western models of mental health services tend to be highly individualized and not offered from a family-centric approach, a factor which may prevent people from safely accessing supports.

As such, non-western cultures become "exotified" as a way of "celebrating" differences often associated with race and ethnicity, while it is subtly suggested that non-racialized people are cultureless. In this case, culture is conflated with ethnicity and race. Such a fixed and narrow understanding divides people into neatly categorized groupings, ignoring the hybridity and fluidity of identity as well as the impact of migratory and integration process.

Working from a cultural competency model may lead practitioners to inadvertently blame trauma survivors' cultural practices for certain behaviours when they recount their stories of trauma. Attributing assumed meaning to people's behaviours and stories therefore leads to a process of culturalization, which then can reinforce and maintain stereotypes.

Cultural awareness, cultural sensitivity and cultural competence models for working with racialized communities, immigrants and refugees fall under the paradigm of a **multicultural framework**. A multicultural framework does little to address and challenge systemic inequities and thus leaves oppressive structures intact. The experiences of immigrants and refugees are shaped by intersecting traumatic systems, such as the racist immigration and refugee policies discussed in the first part of this chapter. The mental health disparities experienced by immigrant and refugee communities are attributed to the challenges associated with settlement and integration, such as lack of credential recognition, under- and unemployment, racial discrimination and family separation. Unfortunately, these structural and institutional issues are not the focus of a cultural competency framework. To view experiences of trauma solely through an individualized lens ignores this systemic reality. The following section will illustrate how an anti-oppression framework is a more effective way to understand the systemic nature of trauma.

## Anti-Oppression Framework

Understanding the impact of trauma at an individual level is imperative to provide support. However, informed support can only be provided if the person's experiences are understood within a broader framework of immigration status, nationality, race, socio-economic status, sexual identity, gender identity, ability and age. As noted by Eyerman (2013), by focusing on individual experiences of trauma, societal, collective or insidious trauma perpetuated by oppression and marginalization often remains deeply hidden. In situations of war, armed conflict, and natural or human-made disasters, one's personal experiences of trauma are deeply tied to the suffering of others; individual trauma is often intensified as one's sense of belonging and collective identity is shattered. Viewing trauma through a societal or systemic lens allows us to understand how power and privilege can be used to cause and perpetuate trauma. One framework that connects individual lived experiences to structural inequities is an anti-oppression framework.

An **anti-oppression framework** is based on the understanding that systemic dominance and oppression exist within our society, resulting in people's unequal access to power (Alexander, 2008). Oppressive values, thoughts and beliefs become embedded in systems and institutions and can shape how those systems implement policies and practices. Oppression, therefore, is not always easily visible. The less subtle forms of oppression are so deeply engrained into the fabric of society and everyday practices that they often go unnoticed and unquestioned. Socio-political and economic positions of power and domination create barriers and disempower marginalized groups.

This lens of understanding people's lived realities encourages service providers to critically analyze how power, including professional power, works, and how such constructs culturalize people's social identity.

## Pressures on Settlement Organizations and Frontline Practitioners

An anti-oppression intervention model informed by principles of social justice can transform existing methods of service delivery and allow for critical analysis of structural oppression. It equips practitioners with tools to counter oppression in the communities they serve and to promote psychological wellbeing in immigrant communities (Ali, et al., 2012) An anti-oppression framework is vital for settlement organizations and frontline practitioners to eliminate professional power as "expert" barriers and "offers a vision of what settlement work could be regardless of the cuts to programs and services, and the repositioning of social workers as settlement workers in the current neoliberal environment" (Clark and Wan, 2011). Increasingly, anti-immigrant sentiments are manifested through legislation, policy and practice implemented by the government of Canada (Chatterjee, 2013). As noted by Danso (2007), "globalization, transnationalization and issues of competition have intensified the migration of highly skilled workers"; however, "neoliberal and institutionalized racist policies and practices" marginalize and oppress immigrants and refugees, resulting in "de-skilled or de-valued" workers in Canada. To address this challenge, Chatterjee (2013) recommends strengthening anti-oppressive social work practice by "explicitly integrating racist state and employment practices as fundamental to global capitalism." These embedded sentiments have a traumatic impact on the process of settlement and integration of immigrants and refugees.

The role of the practitioner in supporting immigrants and refugees involves a fine balance. Settlement organizations recognize the urgency of confronting unjust policies geared towards reducing public expenditure for social services. Funding cuts to settlement programs is a form of discrimination which raises equity and access concerns and which in turn causes preventable trauma on immigrants and refugees.

Funded by the federal and provincial ministries responsible for immigration, settlement organizations provide services to new immigrants. Since the mid-1990s, the settlement sector has regressed into a para-state structure that is funded by contractual arrangements between the government and non-profit settlement agencies. In this context, the contractual agreements force organizations to act as an extension of the government. The current funding priorities set forth by the Canadian government force settlement organizations and frontline practitioners to increasingly adopt  narrow practice approaches that "reflect a reductionist understanding of human need, and run contrary to the wisdom, accumulated knowledge, experience, evidence and ethics of social and community development work" (Lenette and Ingamells, 2014). This results in a dichotomy between the difficulties experienced by individuals during settlement and integration processes, and the "gaps in services, user fees, or the long wait time for some services" (Clark and Wan, 2011). In addition, community-based ethno-specific organizations rarely have sustainable funding to meet the needs of the immigrant and refugee population. The resulting challenge is an inability to call for action and advocacy around refugee and immigrant rights. The traditional approach to supporting immigrant and refugee communities, especially in-dividuals with experiences of trauma, is ineffective because resources to affect change at systemic levels are scarce and scattered.

Frontline workers require structural and organizational support to deliver effective micro-level services and support, particularly for immigrants and refugees experiencing trauma, isolation and poverty. Often, individuals ex-periencing trauma require multi-disciplinary services, including social integration supports, legal services, trauma counselling and medical care. Immigrants and refugees require assistance with medical and historical documentation of torture, with language classes, and also need help to find housing and employment. This has inevitable implications for settlement workers and their clients.

**Implications for Practice**

As discussed, pre- and post-migration trauma affect immigrants and refugees in different ways, and therefore people express differing symptoms of psychological distress that do not necessarily signify mental illness. To make therapeutic services more available to, and accepted by, immigrant and refugee populations, it is important to examine approaches to mental health and ways of healing outside of the western context ("therapy"). Practitioners must also engage in applied research and policy analysis and actively lobby governments to increase funding for targeted and appropriate interventions, including those targeting the labour market (Danso, 2009). Anti-oppressive practice can serve to challenge racist institutional structures and alleviate oppression and inequality. The role of settlement sectors and community organizations is to provide invaluable support and opportunities to newcomers, to reduce isolation and enhance social networks (e.g., conversation circles) and to promote the strengths of immigrants and refugees (e.g., volunteer work) (Clarke and Wan, 2011). Using an anti-oppression framework allows practitioners to promote the rights and entitlements of, and opportunities for, immigrants and refugees living in limbo. In this chapter we discussed the importance of relying on an anti-oppressive approach to practice in order to eliminate the trauma of life in limbo and further "establish supports systems and advocacy services" and "prevent . . . clients from reaching crisis points that cause them to fall into poverty, suicidal ideation, psychosocial and mental health problems" (Danso, 2007). The ways in which we view and understand trauma will affect how we address trauma. The response to trauma must account for the lived experience of refugees and immigrants and validate the experiences of immigrants and refugees living in limbo. This chapter has emphasized the importance of understanding the systemic nature of trauma so that our approach to practice is grounded in an anti-oppression framework. To achieve equity and social justice, we must be cautious and critical of approaches that reduce people's experiences to individual faults. The alternative to pathologizing and culturalizing people's experiences of trauma is to situate their lived experiences in the context of oppression. Practitioners are encouraged to view their roles and responsibilities along a continuum of micro, mezzo and macro approaches, so that change can occur at all levels that impact the lives of individuals living in limbo.

## Conclusion

This chapter has emphasized the importance of understanding the systemic nature of trauma so that our approach to practice is grounded in an anti-oppression framework. To achieve equity and social justice, we must be cautious and critical of approaches that reduce people's experiences to individual faults. The alternative to pathologizing and culturalizing people's experiences of trauma is to situate their lived experiences in the context of oppression. Practitioners are encouraged to view their roles and responsibilities along a continuum of micro, mezzo and macro approaches so that change can occur at all levels that impact the lives of individuals living in limbo.

When migrating and seeking refuge, a person's expectation is that of hope and optimism; however, restrictive and regressive immigration policies exacerbate existing trauma, creating a state of limbo for refugees. In this chapter, we described such experiences as a form of modern-day torture. To understand trauma in the context of immigration policies requires a macro approach to understanding people's lived realities which acknowledges that systems impact people's experiences. However, all too often the trauma experienced by immigrants and refugees is pathologized and culturalized. This keeps our focus at a micro, or individual, level, ignoring systemic power and the impacts of structural barriers. If our goal is social justice, neither of these approaches will suffice. A practice approach to trauma must focus on people's agency, autonomy, knowledge and strengths within the context of systemic oppression experienced by immigrants and refugees upon and after their arrival to Canada. Using an anti-oppression framework ensures that the linkages between individual trauma and issues of equity are acknowledged and addressed.

## References

Abai, M. & Mossallanejad, E. (2013, Spring). Report on Canada's compliance with human rights instruments, for the occasion of the May 2013 periodic review of Canada. *First Light*, 7–20.

Across Boundaries (2009). *Re-conceptualizing "trauma": Examining the mental health impact of discrimination, torture and migration for racialized groups in Toronto*. Retrieved from http://www.acrossboundaries.ca/conference/Trauma%20Report.pdf.

Adelman, H. (2008). *Protracted displacement in Asia: No place to call home*. Aldershot, England: Ashgate.

Ali, A.N., McFarlane, E., Hawkins, R., & Udo-Inyang, I. (2012). Social justice revisited: Psychological recolonization and the challenge of anti-oppression advocacy. *Race, Gender and Class*, 19 (1–2), 322–335.

Alexander, M. (2008). *An integrated anti-oppression framework for reviewing and developing policy: A toolkit for community service organizations*. Springtide Resources. Retrieved from http://www.springtideresources.org/resources/show.cfm?id=241.

American Psychiatric Association (2013). *Post-traumatic stress disorder*. Retrieved from http://www.dsm5.org/Documents/PTSD%20Fact%20Sheet.pdf.

Berg, S.H. (2002). The PTSD diagnosis: Is it good for women? *Affila, 17*(1), 55–68.

Bernard, C. (2005). Review of the book *Culturally Competent Practice with Immigrant and Refugee Children and Families*, Rowena Fong (Ed.). *British Journal of Social Work, 35*, 287–288.

Briere, J.N. & Scott, C. (2012). *Principles of trauma therapy: A guide to symptoms, evaluation and treatment*. Thousand Oaks, CA: Sage Publications.

Bryant-Davis, T. (2007). Healing requires recognition: The case for race-based traumatic stress. *The Counselling Psychologist, 35*(1), 135–143.

Burstow. B. (2005). A critique of posttraumatic stress disorder and the DSM. *Journal of Humanistic Psychology, 45*(4), 429–445.

Burstow, B. (2003). Toward a radical understanding of trauma and trauma work. *Violence against women, 9*(11), 1293–1317.

Capps, D. & Carlin, N. (2010). *Living in limbo: Life in the midst of uncertainty*. Eugene, OR: Cascade Books.

Carpenter-Song, E.A., Schwallie, M., Nordquest, MA., & Longhofer, J. (2007). Cultural competence reexamined: Critique and directions for the future. *Psychiatric Services, 58*(10), 1362–1365.

Craig, G. & Lovel, H. (2005). Community development with refugees: Towards a framework for action. *Community Development Journal, 40*(2), 131–136.

Danso, R. (2009). Emancipating and empowering de-valued skilled immigrants: What hope does anti-oppressive social work practice offer? *British Journal of Social Work, 39*, 539–555.

Duran, E., & Duran, B. (1998). Healing the American Indian soul wound. In Danieli, Y. (Ed.), *Intergenerational handbook of multigenerational legacies of trauma* (pp. 342–372). New York: Plenum.

Edwards A. & Ferstman C. (Eds.). (2010). *Human security and non-citizens: Law, policy and international affairs.* Cambridge: Cambridge University Press.

Eyerman, R. (2013). Social theory and trauma. *Acta Sociologica, 56*, 41.

Fong, R., & Furuto, S. (Eds.). (2001). *Culturally competent social work practice: Skills, interventions and evaluation.* Boston: Allyn & Bacon.

Healy, L.M. (2004) Strengthening the link: Social work with immigrants and refugees and international social work. *Journal of Immigrant and Refugee Services, 2* (1–2), 49–67.

Hinton, D.E. & Lewis-Fernandez, R. (2010). The cross-cultural validity of posttraumatic stress disorder: Implications for DSM-5. *Depression and Anxiety, 0*, 1–19.

Inter-Church Committee for Refugees (1990, October). *Civil rights and refugee claimant backlog: Brief to the United Nations Committee for Human Rights on the occasion of the Canada's examination under article 40 of the International Covenant on Civil and Political Rights.*

Jesuit Refugee Service—Canada (1991, Spring). *Refugee update.*

Joop, T. V. M. De Jong. (2005). Deconstructing critiques on the internationalization of PTSD. *Culture, Medicine and Psychiatry, 29*(3), 361–370.

Kirmayer, L.J. (2012). Rethinking cultural competence. *Transcultural Psychiatry, 49*(2), 149–164.

Kutchins, H. & Stuart, A.K. (2003). *Making us crazy: DSM: The psychiatric bible and the creation of mental disorders.* New York: The Free Press.

Lenette, C. & Ingamells, A. (2014). Mind the Gap! The growing chasm between funding-driven agencies, and social and community knowledge and practice. *Community Development Journal,* doi:10.1093/cdj/bsu024.

Making ends meet in York Region discussion paper (2011). Newmarket, ON: Human Services Planning Board of York Region.

Mossallanejad, E. (2005). *Torture in the age of fear.* Hamilton: Seraphim Editions.

Nguyen, L. (2007). The question of survival: The death of desire and the weight of life. *American Journal of Psychoanalysis, 27*, 53–67.

Ontario Council of Agencies Serving Immigrants (2014). *Understanding and responding to sexual violence in immigrant and refugee communities.* Retrieved from http://learnatwork.ca /course/category.php?id=2.

PRAIDA (2012). A brief concerning Bill C-31, Protecting Canada's Immigration System Act, presented to the Standing Committee on Citizenship and Immigration. Centre de santé et de services sociaux de la Montagne, Programme régional d'accueil et d'intégration des demandeurs d'asile (Regional Program for the Settlement and Integration of Asylum Seekers) (CSSSDLM/PRAIDA). Retrieved from http://www.csssdelamontagne.qc.ca/fileadmin/csss_dlm/Publications/MEMOIRE_SUR_C-31.ENG. CSSDLM_PRAIDA.mai_2012.pdf.

Payne, D. (2011). *Mental health problems of refugees who suffered trauma.* Toronto: Canadian Centre for Victims of Torture.

Pupavac, V. (2002). Pathologizing populations and colonizing minds: International psychological programs in Kosovo. *Alternatives, 27*, 489–511.

Sakamoto, I. (2007). A critical examination of immigrant acculturation: Towards an anti-oppressive social work model with immigrant adults in pluralistic society. *British Journal of Social Work, 37*, 515–535.

Shahsiah, S. & Yee, J.Y. (2006). *Striving for best practices and equitable mental health care access for racialised communities in Toronto.* Retrieved from http://accessalliance.ca/sites/accessalliance /files/documents/EquitableMentalHealthCareAccessResearchReport.pdf.

Sisneros, J., Stakeman, C., Joyner, M.C., & Schmitz, C.L. (2008). *Critical multicultural social work.* Chicago: Lyceum.

Stier, R. & Binyamin, S. (2013). Introducing anti-oppressive social work practices in public services: Rhetoric to practice. *British Journal of Social Work,* doi: 10.1093/bjsw//bct049.

UNHCR (2006, May 2). Security concerns heighten following deadly militia attack near Chad refugee camps. *The UN Refugee Agency.* Retrieved from http://www.unhcr.org/445772944.html.

United Nations Treaty Collection. Convention Against Torture and Other Cruel, Inhuman or Degrading Treatment or Punishment, Article 16.

U.S. Department of Health and Human Services (2001). *Mental health: Culture, race and ethnicity: A supplement to mental health: A report of the Surgeon General.* Retrieved from http://www.ncbi.nlm.nih.gov/books/NBK44243/pdf/TOC.pdf.

CHAPTER TWELVE

# Working as the "Other": Migration, Race, Gender and Wellbeing

## Tania Das Gupta

In this chapter, I examine the experience and meaning of paid work for migrants and immigrants in precarious work, including migrant and immigrant women and undocumented workers, within a framework of capitalist globalization. How is their job strain and employment strain exacerbated by their migration status? Is this contributing to job and employment trauma?

What is the psycho-social impact of devaluation of one's cultural and symbolic capital (Bourdieu, 1986) and resultant underemployment in precarious jobs that do not provide basic security? Specifically, many working class migrants experience linguistic devaluation due to their lack of fluency in English or French or their non-dominant accents. They end up in so-called "3D jobs" (dangerous, dirty, difficult). Their middle-class professional counterparts may be fluent in the official languages but they frequently experience the devaluation of their professional education and experience and are marked as "poor communicators" due to their minority accents. They also end up in precarious jobs, albeit in white-collar sectors (Workers Action Centre, 2007; Das Gupta, Man, et al., 2014). Associated with that, migrants of all class backgrounds experience racism, sexism, other forms of discrimination, violence and bullying on the job. Temporary migrants such as caregivers, agricultural workers, dancers/sex workers, waitresses, mall workers and a range of other service workers who are deemed to be unskilled, work on contract and are tied to their employer for the duration of their contracts, face the additional hardship of being separated from their spouse and child(ren) as part of their condition of employment. They are thus deprived of the benefits of family life, and suffer the lack of what Lewchuk et al. (2006) refer to as "household security," which is considered a human right by United Nations Conventions on Human Rights.

Can negative experiences in the labour market following migration to Canada contribute to trauma? Building on Lewchuk et al.'s notions of "job strain" and "employment strain" (2006), I will argue that indeed an insecure relationship with the state as exemplified through one's migration and/or (lack of) citizenship status contributes to "employment trauma" and "job trauma," concepts that can help explain how one's precarious status in the labour market — that is, uncertainty around the relationship with one's employer, hours of work and wages, the strain of maintaining multiple jobs, lack of union support, and household insecurity or uncertainty and risks in one's workplace — can cause trauma in other areas, such as in social arenas, intimate relationships and one's health and wellbeing. Further, insecurity in one's (im)migration and citizenship status adds to racialization, which also contributes to job and employment strain.

In the first part of the chapter, I will talk about globalization and precarious work and the migration generated as a result from the global south to the global north (otherwise referred to as the "Third World" and the "West" respectively) of those who are unable to sustain themselves any longer within the larger political and economic context. In the second part of the chapter, I will present what scholars have said about precarious work and wellbeing and then present the concepts of "job trauma" and "employment trauma." In the third and last part of the chapter, I will examine the situations of three groups of migrants, including permanent residents, temporary migrants and undocumented workers. Permanent residents may be citizens already or destined to be citizens. However, those who are racialized as "non-whites, non-Christian, not speaking English/French and belong[ing] to the working poor," are almost always assumed to be non-Canadians, since the normative image of a Canadian is as a middle-class, white, Christian man/woman, speaking at least one of Canada's official languages with a specified accent. I will focus on those permanent residents who are racialized and gendered in the labour market. Temporary migrants and undocumented workers are deemed to be "foreign" and thus not belonging to Canada. The latter group is also highly racialized and gendered but additionally designated as "illegal outsiders."

## Globalization, Precarious Work and Migrant Labour

The rise of precarious work and increasing levels of migration of temporary and irregular migrants are features of a neo-liberal, globalized capitalist system. Willis et al. (2010, p. 5) have pointed out that "global neo-liberalism," which includes privatization, sub-contracted labour forms and global work organizations, together with the development of new communication technology have increased international migration since the 1980s. Many countries of the south have been persuaded or indeed coerced by the World Bank and the International Monetary Fund (IMF) to follow policies in order to qualify for loans which, it is promised, will bolster their economies, increase their access to foreign exchange and reduce their unemployment (Velasco, 2002). The net result of these policies has been an increase in migration of those who have been displaced from agrarian economies, some moving internally from villages to cities, including free-trade zones, and working in factories or other non-standard jobs such as in domestic work, while others who are able to gather capital or demonstrate particular skills, such as care-giving, nursing or IT qualifications, migrate to other countries of the global south, such as countries in the Persian Gulf, or to countries of the global north, such as Canada, where they work as contracted workers on time-limited work permits, often lacking civil or human rights. Some, desperate to escape poverty, simply take the risk of crossing the border into other countries without documentation (Keung, 2013). A small minority of middle- and upper-class individuals with exceptionally high education levels and professional qualifications may be accepted as permanent residents with hopes of becoming citizens of countries such as Canada. Some have argued that most migrants and immigrants move not out of free choice but rather out of compulsion or force (Castles, 2003). No matter how qualified or skilled they are, it seems that most of them are concentrated in precarious work sectors and experience different forms and degrees of devaluation, racism and sexism. Many have come to accept this as a part and parcel of the migration experience, the price that must be paid for the sake of the betterment of their family members, most importantly their children.

## Precarious Labour, Health and Wellbeing

Meaningful and decent paid work is a key component of basic economic security (Zaman, 2012). In modern-day capitalist society, not only does paid work define social standing, but it is also fundamental to individual wellbeing and positive self-identity

> ## Case Study 12.1
>
> It took Jameela almost eight years to get her immigration status regularized after she came to Canada. . . . "I never had a chance to look for a good job because I was on a work permit and it limited my time frame for [finding a job]. . . . I worked for three different call centres. . . .The first job I had, like if you go for one, two or three hours and you can't make a sale, and you are trying hard over the phone, but they say 'go home.' So, it's stressful, you know. . . . all those hours I put in — my mouth, my head ache so much I can't talk. When I go to sleep it's just killing me because I've talked so much . . . (Workers' Action Centre, 2007, p. 41).

(Krahn, Lowe and Hughes, 2011). According to Krahn, Lowe and Hughes (2011), there are two schools of thought in conceptualizing "the meaning and experience of work." On the one hand, we have Karl Marx's notion of work under a capitalist labour process being intrinsically alienating, given the estrangement of workers from the tools, relations and products of labour (see Tucker, 1972, p. 56). Raphael (2009) points out that as early as in the mid-1800s, Marx's collaborator, Friedrich Engels, had pointed out that "all conceivable evils are heaped upon the poor. . . . [T]hey are given damp dwellings . . . supplied rotten clothing . . . adulterated and indigestible food . . . and are worked every day to the point of complete exhaustion of their mental and physical energies" (quoted in Raphael, 2009, p. 3). The Marxist thesis was further developed by Braverman (1974), who explained the process of deskilling and degradation of labour under monopoly capitalism. However,

**degradation** was conceptualized primarily in terms of the division and process of labour in a capitalist mode of production, rather than the worker "feeling" psychologically or emotionally degraded. From this perspective, the focus is on how alienated and degraded work can be eliminated with the ending of the capitalist mode of production and its concomitant organizations of work, rather than on the recuperation of workers' psychological, physical and social wellbeing.

The second school of thought is identified by Krahn, Lowe and Hughes (2011) as a social-psychological tradition of alienation research, which emphasizes the organization of work, the particular arrangement of technology, the division of labour and the speed of work, to name a few factors, not in terms of the capitalist mode of production (or the employment relationship per se) but as emanating from ergonomics in the workplace (Blauner, 1964). Further, these scholars have looked at stressful work, work stressors and discussed physical and psychological impacts of one's work experience, including that of unemployment and restructuring. Such conditions as depression, anxiety and other emotional reactions have been shown to be related to poor working conditions, not to mention physical injuries on the job, including fatalities.

Writers from these two schools of thought have pointed out the structural and humanistic aspects of work respectively. Sennett and Cobb (1972), in their classic study, pointed to the "hidden injuries of class" in which the relationship between one's negative work experience and one's self esteem and identity is evident. Their study could be placed in the second school of thought as discussed by Krahn et al. What is evident in all these early discussions is that the working class is seen as a "faceless, monolithic abstraction" (Das Gupta, 1996, p. 4). Most references to workers in these studies represent them as white male nationals. This is a distinct drawback given the diversity of the Canadian workforce.

The connection between economic life and one's health has been further expanded upon in recent years through the "social determinants of health" approach (Raphael, 2009), which seeks to determine the health effects of such factors as employment and working conditions, unemployment, early life, education and food security (p. 7). In addition, Aboriginal status, gender and social exclusion are also seen to be factors connected to health outcomes. Although the connection made between health and poverty, gender, and the fact of Aboriginal peoples and "others" experiencing social exclusion was a step in the right direction, insofar as it acknowledges the diversity of the population, the reality of the intersections of a range of social factors, such as gender, race, ethnicity, Indigeneity, class and migration status that together have an impact on health and wellbeing, remains to be fully developed. Galabuzi (2009) confirms that "a shift in focus from generic notions of poverty as both generic and quantitatively based low income to understanding the differentiated qualitative complexity of poverty and its varied impacts on health of diverse populations within Canada" is required (p. 265). Moreover, he urges the addition of "racism as a social determinant of health."

Focusing on the phenomenon of "precarious work" or "non-standard work," including the rise of part-time, temporary, own-account self-employment (i.e., a self-employed person who does not hire anyone else) and the like, under neo-liberal, globalized capitalist economies, Lewchuk, Wolff, King and Polanyi (2006) have suggested the notion of **employment strain**, departing from the earlier concept of **job strain**. The latter concept had connected health and safety issues at work, particularly those associated with high demands and low control over work and including exposure to toxic chemicals. Lewchuk et al. (2006) refer to a number of studies that indicate a connection between job strain and "exhaustion, depression, lower job satisfaction, and ultimately, to stress-related illness, including cardiovascular disease" (p. 141) The notion of job strain relates to the social-psychological tradition of research on work discussed earlier, as it explores the effects of one's job on one's socio-psychological wellbeing.

Building on the latter point, Lewchuk, et al. argue that the impact of the employment relationship, i.e., that between employer(s) and employee(s), should also be added to the equation, including such factors as employment uncertainty, uncertainty around hours of work and wages, maintaining multiple jobs, lack of union support and household insecurity — all features of precarious work, which they categorize as factors causing employment strain. In suggesting this, they are referring to those aspects that were central to the structural school of work discussed earlier, i.e., the power inequality in the employer-employee relationship. Through the survey of five groups of precarious contract workers, in university, home care, community, a "diverse category" (day labourers, temp agency workers, hospitality workers, high tech workers, health workers) as well as a comparator group of standard full-time, permanent workers, they demonstrated that the "diverse" group reported the highest levels of employment strain and highest levels of poor health, as well as a higher incidence of pain and severity of pain compared to the full-time, permanent waged workers, thus indicating the effects of precarious employment relationships on employment strain. Notably, the "diverse" group members were predominantly racialized, "half were female," non-unionized and "almost one-third had been in Canada for less than ten years" (p. 150). The group of community workers was also predominantly female and racialized but had mostly been in Canada more than ten years. Their level of employment strain was higher than the university, home care and full-time permanent worker groups, but lower than the "diverse group." They experienced uncertainty in terms of work schedules, multiple jobs and working with different groups of co-workers. The university, home care and full-time, permanent groups were predominantly white females, some of whom were unionized and most of whom had lived in Canada for more than ten years. Although not explored explicitly by these authors, their research suggests that the racialization of workers and their years of settlement in Canada have some impact on the level of employment strain they experience and hence level of health enjoyed. Flowing from this work, analogous notions of **job trauma** and **employment trauma** are proposed, precipitated by job strain and employment strain respectively, as described by Lewchuk et al. (2006), but additionally including the marginalization and entrapment created by one's status as "the other," whether the worker is a "racialized other" and/or a "non-citizen other." In this framework, job trauma and employment trauma are additionally determined by one's relationship with the state in the receiving country, that is, through one's (im)migration and citizenship status, which in turn influences one's employment, social and political relationships.

## Permanent Residents

There is now a burgeoning literature on how racialized immigrants hold precarious jobs. As a result, poverty in Canada has become a racialized phenomenon (Galabuzi, 2001; Block, 2010; Block and Galabuzi, 2011). Racialized Canadians are concentrated in sectors of the economy marked by contract, part-time and temporary work with low income and lack of benefits — sectors that in effect fall beyond or in between the cracks of the minimum labour standards.

Jameela's experience, described in the case study above, is testimony to such work arrangements. A call centre job is frequently a starting point for many new immigrants. In the call centres where she worked, Jameela had no assurance of how many hours of work she would be paid for each day, as everything depended on her ability to make sales over the phone. If she was not able to sell, then she could be asked to leave for the day. The pressure of work adversely affected her health, causing insomnia and headaches. Krahn, Lowe and Hughes (2011) discuss how electronic communication systems can be deployed to monitor workers in call centres, including their performance, thus adding to their stress level, burn-out and ill health. Work such as this is frequently irregular, on-call, contractual and temporary. Many are falsely labelled as independent contractors and thus denied minimum labour standards, such as vacation pay, sick leave or contributions to the Canada Pension Plan and Employment Insurance. Employers in such sectors have been characterized as "bad bosses" who subject workers to wage theft and violation of their basic human rights (Workers' Action Centre, 2007). In a neo-liberal globalized economy, such conditions of work are becoming more common, and the once-standard secure, permanent jobs are few and far between. Those who are racialized due to their skin colour and linguistic/educational background are vulnerable to such labour market conditions because of their need to alleviate family poverty and their desire to make a new home in Canada. Perhaps they also dream of sponsoring loved ones to come to Canada or sending money for their support in their countries of origin. In the case of Jameela, she was in the process of being sponsored by her relative, which made her vulnerable in terms of her status in Canada.

Even those who are not so desperate, those who are "admitted" into the nation as permanent residents due to their cultural capital — high levels of educational and professional qualifications, linguistic skills and connections — are routinely devalued and degraded as professional workers and as human beings (Das Gupta, Man, et al., 2007; Zaman, 2012). Their underemployment and unemployment have become a rite of passage into "settling" in Canada. They have learned to settle for less because they have had to learn to accept their subordinate positions as "newcomers" and, hence, supplicants — "less than" — in relation to citizens, the "real" Canadians. These "hidden injuries," to borrow from Sennett and Cobb, are then passed onto children and spouses at home. Kalil, a computer engineer, who immigrated to Canada in 1981 and in 2006 was working as a truck driver and packer, says:

> If you are troubled at work . . . we are human and we transport problems home. . . . My son says "Dad, how is it going?" But how much can I talk to him. I don't want him to feel guilty that I am getting humiliated and troubled just to bring food on the table (Workers' Action Centre, 2007, p. 14).

Kalil also talked about being bullied and harassed at work by his supervisor because he spoke out against unfairness at work. He added that his co-workers did not speak up for fear of losing their jobs as they were new immigrants.

Settling for less is a regular feature of life for most immigrants. Tales of internationally educated doctors, engineers and Ph.D.'s driving taxis and working in gas stations have become urban legends in cities like Toronto where most immigrants end up (Aulakh, 2011). Kalil was advised early on that computer engineering is a "white" space and that he would not find work. Rana, a teacher with over 10 years of teaching experience in India and Dubai, said:

> When I came here with all my skills and education . . . I remember the interviewing officer in Dubai when he looked at my certificates. . . . You'll be in great demand. . . . Fantastic! . . . I had no clue . . . that when I came here, I would be a zero. . . . I had no clue (*Journey To Finding Myself Again*, 2013).

Minara and Asha, two women I have interviewed in the past, similarly told me that they were informed by well-wishers early on that the profession of human resources, in which both had years of education and high levels of  work experience in Bangladesh and India respectively and for which they were given preference for permanent residency in Canada, is "for white people" and for "young people." They were made to feel "out of place" in that sector and urged to switch to another sector of work. What does such treatment do to the professional and personal identities of a person? Zeytinoglu et al. (2007) show in their research with nurses in Ontario that this kind of disjuncture between what workers expect and what they actually end up doing is highly stressful. Devaluation and degradation of immigrants' and migrants' skills and education is tantamount to the symbolic devaluation of them as individuals and as human beings. As Rana says above, when she came to Canada, she became a "zero," stripped of what her identity had been thus far as a professional worker.

Zaman (2012) relates the story of a woman named Mubeena who, upon encountering a similar situation to Rana's, says that "it was a great social and psychological shock" and that her "self confidence declined as a result of continuous negative feedback" in Canada (pp. 78–79). Racism can have lasting psychological effects. Zaman relates a case of a woman who took off her hijab (or veil) in order to get a job because of concerns about Islamophobia, but who found that doing so affected her mentally (p. 78). Syed (2012) has argued that forced assimilation, which is what the involuntary removal of the veil represents, can have negative and traumatic effects. This is because wearing the veil is often associated with self-identity and one's religious practice, elements that may be important for one's wellbeing. The involuntary removal of the veil or of any religious, cultural or spiritual symbol can be perceived as a loss of "self-autonomy," the latter being a precondition for wellbeing.

The appropriation of skills and other cultural and symbolic capital through the systemic and cultural processes described so far in connection with middle-class, professional immigrants is legalized and made explicit in the case of live-in caregivers, agricultural labourers and undocumented workers. This issue will be discussed in the next section.

**Temporary Migrant Workers**

Under the Live-in Caregiver Program (LICP), women trained and experienced in caregiving for children, the elderly and people with disabilities are brought to Canada to provide care to middle- and upper-income Canadian families in the absence of universal childcare programs. One of the most problematic aspects of this program is the requirement of "living in" with their employers (Faraday, 2012; Pratt, 2012; Zaman, 2012), something which is a source of vulnerability and abuse. These caregivers are required to provide the equivalent of two years of full-time caregiving services (amounting to 3,900 working hours) over the course of four years living in Canada (earlier the requirement had been to complete the working hours requirement over only three years), after which they are eligible to apply for permanent residency. As mentioned earlier, participants in the program are not allowed to bring their spouses or child(ren) with them, and thus end up being separated from their loved ones for years at a time in their quest for permanent residency in order to achieve the long-term goal of bettering their family's future prospects in Canada. Many of the participants in the program are also fighting the effects of poverty in their home countries, which have been subjected to neo-liberal globalization that has disrupted their economies (Velasco, 2002; Faraday, 2012; Sharma, 2000).

Most of these caregivers today are Filipino women, the majority being skilled and university-educated, and many of whom are professional nurses and teachers (Zaman, 2012). Despite the fact that many are highly skilled professionals, and must demonstrate experience in caregiving in order to qualify for LICP, the National Occupational Classification (NOC) classifies them under categories C and D, defined as semi-skilled and unskilled. As such, they are not eligible under Canada's immigration regulations to apply directly under Canada's "economic class," which is restricted to categories O, A and B, defined as "skilled." More specifically, the skilled categories include management, professional (requiring university degrees) and "skilled work requiring two or more years of apprenticeship training or on-the-job occupation specific training, or occupations with significant health and safety responsibilities" (Faraday, 2012, p. 21). Their "real" educational and professional qualifications remain unrecognized in this process of addressing "cheap" caregiving needs in the Canadian labour market. Moreover, by law they are prohibited from educating or training themselves any further as temporary workers in Canada, thereby holding them captive as a caregiving labour force. Caregivers earn minimum wage (or maybe lower than minimum) after earnings are deducted by their employers for providing room and board, which by many reports are below the housing standards that Canadians enjoy. Their sense of privacy is often violated when some are expected to live in the same room with whomever they are taking care of, or in some cases living in their employer's office space or basement with no doors or with unlocked doors. Stories of sexual abuse by the "man" of the house are not uncommon (Silvera, 1983), not to mention the fact that they are on-call seven days a week, allegedly being "one of the family." Without their services, middle and upper-middle class Canadian women would not be able to engage in their professional jobs. Studies (Zaman, 2012; Pratt, 2003) have shown that even after gaining permanent residency, caregivers never recover from the systemic devaluation of their professional qualifications and their underemployment, as they continue "to do domestic work as housekeepers and home care health workers." (Pratt quoted in Zaman, 2012, p. 41).

**Temporary Workers and Trauma**

Pratt (2012) has described the situation set out above as one responsible for "state-induced trauma," making use of Jenny Edkins' concept. Prolonged separation from caregivers' own children and spouses have resulted in estrangement, feelings of loss, abandonment and anger in the children, and guilt and loneliness on the part of these women, some of whose marriages also fall apart. Pratt reports that many of the children do not have any memory of when their mothers left them, only that they were taken to bed before their mothers left, or that they cried or felt scared, symptomatic of trauma. "Mothers and children . . . spoke of . . . erasure and the shock of non-recognition" (p. 55) of each other when they later met for short periods of time.

Even after re-unification with their children following the attainment of permanent residency, these mothers and children were virtual strangers trying to begin a new life together. At this point, children face a second trauma of separation from their caregivers, such as grandmothers, aunts and fathers, those who looked after them in their mother's absence. Although many eventually find a balance, others never recover from the trauma of separation. Some young-adult children attempt to cope with drugs and other self-destructive behaviours, which have long-term repercussions for their future. Pratt (2000, p. 70) comments that the separation of caregivers from their children "strips them of their full personhood, including familial relations."

Stories of separation of migrant mothers and fathers from young children are also told by those who come to Canada as farm workers (*El Contrato,* 2003; *Migrant Dreams,* 2013) and as exotic dancers/sex workers (Barrero, 2009). In the film *El Contrato,* a young farm worker tearfully tells his fellow farm workers that his wife had a baby and that he longed to be with them. The film shows him later with his young wife holding their baby after having completed his contract and returned to Mexico. His wife tearfully tells him how every other husband came to see their wives after having given birth to their babies, but hers never came. In family gatherings back in Mexico, migrant farmworkers enjoy the brief reunions that they have with their extended family members, but there is always an underlying pathos of anticipating another separation around the corner. Similarly, in *Migrant Dreams,* there is a powerful scene in which migrant women farm workers in Ontario, sitting in their assigned living space, stare at their cellphones which show pictures of their young children, including those who are babies, far away from them in Mexico. The trauma of their separation from their children is accompanied with tears and guilt, the cost of doing migrant work distant from loved ones.

Apart from this trauma of separation from loved ones, migrant farm workers are often compelled to work while being sick or injured because of the prospect of being deported if deemed unable to perform their jobs. Based on a survey of 600 farm workers, Faraday (2012) reports that 55% of respondents worked while being sick or injured (p. 91), and 45% said that their colleagues worked while sick or injured. "Only 24% of workers injured on the job made claims to workers' compensation . . . for fear of losing their job, and fear of being excluded from the Seasonal Agricultural Worker Program . . . as a result of raising a complaint" (p. 92). This is indicative of job trauma combined with employment trauma.

## Undocumented Workers

Thousands of workers in Canada are undocumented or working without legal permission. A variety of reasons account for the growth of this population. There are those whose temporary work permits have expired, those who were compelled to leave their employment due to abuse, those denied refugee status or those who crossed the border and came to Canada to escape poverty. Despite the fact that, financially, the lives of these workers are much better than what might have been the case in their countries of origin, in other ways — socially, politically, legally and, most significantly, psychologically — they are completely marginalized and criminalized as "illegals."

The undocumented live in a constant state of fear. If caught, they most certainly face deportation. So they rarely report a crime, go to a doctor's office or complain about unfair treatment by employers. They avoid the public library, or any other government service, for fear it will prompt questions about their status.

Some parents go as far as to keep their children home from school (Keung, 2013).

Despite official policy providing un-documented children access to Canadian schooling, in real life these rights are often non-existent (Keung, 2013). Agencies that supply work to those with no official documents, as well as the workers' direct employers, often subject these workers to wage theft, through the form of unpaid wages, by charging unfair fees and by not paying overtime, and also to sexual and racial harassment because they know that the workers will not complain to the authorities given their vulnerable status. Family life and the sharing of such rites of passage as births and deaths are denied to those without official status because of their fear that if they leave Canada, they may be deported and may never be able to re-enter the country again. Such a constant state of fear and economic vulnerability undeniably contribute to trauma at every level, with regard to the government's actions, at work, at home and at an individual, physical and psychological level.

---

**Reflective Questions**

1. What are the different schools of thought regarding the experience of work, health and wellbeing?
2. How do immigration status, race, ethnicity and class have an impact on the experience of work?
3. Differentiate between Lewchuk et al.'s notions of "job strain" and "employment strain," giving examples.
4. What is meant by the terms "job trauma" and "employment trauma"?
5. Share an experience of job trauma and employment trauma.
6. How is Jenny Edkins' notion of "state-induced trauma" connected to the notions of employment trauma and job trauma?

---

## Conclusion

The ongoing process of globalization under capitalism has given rise to an unprecedented level of human displacement and migration on both the national and international scale, caused by the dismantling of indigenous forms of sustenance, environmental destruction and the appropriation of land for mining, oil exploration, and industrial and urban development, to name only a few factors. Many who migrate across borders from the global south to the global north, including countries like Canada, find their economic, social and political lives to be precarious given their status as "outsiders" and "non-citizens." They are thus racialized as "foreign." The trauma of surviving within precarious working conditions, including unsafe health and safety conditions, and the constant devaluation and degradation of one's skills and capabilities and one's sense of self thus have repercussions on an individual's health and wellbeing, relations with loved ones, sense of basic (in)security, and professional, personal and social identity, which become fractured, unstable and often a source of shame. Limitations of rights accorded to temporary and undocumented migrants and the strain of living with the constant threat of being deported further exacerbate the sense of entrapment and trauma. Moreover, being seen as "the other" in relation to permanent residents and citizens — as "one who does not belong" — adds another dimension to a person's trauma and emphasizes separation from family and community. In the final analysis, job trauma and employment trauma are "state-induced" (Pratt, 2012), determined by immigration and/or citizenship status, resultant racialization and (lack of) rights. The more vulnerable one's status is in Canada, the greater the chances of a high level of job and employment strain and corresponding levels of job and employment trauma.

# References

Aulakh, A. (2011, October 27). Meet Dr. Balvinder Singh Ahuja. *Toronto Star*, p. A11.

Barrero, G.P.D. (2009). Dancing here, "living" there: Transnational living and working conditions of Latina migrant exotic dancers. In Goldring, L. & Krishnamurti, S. (Eds.), *Organizing the transnational: Labour, politics and social change*. Vancouver: University of British Columbia Press.

Blauner, R. (1964). *Alienation and freedom: The factory worker and his industry*. Chicago: University of Chicago Press.

Block, S. (2010). *Ontario's growing gap: The role of race and gender*. Ottawa: Canadian Centre for Policy Alternatives.

Block, S., & Galabuzi, G. (2011). Canada's colour coded labour market. Toronto: Wellesley Institute.

Bourdieu, P. (1986). The forms of capital. In Richardson, J. (Ed.), *Handbook of theory and research for the sociology of education*. New York: Greenwood Press.

Braverman, H. (1974). *Labour and monopoly capital: The degradation of work in the twentieth century*. New York: Monthly Review Press.

Das Gupta, T., Man, G., Mirchandani, K., & Ng, R. (2014). Class borders: Chinese and South Asian professional immigrant women navigating the labour market. *Journal of Pacific Migration Review, 23* (1).

Das Gupta, T. (1996). *Racism and paid work*. Toronto: Garamond Press.

*El Contrato* (2003). National Film Board, Canada.

Faraday, F. (2012). *Made in Canada: How the law constructs migrant workers' insecurity*. Toronto: Metcalf Foundation.

Galabuzi, G. (2001). *Canada's creeping apartheid*. Toronto: CSJ Foundation for Research and Education. Retrieved from www.socialjustice.org.

Galabuzi, G. (2009). Social exclusion. In Raphael, D. (Ed.). *Social determinants of health*. Toronto: Canadian Scholars' Press.

*Journey To Finding Myself Again* (2013). Documentary film by Srabani Maitra and Tania Das Gupta, York University. Retrieved from http://www.youtube.com/watch?v=vwY11Ykxs8c&feature=em-share _video_user.

Keung, N. (2013, July 14). The undocumented. *Toronto Star*, p. A1.

Krahn, H. J., Lowe, G.S., & Hughes, K. D. (2011). *Work, industry and Canadian society*. Toronto: Nelson.

Lewchuk, W., de Wolff, A., King, A., & Polanyi, M. (2006). The hidden costs of precarious employment: Health and the employment relationship. In Vosko, L. F. (Ed.), *Precarious employment: Understanding labour market insecurity in Canada*. Montreal: McGill-Queen's University Press.

Pratt, G. (2012). *Families apart: Migrant mothers and the conflicts of labour and love*. Minneapolis, MN: University of Minnesota Press.

Raphael, D. (2009). *Social determinants of health*. Toronto: Canadian Scholars' Press.

Sennett, R. and Cobb, J. (1972) *The hidden injuries of class*. New York: Knopf.

Sharma, N. R. (2000). Race, class, gender and the making of difference: The social organization of "migrant workers" in Canada. *Atlantis, 24* (2), 5–26.

Silvera, M. (1983). *Silenced*. Toronto: Williams-Wallace Publishers.

Syed, I.U.B. (2012). Forced assimilation is an unhealthy policy intervention: The case of the hijab ban in France and Quebec, Canada. *The International Journal of Human Rights*. DOI:10.1080/13642987. 2012.724678.

Tucker, R.C. (Ed.) (1972). *The Marx-Engels reader*. New York: W.W. Norton.

Velasco, P. (2002). Filipino migrant workers amidst globalization. *Canadian Woman Studies, 21/22* (4), 131–135.

Workers' Action Centre (WAC). (2007). *Working on the edge.* Toronto: Workers' Action Centre.

Zaman, H. (2012). *Asian immigrants in "two Canadas": Racialization, marginalization, and deregulated work.* Halifax: Fernwood Publishing.

Zeytinoglu, I.U., Denton, M., Davies, S., Baumann, A., Blythe, J., & Boos, L. (2007). Associations between work intensification, stress and job satisfaction: the case of nurses in Ontario. *Relations Industrielles/Industrial Relations, 62* (2), 201–25.

# Part Three

# Action, Policy and Practice

CHAPTER THIRTEEN

# Ethical Considerations
# in Working with Refugees

*Donald Payne*

Ethical issues repeatedly intersect the lives of refugees. These include ethical issues related to the international political situation and the situation in countries from which refugees are forced to flee, ethical issues related to the process of migration, and ethical issues related to the refugee determination process in the receiving country. Within the receiving country, there are ethical issues related to the refugee's community, interpersonal relationships and the provision of service delivery to refugees. Refugees also face their own personal ethical dilemmas throughout the process, such as decisions on personal security versus family and national loyalty.

In this chapter, I will first explore the development of ethics codes, protocols and standards that social workers, health care workers, legal advocates and community development workers should be familiar with as they work with and alongside refugees in Canada. I will then explore ethical problems and limitations embedded in the practical application of the codes. I will outline ethical issues related to Bill C-31, which changed Canada's policy in accepting refugees. The chapter finally explores ethical issues as they relate directly to working with and alongside refugees. The main focus of this chapter is on refugees who are forced to flee for their safety in the absence of state protection, whether intentional or unintentional. It does not include economic or environmental refugees, although these conditions often lead to political repression and war with resulting migration.

## International Codes and Standards

Ethical codes have existed since the early days of human history, reflecting the need for societies to establish rules of conduct and fairness. The *Code of Hammurabi*, a well-preserved Babylonian law code, dating back to about 1772 B.C., consists of 282 laws, with graded punishments, depending on whether a man's status was slave versus free. The code deals with the ethics of fairness in the organization of society. Aspects of the code have been incorporated by later societies. Nearly one-half of the code deals with matters of contract and liability for personal and economic damages to individuals. A third of the code addresses issues concerning household and family relationships, such as inheritance, divorce, paternity and sexual behavior. The code is one of the earliest examples of the idea of presumption of innocence, and it also suggests that both the accused and accuser have the opportunity to provide evidence. The laws set out in the code were arranged in orderly groups, to ensure that readers would know what was required of them.

Written codes of medical ethics date back at least to the late fifth century B.C.

### United Nations Declarations and Conventions Contained in General Assembly Resolutions

- Universal Declaration of Human Rights (1948)
- Geneva Conventions related to armed conflict (1949)
- Convention Relating to the Status of Refugees (1951)
- International Covenant on Civil and Political Rights (1966)
- International Covenant on Economic, Social and Cultural Rights (1966)
- Declaration on the Protection of Women and Children in Emergency and Armed Conflict (1974)
- Convention against Torture and Other Cruel, Inhuman and Degrading Treatment or Punishment (1984)
- Convention on the Rights of the Child (1989)
- Declaration on the Rights of Indigenous Peoples (2007)

with the *Hippocratic Oath*, widely believed to have been written either by Hippocrates, often regarded as the father of western medicine, or by one of his students (Amnesty International, 2011, p. 3). This oath, whether in the original or modernized versions, has historically been taken by physicians and other health care professionals, who swear to practice medicine honestly, including treating the sick to the best of their ability and preserving patient privacy. A modern revision, the *Declaration of Geneva*, was first drafted in 1948 by the World Medical Association (WMA) and has been revised since then (WMA website). The *Oath of Maimonides*, composed by Moses Maimonides (A.D. 1135–1204) a rabbi, physician and philosopher in Morocco and Egypt, declared:

> May the love for my art actuate me at all time; that neither avarice nor miserliness, nor thirst for glory or for a great reputation engage my mind. . . . May I

never see in the patient anything but a fellow creature in pain. Grant me the strength, time and opportunity always to correct what I have acquired (Amnesty International, 2011, p. 4).

## Did You Know?

The first review of Canada's human rights record was held in 2009. Canada accepted fewer than half of the 68 recommendations from the 2009 review, partially rejected 22 and completely rejected 14. Rejected recommendations touched on issues that included racial discrimination, Aboriginal rights, poverty reduction, and seeking clemency for Canadians who face the death penalty overseas (Edwards, 2009). The second review in 2013 made 88 recommendations (UN General Assembly, 2013). Amnesty International noted that the review raised critical, concrete recommendations touching on numerous human rights shortcomings that are well known to Canadians. This included alarming levels of violence against Indigenous women and girls, nationwide poverty and homelessness, and Canada's lagging record of ratifying international human rights treaties. Other areas included the rights of Indigenous peoples, refugee protection, corporate accountability, national security and women's equality (Amnesty International, 2013).

## Reflective Questions

1. What are some of the implications of Canada's human rights record as it relates to working with clients, especially refugees?
2. How important to you is it that Canada accepts the United Nations' recommendations?

These medical codes focus not only on fairness, but extend to giving priority to the needs and rights of those being cared for.

The *Universal Declaration of Human Rights*, adopted by the UN General Assembly on December 10, 1948, arose as a response to the atrocities that occurred during the Second World War, with the aim of never allowing their recurrence. This declaration focuses on the rights of all individuals and the need to have their rights protected. The table on the preceding page lists declarations and conventions relevant to refugees.

A UN General Assembly **declaration** is essentially an expression of political commitment on the part of states that voted in favour of its adoption on matters of considerable significance, such as climate change, poverty and the rights of Indigenous peoples. Unlike a treaty or covenant, a declaration is not legally binding. States do not sign or ratify declarations adopted by the UN General Assembly. On the other hand, a United Nations **convention** is legally binding, from an international perspective, on the states that ratify it and requires states to implement conforming legislation as part of their domestic law (United Nations, n.d.).

All UN Conventions have not been ratified by all countries. For example, the United States has not ratified the *Convention on the Rights of the Child*. Despite the good intentions implicit in them, the major shortcoming of conventions is the fact that there is no legal mechanism to enforce them. However, the United Nations Human Rights Council, composed of 18 experts, conducts a "Universal Periodic Review" every four years, looking at all individual UN members' human rights records in terms of their conformity to the United Nations' human rights standards.

The International Criminal Court, a permanent tribunal established by the Rome Statute which came into force on July 1, 2002, was established to prosecute individuals for genocide, crimes against humanity and war crimes (International Criminal Court, 2013). The Court is located in The Hague, Netherlands, but its proceedings may take place anywhere. It is intended to complement existing national judicial systems, and may exercise its jurisdiction only when national courts are unwilling or unable to investigate or prosecute such crimes. It has jurisdiction only over states who have agreed to be party to it. Some states have decided not to be party to the ICC, including India, China, Israel, Sudan and the United States.

## Ethical Issues Associated with the United Nations Convention Relating to the Status of Refugees

The following section will explore the *United Nations Convention Relating to the Status of Refugees* (UNCRSR) and ethical considerations related to its implementation. The section will first provide brief background information on the convention itself and then explore ethical quandaries that arise when the spirit of the convention is not upheld. This will be followed by an examination of the implications of the convention for refugees as well as refugee practitioners generally, and for those working in Canada in dealing with Bill C-31 specifically.

THE UNITED NATIONS CONVENTION RELATING TO THE STATUS OF REFUGEES. The UNCRSR, or the Refugee Convention, adopted in July 1951 and implemented in 1954 with some later revisions, is an international convention that defines who is a refugee (United Nations, 2010). It sets out the rights of individuals who are granted asylum and the responsibilities of nations that grant asylum. Countries that have ratified the Refugee Convention are obliged to protect refugees that are on their territory and not impose penalties pertaining to the illegality of their entry or presence in a country if it can be shown that there was ample cause for their illegal entry and/or presence, such as escaping threats on their lives or freedom.

The main ethical principle in dealing with refugees should be establishing their right to justice and protection for individuals fleeing persecution. Problems arise in the application of the convention when states view refugee protection as something thrust upon them, and therefore avoid accepting responsibility for having caused refugee flows. In this view, accepting refugees is presented as a charitable act rather than a justice and human rights obligation. States often feel justified in providing only the minimal obligations required under the convention, regarding refugees as a burden, rather than being guided by the ethical spirit of the convention in providing adequate levels of rights-based assistance and justice to individuals fleeing from persecution.

In practice, the broader ethical issues in dealing with refugees are usually overlooked, or reduced to the state's ability to decide who is a "genuine" refugee needing protection (Gibney, 2004). The ethical issues regarding refugees tend to be framed in a manner that assumes that a state has absolute control over its borders, that western countries have absolutely no connection with the creation of refugee flow, and that the absorption capacity for refugees in their country has been surpassed. From this perspective, refugee flows are seen as being the consequences of actions of "others" while ignoring history, including the fact that European settlers invaded every corner of the globe from the fifteenth century onward, that western countries have meddled in the politics of other countries in supporting dictatorships, that western countries have provided arms in one civil war after another, and that billions of dollars in foreign aid have been given to corrupt and brutal dictatorships by governments and the World Bank. States should accept the ethical responsibility for having caused, and continuing to cause, many of the refugee problems through their direct or indirect actions, rather than turning a blind eye to these actions and regarding the refugee problem only as something thrust upon them.

When a state grants refugee status to individuals, this does not necessarily equate to the state acting ethically in regard to refugees. States can interpret their obligations to refugees in a way that defeats the purpose of refugee admissions, which is to protect people. States have gone to great lengths to try to eliminate the possibility of individuals being able to apply for refugee status, such as the requirement of visas for refugee-producing countries and the strict inspection of passports prior to boarding a plane bound for the receiving country. In the past decade, governments have developed regulations that penalize airlines and ferry companies for carrying "illegal" immigrants. These provisions have serious implications for those fleeing persecution and seeking asylum. In Canada there is an administrative fee of $3,200 that airlines must pay as well as all removal costs, living expenses and medical expenses incurred while the "illegal" immigrant is in Canada (Canadian Border Services Agency, 2012). The problem thus created of restricting access to Canada has been heightened by so-called "safe" third country agreements, such as the December 2004 Canada-U.S. Safe Third Country Agreement, under which persons seeking refugee protection must make a claim in the first country they arrive in (the United States or Canada), unless they qualify for an exception to the agreement. The designation of "safe" countries of origin in Bill C-31 (2012), discussed elsewhere in this volume, greatly adds to the difficulties of access.

At the refugee determination stage, some refugee claimants have documents and/or other evidence that strongly support their claims. Others have little documentation or evidence to support their claims. In the latter case, the decision rests on an appraisal of the claimant's credibility. This is a subjective judgment that is subject to error and vulnerable to bias. For example, the stereotypical perception that Roma claimants are "unfounded" refugees can prejudice the decision on an individual Roma's claim and limit their ability to appeal a negative decision. At the ethical level, the refugee determination system has to decide whether to enforce a very strict assessment of credibility which will exclude some genuine claimants, or a more liberal assessment regime which will admit more genuine claimants but may also allow into Canada some claimants who have been deceptive in their claims. Under political pressure and financial restraint, there is the great risk of a shift to a very strict assessment of credibility.

In Canada, there is no guarantee for provision of adequate legal representation for refugee claimants at their hearings, and there is limited recourse when a claimant receives poor or harmful advice from a refugee consultant. The changes in Bill-31, discussed later, add to the difficulties in the claimant's case being heard in a fair and just manner. This is particularly true for claimants who require more time to disclose information and prepare their cases due to psychological problems resulting from trauma and/or shame over sexual abuse.

States have not taken on responsibility for meeting the needs of the large number of refugees in the world requiring protection. They provide statistics on how many individuals are given refugee protection, but not on how many individuals are in need of such protection. Although the Canadian government has promised to resettle more refugees, there was a dramatic decrease in the number of refugees resettled to Canada in 2012, down to 9,624, the second-lowest number resettled in Canada in over 30 years, despite a target of 13,000. In 1980, 40,271 refugees were resettled and in 1989, 35,439 refugees were resettled, the majority in both years being privately sponsored (Canadian Council for Refugees, 2013). This decrease in the number of refugees resettled in Canada occurs at a time when there are an estimated 45.2 million refugees, 80% of them women and children, scattered around the world in refugee camps, the highest number in nearly two decades (Smithsonian Institution, n.d.). While the phrase "refugee camp" implies a temporary situation, some refugees remain in these camps for many years, and for many young refugees, these camps are the only homes that they know.

Although governments claim they do not send individuals back to countries where they believe they will be harmed, determining whether it is safe to return a failed claimant to their home country is a judgment call by the deporting government. There are many instances where such judgments have been inaccurate and where the deported individuals have faced persecution, imprisonment and even death. Up to this point, the Canadian government has not kept statistics on the fate of returned refugee claimants, considering it an issue outside its jurisdiction, and thus relieving itself of the responsibility of dealing with the reality that returned refugee claimants may face further persecution and even death.

## Ethical Issues Related to Canada's Bill C-31

Governments are under pressure from many competing interests. The desire to maintain political power, and to maintain or increase voter popularity, is a constant pressure. There are legitimate restrictions on the number of refugees that can be received in Canada and the resources that can be allotted to them, but how are these limits to be determined? Under the utilitarian principle of "the greatest good for the greatest number of people," should "people" be defined as Canadian taxpayers, all the people in the world or only the "desirable" people in the world? Government policy-makers want to appear moral and use ethical arguments to support their policies, such as using the necessity of protecting the integrity of Canada's immigration system as the rationale for Bill C-31, the *Protecting Canada's Immigration System Act.*

Bill C-31 came into effect on December 15, 2012 and contained important changes to Canada's *Immigration and Refugee Protection Act.* Bill C-31 adds greatly to the difficulty for refugee claimants in gaining access to Canada, while making it easier for them to be removed (Citizenship and Immigration Canada, 2012). The changes indicate that Canada is assuming a more restricted ethical responsibility for refugee protection. From the government's perspective, the important ethical principle is the protection of the safety and security of Canadians as well as the safeguarding of the integrity of Canada's immigration system. These goals are accomplished by making it much easier to keep "unfounded" refugees out of Canada or to remove them quickly. Bill C-31 makes this protection a much higher priority than the ethic of responsibility for the protection of refugees.

Below is a summary the government has provided of the changes in its policies and procedures under Bill C-31 (Citizenship and Immigration Canada, 2012):

- Detaining individuals in the designated "irregular arrival" group, with detention reviews within 14 days followed by another review only every six months until a decision is made on the refugee claim.
- Preventing these "irregular arrivals" from applying for permanent resident status for a period of five years, which intentionally prevents people from sponsoring family members during that time, reducing the attraction of coming to Canada by way of a designated irregular arrival.
- Denying access to the Refugee Appeal Division when the Refugee Protection Division of the Immigration and Refugee Board decides that a refugee claim is manifestly unfounded.
- Removing most failed asylum claimants from Canada within 12 months of a final decision from the Immigration and Refugee Board. It is claimed that timely removals will reduce costs and deter abuse. Making an unfounded asylum claim will no longer be seen as an automatic way to stay in Canada for long periods.
- Using biometrics will strengthen the integrity of Canada's immigration program by helping prevent known criminals, failed refugee claimants, and those deported in the past from using a different identity to obtain a visa.

From the perspective of refugee protection, the legislated changes have raised grave ethical concerns, as they emphasize speed and categorizations over fairness and individual protection. The Canadian Council for Refugees (CCR) has expressed the following concerns (2013):

- **Impossibly tight timelines** for preparation of refugee hearings and for processing refugee claims, especially for refugees who have experienced serious trauma and need time to build trust before they can tell their stories.

- **Designated countries of origin,** identified at the minister's discretion, will push people from those countries through the system more quickly than others. It makes Canada's system of independent decision-making for refugees vulnerable to political, trade, military, diplomatic and other considerations.
- **Irregular arrivals** (groups of two or more identified at the government's discretion) will face mandatory detention under the new law. While an amendment will provide for review of detention within 14 days and then after six months, legal experts are concerned that this will not meet the requirements of the *Canadian Charter of Rights and Freedoms.*
- **Barriers to appeal**: An appeal will be inaccessible to "irregular arrivals" and to refugees from "designated countries of origin."

The CCR[1] notes that there are also ethical concerns around the undermining of public support for refugees because of the language used in Bill C-31, language which is presented in a way that spreads damaging misinformation about refugees and about Canada's obligations towards refugees. It portrays refugee claimants as being dangerous and a risk to the security and safety of our streets and communities. It is ethically wrong to label refugee claimants as queue-jumpers as there is no queue for refugees. To not allow individuals to flee an urgent threat to their lives, but make them wait in line to be accepted at some point in the future, would be similar to closing the emergency wards of hospitals and making everyone wait for an indefinitely distant doctor's appointment. We have a refugee determination system because international law guarantees to people fleeing persecution the right to go to another country and seek asylum.

The Canadian government still has the problem of dealing fairly and ethically with the backlog of some 38,000 refugee claims accumulated under the former refugee determination system (Canadian Council for Refugees, 2013). Although Bill C-31 may push claimants through too quickly, many in the old system have languished too long without having their claims heard.

## Case Study 13.1

*This composite case presents some situations with ethical issues encountered by refugees migrating to Canada. How many can you identify?*

Ms. D, along with friends, became politically active after they had become very angry at

---

[1] The Canadian Council for Refugees (CCR) is a non-profit umbrella organization committed to the rights and protection of refugees in Canada and around the world, and to the settlement of refugees and immigrants in Canada. The membership is made up of organizations involved in the settlement, sponsorship and protection of refugees and immigrants.

the repression in her country. She was detained at a demonstration and was tortured in detention in an attempt to extract names of other politically active people with whom she had contact. Her family paid a bribe to have her released. Following her release, she was fearful of being detained again and thought of leaving the country as she knew she was being watched. However, she decided to remain with her mother who was ill and needed her help. When she heard that the authorities were actively looking for her, she recognized that she needed to leave to save her life and did so with the help of an agent. After she arrived in Canada, she learned that her father had been detained and tortured in an attempt to get him to reveal her whereabouts. He died of a heart attack as a result of the torture. His death, indirectly resulting from her fleeing, produced in her ambivalent feelings of guilt as well as relief at being in Canada.

In Canada, she applied for convention refugee status, but did not have documentation to support her claim and got poor advice from a refugee consultant. She required an interpreter in preparing her case, but the only ones available to her were from her country and she had difficulty trusting them. As a result she did not reveal her sexual abuse in detention. She had the stress of enduring harsh cross-examination at her hearing and her admission of sexual abuse at the hearing was treated with skepticism as it was not in her initial report (personal information form). She was under great distress until she learned that she had been accepted. She was making good progress at her ESL classes where she had a good relationship with her teacher, but soon had to change programs due to the eligibility criteria – the class was not for accepted refugees.

## Ethical Issues Associated with Health Care for Refugees in Canada

In addition to ethical issues for refugees coming to Canada, ethical conflicts can arise in regard to the provision of health care to refugees in Canada. On the one hand, health professionals are ethically required to provide health care to everyone regardless of their circumstances. On the other hand, the current federal government's policy holds that it is ethically justified in making spending cuts to heath care on the basis of cost, deterrence of refugees coming to Canada and equity issues for other Canadians. Refugee health care can be seen as a responsibility to be discharged at as low a cost as possible for Canadian taxpayers. The ethical focus becomes one of discharging minimal obligations rather than on meeting the needs and rights of refugees for health care. The equity argument pits Canadian citizens against refugees, and ignores the tremendous hardship experienced by most refugees. Health care professionals have a responsibility to uphold their ethical standards in treating all individuals regardless of their status, to protest government policy and to challenge those who seek to prevent them from fulfilling their ethical duties through attempting to limit necessary health care (University of Toronto Department of Psychiatry, 2012).

The problems associated with health care for refugees, and especially the cutbacks in the Interim Federal Health Program (IFHP) and their implications, are explored in more detail elsewhere in this book.

## Ethical Issues for Refugee Practitioners in Canada

In Canada, national and provincial professional organizations and regulating bodies set out ethical standards for professionals who work with individuals (Canadian Medical Association, 2004; Canadian Psychological Association, 2000; Canadian Nurses Association, 2008; Canadian Association of Social Workers, 2005). If there is a conflict between the professional college's requirements and the employing agency's requirements, the college's requirements take precedence. Close attention must be paid to these standards in working with refugees, specifically as they relate to issues such as the cultural understanding of trauma and treatment, diverse cultural expressions of distress, concerns regarding confidentiality, the practitioner's emotional reactions to the refugee's situation, and the vulnerability of the individuals.

Ethical issues in health care involve respecting the autonomy and dignity of those being helped without discriminating against them or imposing cultural, religious or personal beliefs. The principal imperative of medical ethics, *primun non nocere* ("do no harm"), reminds health care providers that they must consider the possible harm that any intervention might do. In working with individuals, ethical practice means providing the best care and best manner of care for the individual. Those providing help need to be aware of factors, often assumed or unconscious, that can ethically interfere with this best care.

ETHICS AND CULTURAL DIFFERENCES. There are culturally diverse ways of understanding, expressing and managing physical and emotional distress. Western psychological models are embedded with western cultural values and beliefs. Western practitioners, indeed all practitioners, should be aware of cultural differences as an ethical point of departure, to avoid falling into the trap of comparing other cultures to one's own as if one's own were the standard. Some aspects of a different culture may appear strange and irrational to us, but to someone in that culture, our culture can appear just as strange and irrational. As an example, being told that one has a terminal illness may be perceived as a right in western culture, but as a disrespectful ethical violation in a different culture. Some cultures focus on "active forgetting" and others on "processing trauma."

Individuals from different cultures, and within cultures, can have differing understandings of health and illness, and different ways of expressing and coping with their distress. Some consider their suffering and trauma their own fault, either because they regard it as a punishment for their wrongdoing or the result of a situation that they should have been aware of so as to avoid the suffering. Some place virtue on handling their distress in a stoical, uncomplaining fashion, regarding it as a sign of personal strength, whereas showing emotion or asking for help would display a personal weakness. Often a stigma is placed on psychological symptoms, making it difficult for workers to promote support for mental health problems. Emotional distress can be experienced culturally primarily through physical symptoms, such as headaches and stomach distress, especially if psychological symptoms are seen as a weakness (American Psychological Association, 2009; Shahid, 2013).

The term **culture** can mean different things and it is important to recognize the context in which it is being used. It can refer to dominant culture, legislated culture, traditional and/or religious culture or the culture of one's local group or family. It is important not to be distracted by generalizations about an individual's culture. What is important is the individual's worldview and how that individual experiences his/her culture. Within cultures, there is great diversity in worldviews. Worldviews differ between and among men and women, and older and younger generations. They are affected by factors including the amount and manner of education, lived condition and life experience, political views, or degree of affluence and one's status in society. In order to understand an individual and his/her worldview in an informed manner, one has to listen carefully to the individual's description of her/his life, being aware of one's own preconceptions.

A continuum exists between ethical relativism and ethical universalism. **Ethical relativism** holds that morality is relative to the norms of one's culture, and that there are no universal moral standards that can be applied to all peoples at all times. Whether an action is right or wrong depends on the moral norms of the society in which it is practiced. The same action may be morally right in one society but morally wrong in another. For example, within some patriarchal societies, even if there are appropriate laws that make gender-based violence a crime, governments often take no or little action to punish honour-killers. Other problematic situations range from war to legal punishments to revenge killings and euthanasia. Under cultural or ethical relativism, practices such as polygamy and sexual orientation would ethically be held as relative to the community culture (Markkula Center, 1992). The norms of the culture can vary depending on whether the culture is regarded as the dominant culture, the legislated culture or the traditional/religious culture.

**Ethical universalism** holds that there is a code of moral conduct that applies universally, that is, for all similarly situated individuals regardless of culture, race, sex, religion, nationality, sexuality or other distinguishing feature. Examples would include the "golden rule", the UN Declaration of Human Rights and medical ethical standards. States appear to hold that their responsibility to admit refugees is relative to the state's situation rather than being a universal obligation.

The practitioner may be challenged by the practices or beliefs of individuals from different cultures that are in opposition to their own values. These can include views about family roles, views on "respect" for authority, or explanations for illness and for bad things happening. These differences could result in providing care and advocating for a refugee whose belief system is abhorrent to one's own. While appreciating these differences, helpers have a role in educating refugees about how Canadian society, including its laws, operates. This education can include informing refugees about the most productive manner to deal with government officials and others in authority, situations where one is required to be assertive, and what behaviour should not be tolerated from anyone.

Refugees and professionals working with them can encounter ethical dilemmas. A dilemma is a situation presenting two or more equally conclusive alternatives, where the choice of one excludes the other and where there is no "right" choice. It is ethically important for the helper to not try to resolve the dilemma by proposing what they believe to be the right choice according to their own beliefs, but to allow the refugees to articulate and work out the dilemmas for themselves over time. The following cases demonstrate dilemmas that may arise in working with refugees. When reading Case Study 13.2, contemplate the following questions:

1. What are some of the underlying causes of the ethical dilemma that Ms. B is facing?
2. How would you assist Ms. B?
3. What would be some of your professional dilemmas in helping Ms. B?
4. In what way could your own personal/cultural ethics interfere with helping Ms. B?

## Case Study 13.2

Ms. B has been in Canada for several years. She is very busy looking after her four young to early adolescent children, as well as her husband. She would like to get out more, but her husband does not permit her to go out on her own without him or to have friends visit her at their home. She feels very restricted by his demands and has had thoughts of separating, but at the same time feels a strong need to not compromise her family values. As well, if she were to separate, she would feel guilty for having created a major disruption in the family. There is an internal conflict between, on the one hand, maintaining her ingrained beliefs regarding her caregiving role and responsibility to her family and, on the other hand, her awareness that she also has a right to pay attention to her own needs.

Another situation that may raise an ethical dilemma is when couples are involved in mixed cultural relationships and they need to arrive at some joint decision in regard to their children. The case of Mr. C will put this into perspective.

## Case Study 13.3

Mr. C was a political prisoner in Latin America where he was severely tortured. He came to Canada, has been settled here for many years and is married with two adolescent sons. A conflict has arisen between himself and his wife over telling their sons about his past. His Canadian wife with her cultural beliefs about disclosure strongly believes that he has an ethical obligation to tell them about his past as they have a right to know as part of their family heritage. He strongly resists this, refusing to share his past which he wants to leave behind him. He also does not want to burden his children with his past. With his cultural values, he believes in "actively forgetting" and he believes his role as a man is to protect his family members from distress. There is an ethical dilemma over his personal/cultural belief preventing him from sharing his past pain and his wife's personal/cultural belief that children have a right to know.

As a professional:

1. How could you assist Mr. C and his wife in dealing with their situation?
2. What compromises could be possible to resolve the dilemma that would respect the values of both parents?

CONFIDENTIALITY. For individuals who have suffered trauma, confidentiality is a very important issue. This is greatly intensified if there are feelings of fear or shame associated with their experiences. Many new refugees are unaware of how confidentially is regarded within professional ethical codes. Concerns often centre on the possible or potential consequences of other people in their community finding out about their experiences, or on information they have provided getting back to the authorities in their country. Because of confidentially concerns, it may be necessary at times to have them sign a release of information form. They may have real or imagined fears regarding the implications of signing a paper. This is heightened if they have been forced to sign a document, especially a confession, in the past, or if the consent form is written in complicated legalistic terms. Not only must confidentiality be practiced, but the individual must be confident that confidentiality is occurring in order to develop trust. An ethical problem regarding confidentiality can arise when government agencies request personal information about those receiving services, something that has been strongly resisted by agencies providing services.

Problems may arise when a husband or male member of a family, or parents and guardians of children over the age of 16, expect to be able to give consent for treatment of their family members, including an adult female. Although professionals can respect certain practices, they need to educate their clients by providing them with information about the law, institutional practices, procedures and processes in Canada.

Practitioners also need to provide their clients with information about family law, children's rights, criminal law, immigration law, school policies, housing rights and any other information that might be assist with the integration process. This extends to issues that are deemed criminal in Canada, such as female genital mutilation.

Professionals need to respect confidentiality except when required to do otherwise by law. In Canada, legal requirements for reporting are the responsibility of the provincial professional colleges. For example, in Ontario, physicians are legally required to report certain situations, including communicable diseases, child abuse, sexual abuse of a patient by a health professional, impaired driving ability and gunshot wounds (College of Physicians and Surgeons of Ontario, 2012). There is also an obligation to certify suicidal/homicidal individuals to hospitalize them against their will. Other professional colleges have related requirements for reporting. Social workers and social service workers, for instance, are required to report cases of child abuse and neglect, harm to self and harm to others.

USE OF INTERPRETERS. The use of interpreters raises particular concerns about confidentiality. Ideally the interpreter would be proficient in the language of the refugee, but not from the same culture and community. In practice, this is difficult to achieve due to lack of availability and limited government funding. Even if the interpreter is from the same culture, but without direct contact with the refugee or his community, there can still be the fear that information could get back to the government of the country they fled. For example, Iranians have realistic fears about Iranian government agents in Canada. If the interpreter is from the same community, there is concern that the community gossip network will spread information about them. In this situation, important information that is regarded as private or shameful may not be revealed to the worker.

The situation can worsen when family members are used as interpreters as this can put the individual in conflict over how much to reveal, and greatly limits the information that the individual may be willing to reveal. This problem is intensified when children are used as translators. Moreover, revealed information may stir up conflict within the family, adding to the individual's distress. Increased distress can be produced if a male interpreter is used in talking with a woman, especially if she has suffered sexual abuse. Refugees may have difficulty trusting that an interpreter will interpret correctly if the interpreter is from a culture with which their culture has had conflict, such as an Ethiopian interpreting for a Somali refugee or vice versa. There is major concern regarding untrained interpreters, as they often provide only a summary of what was said, edit the information to include only what they feel the helper wants to hear, or provide the history themselves to relieve stress on the individual in reporting it himself or herself. Interpreters can be helpful in providing the cultural context of what is being interpreted rather than just providing a literal interpretation.

POWER IMBALANCE. The power imbalance in any engagement between refugees and those working with them needs to be recognized. Professional ethical standards recognize this imbalance and have prohibitions against abusing it. Refugees may feel a need to submit and not voice their feelings and opinions out of respect for the professional. They may come from cultures where respect for those providing help is regarded as involving submission and being grateful, rather than being able to honestly express what they feel even if it is critical or what they think the helper does not want to hear. At the same time, the power of the helper can be exaggerated so that he/she is seen as the person who can solve all their problems and provide all the answers, rather than the client being actively involved in the helping process.

The power imbalance can lead to the problem of **coercion**. Coercion acts against individuals freely making decisions and choosing courses of action themselves. Professional ethical codes disapprove of coercion, but there are different understandings of what constitutes coercion. In the worst situation, coercion can lead to open or veiled threats of hospitalization or the involvement of the Children's Aid Society if the refugee does not conform to the helping person's desires, whether those desires benefit the refugee or not. In the best situation, there is a problem of how far one should go in trying to convince someone to do or not do something, especially if the consequences seem inevitable and serious to the refugee. There can be a thin line between well-intentioned helping and coercion. How much can a helper discourage what he/she regards as a very damaging relationship before it becomes coercion?

PATHOLOGIZING RESPONSE TO STRESS RATHER THAN LOOKING AT RESILIENCE. Western models tend to treat suffering and adversity in terms of psychopathology rather than as legitimate responses to stress and upheaval (Pain, 2013). Refugees are often asked about their distress in medical terminology expressed according to the definitions set out in the *Diagnostic and Statistical Manual of Mental Disorders* (the DSM-5 for short) (American Psychiatric Association, 2013). Refugees may feel that they have to describe their distress using medical terms in order for their distress to be accepted as genuine. This can be reinforced when refugees feel that they have to present enough medical symptoms in order to be admitted to a program or obtain a benefit, especially when a medical diagnosis is required to open the door for services and benefits. The diagnosis of post-traumatic stress disorder (PTSD), although useful in some contexts, such as refugee determination hearings, can pathologize a normal response to extreme events. Victims of trauma often need to be reassured that the distressing symptoms they are experiencing are a normal response to their extreme situation.

## Case Study 13.4

A 23-year old engineer and refugee who had been in Canada for three months was seen for psychiatric assessment for marked distress. His father had been killed in front of him, his leg had been severed in a bomb blast and his girlfriend had been killed by her family for dating him. He was well qualified for a PTSD diagnosis. When asked about current problems, he reported that he had been spoiled as a child and had never learned to cook. The situation causing his greatest distress was having been placed with a roommate where he was required to cook, and thus having to face extreme embarrassment and anxiety over not being able to cook. He was greatly helped by a cooking course rather than requiring treatment for his marked previous trauma (Pain, 2014).

Refugees usually have experienced a long series of traumatic situations in the general context of instability, insecurity and deprivation, rather than being exposed to one single traumatic event. This reality does not "fit" the Western understanding of how PTSD usually develops. This can lead to excessive focus on the most traumatic event, rather than the whole series of traumatic experiences in their lives. When a refugee provides a history of marked trauma and symptoms of PTSD, it can be easy to project one's own imagined response to the horrible story and regard the trauma as the main problem, rather than looking for other sources of difficulty in the individual's current life. Refugees who have suffered from trauma are usually more concerned about immediate problems, such as housing, work, school and family reunification, rather than wanting help in dealing directly with the traumatic experiences of their past. Case Study 13.5 will put this into further perspective.

Some agencies prefer to use the term "survivor of torture" rather than the term "victim of torture" in order to focus on the resilience present rather than the pathology. In order to understand refugees as individuals, one needs to look at their hopes, dreams and ambitions as well as their distress.

EMOTIONAL REACTIONS TO REFUGEES AND MAINTAINING APPROPRIATE BOUNDARIES. Working with trauma victims can stir up strong emotional feelings in the helper that can interfere with helping the individual in an objective manner. Because of strong positive feelings for the individual, there is risk of over-identification with the individual, over-idealizing the individual or becoming too enmeshed in his/her life. This can lead to blurring of role boundaries, rescue tendencies, focusing exclusively on traumatic events rather than current problems, distortion of the client's psychodynamics, a narcissistic need for recognition, guilt reactions and excessive responsibility for the outcome. Burn-out is an occupational hazard in working with refugees. Empathic strain, in being repeatedly helpful in an emotionally tense situation, can lead to emotional avoidance and detachment, with withdrawal and distancing in the relationship. The strain is increased for individuals working on their own without supervision and a supportive community of colleagues.

Maintaining appropriate boundaries is important in ethical practice, especially with individuals who have suffered trauma. Providing help can evoke strong emotional reactions of dependence and gratitude in clients as well as powerful emotional reactions in helpers. One needs to have a humanizing attitude of openness and support in order to provide an appropriate healing experience to counteract the dehumanization of torture and ill-treatment. An attitude of absolute neutrality in dealing with traumatized individuals is too distancing and unsupportive. The neutrality does not provide a genuine human relationship and can be seen as minimizing or denying the injustice that was done to the person. There is great benefit in bearing witness to the individual's suffering and taking a stand as to its injustice and criminality.

ETHICS IN PRACTICE. Ethical issues that are clear-cut usually do not create a dilemma in practice. The situation becomes more complicated when there are competing ethical demands, such as the need to protect the patient and the need to report to authorities. These situations require clinical judgment as well as awareness of the ethical issues. Consultation with a supervisor, experienced colleagues or professional regularity body can be helpful. Under the pressures of dealing with clients, professionals can be caught up in situations where they have to make ethical decisions on the spot with the luxury of time to reflect on them. The following case study will put this into perspective.

## Case Study 13.5

Ms. C. is being seen for help in dealing with practical problems in adjusting to life in Canada. At times, she has complained that her husband treats her roughly by shoving her around when he is emotionally upset, but does not hit her. He is reportedly irritable and yells at the children when he is upset. When she is settled, she minimizes the difficulty, denying that there is a significant problem and wanting to ignore it.

In your opinion:

1. How does one determine that one is not over-reacting by reporting the abuse or under-reacting by going along with Ms. C.'s minimizing of it?
2. What criteria should one use to assess whether or not it should be reported?
3. What level of physical roughness could be tolerated before it is reported?

## Conclusion

In conclusion, it is important to remember that professionals are faced with ethical issues in dealing with refugees, with the requirement to place the needs of clients before their own desires. They have an obligation to be aware of their own biases and avoid possible harm to their clients. When relating to clients, professionals need to have an awareness of the ethical issues involved in their relationship with their clients and in relation to their professional decision-making. The professional obligation, however, requires us to support our clients and their families in the best of our ability as they thrive to integrate into the Canadian society and eliminate barriers by expanding their knowledge and providing alternative options.

## References

American Psychiatric Association (2013). *Diagnostic and statistical manual of mental disorders* (5th ed.). Washington, D.C.: American Psychiatric Association.

Amnesty International (2011). *Codes of ethics and declarations relevant to the health professions* (5th ed.). London: Amnesty International Publications.

Amnesty International (2013, Sept. 19). Canada gives human rights the cold shoulder: Disgraceful response to UN human rights review contains no new commitments. Retrieved from http://www.amnesty.ca/news/news-releases/.

American Psychological Association (2009). *Task force report, working with refugee children and families: Update for mental health professionals.* Retrieved from http://www.apa.org/pubs/info/reports/refugees-health-professionals.pdf.

Canadian Association of Social Workers (2005). *Code of ethics.* Retrieved from http://www.caswacts.ca/sites/default/files/attachements/CASW_Code%20of%20Ethics.pdf.

Canadian Border Services Agency (2012) *Guide for transporters*. Retrieved from http://www.cbsa-asfc.gc.ca/publications/pub/bsf5023-eng.html#s1x9.

Canadian Council for Refugees (2013). Overview of C-31 refugee determination process. Retrieved from http://ccrweb.ca/en/refugee-reform.

Canadian Medical Association (2004). *Code of ethics*. Retrieved from policybase.cma.ca/dbtw-wpd/PolicyPDF/PD04-06.pdf.

Canadian Nurses Association (2008). *Code of ethics*. Retrieved from www.cna-aiic.ca.

Canadian Psychological Association (2000). *Code of ethics*. Retrieved from www.cpa.ca.

Citizenship and Immigration Canada (2012). Legislation to protect Canada's immigration system receives royal assent. Retrieved from http://www.cic.gc.ca/english/department/media/releases/2012/2012-06-29.asp.

*Code of Hammurabi*. King, L. (Trans.). Retrieved from http://avalon.law.yale.edu/ancient/hamframe.asp.

College of Physicians and Surgeons of Ontario. (2012). *Mandatory and Permissive Reporting*. Retrieved from http://www.cpso.on.ca/policies/policies/default.aspx?ID=1860#sexual.

Edwards, S. (2009, June 9). Canada rejects UN human rights recommendations. Retrieved from http://www.canada.com/news/Canada+rejects+human+rights+recommendations/1678153/story.html.

Gibney, M. J. (2004) *The ethics and politics of asylum: Liberal democracy and the response to refugees*. Cambridge: Cambridge University Press.

Government of Canada (2012). *Protecting Canada's immigration system*. Retrieved from http://www.cic.gc.ca/english/refugees/reform.asp.

International Criminal Court (2013). Retrieved from http://www.icc-cpi.int/en_menus/icc/Pages/default.aspx.

Markkula Center for Applied Ethics (1992). *Ethical relativism*. Developed by M. Velasquez, C. Andre, T. Shanks, & M. J. Meyer. Retrieved from http://www.scu.ed u/ethics/practicing/decision/eth icalrelativism.html.

Shahid, A., Bhugra, D., Syed, E. U., & Zalai, D. (2013). *Cultural aspects of psychiatry*. Thornhill, ON: Joli Joco Publications.

Smithsonian Institution (n.d.). *Where are the 50 most populous refugee camps?* Retrieved from http://www.smithsonianmag.com/ideas-innovations/Where_are_the_50_Most_Populous_Refugee_Camps.html.

Pain, C., Kanagaratnam, P., & Payne, D. (2014). The debate about trauma and psychosocial treatment for refugees. In Simich & Andrmann (Eds.), *Refuge and resilience* (pp 51–60). New York: Springer.

United Nations (n.d.). *Declarations and Conventions Contained in General Assembly Resolutions*. Retrieved from http://www.un.org/documents/instruments/docs_en.asp.

United Nations (2010). *United Nations Convention Relating to the Status of Refugees*. Retrieved from http://www.unhcr.org/3b66c2aa10.html.

University of Toronto Department of Psychiatry (2012). *Interim federal health program cuts and Bill C-31: U of T Psychiatry position statement*. Retrieved from www.utpsychiatry.ca/bill-c31-uoft-psychiatry-position-statement.

World Medical Association. (2006). *Declaration of Geneva*. Retrieved from http://www.wma.net/en/30publications/10policies/g1/.

UN General Report of the Working Group on the Universal Periodic Review: Canada. (2013). Retrieved from http://www.refworld.org/docid/52271e254.html.

## CHAPTER FOURTEEN

# Barriers to Accessing Health Care for Refugees, Government Policy and the Health Care Communities' Response

*Doug Gruner, Janet Cleveland, Laïla Demirdache and Kevin Pottie*

Canada has for many years had an international reputation for ensuring the most vulnerable have reasonable access to health care. Fundamental Canadian values, according to many, include offering protection to refugees, fair and equal treatment for all people regardless of differences, and universal access to health care. Although these are lofty goals, many Canadians, including health care practitioners, continue to adhere to and implement these values even in the context of increasingly difficult political challenges. This chapter aims to identify and explore the policy, legal, and health care implications surrounding the reception and resettlement of refugees in Canada. It uses a series of case studies to illustrate barriers in accessing the health care system that refugees face as well as the challenges confronted by health care practitioners while providing care to refugees.

The chapter will first outline Canadian government policy towards refugees, followed by more in-depth background information on the challenges refugees encounter in Canada, particularly in relation to accessing the health care system. The chapter will further focus on recent cuts to government funding for refugee health care, and the response from health care practitioners and others concerned with the consequences for refugees and Canadian society overall. The latter part of the chapter provides a detailed account of the legal challenges and recommendations for routes forward.

### Federal Government Policy Toward Refugees

In terms of government policy towards refugees, Canada's record has been mixed. In 1986, thanks to the joint efforts of individuals, community members, faith groups and various levels of governments, Canada received the Nansen Award for "the major and sustained contribution of the People of Canada to the cause of refugees" (Immigration and Refugee Board of Canada, 2009) in promoting the settlement of 110,000 Southeast Asians, known as the "Boat People" (Dorais, 2000). Over the years Canada has maintained programs for the resettlement of refugees, either through government or private sponsorship, as well as providing protection to people determined to be Convention refugees by the Immigration and Refugee Board (IRB). In terms of resettled refugees, the number accepted in Canada is relatively small considering that about 36 million people are currently living outside of their country of birth as a result of forcible displacement linked to internal armed conflict or individual violence (United Nations High Commissioner for Refugees, 2013). More than 10 million displaced people have also fled to neighbouring countries of the global south where they are often housed for years in refugee camps with restricted political rights and in conditions of destitution and disempowerment.

Canadian policies have historically been less welcoming towards people who take the initiative of coming to Canada and making a claim for refugee protection. Receiving countries who are signatories to the *Convention Relating to the Status of Refugees*, including Canada, are not allowed to penalize refugee claimants for entering the country without authorization or with false documents (*Convention Relating to the Status of Refugees*, 1951; Hathaway, 2005). This recognizes the reality that people whose life is in danger may have to leave their country rapidly or in secret, without official documents. Since the 1990s governments in receiving countries in the global north, including Canada, have increasingly adopted restrictive border control policies, practiced immigrant detention, restricted visas and taken other measures designed to limit the flow of refugee claimants (Crépeau, Nakache, and Atak, 2007; Edwards, 2011; Phillips, 2011). At the same time, the neoliberal and resultant anti-refugee discourse portrays individuals in need of protection as "illegal" and potentially dangerous intruders, "bogus" refugees bent on taking advantage of the local population (Hyndman and Mountz, 2008; Kenney, 2011; Kenney, 2012; Wherry, 2012). This discourse tends to reinforce implicit xenophobic stereotypes, and may contribute to hostility toward refugee claimants in receiving countries (Rousseau, Hassan, Moreau, and Thombs, 2011).

However, Canada has for many years maintained a number of positive policies towards refugees, such as access to employment, social assistance, education, and until recently, access to health care through the Interim Federal Health Program (IFHP). Since 1957, the IFHP had provided temporary coverage of medical costs for refugees without financial means while they await qualification for provincial or territorial coverage (Citizenship and Immigration Canada, 2012; Order Respecting the Interim Federal Health Program, 2012). The IHFP applied to all resettled refugees and refugee claimants, including refused claimants, and covered doctor's visits, diagnostic tests like x-rays and blood tests, and subsequent treatment plans which often included medications and other necessary therapies. It also provided access to emergency dental and basic vision care. This health care coverage was similar to that of low-income Canadians.

Since 2006, the Conservative government in Canada has hardened their policies toward and discourse concerning refugee claimants. For the Conservative government, legitimate refugees are those who wait patiently in refugee camps, often for 10 years or more, in hopes of return or resettlement. As noted above, refugee claimants who come to Canada through their own means seeking refugee protection or asylum are portrayed as illegitimate: "bogus" and "illegal" (Kenney, 2011; Kenney, 2012; Wherry, 2012). Among the many restrictive policies adopted in recent years, one of the most egregious is the deep cuts to the IFHP instituted in June 2012.

In order to fully examine the IFHP cuts, we will first present an overview of definitions and issues facing refugees, specifically related to health. We will present some of the systemic barriers to accessing health care services, and show how the Canadian government's 2012 cuts to the IFHP have created additional health care barriers causing major trauma for refugees and their families. We will then explore the response by the health care community, which has mobilized to fight back against unfair and restrictive policies. Health care practitioners, traditionally shy of activism, have taken centre stage in the fight to rescind the cuts, forcing the government to respond to allegations that it is not living up to its responsibility inherent in the *Canadian Charter of Rights and Freedoms* (1982) as well as the *Convention Relating to the Status of Refugees* (1951) and the *Convention on the Rights of the Child* (1989). In addition, through their national and provincial organizations, doctors, nurses and other health practitioners have reminded the government that cuts to refugee health care have profoundly undermined the ideal of a universal health care system in Canada.

## Refugees in Canada: An Overview

Refugees, especially in their first years in Canada, require programs and policies that ensure timely access to quality health care and other basic social supports. Their vulnerability stems from pre-migratory factors such as threatened or actual physical or sexual assault, intimate violence, armed conflict, arbitrary imprisonment, torture, death threats, murder of loved ones or other forms of violence, often in the context of mass conflict or state failure (Fazel, Reed, Panter-Brick, and Stein, 2012; Fazel, Wheeler, and Danesh, 2005; Steel, Chey, Silove, Marnane, Bryant, and van Ommeren, 2009). Throughout their migrant journey, many refugees experience violence or hardship in refugee camps, along the way, or in transit countries. Upon arrival in refugee-receiving countries such as Canada, refugees may face multiple forms of discrimination and restrictions on political rights (Cleveland, Rousseau, and Guzder, 2013; Viruell-Fuentes et al., 2012), including restricted access to health care and essential medications. While refugees demonstrate considerable human resilience and contributions to host societies (Beiser 1999), restrictions on political rights remain associated with diminished long-term health outcomes (Viruell-Fuentes et al., 2012).

Refugees arrive in Canada by two main routes: First, **resettled refugees,** typically arriving from refugee camps, are sponsored by the government (**government assisted refugees**, or **GARs**) or by church or community groups (**privately sponsored refugees**, or **PSRs**). About 7,000 are brought to Canada yearly as GARs, and about 4,000 as PSRs (Citizenship and Immigration, 2013a). These individuals become permanent residents upon arrival in Canada. Second, **refugee claimants** (or asylum seekers) come to Canada by their own means and make a claim for refugee protection at the border or from within Canada.

Under Canadian law (*Immigration and Refugee Protection Act*, 2001) and the *Convention Relating to the Status of Refugees* (1951), refugee claimants cannot be sent back to their country of nationality if they have a well-founded fear of persecution for reasons of race, religion, nationality, membership in a particular social group (for example gender or sexual orientation) or political opinion. Canada also adheres to the *Convention Against Torture* (1984), which prohibits returning claimants to their country of nationality if they would be exposed to a risk of torture or of cruel and unusual treatment or punishment.

Until recently, about 20,000 to 25,000 people claimed refugee status annually in Canada, but numbers dropped sharply to about 10,000 in 2013, probably because of hardening of various government policies. On average, about 40% of claimants are accepted as refugees (The Refugee Forum, 2012). Refugee claimants have the right to remain in Canada until final adjudication of their claim by the Immigration and Refugee Board (IRB). Some, but not all, refused refugee claimants also have a right to remain in Canada until they have exhausted their right to appeal or judicial review proceedings. If their claim is definitively rejected, **refused claimants** are allowed to remain in Canada until the deportation order issued against them becomes enforceable. Individuals who choose to stay in Canada after their deportation order becomes enforceable are known as **undocumented, non-status** or **illegal migrants**. These individuals have no legal rights or access to public services, including the health care system. In this chapter, we will focus only on refugees (including refugee claimants and refused claimants who are not under an enforceable deportation order), and will not be discussing the situation of non-status migrants.

As indicated earlier, studies show that resettled refugees and refugee claimants are highly resilient (Beiser, 1999, 2009; Cleveland, Rousseau, and Guzder, 2013; Rousseau and Drapeau, 2003). Positive conditions in the receiving country such as access to secure migratory status, employment, health care, social assistance and schooling, as well as speedy family reunification, play a crucial role in mitigating the impact of pre-migratory trauma while fostering recovery and integration into the new society (Porter and Haslam, 2005; Steel, Momartin, et al., 2011). On the other hand, negative conditions in the receiving country such as precarious status, detention, protracted separation from family, and limited access to employment, health care and social services, can exacerbate pre-existing vulnerabilities and have a serious adverse and often traumatic effects on refugees' health and well-being (Cleveland and Rousseau, 2013; Cleveland, Rousseau, and Guzder, 2013; Laban et al., 2005; Ryan et al., 2009).

Many refugees arrive from refugee camps and countries where a number of infectious and chronic conditions are endemic, with rates of tuberculosis, hepatitis B and HIV being about twice as high among refugees as among other immigrants (Greenaway et al., 2011; Pottie et al., 2011; Rossi et al., 2012; Toronto Public Health and Access Alliance, 2011; Zencovich, et al., 2006). Refugee claimant mothers have a higher level of psychosocial risk and unaddressed postnatal concerns than other immigrant or Canadian-born mothers (Gagnon et al., 2013). This is of particular concern because about 70% of female claimants are of childbearing age (Citizenship and Immigration Canada, 2013b). In Canada, refugees are at higher risk than other immigrants for a rapid decline in self-reported health after arrival (Pottie et al., 2008). Large-scale meta-analytic studies have shown that adult resettled refugees are about 10 times more likely than North Americans to suffer from symptoms of post-traumatic stress disorders (PTSD), which also affects nearly 11% of refugee children (Fazel et al., 2012; Fazel et al., 2005; Rousseau, Pottie, et al., 2011). Rates of PTSD and depression also tend to be high among refugee claimants (Cleveland and Rousseau, 2013; Ouimet, Munoz, Narasiah, Rambure, and Correa, 2008). This reflects the high level of pre-migration and post-migratory trauma and the multiple ongoing stressors in receiving countries including poverty, separation from family, loss of social support, limited access to employment and health services, language and cultural difficulties as well as fears of deportation, should their claim be rejected.

It is therefore imperative that refugees be able to access health care, especially primary and preventative care to ensure that health conditions are identified early and treated, thereby protecting public health as well as the health of the refugee.

## Cuts to the Interim Federal Health Program

On June 30, 2012, the Canadian government significantly reduced the scope of the IFHP. Coverage of basic medication was eliminated, except for conditions threatening public health or safety, for almost all IFHP beneficiaries. Medical services were no longer covered for refugee claimants from certain designated countries and for refused claimants except for conditions posing a risk to public health or safety. The new IFHP also created administrative complexities and health care practitioner confusion that aggravated systemic barriers to health care access for refugee claimants. This is likely to lead to delayed health care seeking, cost-related non-adherence to prescription medication, higher morbidity, increased reliance on hospital emergency departments and worse health outcomes.

The June 2012 changes instituted three main types of IFHP coverage. Only GARs retained the same benefits as before the cuts (**Expanded Coverage**). Refugee claimants from countries other than Designated Countries of Origin (DCO) and PSRs were eligible for IFHP **Health Care Coverage**, which covered all medical services except elective surgery, rehabilitation, home and long-term care. Medications were not covered, except for conditions posing a risk to public health or safety. Public health conditions are defined as 34 communicable diseases on the Public Health Agency of Canada's notifiable disease list, including tuberculosis, HIV/AIDS, sexually transmitted infections and vaccine-preventable infections (see Appendix 1 to this chapter). Public safety conditions are psychotic states involving potential danger to others. There was no coverage of other supplemental benefits such as dental care. Claimants remained entitled to Health Care Coverage until final adjudication of their claim, which may include appeals to the Immigration and Refugee Board and judicial review proceedings before the Federal Court of Canada.

The third type of coverage, **Public Health and Public Safety Coverage**, applied to refused (unsuccessful) refugee claimants from the date of final rejection of appeals until the date on which they are ordered to leave the country. Public Health and Public Safety Coverage also applied to refugee claimants from DCOs who made a refugee claim after December 15, 2012. Claimants from DCO countries are subject to an expedited process, limiting their ability to fully present their case, as well as no right of appeal to the Immigration and Refugee Board. There are currently 42 countries on the DCO list, including Mexico and almost all European countries. The Minister of Citizenship and Immigration has the power to place a country on the list based mainly on low acceptance rates from the country (under 25%). The country's human rights record is generally not taken into account. Many people from DCOs who have suffered violence and would be in danger if sent back to their home country will now have very limited access to refugee protection and, under the June 2012 IFH system, had almost no access to basic health care.

For people in the Public Health and Public Safety category, there was no coverage of any medical services, medication or hospital care, even for life-threatening emergencies, unless they were diagnosed with one of the 34 listed communicable diseases or a psychotic state involving danger to others. Neither prenatal nor paediatric care were covered. This policy seems all the more absurd given that most babies born in Canada will qualify as citizens by birth (*Citizenship Act*, 1985, s.3(1)(a)). Lack of prenatal and paediatric care places the health of these Canadian babies at risk.

The Canadian provinces have taken over payment of many of the costs no longer assumed by the federal government. Low-income refugee claimants can in most cases access medications and certain other supplemental services through provincial programs, notably income assistance. In Manitoba and Alberta, access to these provincial programs has also been extended to privately sponsored refugees. Quebec is the only province that immediately stepped in to cover all medical no longer covered by the IFHP, for all refugee claimants including those from DCO countries and refused refugee claimants. In Quebec, health coverage for all refugee claimants is now identical to provincial health insurance. In January 2014, Ontario adopted a program to compensate for the IFHP cuts, but refugee claimants must wait three months before qualifying for the program, except for children under 18, pregnant women (for prenatal and perinatal care), and individuals with a life-threatening medical condition requiring immediate attention. The exact scope of this latter exemption is unclear.

Kendra, the government assisted refugee whose situation is discussed in Case Study 14.1, faces a number of health care access and navigation barriers. Health practitioners may be reluctant to accept her as a new patient due to unfounded concerns regarding refugee health care compensation; hospitals may fail to provide full and quality services due to Kendra's limited English/French language skills. Kendra may find it challenging to find a female practitioner and may also struggle to find a community-based clinic where there is an interpretation service. If a family member or friend accompanies her for interpretation support there are significant concerns related to fidelity of interpretation and confidentiality. Kendra comes from a region of the world where there is little to no preventative care — the very concept of preventative care will be unfamiliar — and thus she will be unprepared to seek and request the best possible care.

Fortunately, Kendra was able to find a practitioner. The practitioner discovered she had high blood pressure, which was the likely cause of her headaches and visual disturbances. These symptoms are significant in light of her pregnancy, as untreated high blood pressure can lead to a condition known as eclampsia, which may result in seizures and death. Thankfully, she is a government assisted refugee (GAR) and as such, qualifies for basic medication coverage. If she were a refugee claimant, her blood pressure medication would not be covered, thus leading to potentially deadly consequences. Even before the cuts to the IFHP came into effect, most refugees struggled to effectively access the health care system due to issues related to language, culture, gender, and financial means, but these have been exacerbated and more barriers are being created by the government's policy changes to the IFHP.

> ## Case Study 14.1
> ## Kendra: A Government Assisted Refugee
>
> Kendra, a 28-year-old woman from sub-Saharan Africa, is 32 weeks pregnant. She is a government assisted refugee (GAR) who arrived in Canada nine weeks ago, speaks Swahili, but does not speak English or French. She is Muslim and as such is not comfortable with a male health provider, and has never had preventative screening, including pap tests, in the past. About four to five days ago she began to have headaches and for the past two days has also noted some visual disturbances; she decides to go see a doctor.
>
> ## Reflective Question
>
> How might Kendra's status as a GAR affect how her cultural and gender-specific needs are addressed?

The ability of refugees like Jose (whose situation is discussed in Case Study 14.2) to access medication coverage depends on which province they live in. Jose lives in Ontario, and prior to 2014 his medication would not have been covered. Without medication, Jose's seizures returned and he was rushed to the hospital by ambulance, triaged by the nurses in the emergency room, treated by the emergency room doctors and later by consulting neurologists. He was admitted to the hospital for two days at a total cost of tens of thousands of dollars.

His family was unable to cover the medical bills and thus the hospital and ultimately taxpayer ended up covering the medical costs. The cost of the medication to prevent the seizures was less than a dollar a day: $26 a month. This case illustrates how the cost of preventing serious disease is often much less than the cost to treat it. The federal government has suggested one of the main justifications for the cuts to refugee health care services is to save taxpayers money. This case would suggest otherwise. Further, while hospitals have waived costs for such families, in other cases, collection agencies were hired to track down families to recoup hefty medical bills. This latter injustice places refugee families in an even more precarious situation.

Since Ontario has stepped in and now covers the costs of medication, the overall costs to the taxpayer and refugees will be reduced. In fact, Ontario has in turn billed the federal government to reimburse the province for this blatant downloading of costs. This new reality is a direct result of the advocacy efforts of health care providers and others in civil society.

Franco, whose situation is discussed in Case Study 14.3, was diagnosed as having a heart attack, but before treatment was started it was discovered that he is a refugee from a DCO (safe) country and so prior to 2014 would not have had coverage for the treatment of his heart attack. This federal policy thus forced the doctor into a precarious position: do you deny health care to a man having a heart attack or do you treat him knowing full well that he (or the government) will never

## Case Study 14.2
## Jose: A Refugee Claimant

Jose is an 11-year-old boy, a refugee claimant from Colombia. He has a seizure disorder and without his medication he would have seizures daily. Because Jose is a refugee claimant and his condition does not pose a risk to public health or safety, his family is told by the pharmacist that with the new changes to the IFHP the boy's medication is no longer covered. His mother does not have the resources to pay for the medication and leaves without acquiring the anti-seizure drugs.

### Reflective Questions

1. What will happen to Jose when he has a seizure?
2. What are the barriers Jose and his family face when trying to access the health care system?

## Case Study 14.3.
## Franco: A Refugee Claimant from a Designated Country of Origin

Franco is a refugee claimant from Hungary, a country on the DCO list. He was told a few years ago while still in Hungary after having some chest pains that he has a mild form of angina and told to go the doctor if ever he has chest pain again. Now in Canada and awaiting his IRB hearing which clearly is causing him stress, he develops chest pain. He goes to the emergency room of the closest hospital and the triage nurse takes him in right away. An ECG (heart tracing) shows clear signs of a heart attack.

### Reflective Questions

1. How might the federal policy of June 2012 affect Franco's care and how has this changed in 2014?
2. What key issues remain in terms of funding health care for refugees after 2014?

pay for your professional medical services? Clearly there is a duty of care and the physician will treat this individual. However, the refugee is charged and given a bill, which they are usually unable to pay; and so both the hospital costs and the doctor's services will go unpaid and the cost will be transferred to the province or absorbed by the hospital. In the end, there was little in the way of savings for the taxpayer, despite the fact the government claimed that such savings justified the cuts.

As we will discuss below, as of November 2014, the federal government must abide by the Federal Court ruling in July 2014 which deemed the cuts unconstitutional. The medical and hospital costs would now be covered by IFH so not only would Franco have his emergency care visit covered but, since he is now able to access primary and preventative care, he would have been able to have his risk factors managed more effectively. This would likely have prevented the heart attack in the first place, again saving the system thousands of dollars.

## Systemic Barriers to Health Care Access

As illustrated in the preceding cases, migrant populations are often vulnerable and require special social and health care considerations in order to overcome barriers related to knowledge, language and cultural structures, and to mitigate the effects of limited social and cultural capital, lower income and discrimination (Anderson, 1995; Ng Health Reports, 2011). Resettled refugees and refugee claimants face many of the same disparities faced by other immigrant populations, such as barriers to health information and health services due to language issues (Pottie et al., 2008), or limited access to health services due to lack of knowledge or social and cultural capital in their new setting (McKeary and Newbold, 2010). Many resettled refugees and refugee claimants arrive with few resources and have very low incomes during their first years in Canada. Refugee claimants generally have to wait months before obtaining a work permit, the temporary nature of which restricts their ability to find a job, and they are often obliged to seek social assistance.

As previously noted, even under the old IFHP, resettled refugees and refugee claimants often had great difficulty accessing health care. For example, pregnant refugee claimants were often refused care or charged fees, in part because of confusion among practitioners about the extent of IFHP coverage (Merry, Gagnon, Kalim, and Bouris, 2011). In many instances, fees were charged for medical care for infants, despite the fact that children born in Canada are citizens entitled to provincial health insurance. For many years the IFHP billing process has been perceived as time-consuming, slow and unpredictable, leading many clinicians to either deny care or to charge fees to IFHP recipients (Caulford and d'Andrade, 2012; McKeary and Newbold, 2010; Rousseau et al., 2008; ter Kuile et al., 2007). Migrants who experience refusals of care or demands for fees may subsequently postpone or forgo medical consultation (Richardson and Norris, 2010; ter Kuile et al., 2007). Since the IFHP cuts, refugee claimants have even more difficulty accessing health care, because of two main factors. The first factor is the decreased health care coverage that results directly from the cuts, outlined in detail above. The second main factor is that the IFHP cuts have contributed to increased health system barriers. A high proportion of walk-in clinics in Toronto (45%) and Ottawa (65%) no longer accept people with IFHP coverage as patients, according to informal surveys conducted by members of Canadian Doctors for Refugee Care (Rashid, personal communication 2013). The clinics that do accept such patients often demand fees, even for services covered by the IFHP. In Toronto, for example, a pregnant diabetic refugee claimant who was entitled to free prenatal care, covered by the IFHP, was nonetheless refused care by eight family doctors (Caulford, 2012). Some demanded a fee while others simply told her they no longer accept any refugee claimants. In Ottawa, before the cuts were implemented, all 33 walk-in clinics in the city saw refugee claimants. Since the cuts, 80% of these clinics refuse to treat refugee claimants, and the nine clinics who still accept them as patients all charge a $60 fee up front before they are able to see a doctor (Bradley, personal communication 2012). Many of these individuals cannot afford to pay and end up going to the emergency department for their care or, even worse, do not access any form of health care at all until their condition deteriorates. Others go into debt to obtain treatment, which then places a burden on families that are often already living in poverty. Hospitals providing treatment to this population may have to absorb the cost if patients are unable to pay (Keung, 2013).

Outright refusal of care or demands for fees may be linked to a number of factors. These include confusion about which services are covered, difficulties checking the person's status, concerns that services may not be reimbursed by the IFHP, and time-consuming billing procedures. Faced with uncertainty and additional effort, many clinicians prefer to refuse people with IFHP coverage or to demand fees. The Registrar of the Alberta College of Physicians and Surgeons recently urged doctors to treat refugee patients even when they are not sure of being paid, reminding them that denying care may be contrary to professional ethics and legal obligations ("Doctors should treat," 2013).

In short, the federal government has shifted health care costs to provincial governments, hospitals, and to refugees themselves, who are a very low-income and vulnerable population. Health care providers and hospitals find themselves facing a painful dilemma. On the one hand, there may be an ethical and legal duty to provide care, especially for life-threatening conditions. On the other hand, hospitals and other health care institutions must manage limited resources for the good of the entire population.

The Quebec government's decision to assume the costs of medical, diagnostic and hospital services no longer covered by the IFHP partially resolves this dilemma and might serve as a model for other provinces, but remains incomplete as supplemental services are not covered. Also, cost transfers from the federal to provincial governments should normally be accompanied by compensation. Provinces and hospitals being forced to provide care for refugees without receiving compensation creates the risk that the health care they receive will be of low quality, a situation that in itself is unsustainable.

## Resistance from Health Professionals and Other Community Members

Health care practitioners across Canada have expressed outrage at the IFHP cuts, which put the lives of refugees at risk, cost taxpayers more money and threaten public health.

Over 20 national and provincial health care associations have written to the federal Minister of Citizenship and Immigration to express concern that IFHP changes may compromise access to health care for a vulnerable population, and have a negative impact on the pan-Canadian health care system, increasing the burden on provinces and territories (see Appendix 2 to this chapter).

On May 11, 2012, there was a sit-in at the Toronto office of Joe Oliver, a federal cabinet minister, by more than 90 doctors. Following an overwhelmingly positive response from the medical community and the public at large, further protests at various ministerial announcements took place during the summer of 2012. This involved interrupting the minister's announcement in some cases, or simply asking pointed questions after the announcement, with media present, holding the Canadian government to account. On June 18, 2012, health care providers organized a National Day of Action in 13 cities across the country, from Iqaluit in the north to St. John's, Newfoundland on the east coast to Vancouver on the west coast. The focus of the day was to highlight the injustice of this policy change and to demand that the IFHP cuts be rescinded. On June 17, 2013, a second National Day of Action was held in 19 cities across Canada.

This ad hoc group has now formed a non-partisan incorporated advocacy group, Canadian Doctors for Refugee Care (CDRC). The CDRC continues to document cases where refugees are being affected by the cuts, and to inform the public and media about these cases on a regular basis. Cases include  cancer patients being refused care, others with urgent conditions affecting their vision requiring emergency surgery, and similar serious denials of care.

The Canadian government did back-track with respect to one group of refugees, the government assisted refugees (GARs), and rescinded the cuts for this group. This was a partial victory for all the advocacy efforts to date. However, GARs traditionally account for less than 20% of refugees in Canada, and an even smaller proportion (about 8%) of IFHP beneficiaries (Citizenship and Immigration Canada, 2013a; Order Respecting the Interim Federal Health Program, 2012).

One of the roles physicians play is that of being an advocate for their patients. One such example of this advocacy is the recent activism related to the IFHP cuts, where there has been an unprecedented response within the health care community that in fact brought the community together to address a clear injustice to some of its most vulnerable patients. The activism has also led to collaboration with other professionals, including the legal community.

## Legal Mobilization: Court Challenge Against the IFHP Cuts

On February 25, 2013, a legal challenge to the Canadian government's cuts to the IFHP was launched in the Federal Court (Notice of Application between Canadian Doctors for Refugee Care, the Canadian Association of Refugee Lawyers, Daniel Garcia Rodriguez, Ahmad Awatt and Hanif Ayubi, 2013 [hereinafter "Notice of Application"]). The legal challenge was filed by three individuals who have had critical health care denied to them since the government's cuts to the IFHP in June 2012 (Notice of Application, paras. 18–21). They were joined by two public interest groups, the Canadian Doctors for Refugee Care and the Canadian Association of Refugee Lawyers (Notice of Application, para. 1).

The legal challenge raised two main arguments: First, that the denial of IFHP coverage to refugee claimants and PSRs is unconstitutional, in that it violates the *Canadian Charter of Rights and Freedoms* (1982); and second, that the denial of IFHP coverage to refugee claimants and PSRs is in breach of Canada's international obligations under the *Convention Relating to the Status of Refugees* (1951) and the *Convention on the Rights of the Child* (1989). Let us consider those arguments in turn.

THE CUTS TO THE IFHP VIOLATE THE CHARTER. Section 7 of the *Canadian Charter of Rights and Freedoms* provides that "[e]veryone has the right to life, liberty and security of the person and the right not to be deprived thereof except in accordance with the principles of fundamental justice." As indicated, section 7 of the Charter applies to "everyone" in Canada, including non-citizens. In their application before the Federal Court, the applicants argued that because of the changes to IFHP, individuals do not have access to basic and necessary health care, a situation which affects them both physically and psychologically (Notice of Application, paras. 18–21, 22, 23, 24, and 25).

Even if one assumes that the aim of the cuts to the IFHP is to discourage "bogus" refugee claims, there is no evidence that these cuts will have the desired result (Notice of Application, paras. 18–21, 22, 23, 24, and 25). As such, the Canadian government's decision to deny IFHP coverage to refugee claimants and PSRs can be said to be arbitrary and inconsistent with the principles of fundamental justice.

Section 12 of the Charter provides that "[e]veryone has the right not to be subjected to any cruel and unusual treatment or punishment." According to Canadian jurisprudence, "treatment" may be interpreted broadly to include any conduct, action or behaviour by the government towards people under its control (Notice of Application, para. 39).Treatment can also extend to all forms of disability, disadvantage or hardship caused by a government's action or inaction (Notice of Application, para. 39).

According to the Supreme Court of Canada, treatment or punishment is cruel and unusual if it is "so excessive as to outrage our standards of decency"(*R. V. Smith*, 1987 1 SCR 1045). The changes to the IFPH reduce or deny basic and life-sustaining health coverage for refugee claimants, thereby causing significant and unnecessary pain, trauma, and suffering (Notice of Application, para. 54). As such, it is argued that the changes made to the IFHP constitute cruel and unusual treatment (Notice of Application, para. 54).

Section 15 of the Charter provides that "[e]very individual is equal before and under the law and has the right to the equal protection and equal benefit of the law without discrimination and, in particular, without discrimination based on race, national or ethnic origin, colour, religion, sex, age or mental or physical disability." Discrimination exists when a government widens a gap between a historically disadvantaged group, such as refugee claimants, and the rest of society, rather than narrowing it (Notice of Application, para. 61).

The 2012 IFHP creates two distinctions. The first is between refugee claimants from DCO countries and those that are not from a designated country of origin. This distinction is clearly based on a person's national or ethnic origin (Notice of Application, paras. 62 and 63). The second distinction is based on an individual's immigration status — specifically, they are being denied health care because they are in Canada for the purpose of claiming protection.

Furthermore, the distinction creates disadvantages by perpetuating prejudice or stereotype, marginalizing minorities, and widening the gap between historically disadvantaged groups and the rest of society (Notice of Application, paras. 70—73). By denying refugee claimants and PSRs basic health care services at the same level as other persons lawfully in Canada, the 2012 IFHP is discriminatory and violates section 15 of the Charter.

THE CUTS TO THE IFHP VIOLATE CANADA'S INTERNATIONAL OBLIGATIONS. Canada is a party to both the *Convention Relating to the Status of Refugees* (1951) and the *Convention on the Rights of the Child* (1989). There are, therefore, certain international obligations which Canada must abide by. First, the changes to the IFHP by the Canadian government discriminate among and between refugees contrary to article 3 of the *Convention Relating to the Status of Refugees* which stipulates that "Contracting States shall apply the provisions of this Convention to refugees without discrimination as to race, religion or country of origin" (Notice of Application, para. 77). Second, given that the changes to the IFHP apply to children and pregnant women, it is argued that Canadian government is also in breach of *Convention on the Rights of the Child* (Notice of Application, para. 82, 83, and 86), which stipulates that countries which are parties to the treaty must:

1. Respect and ensure the rights of each child within their jurisdiction without discrimination of any kind (article 2);
2. Ensure that in all actions concerning children, the best interest of the child is a primary consideration (article 3);
3. Ensure that a child who is seeking refugee status shall receive appropriate protection and humanitarian assistance (article 22);
4. Recognize the right of the child to the highest attainable

standard of health, including the requirement that the government strive to ensure that no child is deprived of his or her right of access to such health care services (article 24(1));

5. Provide necessary medical assistance and health care to all children as well as the appropriate pre-natal and post-natal health care for mothers (article 24(2)).

## The Federal Court Decision

The Federal Court decision in the matter of *Canadian Doctors for Refugee Care v. Canada (Attorney general)* 2014 FC 651 was released on July 4, 2014. The cuts to the IFHP were deemed unconstitutional in that they were found to violate sections 12 and 15 of the Charter. With respect to section 12 of the Charter, the Federal Court held that the impact of IFHP cuts on refugees and especially children amounts to "cruel and unusual" treatment. It was found that the more severe health cuts to refugee claimants from Designated Countries of Origin were discriminatory and without legal justification, thereby violating section 15 of the Charter. The health cuts were thus deemed to be invalid and the federal government was given four months to reinstate the previous Interim Federal Health Program.

Instead, the federal government decided to appeal the decision to the Federal Court of Appeal (FCA) and asked for a stay of the judgment which would allow the government to keep the cuts in place until the appeal was heard. On October 31, 2014, the federal government's application for a stay was denied by the Federal Court of Appeal (2014 FCA 252) and, therefore, in order to comply with the Federal Court's ruling, the government had until November 4, 2014, to reinstate the IFHP as it was prior to the 2012 cuts.

Surprisingly, the federal government did not fully reinstate the IFHP as it had been configured prior to the 2012 cuts, but, rather, expanded the current program. In so doing, the federal government is not respecting the Federal Court's order, and is in breach of the rule of law.

## Conclusion

Refugees face many challenges as they attempt to integrate into their new country. Access to and navigation of the health care system is one important challenge. Refugees are a vulnerable group because of their experience of pre-migration trauma, migration and refugee camp hardships, and the multiple barriers they face in Canada, which now include restrictions to health care services. Yet despite these challenges they continue to strive to move forward and contribute to Canadian society. Canadians can choose to facilitate their integration, welcome them as they strive to create a new home in a safe environment for themselves and their children, and as a community grow with them and learn from them. Or Canadians can choose to heighten the existing barriers, make it more difficult to build community, and thus create divisions between Canadians born in Canada and newcomers. The cuts to the IFHP by the Canadian government are an example of taking the latter path, making life more challenging for an already vulnerable group. As an unexpected outcome, the federal government's refugee health care cuts have resulted in a galvanization of the health care practitioner community, something which has in turn helped to strengthen the resolve of refugees and refugee serving organizations. Canadians face a fundamental choice as to whether they want to build a society based on inclusion or exclusion.

## Appendix 1. IFHP Public Health and Public Safety Coverage

**Public health conditions** are defined as the 34 communicable diseases on the list of national notifiable diseases of the Public Health Agency of Canada which are transmissible person-to-person and/or vaccine-preventable. These 34 conditions are:

Tuberculosis • Syphilis • HIV/AIDS • Meningitis (Other Bacterial) • Chancroid • Genital Chlamydia • Cholera • Gonorrhoea • Leprosy • Invasive Group A Streptococcal Disease • Meningitis (Viral) • Diphtheria • Tetanus • Pertussis • Measles • Mumps • Rubella • Chickenpox (Varicella)/Herpes Zoster • Acute Flaccid Paralysis (Poliomyelitis) • Haemophilius Influenzae Type B • Influenza • Invasive Meningococcal Disease • Invasive Pneumococcal Disease • Hepatitis B • Noroviral Infection • Viral Hemorrhagic Fevers • Smallpox • Viral Hepatitis • Cryptosporidiosis • Giardiasis • Verotoxigenic E • Shigellosis • Salmonellosis • Clostridium difficile

**Public safety conditions** are defined as "a mental health condition in a person who has been examined by a physician licensed in Canada and for which the physician is of the opinion that the person will likely cause harm to others." This typically means psychotic conditions in which the person may be dangerous to others (Source: Medavie/Blue Cross Public Health and Public Safety benefits grid, Note 3).

## Appendix 2. National Health Care Organizations Opposed to the Cuts

Canadian Medical Association • College of Family Physicians of Canada • Royal College of Physicians and Surgeons of Canada • Canadian Association of Optometrists • Canadian Association of Social Workers • Canadian Dental Association • Canadian Nurses Association • Canadian Pharmacists Association • Canadian Association of Community Health Centres • Canadian Doctors for Medicare • Canadian Association of Midwives • Registered Nurses Association of Ontario • Canadian Federation of Nurses Union • Canadian Psychiatric Association • Canadian Paediatric Society • Association of Medical Microbiology and Infectious Diseases Canada • Médecins du Monde • Public Physicians of Canada • Ontario's Council of Medical Officers of Health • Canadian Association of Occupational Therapists

## References

Association of Medical Microbiology and Infectious Diseases Canada (2012, June 18). Letter to the Minister of Citizenship and Immigration, Jason Kenney. Retrieved from http://www.ammi.ca/media/44418/ammi%20canada%20response%20to%20ifhp.pdf.

Beiser, M. (1999). *Strangers at the gate: The "Boat People's" first ten years in Canada*. Toronto: University of Toronto Press.

Beiser, M. (2009). Resettling refugees and safeguarding their mental health: Lessons learned from the Canadian Refugee Resettlement Project. *Transcultural Psychiatry, 46*(4), 539–583.

*Canadian Charter of Rights and Freedoms* (Constitution Act, 1982). 1982, c. 11 (U.K.), Schedule B. Retrieved from http://laws-lois.justice.gc.ca/eng/Const/page-15.html.

Canadian Association of Midwives (2012, May 22). Letter to the Minister of Citizenship and Immigration, Jason Kenney. Retrieved from http://www.canadianmidwives.org/DATA/DOCUMENT/Jason_Kenny_Citizenship_Immigration_2012_letter.pdf.

Canadian Medical Association, Royal College of Physicians and Surgeons of Canada, College of Family Physicians of Canada, Canadian Nurses Association, Canadian Association of Social Workers, Canadian Association of Optometrists, Canadian Dental Association, Canadian Federation of Medical Students, and Canadian Pharmacists Association (2012, December 5). Letter to the Minister of Citizenship and Immigration, Jason Kenney. Retrieved from http://www.casw-acts.ca/sites/default/files/open_letters/Letter%20-%20Minister%20Kenney%20re%20Changes%20to%20the%20Interim%20Federal%20Health%20Program_Dec%205_12.pdf.

Canadian Psychiatric Association (2012, June 6). Letter to the Minister of Citizenship and Immigration, Jason Kenney. Retrieved from http://www.cpa-apc.org/media.php?mid=1742.

Caulford, Paul (2012, November 22). Refugee diaries: Canada [Web log post]. Retrieved from http://refugeediaries.ca/.

Caulford, P., & D'Andrade, J. (2012). Health care for Canada's medically uninsured immigrants and refugees: Whose problem is it? *Canadian Family Physician, 58*(7), 725–727.

Citizenship and Immigration Canada (2012). Summary of changes to the Interim Federal Health Program. Retrieved from http://www.refugeehealth.ca/sites/default/files/CIC's%20Summary%20of%20changes%20to%20IFH.pdf.

Citizenship and Immigration Canada (2013a). Permanent residents by category, 2008-2012. Retrieved from http://www.cic.gc.ca/english/resources/statistics/facts2012-preliminary/01.asp.

Citizenship and Immigration Canada (2013b). Facts and figures 2012: Immigration overview – Permanent and temporary residents. Retrieved from www.cic.gc.ca/english/resources/statistics/menu-fact.asp.

Cleveland, J., Dionne-Boivin, V., & Rousseau, C. (2013). Droit d'asile et incarcération: l'expérience des demandeurs d'asile détenus au Canada. *Criminologie, 46*(1), 107–129.

Cleveland, J., & Rousseau, C. (2013). Psychiatric symptoms associated with brief detention of adult asylum seekers in Canada. *Canadian Journal of Psychiatry, 58*(7), 409–416.

Cleveland, J., Rousseau, C., & Guzder, J. (2013). Cultural consultation for refugees. In Kirmayer, L. J., Guzder, J., & Rousseau, C. (Eds.), *Cultural consultation: Encountering the other in mental health care*. New York: Springer.

*Convention against Torture and Other Cruel, Inhuman or Degrading Treatment or Punishment* (1984). 1465 UNTS 85. Retrieved from http://www.refworld.org/docid/3ae6b3a94.html.

*Convention on the Rights of the Child* (1989). 1577 UNTS 3. Retrieved from http://www.refworld.org/docid/3ae6b38f0.html.

*Convention Relating to the Status of Refugees* (1951). 189 UNTS 137. Retrieved from http://www.unhcr.org/protect/PROTECTION/3b66c2aa10.pdf.

Crépeau, F., Nakache, D., & Atak, I. (2007). International migration: Security concerns and human rights standards. *Transcultural Psychiatry, 44*(3), 311–337.

Doctors should treat uncovered refugees, college head says (2013, April 30). *CBC News*. Retrieved from http://www.cbc.ca/news/canada/calgary/story/2013/04/30/calgary-college-refugee-obligation.html.

Dorais, L. J. (2000). The Cambodians, Laotians and Vietnamese in Canada. In Perin, R. (Ed.), *Canada's ethnic group series*, Vol. 28. Ottawa: The Canadian Historical Association. Retrieved from http://www.collectionscanada.gc.ca/obj/008004/f2/E-28_en.pdf.

Edwards, A. (2011). *Back to basics: The right to liberty and security of person and "alternatives to detention" of refugees, asylum-seekers, stateless persons and other migrants*. Geneva: Office of the United Nations High Commissioner for Refugees.

Fazel, M., Reed, R. V., Panter-Brick, C., & Stein, A. (2012). Mental health of displaced and refugee children resettled in high-income countries: Risk and protective factors. *The Lancet, 379* (9812), 266–282.

Fazel, M., Wheeler, J., & Danesh, J. (2005). Prevalence of serious mental disorder in 7000 refugees resettled in western countries: A systematic review. *The Lancet, 365* (9467), 1309–1314.

Gagnon, A., Dougherty, G., Wahoush, O., Saucier, J. F., Dennis, C. L., Stranger, E., . . . & Stewart, D.E.

(2013). International migration to Canada: The post-birth health of mothers and infants by immigration class. *Social Science & Medicine, 76*(1), 197–207.

Greenaway, C., Sandoe, A., Vissandjee, B., Kitai, I., Gruner, D., Wobeser, W., . . . & Schwartzman, K. (2011). Tuberculosis: Evidence review for newly arriving immigrants and refugees. *Canadian Medical Association Journal, 183*(12), E939–E951.

Hathaway, J. C. (2005). *The rights of refugees under international law.* Cambridge: Cambridge University Press.

Immigration and Refugee Board of Canada (2009). *Nansen Medal awarded to the "People of Canada."* Retrieved from http://www.irb-cisr.gc.ca/Eng/NewsNouv/NewNou/2009/Pages/Nansen.aspx.

Immigration and Refugee Protection Act (2001). S.C. 2001, c. 27. Retrieved from http://laws-lois.justice.gc.ca/eng/acts/I-2.5/.

Kenney, J. (2011, September 27). Jason Kenney: Our plan to combat human smuggling. *The National Post.* Retrieved from http://fullcomment.nationalpost.com/2011/09/27/jason-kenney-our-plan-to-combat-human-smuggling/.

Kenney, J. (2012, February 16). Speaking notes for The Honourable Jason Kenney, P.C., M.P. Minister of Citizenship, Immigration and Multiculturalism following the tabling of Bill C-31, *Protecting Canada's Immigration System Act.* Retrieved from http://www.cic.gc.ca/english/department/media/speeches/2012/2012-02-16.asp.

Keung, N. (2013, June 8). Ontario hospitals absorb health costs to treat refugees. *The Toronto Star.* Retrieved from http://www.thestar.com/news/immigration/2013/06/08/ontario_hospitals_absorb_health_costs_to_treat_refugees.html.

Laban, C. J., Gernaat, H. B. P. E., Komproe, I. H., van der Tweel, I., & De Jong, J. T. V. M. (2005). Postmigration living problems and common psychiatric disorders in Iraqi asylum seekers in the Netherlands. *Journal of Nervous and Mental Disorders, 193*(12), 825–832.

McKeary M., & Newbold, B. (2010). Barriers to care: The challenges for Canadian refugees and their health care providers. *Journal of Refugee Studies, 23*(4), 523–545.

Medavie Blue Cross and Citizenship and Immigration Canada (2012). *Interim Federal Health Program: IFHP outline of services – What does the IFHP cover?* Retrieved from https://www.medavie.bluecross.ca/cs/ContentServer?c=ContentPage_P&pagename=IFHP_CIC_Public%2FContentPage_P%2FIFHP_CICOneColumnFull&cid=1181930640540.

Merry L. A., Gagnon A. J., Kalim N., & Bouris S. S. (2011). Refugee claimant women and barriers to health and social services post-birth. *Canadian Journal of Public Health, 102*(4), 286–290.

Notice of Application between Canadian Doctors for Refugee Care, the Canadian Association of Refugee Lawyers, Daniel Garcia Rodriguez, Ahmad Awatt and Hanif Ayubi, Registry No. T-356-13, filed February 25, 2013.

Ontario Medical Association (2012, June 17). Refugee health changes a concern: Ontario doctors. Retrieved from https://www.oma.org/Mediaroom/PressReleases/Pages/RefugeeHealthChangesaConcernOntarioDoctors.aspx.

Order Amending the Order Respecting the Interim Federal Health Program (2012). P.C.2012-945, June 28, 2012 - SI/2012-49. Canada Gazette, Part II, Vol. 146, No. 15, July 18, 2012. Retrieved from http://canadagazette.gc.ca/rp-pr/p2/2012/2012-07-18/html/si-tr49-eng.html.

Order Respecting the Interim Federal Health Program (2012). P.C. 2012-433, April 5, 2012 - SI/2012-26. Canada Gazette, Part II, Vol.146, No. 9, April 25, 2012. Retrieved from http://www.gazette.gc.ca/rp-pr/p2/2012/2012-04-25/html/si-tr26-eng.html.

Ouimet, M. J., Munoz, M., Narasiah, L., Rambure, V., & Correa, J. A. (2008). Pathologies courantes chez les demandeurs d'asile à Montréal: Prévalence et facteurs de risque associés. *Canadian Journal of Public Health, 99*(6), 499–504.

Phillips, J. (2011). Asylum seekers and refugees: What are the facts? Retrieved from http://www.aph.gov.au/binaries/library/pubs/bn/sp/asylumfacts.pdf.

Porter, M., & Haslam, N. (2005). Predisplacement and postdisplacement factors associated with mental health of refugees and internally displaced persons: A meta-analysis. *Journal of the American Medical Association, 294*(5), 602–612.

Pottie, K., Ng, E., Spitzer, D., Mohammed, A., & Glazier, R. (2008). Language proficiency, gender and self-reported health: An analysis of the first two waves of the longitudinal survey of immigrants to Canada. *Canadian Journal of Public Health, 99*(6), 505–510.

Pottie, K., Greenaway, C., Feightner, J., Welch, V., Swinkels, H., Rashid, M., . . . & co-authors of the

Canadian Collaboration for Immigrant and Refugee Health (2011). Overview: Evidence-based clinical guidelines for immigrants and refugees. *Canadian Medical Association Journal, 183*(12), E824–E925.

*R. v. Smith*, 1987 1 SCR 1045.

Richardson, L.D., & Norris, M. (2010). Access to health and health care: How race and ethnicity matter. *Mount Sinai Journal of Medicine: A Journal of Translational and Personalized Medicine, 77*(2), 166–177.

Rossi, C., Shrier, I., Marshall, L., Cnossen, S., Schwartzman, K., Klein, M. B., . . . & Greenaway, C. (2012). Seroprevalence of chronic hepatitis B virus infection and prior immunity in immigrants and refugees: A systematic review and meta-analysis. *PloS One 7*(9).

Rousseau, C., & Drapeau, A. (2003). Are refugee children an at-risk group? A longitudinal study of Cambodian adolescents. *Journal of Refugee Studies, 16*(1), 67–81.

Rousseau, C., Hassan, G., Moreau, N., & Thombs, B. D. (2011). Perceived discrimination and its association with psychological distress among newly arrived immigrants before and after September 11, 2001. *American Journal of Public Health, 101*(5), 909–915.

Rousseau, C., Pottie, K., Thombs, B., Munoz, M., & Jurcki, T. (2011). Guidelines for Immigrant Health, Appendix 11. Post traumatic stress disorder: Evidence review for newly arriving immigrants and refugees. *Canadian Medical Association Journal, 183*(12), E824–E925.

Rousseau, C., ter Kuile, S., Munoz, M., Nadeau, L., Ouimet, M. J., Kirmayer, L., & Crépeau, F. (2008). Health care access for refugee and immigrant with precarious status : Public health and human right challenges. *Canadian Journal of Public Health, 99*(4), 290–292.

Ryan, D.A., Kelly, F. E., & Kelly, B. D. (2009). Mental health among persons awaiting an asylum outcome in western countries. A literature review. *International Journal of Mental Health, 38*(3), 88–111.

Samson, L., & Hui, C. (2012). *Cuts to refugee health program put children and youth at risk.* Retrieved from http://www.cps.ca/advocacy/CPS_RefugeeHealth.pdf.

Steel, Z., Chey, T., Silove, D., Marnane, C., Bryant, R. A., & van Ommeren, M. (2009). Association of torture and other potentially traumatic events with mental health outcomes among populations exposed to mass conflict and displacement: A systematic review and meta-analysis. *Journal of the American Medical Association, 302*(5), 537–549.

Steel, Z., Momartin, S., Silove, D., Coello, M., Aroche, J., & Tay, K. W. (2011). Two year psychosocial and mental health outcomes for refugees subjected to restrictive or supportive immigration policies. *Social Science and Medicine, 72*(7), 1149–1156.

ter Kuile S., Rousseau C., Munoz M., Nadeau L., & Ouimet, M. J. (2007). The universality of the Canadian health care system in question: Barriers to services for immigrants and refugees. *International Journal of Migration, Health and Social Care, 3*(1), 15–26.

The Refugee Forum. (2012). *By the numbers: Refugee statistics 1989-2011.* Retrieved from http://www.cdp-hrc.uottawa.ca/projects/refugee-forum/projects/documents/REFUGEESTATSCOMPREHENSIVE1999-2011.pdf.

Toronto Public Health and Access Alliance Multicultural Health and Community Services. (2011). *The global city: Newcomer health in Toronto.* Retrieved from http://www.toronto.ca/health/map/pdf/global_city/global_city.pdf.

United Nations High Commissioner for Refugees (2013). *UNHCR Global Appeal 2013. Update: Populations of concern to UNHCR.* Retrieved from http://www.unhcr.org/50a9f81b27.html.

Wherry, A. (2012, July 16). Bogus refugee claimants receiving gold-plated health care benefits [Web log post]. Retrieved from http://www2.macleans.ca/2012/07/16/bogus-refugee-claimants-receiving-gold-plated-health-care-benefits/.

Zencovich, M., Kennedy, K., MacPherson, D., & Gushulak B. (2006). Immigration medical screening and HIV infection in Canada. *International journal of STD & AIDS. 17*(12), 813–816.

CHAPTER FIFTEEN

# Race-Based Stigma as a Determinant of Access and Support in Black Mothers' Experience of Loss to Gun Violence

*Annette Bailey, Jennifer Clarke and Bukola Salami*

G un violence trauma is rooted in colonization. Global migration and displace-ment are forms of neo-colonization and neo-colonial relations that structure and sustain the exploitation of members of the Black race across the globe (Fekete, 2001). In earlier days, colonization and its concomitant displacement were en-forced through brutal acts. Today, various forms of economic inequalities influence individuals to migrate in search of access to needed resources (James and Davis, 2012). Fekete (2001) defined these individuals as **economic mi-grants**. Although some may argue that Caribbean people in Canada are "voluntary" economic migrants, we argue that the historical imprinting of slavery and colonization has created appalling economic and social conditions that con-tinue to force people from their homelands and families to seek a better life else-where. Caribbean immigrants' decisions to come to Canada are not simply born of mobility but of displacement (James and Davis, 2012). Therefore, it is impossible to separate the historic and material conditions that have shaped Black women's migration from their present-day experiences related to gun-violence trauma. For Black mothers (a more encompassing term preferred by those mothers them-selves) who have lost children to gun violence, the historical context of colonization and slavery, as well as the present day neo-colonial structure of their lives, predisposes their families to violence, and deprives them of valuable grieving and coping resources. Racism and stigma, which are rooted in colonial discourses, persist in complicating Black mothers' traumatic loss experiences by creating mul-tiple interlocking structures of domination and oppression (Henry and Tator, 2010).

Recent studies show that after losing children to gun violence, Black mothers' trauma experiences were shaped and compounded by race, the stigma of gun violence loss, negative social interactions and lack of access to victim compensation and social support. These factors persisted in their subsequent experiences, making coping a treacherous undertaking (Bailey et al., 2013; Bailey and Velasco, 2014). Their race, in particular, dominated and intersected with their trauma experiences. The social construction of race influenced how these Black mothers accessed necessary resources and coped with their loss. Their access to coping resources and social supports was perpetually shaped by the social discourse of race and the disproportional occurrence and reporting of the deaths of young Black males to gun violence (Ezeonu, 2010). Their immigrant status, combined with racism, created feelings of powerlessness and victimization in their grief and trauma experiences. Given that Black mothers have borne and continue to disproportionately bear the social, emotional and financial burden of loss of children to gun violence (Phillips, 1997; Sharpe and Boyas, 2011; Sheptycki, 2009), understanding the role of race in their trauma experiences is critical.

This chapter explores race-based stigma as a determinant of access to resources and support in Black mothers' experiences of losing a child to gun violence. It commences with a discussion of race, stigma and trauma, and follows with discussions on the role of race in Black mothers' access to resources and support during their grief process. In demonstrating the intersecting and dominating role of race in Black mothers' grief experiences, and its unique impact on their access to coping resources and supports, we draw on the narrative of 12 Black mothers from a recent study that explored their experiences of losing a child to gun violence in Toronto. We explore these mothers' realities in accessing resources and supports, as well as the role of race in their lived experiences. The relevance of immigration status in their lived experiences is also discussed. A case study focusing on one of the mothers is included, with critical reflection questions found at the end of the chapter.

## Case Study 15.1
## In Her Own Words:
## The Case of a Toronto Mother Bereaved by Gun Violence

My son was shot in the stomach in an apartment building. After the shooting he got into the elevator. The elevator went up instead of down. When the elevator door opened on the eighth floor, he fell forward to the ground. His teeth smashed and he choked. He died there in front of the elevator. I wonder, what if the elevator had gone down?

When he was shot I didn't hear from the police. I drove to several hospitals and police stations in Toronto in the snow storm, trying to get information. When we finally got to the right police station, we were told it would take 24 to 48 hours before I was notified. So, we drove down to police headquarters. I was told that I had no right to be there. I had to persist intensively before I was informed that my son had died and I was able to see the body.

This loss affected my relationship with family and friends. My remaining son let go of all his dreams. He is now very distant. The loss also created distance between me and my parents. They became very non-emotional. They kept saying, you lost your son but you have to get over it. One day I just said I am done with you. I lost most of my friends. At the beginning of my grief everyone was there to lend support and mourn with me. Eventually people went back to their lives and I was left stuck in a void.

I lost three or four jobs because I couldn't muster up the energy to survive. I lost my house three years ago. I never filled out those Victim Compensation forms I got in the mail. I tried to complete them but I just couldn't bring myself to do it. I was in a bubble. I felt like I couldn't even read; nothing was clear. The two years lapsed and I did not find anybody to help me complete the forms. I couldn't muster up the energy to go see a counsellor, and no one came to encourage me.

I have been sad for so long. Over the last five years I had many thoughts of suicide. However, it didn't make sense to leave my three children. I started to smoke and drink. My grief prolonged my children's grief. The fact that I couldn't lift my head many times, made my kids lay down with me. Not only did they lose their brother they were losing me. I didn't want to become a statistic, even though I knew that as a single mom, I am a statistic. I couldn't let my kids grow up with a checked-out mother. I had to turn that around.

I believe that God helped me to survive my son's passing. My relationship with God sustained me throughout many thoughts of suicide, even though I didn't know He was sustaining me. Very quietly He sustained me. I don't feel like a survivor. However, I don't feel like I am fighting myself to survive anymore. I fight every day to be productive and positive, but I feel like my heart is still scared.

## Race, Stigma and Trauma

Blacks are almost five times more likely to lose a loved one to homicide than Caucasians — 11.6% of African Americans compared to 2.4% of Caucasians (Laurie and Neimeyer, 2008). Blacks' susceptibility to gun violence loss is shaped by unemployment, economic struggles and lack of social support structures (McDevitt-Murphy et al., 2012). Similarly, Black mothers' trauma experiences following loss to gun violence are shaped by these and other key determinants associated with their children's murders. Social differences in education, neighbourhood of residence, and income are representative disadvantages of most Black mothers who survive gun violence in Canada (Chettleburgh, 2007; Janhevich, Bania and Hastings, 2008). These social circumstances, present in Black mothers' lives prior to their loss, indicate that systemic and structural barriers play a preceding role in their trauma experiences.

RACIAL STIGMA AND TRAUMA. Research with Black mothers in Toronto (Bailey et al., 2013), as well as research in the United States with African American victims and survivors of homicide (Rosenblatt and Wallace, 2005; Sharpe and Boyas, 2011; Sharpe, 2013) have shown that factors such as poverty, lack of social support and racism are implicated in their loss and trauma experiences. The racial stigma of gun violence, in particular, persists in Black mothers' trauma experiences and forms the root of their social barriers, identity and struggles as survivors of gun violence (Bailey et al., 2013). In the context of many of these mothers' elusive and enduring adjustments as immigrants in Canadian societies, dealing with social disadvantages, the sudden death of a child, and the racial stigma of gun violence can create a wave of secondary victimization that greatly hampers their ability to cope.

The racial stigma of gun violence is propagated by the media in a manner that projects blame, and devalues and diverts attention from Black mothers' trauma. Prevailing media images of Black males as either the victims or perpetrators of gun violence, and Black mothers as complicit or helpless victims, have become ingrained into public consciousness. Television viewers empathetically or blamefully watched as Lorraine Small collapsed upon receiving the terrible news that her 15-year-old son Jordan Manners had been found shot in the stairwell of his Toronto high school. Trayvon Martin's mother stood in disbelief as the self-appointed Neighbourhood Watch volunteer who killed her son walked free from a Florida court room. When Black youths like Jordan and Trayvon become victims of gun violence, the public is exposed to a social discourse of race and gun violence. Predominantly, in countries like Canada, the United States and Britain, this discourse as expressed in the media facilitates a social perception of gun violence as a "Black thing," a fact that perpetuates the racial stigma that negatively affects the Black community.

IMMIGRATION STIGMA AND TRAUMA. Public discourses of "foreignness" as being responsible for high crime rates in certain parts of North America are reinforced by political figures. For example, Jason Kenney, the former Canadian minister of citizenship and immigration, after a shooting incident in Toronto in 2012 that killed two young people and wounded 23 others, tweeted that "foreign gangsters should be deported w/out delay" (Bryden, July 21, 2012). This statement has been criticized for wrongfully stigmatizing racialized immigrants, particularly Caribbean immigrants, as being responsible for crimes in Toronto. We also saw this discourse of race in British prime minister Tony Blair's assertion that the increase in violence was not the result of poverty but of Black youth, and, more precisely, a distinctive Black culture (Wintour and Dodd, 2007). Such statements contribute to a widely held stigmatization of immigrant Blacks as criminals and the construction of images of "good" and "bad" Canadians, based on race, class and nationality. Black mothers have reported that these social images and associated racial discourse have severely impacted their sense of vulnerability to violent loss, and have added to a system of oppression that dominated their grieving processes, affected their social interactions and constrained their access to resource and supports (Bailey et al., 2013).

Persistent differential treatment and resource access related to the **political significance of immigration status** is a challenge for Black immigrant survivors coping with the loss of loved ones to gun homicide. Despite studies that have shown that immigrants are less likely to be perpetrators of crime than their domestic-born counterparts (Almeida, Johnson, McNamara, and Gupta, 2011; Feldmeyer, 2009; Lee, Martinez and Rosenfeld, 2001), public discourse still widely supports the view that racialized immigrants are largely responsible for crimes in North America (Horowitz, 2001). Such public scrutiny fuels race-based stigma and inequalities, which research has shown often limit access to available supports for African American victims and survivors of homicide (Sharpe, 2008; Sharpe, 2013). For Black mothers whose children have been victims or perpetrators of gun violence, such perceptions instill blame and shame that can alienate them from community and social support, and jeopardize their access to needed institutional resources for healing and recovery (Bailey et al., 2014).

The success of their children in Canada is one of the primary motivations behind many Black mothers' migration, despite their own experiences with deskilling, downward occupational mobility, and poverty (Pratt, 2012). Their trauma experiences are accentuated by both losing children to gun violence and witnessing the devastating social, educational and economic impact that the loss imposes on their remaining children. Some Black mothers in Toronto revealed that after the loss of their children, surviving children have dropped out of school, engaged in retaliation and have relinquished their passion and dreams. Intense traumatic grief from gun violence not only poses a serious threat to mothers' wellbeing, but to surviving siblings' ability to cope (Jenkins, 2002; Lohan, and Murphy, 2002; Mohr, Fantuzzo, and Abdul-Kabir, 2001). With little support of any kind available to immigrant families in Canada (Simich, Hamilton, and Baya, 2006), the death of a loved one to gun violence can easily cause a breakdown in family structures.

As immigrant women living in Canada, a society that is largely oriented towards the principles of individualism, the scant support Black mothers receive is in sharp contrast to the tight-knit community ties they would have been able to draw upon in the collectivist-oriented cultures in their countries of origin (Christiansen, 2010). Upon migrating to Canada, Black women experience a sharp decline in their income and social status, even if they are highly educated (Chui, 2011; Houle and Yssaad, 2010; Picot, Hou, and Coulombe, 2008). They experience a higher poverty rate than Canadian-born women due to barriers in credential recognition (Picot, Hou, and Coulombe, 2008). Loss to gun violence further intensifies their economic situation by burdening them with legal fees and burial expenses, and often resulting in multiple job losses. Low socio-economic and immigrant status poses further challenges to mothers' grieving processes, as the intersection of societal blame, race, social class, gender and nationality becomes all too apparent.

One might expect the intensity of Black mothers' gun violence trauma to last only so long, and to diminish in intensity over time. However, research suggests that is not the case. Black mothers' pain, like that endured by other gun violence trauma sufferers, does *not* abate over time (McDevitt-Murphy et al., 2012; Sharpe, et al., 2014). Yet there continues to be a fundamental distinction between the public discourse concerning Black men's deaths from gun violence, and the private suffering of Black mothers. To a considerable extent, the factors that complicate Black mothers' trauma responses — such as unmet migration expectations, their children's unrealized futures, stigmatized social treatments and their economic vulnerability — remain seriously hidden from public domain and discourse.

## Access and Support for Survivors

Psychological challenges faced by homicide survivors support the need for available, accessible resources and services to buffer their distress (Armour, 2002; Currier, Holland and Neimeyer, 2006; Murphy, Johnson and Lohan, 2003). The World Health Organization (2002) reports that for each individual that dies from violence, grieving survivors experience a range of physical, social, and mental health issues. The Ontario Office for Victims of Crime (2010) acknowledges that promoting healing and resilience for grieving victims/survivors requires services that are accessible, free of barriers and consistent across groups and contexts. Access to services and supports is a central dimension of coping and recovery for survivors. Survivors of gun violence require services that extend across hospital care, mental health care, crisis intervention, rehabilitation, legal and other social support services (Asaro, 2001; Buchanan, 2014; Oliver, 2000). Examination of gun violence survivors' grief, trauma, and rehabilitation experiences in over 20 countries confirmed that in both high- and low-income countries, survivors of gun violence faced challenges in accessing resources such as social assistance, long-term psychological rehabilitation, victim compensation and peer support (Buchanan, 2014). These challenges are largely due to the lack of available services and under-usage of services.

A 2004 Canadian survey on victimization revealed that only 9% of those involved in violent crimes sought support from formal service providers (Department of Justice Canada, 2010). Studies have shown that an under-utilization of services among gun homicide population and other victims of crime is due to actual or perceived barriers (Asaro, 2001; Department of Justice Canada, 2010; Horne, 2003; Kelly et al., 2010; Sharpe, 2008; Sims, Yost, and Abbott, 2006). Although crime victims were aware of the benefits of service utilization, many still faced barriers in accessing services. Accessing social support services may be even more complicated for immigrant families as they navigate the system and establish their identity (Christiansen, 2010). In urban centres, where immigrants mostly settle, barriers included limited mental health services and a lack of a coordinated and seamless service system that caters to the physical, mental and psychosocial needs of survivors (Kelly et al., 2010). The lack of a coordinated system can lead to poor follow-up for missed appointments and limited communication between medical providers and mental health programs, both of which create more barriers in accessing and/or receiving needed services (Kelly et al., 2010).

According to Kelly et al. (2010), six to 12 months after a violent incident, just under one-third of crime victims were utilizing mental health services, with very low usage among Blacks and other ethnic minorities. Underutilization of services was attributed to the belief that counselling was not effective, lack of awareness of existing services, and lack of culturally relevant services (Department of Justice Canada, 2010; Kelly et al., 2010; Sims et al., 2006). The findings in our study with Black mothers support these conclusions. For these mothers, barriers to access tended to be related to the stigma of gun violence as a "Black thing." The marginalization and stigmatization they faced limited their access to available resources and support (Sharpe, 2008; Sharpe and Boyas, 2011). One mother noted, "People in service judge you as a Black person. If your son died from guns, he was either a criminal or a drug dealer. I don't want to come home feeling like a murderer" (Participant 3, interviewed February 20, 2012).

A certain range and amount of trauma resources are made available to all survivors of gun violence in order to facilitate coping and healing, with the idea being that these resources are to be shared among survivors to support recovery. Such access, if provided, can mark the beginning of the survivors' healing process and the easing of their trauma experience. Compromised access to trauma resources and services therefore reinforces marginalization, alienation, and makes it difficult for survivors of gun violence to break the cycle of violence (Buchanan, 2014). Fair and equitable access to the total range and amount of available resources can promote healing and end the trauma experience.

## Race Influences Access to Resources

The demographics of victims and survivors of gun violence are reflective of low socioeconomic status and social challenges, both of which add to the complexity of their coping. Seventy-five percent of Black mothers (n=48) involved in a recent research project on gun violence trauma and resilience in Toronto lived in economically deprived neighbourhoods. Ninety-two percent were immigrants, mainly from Caribbean countries. They grappled with low economic status, low levels of education, and low levels of employment (Bailey, Sharma and Jubin, 2013). Access to victim compensation and other financial services are of paramount importance for these and other Black survivors, especially when research shows that race is a barrier to accessing services (Ahmed, Mohammed, and Williams, 2007; Sharpe, 2008; Williams and Mohammed, 2009). Regretably, while principles of human rights, compassion, fairness and respect ground victim services in Canada (Correctional Service Canada, 2014), there remain gaps in democratizing meaningful access to all victims of violent crimes. Ninety percent (43 out of 48) of Black mothers in Toronto who lost children to gun violence reported being denied victim compensation because their children were known to the police and/or because the mothers did not manifest mental shock as demonstration of their grief (Bailey and Velasco, 2014). One mother informed us, "I was told that when you lose someone to a criminal act then you are entitled to a criminal compensation . . . but I was told that my son caused his own death and because of that reason, I didn't get it" (Participant 6, interviewed April 10, 2012). Another mother cried, "I was told that I was not grieving enough. Breaking down was not an option for me as a black woman" (Participant 8, interviewed May 20, 2012). Black mothers, due to their cultural imperative to be strong in the face of racism and oppression, may not publicly demonstrate their grief (Bailey et al., 2013; Bailey and Velasco, 2014). Also, given Black male youths' economic and social vulnerability as victims, witnesses and survivors of gun violence (Ezeonu, 2010; Sharpe and Boyas, 2011; Sheptycki, 2009), these criteria are precisely those that disadvantage Black mothers and exacerbate their grief and trauma experiences.

Black mothers felt that at the height of their trauma, race-based stigma influenced their access to trauma resources, perpetuated their marginalization, and threatened their coping repertoire (Bailey et al., 2013). When exclusionary criteria are applied to compensation policies and practices that affect Blacks more than other groups, Black mothers' difficulties in gaining access to compensation and other victim resources are accentuated. Steve Sullivan, executive director of Ottawa Victim Service, noted that "negative perceptions held by service providers of mothers whose sons die from gun violence, especially those in gangs, can adversely influence their access to victim services" (Sullivan, interviewed, June 11, 2012). This comment substantiates the conclusion that the discourse of stigma attached to Black bodies and gun violence becomes woven into policies, and then enacted in the practice of distributing and denying resources to victims of gun violence. For these mothers, it appears that the bar to accessing victims' compensation has been raised, excluding many of them from a necessary state resource. A lack of compensation impacts on Black mothers' ability to seek and afford long term psychological support. As a result, several mothers went without such support, which in turn weakened their resilience, lessened their civic engagement and crippled their ability to positively appraise their loss (Bailey et al., 2013). "The resource is just not there. . . . I had to make my own resources. . . . We Black mothers are just left to fall into the statistics hole of poverty," said one mother (Participant 3, interviewed February 20, 2012). Preventing mothers from gaining access to an equitable share of the resources required for recovery further exposes them to financial and social stress, accentuating their feelings of inferiority (Ahmed, Mohammed, and Williams, 2007).

**Race Influences Social and System Support**

Research shows that informal support from family and friends (Stroebe, Shut and Stroebe, 2005), as well as formal support systems and networks (Burke et al., 2011) are important mediators for survivors of gun homicide' bereavement outcomes. Barriers in accessing supports tend to be specific to racialized groups, with some historical influence. Black survivors are more likely to suffer from disenfranchised grief, which makes them susceptible to lack of support and negative reactions from others (Miller, 2009). Studies of Black victims of homicide showed that they rarely sought formal support and community services, due to fear of racial stigma and historical mistrust of formal support systems (Laurie and

Neimeyer, 2008; Sharpe, 2008; Sharpe and Boyas, 2011). Our study paralleled these findings and showed that although family and friends serve at first as adequate support for Black mothers, especially when formal services or programs fail to meet mothers' needs, over time these informal support systems eventually became exhausted (Bailey et al., 2014). One mother explained, "[T]here is the immediate grief where everyone . . . lend[s] support and mourn[s] with you. Eventually people go back to their lives and the only person that is stuck in this void is the mother" (Participant 10, interviewed December 12, 2013).

The racial stigma associated with losing a Black child to gun violence also made it difficult for mothers and others in their social circles to talk about the loss. As a result, many mothers retreated from social interactions for fear that they or their deceased children would be judged negatively (Bailey et al., 2013). "[T]hey judge you as a black person who lost a black child," expressed one mother. In light of a long history of racial discrimination, oppression and socio-economic disparities, altruism, caring and informal supports remain critical in the Black community (Sharpe and Boyas, 2011; Burke et al., 2011). However, for best psychological outcomes, formal supports should work in tandem. This is particularly the case for immigrant women who are often at the bottom of the economic ladder (Picot, Hou, and Coulombe, 2008). Not having support at different levels impacts greatly on Black mothers' ability to cope and adds an extra layer of challenge for them to obtain respite from their trauma experience (Bailey and Velasco, 2014).

## Race Intersects and Dominates Access and Support

Literature on the cause and impact of homicide loss is grounded in an **intersectionality perspective** that gives credence to the inter-relational and multi-level complexities of race (Janhevich, Bania and Hastings, 2008; Sharpe, 2013; Sharpe et al., 2014). The processes of racialization, stigmatization and marginalization intersect with poverty, nationality, lack of social support and poor access to social resources to complicate Black mothers' experiences as survivors of gun violence (Bailey, et al. 2013, Bailey and Velasco, 2014). When race intersects with access and social support, Black mothers are placed at a particular disadvantage. Race is salient to determining who gets access to resources. The various policies and procedures that have been put into place have the potential to allocate resources in such a way as to ensure that each survivor receives a fair share (i.e., necessary access to resources and supports). However, in practice, when resources are allocated, it is an unfortunate fact that not all survivors receive equal or equitable access to the resources they require so as to address their trauma needs. Racial stigma leads to biased decision-making, which can affect Black mothers' access to resources and supports. In fact, when racial stigma intersects with access and social support, Black mothers are denied or given limited access to resources and support, despite the fact that there are policies and definitions that should guide decision-making practices to ensure equitable access in Canada (Oxman-Martinez, et al., 2005). The denial of victims' compensation to mothers who lose children to gun violence because of the criterion that their children were responsible for their own deaths is an example of the systemic barriers faced by Black mothers when trying to access needed resources. "If your child contributed to his death, what does this have to do with the mother's grief? What does that have to do with your needs? Doesn't that mother still have the same grieving needs as any other?" questioned one mother (Participant 3, interviewed February 20, 2012).

Race is a powerful predictor of access to resources. We have come to understand that on a number of health indicators, racialized groups have worse outcomes than members of non-racialized groups (Toronto Public Health, 2013; Williams and Mohammed, 2009). In the case of gun violence, the discourse of race intersects and interlocks with access and support, ultimately playing a dominant role in the distribution of health resources such as victims' compensation, which can impact the health outcomes of victims. For Black mothers, being hindered from accessing their fair share of the resource pie because of race-based stigma and preconceived judgment of their worthiness as victims can have lasting social, biological and psychological outcomes (Mastrocinque et al., 2014). As Steve Sullivan stated: "There is the notion of 'good victims' and 'bad victims.' A lot of people don't see these mothers as good victims. We see it played out quite often in victim services, especially with the shootings in Toronto. We do make service decisions on who the good victims are and who the bad victims are" (Sullivan, interviewed June 11, 2012). In Sullivan's view, the perception of the "good" citizen shapes decisions about who has access to available resources and what kind of resources they have access to. More broadly, the influence of public perceptions of who is considered "good" within a society influence the type of access to resources and supports that survivors or victims of gun violence receive from the state.

Dignified and empathetic treatments for victims — in Canada defined as a "persons who, as a result of the commission of a crime by another, suffer emotional or physical harm, loss of or damage to property or economic harm" — should not vary based on the perceived worthiness of the victim (*The Correctional and Conditional Release Act,* 1992, p. 4). Yet this definition gets played out differently in service access when racial stigma associated with gun violence informs decision-making. As one mother puts it, "sometimes the negativity that comes because most of the mothers are Black mothers, the negativity that the society, the government has, it seems like we are second class citizen[s]. We are not being treated as any normal person." Butler and Spivak (2007) confirm that immigrants, particularly racialized immigrants, are often treated as second-class citizens in society, despite their contribution to the economic success of a country. In an imperialistic society that sustains exploitation, there is a need for Black immigrant women to provide much-needed "lower" skilled services, but without access to the necessary resources and rights afforded to their domestic Caucasian counterparts (Butler and Spivak, 2007). Consciously or unconsciously, the determination of who is most worthy of victims' compensation reflects who is more valued and accepted in society.

In order to understand how race dominates, we must acknowledge that racism gets articulated in a myriad of ways in organizational structures through policies and practices. In the context of violence and crime, social construction of the "good victim" identity is instituted pervasively in practice and delivery of victim services. This construction shapes how individuals are perceived and the kind of access they receive, thus dominating survivors' broad resource-access experience. Decision-makers have the power to determine how trauma recovery resources are allocated. If that power is used in a compassionate and fair way, the intent would be to provide equitable access to survivors based on inherent and demonstrated need. However, while decision-makers have the power to divide and distribute resources equitably for survivors of gun violence, in the case of Black mothers considered unworthy because of their children's alleged involvement in the crime, all too often the allocation of resources is carried out in a way that is dominating, oppressive, and that limits access to needed resources. The end result is to exacerbate Black mothers' trauma experiences.

## Discussion

The traumatic, meaningless and socially involved nature of gun violence makes the needs of survivors relevant, immediate, pressing and unique. Gun violence trauma and survivorship are not experienced equally by all survivors. Black mothers' experiences are influenced by the intersecting and interlocking effects of race, gender, culture, nationality, marginalization, social and economic deprivations, and the stigma of gun violence. The intersecting and interlocking nature of these experiences can impede Black mothers' independence, self-determination and resilience to continue contributing to their families, communities and society following loss of their children to gun violence. The dominance of race creates social and psychological complexities that complicate their access to services and supports. The resulting trauma is debilitating and persistent, and requires changes in policies, practices and services toward greater fairness and equity to address their health and social needs.

The influence of race in gun violence trauma does not begin at the cusp of the loss. Many Black mothers came to understand in a new way the reality and seriousness of racism in impacting their grief and loss experience, livelihoods as survivors, and their coping and resilience following their loss. They came to realize that rather than receiving a victim status, they received a status of victimization (Bailey et al., 2013). Many mothers were left feeling blamed. Whether this blame is perceived or real, it contributes to loss of social support, negative reactions from other people, and lack of access to services because of the disruption of their ability to find or make meaning of their children's deaths (Bailey et al., 2013; Miller 2009). As support is vital to the grief and trauma experiences of Black mothers, it is important to understand how race intersects with resources and support to affect their ability to cope.

Access to finances is essential to homicide victims' coping and survivorship, especially in the immediate aftermath of the loss. Because many Black mothers are unable to work after the loss of their children to gun violence, their socio-economic situation compromises their coping abilities. Research shows that low-income Black survivors of homicide loss suffer more intense symptoms of PTSD and complicated grief (McDevitt-Murphy et al., 2012). A denial of victims' compensation exacerbates existing financial challenges and coping difficulties. Being denied compensation leaves Black mothers without resources to adequately deal with their loss. Although mothers can appeal the denial of compensation, the intensity of their trauma, and the lack of formal and informal supports rendered them, disempowers them, and also prevents them from meeting appeal requirements. As one mother puts it, "the compensation policy that they have is one sided. It works for one section of society but not for the other. I think criminal compensation should be what they say it is, and it shouldn't be in the fine print" (Participant 11, interviewed, February 13, 2014). What is clear in these mothers' narratives is that at the root of this denial is the discourse of race. Black mothers felt victimized when their sons were perceived as complicit in their own deaths. An applied psychological category of mental shock creates blame and exclusion from access to resources. Victim compensation policies based on these criteria, especially on the actions of the deceased, can negatively impact survivors' needs, and should be changed so that survivors are not denied access to resources for dealing with their grief. Black mothers felt that these policies were predicated by racism. Failing to centre race de-historicizes Canada's colonial past and the racism that people of African descent have experienced and continue to experience in their everyday interactions with mainstream institutions (Henry et al., 2000; Thobani, 2009).

Many Black mothers, especially those who did not receive victim compensation, were not able to seek further counselling because of financial challenges. Sustained counselling that incorporates culturally relevant models and processes for dealing with the impact of social stigmas and Black mothers' unique needs are important for healing and resilience. Regardless of race, victims of violence need to have their grief acknowledged and their cultural values respected as they interact with and try to access systems of social support. Services should be accessible and adequate and service providers need to be caring and compassionate. Psychological rehabilitation services need to be long-term, culturally relevant and specific to the unique needs of survivors of gun violence (Buchanan, 2014).

With the withdrawal of support from friends and families and, at times, significant others, some Black mothers reported feeling isolated. However, solutions for their isolation were rarely sought through formal services and programs. Although Black mothers believe that support from community-based survivor groups can be effective, they articulated that there is a lack of funding for long-term support in these groups and in non-profit organizations. Black mothers believe that racial stigma is pervasive at all levels of support and across all institutions and sectors because most survivors are Black. We advocate that policymakers and service providers endeavour to challenge racial stigma and discrimination in their criteria and decision-making processes, and provide more services and equitable compensation for Black mothers to help counteract the impact of "triple jeopardy" — the intersection of race, gender and class. This goes beyond an equal sharing of resources to a comprehensive review of victim services to ensure that everyone affected by gun violence receives equitable access to the resources and supports that are needed for positive grief and trauma outcomes. Social, psychological and financial resources are fundamental for strengthening Black mothers' ability to cope with gun violence loss and building their resiliency.

## Reflective Questions

The following reflective questions are tied to Case Study 15.1 as well as the content of the chapter as a whole.

1. Explain why several levels of support to deal with grief are critical for Black mothers who lose children to gun violence. Discuss your answers using evidence from the case study.
2. It can be argued that services are rendered on protocol rather than individual needs. How do you think this practice would specifically affect survivors of gun violence?
3. What are the three most significant indicators of traumatic grief experienced by the mother in the case study?
4. Based on your knowledge of families and the impact of gun violence on families, describe three strategies that should be considered in supporting the family in the case study.

## Acknowledgements

A seed grant provided by Ryerson University, Faculty of Community Services, helped to make this chapter possible. Levar Bailey designed a piece of artwork that was very helpful in conceptualizing and visualizing the core concept of the chapter.

## References

Ahmed, A., Mohammed, S. A., & Williams, D. (2007). Racial discrimination and health: Pathways and evidence. *Indian Journal of Medical Research, 126*(4), 318–27.

Almeida, J., Johnson, R. M., McNamara, M., & Gupta, J. (2011). Peer violence perpetration among urban adolescents: Dispelling the myth of the violent immigrant. *Journal of Interpersonal Violence, 26*(13), 2658–2680.

Armour, M. P. (2002). Experiences of co-victims of homicide: Implications for research and practice. *Trauma, Violence, and Abuse, 3*(2), 109–124.

Asaro, M. R. (2001). Working with adult homicide survivors, part I: Impact and sequelae of murder. *Perspectives in Psychiatric Care, 37*(3), 95–101.

Bailey, A., Hannays-King, Clarke, J., Lester, E., & Velasco, D. (2013). Black mothers' cognitive process of finding meaning and building resilience after loss of a child to gun violence. *British Journal of Social Work, 43*(2), 336–356.

Bailey, A., Sharma, M., & Jubin, M. (2013). The mediating role of social support, cognitive appraisal, and quality health care in Black mothers' stress-resilience process following loss to gun violence. *Violence and Victims, 28*(2), 233–247.

Bailey, A., & Velasco, D. (2014). Gun violence in Canada. In Buchanan, C. (Ed.), *Gun violence, disability and recovery*. Freshwater, NSW, Australia: Surviving Gun Violence Project.

Bailey, A., Hanays-King, C., Clarke, J., Lester, L., Akhtar, M., & Le, K. (2014, under review). Social support and Black mothers' psychological well-being following loss to gun violence. *Bereavement Care Journal*.

Bryden, J. (2012, July 21). Jason Kenney tweet on "foreign gangsters" and Toronto shooting lands minister in hot water. Canadian Press. Retrieved from http://www.huffingtonpost.ca/2012/07/20/jason-kenney-twitter-toronto-shooting-foreign-gangsters_n_1690660.html.

Buchanan, C. (2014). *Gun violence, disability and recovery*. Freshwater, NSW, Australia: Surviving Gun Violence Project.

Burke, L. A., Neimeyer, R. A., McDevitt-Murphy, M. E., Ippolito, M. R., & Roberts, J. M. (2011). Faith in the wake of homicide: Religious coping and bereavement distress in an African American sample. *International Journal for the Psychology of Religion, 21*(4), 289–307.

Carniol, B. (2010). *Case critical: Social services and social justice in Canada* (6th ed.). Toronto: Between the Lines Press.

Chettleburgh, M.C. (2007). *Young thugs: Inside the dangerous world of Canadian street gangs*. Toronto: HarperCollins Publishers.

Christiansen, D. E. (2010). Adolescent Cape Verdean girls' experience of violence, incarceration, and deportation: Developing resources through participatory community-based groups. *International Journal of Intercultural Relations, 34*(2), 127–140.

Chui, T. (2011). *Women in Canada: A gender-based statistical report: Immigrant women*. Ottawa: Statistics Canada. Retrieved from http://www.statcan.gc.ca/pub/89-503-x/2010001/article/11528-eng.pdf.

Clarke, J., Aiello, O., Chau, K., Atcha, Z., Rashidi, M., & Amarel, S. (2012). Uprooting social work education. *LEARNing Landscapes, 6*(1), 81–105.

Correctional Service Canada (2014). Victim services. Retrieved from http://www.csc-scc.gc.ca/victims/index-eng.shtml.

Currier, J. M., Holland, J. M., & Neimeyer, R. A. (2006). Sense-making, grief, and the experience of violent loss: Toward a mediational model. *Death Studies, 30* (5), 403–428.

Department of Justice Canada (2010). Every victim matters. *Victims of Crime Research Digest, 3*, 1–32. Retrieved from http://www.justice.gc.ca/eng/index.html.

Ezeonu, I. (2010) Gun violence in Toronto: Perspectives from the police. *Howard Journal, 49*, 147–165.

Fekete, L. (2001). The emergence of xeno-racism. *Race and Class, 43*(2), 23–40.

Feldmeyer, B. (2009). Immigration and violence: The offsetting effects of immigrant concentration on Latino violence. *Social Science Research, 38*(3), 717–731.

Henry, F., & Tator, C. (2010).*The colour of democracy: Racism in Canadian society*. Toronto: Nelson.

Henry, F., Tator, C., Mattis, W., & Rees, R. (2000). *The colour of democracy: Racism in Canadian society*. Toronto: Harcourt Brace.

Horne, C. (2003). Families of homicide victims: Service utilization patterns of extra- and intrafamilial homicide survivors. *Journal of Family Violence, 18*(2), 75–82.

Horowitz, C. F. (2001). The examination of U.S. immigration policy and serious crime. Washington: Center for Immigration Studies. Retrieved from http://www.cis.org/articles/2001/crime/toc.html.

Houle, R. & Yssaad, L. (2010). Recognition of newcomers' foreign credentials and work experience. *Perspectives on Labour and Income, 11*(9), 18–33.

James, C., & Davis, A. (2012). *Jamaica in the Canadian experience: A multiculturalizing presence*. Halifax: Fernwood Publishing.

Janhevich, D., Bania, M., & Hastings, R. (2008). Rethinking newcomer and minority offending and victimization: Beyond hate crimes. Retrieved from http://canada.metropolis.net/pdfs/janhevich_rethinking_minority_crime_e.pdf.

Jenkins, E. J. (2002). Black women and community violence: Trauma, grief, and coping. *Women and Therapy, 25* (3/4), 29–44.

Kelly, V. G., Merril, G. S., Shumway, M., Alvidrez, J., & Boccellari, A. (2010). Outreach, engagement, and practical assistance: Essential aspects of PTSD care for urban victims of violent crime. *Trauma, Violence and Abuse, 11*(3), 144–156.

Laurie, A., & Neimeyer, R. A. (2008). African Americans in bereavement: Grief as a function of ethnicity. *OMEGA: Journal of Death and Dying, 57*(2), 173–193.

Lee, M. T., Martinez, R., & Rosenfeld, R. (2001). Does immigration increase homicide? Negative evidence from three border cities. *Sociological Quarterly, 42*(4), 559–580.

Lohan, J. A., & Murphy, S. A. (2002). Family functioning and family typology after an adolescent or young adult's sudden violent death. *Journal of Family Nursing, 8*(1), 32–49.

Mastrocinque, J. M., Metzger, J. W., Madeira, J., Lang, K., Pruss, H., Navratil, P. K., Sandys, M., Cerulli, C. (2014). I'm still left here with the pain: Exploring the health consequences of homicide on families and friends. *Homicide Studies,* 1–24.

McDevitt-Murphy, M., Neimeyer, R.A., Burke, L. A., Williams, J. L., & Lawson, K. (2012). The toll of traumatic loss in African Americans bereaved by homicide. *Psychological Trauma: Theory, Research, Practice, and Policy, 4*(3), 303–311.

Miller, L. (2009). Family survivors of homicide: I. Symptoms, syndromes, and reaction patterns. *The American Journal of Family Therapy, 37*(1), 67–79.

Mohr, W. K., Fantuzzo, J. W., Abdul-Kabir, S. (2001). Safeguarding themselves and their children: Mothers share their strategies. *Journal of Family Violence, 16*(1), 75–92

Murphy, S. A., Johnson, L. C., & Lohan, J. (2003). Finding meaning in a child's violent death: A five-year prospective analysis of parents' personal narratives and empirical data. *Death Studies, 27*(5), 381–404.

Oliver, W. (2000). The public health and social consequences of black male violence. *Journal of African American Men, 5*(2), 71–92.

Ontario Office for Victims of Crime (2010). Victims' bill of rights. Retrieved from http://www.attorneygeneral.jus.gov.on.ca/english/ovss/rights.asp.

Oxman-Martinez, J., Hanley, J., Lach, L., Khanlou, N., Weerasinghe, S., & Agnew, V. (2005) Intersection of Canadian policy parameters affecting women with precarious immigration status: A baseline for understanding barriers to health. *Journal of Immigrant Health, 7*(4), 247–258.

Phillips, J. (1997). Variation in African-American homicide rates: An assessment of potential explanations. *Criminology, 35*(4), 527–556.

Picot, G., Hou, F., & Coulombe, S. (2008). Poverty dynamics among recent immigrants to Canada. *International Migration Review, 42*(2), 393–424.

Pon, G., Gosine, K., & Phillips, D. (2011). Immediate response: Addressing anti-Native and anti-Black racism in child welfare. *International Journal of Child, Youth and Family Studies, 3 & 4*, 385–409.

Pratt, G. (2012). *Families apart: Migrant mothers and the conflict of labor and love.* Minneapolis, MN: University of Minnesota Press.

Rosenblatt, P. C., & Wallace, B. R. (2005). Narratives of grieving African-Americans about racism in the lives of deceased family members. *Death Studies, 29*(3), 217–235.

Sharpe, T. L., Osteen, P., Frey, J. J. & Michalopoulos, L. M. (2014). Coping with grief responses among African American family members of homicide victims. *Violence and Victims, 29*(2), 332–47.

Sharpe. T. L. (2013). Understanding the sociocultural context of coping for African American family members of homicide victims: A conceptual model. *Trauma, Violence, and Abuse,* 1–12.

Sharpe, T. L. (2008). Sources of support for African-American family members of homicide victims. *Journal of Ethnic and Cultural Diversity in Social Work, 17*(2), 197–216.

Sharpe, T. L., & Boyas, J. (2011). We fall down: The African American experience of coping with the homicide of a loved one. *Journal of Black Studies, 42*(6), 855–873.

Sheptycki, J. (2009). Guns, crime and social order: A Canadian perspective. *Criminology and Criminal Justice, 9*(3), 307–336.

Simich, L., Hamilton, H., & Baya, B.K. (2006). Mental distress, economic hardship and expectations of life in Canada among Sudanese newcomers. *Transcultural Psychiatry, 43*(3), 418–444.

Sims, B., Yost, B., & Abbott, C. (2005). Use and nonuse of victim services programs: Implications from a statewide survey of crime victims. *Criminology and Public Policy, 4*(2), 361–384.

Stroebe, W., Schut, H., & Stroebe, M. S. (2005). Grief work, disclosure and counseling: Do they help the bereaved?. *Clinical Psychology Review, 25*(4), 395–414.

Toronto Public Health (2013). *Racialization and health inequities in Toronto.* Retrieved from www.toronto.ca/health/reports.

Thobani, S. (2009). *Exalted subjects.* Toronto: University of Toronto Press.

Todd, J. L., & Worell, J. (2000). Resilience in low-income, employed, African American women. *Psychology of Women Quarterly, 24*(2), 119–128.

World Health Organization (2002). *World report on violence and health.* Retrieved from http://www.who.int/violence_injury_prevention/violence/world_report/en/.

Williams, D. R., & Mohammed, S. A. (2009). Discrimination and racial disparities in health: Evidence and needed research. *Journal of Behavioral Medicine, 32*(1), 20–47.

Wintour, P., & Dodd, V. (2007, April 12). Blair blames spate of murders on black culture. *The Guardian.* Retrieved from: http://www.theguardian.com/politics/2007/apr/12/ukcrime.race.

CHAPTER SIXTEEN

# From Displacement and Residential Schools to Art, Archive and Healing

## Jonathan Dewar

For Canadian First Nations, Inuit and Métis, migration as well as forced displacement and dislocation are historical and contemporary realities. The Indian Residential Schools (IRS) era (1831–1996) and the post-IRS, contemporary experiences are significant parts in the story of displacement and dislocation. In contrast, the lengthy history of nomadic movements and migrations pre- and post-contact are not the focus here. However, this "forever history" context should be noted as it relates and compares to post-contact movements, settlements, displacements and dislocations that took place due to disease, missionary zealotry, trade, extinctions of game, and pre- and post-Confederation legislation and policy (Milloy, 1999; Dickason and McNab, 2009).

To understand contemporary implications of displacement for Indigenous people, then, the history and living legacy of Indian Residential Schools is of key significance, as are the terms that have come to define that legacy in recent years — trauma, healing, truth and reconciliation. First Nations, Inuit and Métis children were all subject to the assimilatory goals of the government and the proselytizing efforts of the various church entities through schooling (Chartrand et al., 2006; Legacy of Hope Foundation, 2012). It is important to note that while the government of Canada has formally apologized for the Residential School experience, the Day School experience, which affected many more Métis students

**Reflective Questions**

1. What role did Residential Schools play in the displacement of Indigenous people in Canada?
2. How can art and archival work serve as a strategy to confront the displacement and trauma generated during the Residential School period?
3. What are some of the challenges and successes of the Shingwauk Educational project in Northern Ontario?
4. Name and explore three key policies or reports foundational to the development of a position on Indigenous peoples, cultural, economic, political and territorial rights.

proportionately, as well as some First Nations and Inuit students, has not been formally addressed.

The history, legacy and particularly the intergenerational effects of Residential Schools, and the ignorance about this experience that still abounds, must be placed within both the pre-contact history of First Nations and Inuit peoples and the context of Canada's colonial history. Thousands of Residential School Survivors ("Survivor" is the term that former students have chosen for themselves) have been tireless in their advocacy and agency, often through truly grassroots efforts, to offer opportunities to all affected by Residential Schools, including the Canadian public, to respond to the trauma of forced removal from family and community, discrimination, abuse (physical, sexual, spiritual, and psychological), and demonization of culture and languages, and to share, heal and learn.

In this chapter I will discuss the history of Indian Residential Schools and the efforts of Survivors to respond to the trauma they experienced, with a particular emphasis on the important role the collection and sharing of Residential Schools photographs, records and artefacts has played within the healing movement. The first section introduces the notion of the "profound silences" around Residential Schools history, then moves on to the most recent official effort to unveil the truth of both the policy of assimilation and the experiences of former students, emphasizing the importance of the arts, and particularly the "Survivor memoir." The second section explores as a case study a specific example of grassroots healing efforts in Northern Ontario. Readers are then introduced to the concepts of Apology and Redress, and the implementation of the Indian Residential Schools Settlement Agreement and the establishment of the Indian Residential Schools Truth and Reconciliation Commission of Canada. The penultimate section returns to the perspectives of artists who have been engaged in art practices that explore the role that artists and their work have played in healing and redress movements. The chapter closes by highlighting the ongoing need for further efforts to promote truth, healing and reconciliation, while continuing to exercise caution for the benefit of those impacted by the Residential Schools experience and its legacy. Before beginning the first section, however, I will provide a few notes on key terminologies associated with this chapter.

## Notes on Terminologies

The following terms require clarification for readers unfamiliar with the implications of discourse related to Indigenous people's experiences in Canada. The term **Indian**, for example, remains the legal term for First Nations people, identified by the federal government under the *Indian Act* as **status Indians**. Individuals may also refer to themselves as **non-status Indians**, although this term holds no legal standing as such. I will use the more culturally appropriate term **First Nations** to discuss both groups. In Canada, the term **Aboriginal** refers, constitutionally, to First Nations, **Inuit** (once known as Eskimo) and **Métis**. It is also essential to note that the term **Métis**, that is, with a capital "M," denotes a specific history and culture of mixed racial and/or cultural heritage that is not to be confused with the derogatory "halfbreed," sometimes used interchangeably in Canada, and "mixed blood," which is largely American terminology. Small "m" **métis** has some currency in Canada when referring to mixed heritage, generally, as in *métissage*, but it is often misused or misunderstood.

**Indian Residential School** is the official term used by the government of Canada for the Residential Schools that First Nations, Metis and Inuit were forced to attend. There are some variants, including the inclusion of Inuit as a descriptor. Hereafter, I will use the broader, inclusive term Residential Schools to ensure that all of Canada's Aboriginal peoples are included. The term **Residential Schools** refers to all government-funded, Church-run "schools" where children were in residence, including industrial schools, boarding schools, student residences, hostels, billets and even Inuit tent camps in the North.

Indian Residential School is a historical and legal term; I will use Residential School, except where necessary, to refer to the policy and system. The term will not be capitalized when referring to one or more schools informally.

**Genocide** is a term that has been used to describe the effects of Residential Schools (Lemkin, 1944). While there is debate about the meaning of the term genocide in relation to Residential Schools, the final item in the list of "acts committed with intent to destroy, in whole or in part, a national, ethnical, racial or religious group" (Convention on the Prevention and Punishment of the Crime of Genocide, Article II) is drawn upon as proof of genocide. Others, more narrowly, define "forcibly transferring children of the group to another group" as **cultural genocide** (Chrisjohn and Young, 1997).

I will now explore the ways in which significant issues about Residential Schools are hidden. This notion of **profound silences** includes the multiple ways in which Aboriginal people have been negatively affected, displaced, and dispossessed.

## Profound Silences: Residential Schools History, Trauma and Healing

Profound silences with regard to Residential Schools are still very present. These silences are deeply personal, but also communal, felt for decades within families and Aboriginal communities and within the body politic. Beyond mere ignorance, which is an essential component of the Residential Schools story, deliberate silences have also existed on all sides of this issue. Those silences are reflected in the creative works of many Aboriginal artists, past and present. Despite the fairly recent attention paid to Aboriginal arts and literatures, there was a period of time when virtually no one was using Residential Schools as a context or, more boldly, as a character in literature. Contemporarily, however, there have been watershed moments in which these themes have emerged both within the art, as well as the scholarship that goes with it. We can safely say that concepts of health and healing are explored by First Nations, Inuit and Métis artists and scholars and have been present since time immemorial. This idea cannot be overemphasized; Indigenous peoples rightly seek to have others understand and accept that their ways of being and knowing — their knowledge, knowledge systems and cosmology — stand as distinctly Indigenous paradigms. Contact and the resultant forces of colonization are, for many Canadian Indigenous peoples, seen as recent history when placed within the context of a forever history.

In 2012, Canada's Indian Residential Schools Truth and Reconciliation Commission (TRC) released two publications: its *Interim Report* and *They Came for the Children,* the latter of which summarizes the historical facts and the trauma that ensued as follows:

> To put it simply: the needs of tens of thousands of Aboriginal children were neglected routinely. Far too many children were abused far too often. . . . Residential schools disrupted families and communities. They prevented elders from teaching children long-valued cultural and spiritual traditions and practices. They helped kill languages. These were not side effects of a well-intentioned system: the purpose of the residential school system was . . . to destroy their culture. The impact was devastating. Countless students emerged from the schools as lost souls, their lives soon to be cut short by drugs, alcohol, and violence. The last of the federally supported schools and residences, of which there were at least 150, closed in the 1990s (TRC, 2012).

The above passage describes a significant historical and contemporary swath of the landscape occupied by First Nations, Inuit and Métis. This landscape, from which, and into which, they engaged, is forever changing. The most significant recent development is the implementation of the historic Indian Residential Schools Settlement Agreement. With it, and its five components — most notably a Truth and Reconciliation Commission — we can safely say that a bright spotlight has begun to illuminate the truths of the experience and its legacy, although this spotlight has come with a price.

Basil Johnston's 1988 novel *Indian School Days* is one example of this illumination that came with a price. It was not the first autobiography, memoir or example of life writing that tackled the topic of Residential Schools to some degree (McCall, 2011; McKegney, 2007; Reder, 2009); however, this relatively well-known Anishinaabe writer shone a significant light toward the shadows. This text can be also understood as deliberately withholding some part of the story, even as it details many of the facts, figures and traumas, details we now accept as indisputable truths of the Residential Schools policy and lived experiences. Only recently have we begun to hear Johnston's account of what still lurked in those shadows:

> [*Indian School Days*] was intended to amuse readers, to recount and to relive some of the few cheerful moments in an otherwise dismal existence, a memorial to the disposition of my people, the Anishinaubaek, to find or to create levity even in the darkest moments. And this is how I

would like my book to be seen. Had I known what I now know, perhaps I might have written an entirely different text (Johnston in McKegney, 2007, p. viii).

When it was published, there were no references to sexual abuse. It was only later that Johnston began to discuss the subject, as he does in the frank foreword to Sam McKegney's *Magic Weapons: Aboriginal Writers Remaking Community after Residential School* (2007):

> I girded myself to tell the story I had never told before [to the lawyer representing hundreds of complainants from the Spanish Residential School in a class action lawsuit], without breaking down. But I broke down. I wept . . . For years I had laboured under the conviction that I was the only one to be debauched in Spanish Residential School. . . . During the negotiating meetings, not only did I learn that I was not the only one who had been befouled and desecrated, but that we had all been damaged in some way. Even those who had not been ravished suffered wounds, scars, and blemishes to heart, mind, and spirit that would never fully heal (pp. ix–x).

This type of experience, where individuals realized they were not the only ones to be damaged, continues even today, as Survivors continue to reconcile their own experiences and the scope of the abuse scandals. Increasingly, creative practice is being used as a way to further explore and come to terms with what happened to people. I will now turn my attention to a case study on organizational and creative methods for healing from abuse.

## Sharing, Healing and Learning in Northern Ontario: A Case Study

As the subject of Residential Schools has been explored through the arts, literature and scholarship, concepts of healing and reconciliation also began to develop and evolve in different ways and at different paces across the country. One of the most foundational was the work by the Aboriginal Healing Foundation's research and evaluation unit. Healing, in particular, became well-defined in grassroots efforts. The following section will explore such efforts, focusing on the Shingwauk Project in Northern Ontario, and will also touch on national, governmental and non-governmental efforts, most notably in the name, mandate and publications of the Aboriginal Healing Foundation.

The various healing movements, as others have described them (Legacy of Hope, 2012), overlap and are inextricably woven through and within the experience and legacy of Residential Schools. In fact, one may also argue that these healing movements are among the few positive legacies of Residential Schools, in contrast to the many painful and destructive legacies, which were first meaningfully illuminated at a grassroots levels during the late 1970s and early 1980s when former students came together for the first well-attended reunions or gatherings. This is particularly true in northern Ontario at the site of the former Shingwauk

Indian Residential School, now Algoma University (AU) in Sault Ste. Marie.

In 1979, Survivors and their supporters began to develop the Shingwauk Project, "a cross-cultural research and educational development project of Algoma University [then Algoma University College (AUC)] and [Survivors who would later form] the Children of Shingwauk Alumni Association (CSAA)." This was followed by the 1981 Shingwauk Reunion. The Survivors involved in this initiative deliberately chose the word "reunion" but later changed the terminology for future events, settling on the term "gathering." (It is also important to note that the idea of reunions was not taken up in other parts of Canada.) That reunion led to the development of Remember the Children: National Residential Schools Photo Identification Project, which built upon the fortuitously discovered positive – and healing – experience of Survivors sharing their stories with each other as they pored over photographs, identifying themselves and others, adding details and dates as notations to accompany the images and, ultimately, beginning the process of collecting, preserving and sharing this process programmatically with others affected by the legacy.

This form of documentation is an idea that was later picked up by Iroquois (Onondaga) curator, photographer and cultural critic Jeff Thomas in his critically acclaimed exhibition, Where Are the Children? Healing the Legacy of Residential Schools, developed for Library and Archives Canada and the Aboriginal Healing Foundation. He has spoken and written at length about both the challenges but also the power of working with archival photographs:

> When I began research for Where Are the Children? I found a large number of residential school photographs, but none that illustrated the kinds of experiences that Survivors have described or that directly imaged the abuses Survivors were disclosing. . . .
>
> Instead, I had to weave a story from photographs that had originally intended to show the so-called "good work" taking place at the schools and make that story meaningful to the indigenous community; not only the survivors, but their children and grandchildren, as well as the youth who are feeling the inter-generational impacts of that horrific history.
>
> The challenge of re-purposing the archival photographs was compounded by a traditional Indigenous suspicion of so-called "documentary" evidence – photographs, written reports, and tape recordings had been used for centuries by anthropologists and government agents in ways that did not speak to indigenous experiences or benefit their communities. I chose the story-telling tradition I learned from my elders as the exhibition framework. The photographs would tell a story, but not always the one they were originally intended to tell (LHF, 2011).

This lesson and Thomas' efforts to share his learning experience have, along with the Shingwauk Project proponents, greatly informed debates around the importance of archival photographs, and the challenges their application can engender. The Shingwauk Survivors and their allies were from all over Canada, sent to the Shingwauk School at the whim of Indian agents and school administrators. They were, and remain, Anishinaabe, Mushkegowuk, Haudenosaunee and many other national identities. But they also saw and continue to see themselves as a community — even a family — and part of something larger: *Shingwauk's Vision*.

The Shingwauk School, or "Teaching Wigwam," was originally envisaged by the great Ojibway Chief Shingwaukonse (1773–1854), also known as Shingwauk, as a crucible for cross-cultural understanding and synthesis of traditional Anishnabek and modern European knowledge and ways. Commissioned in 1832, in co-operation with the colonial government and Anglican Church as part of St. John's Mission to the Ojibway, the Shingwauk School was built by Rev. William McMurray and Shingwauk's Band and opened in Sault Ste. Marie in 1833, relocating to the current site as the Shingwauk and Wawanosh Industrial Homes (Shingwauk 1874–1935 and Wawanosh 1876–96/1896–1935) and the Shingwauk Indian Residential School (1935–70). As part of Chief Shingwauk's new strategy of Aboriginal rights, self-determination and modern community development, the School's cross-cultural educational project was also regarded by Shingwauk as essential to the restoration of cosmological balance and harmony between Aboriginal and non-Aboriginal Peoples, and between both Peoples and the natural environment (Miller, 1996).

As the former students of the Shingwauk School sought to reclaim a sense of community, to forge an identity as alumni of a school rather than deliberately forgotten and unceremoniously dismissed inmates of an institution of assimilation and conversion, they saw themselves as part of that greater vision. The Shingwauk Residential Schools Centre (SRSC) is a recent consolidation of two major initiatives of Algoma University and its partners, the Children of Shingwauk Alumni Association (CSAA) and the National Residential Schools Survivors Society (NRSSS): the Shingwauk Project, founded in 1979; and the Residential School Research, Archive and Visitor's Centre, founded in 2005. The founders of these decades-long efforts were brought together by their recognition of the profound importance of the commitment to the Shingwauk Trust and the relationship with Canada's Aboriginal Peoples that AU assumed upon its relocation in 1971, in partnership with the Keewatinung Anishnabek Institute, to the site of the former Shingwauk and Wawanosh Indian Residential Schools.

For over three decades the SRSC and its predecessors have partnered with many organizations including the Aboriginal Healing Foundation (AHF), the Anglican Church of Canada, the Dan Pine Healing Lodge, Nishnawbe-Aski Nation (NAN) and others to research, collect, preserve and display the history of Residential Schools across Canada; develop and deliver projects of "sharing, healing and learning" in relation to the impacts of the Schools, and of individual and community restoration; and accomplish "the true realization of Chief Shingwauk's Vision." All of this is built upon a foundation of the need and desire to create a surrogate community and family of fellow students and Survivors, broadly and specific to individual schools, to encompass all those with the common experience of being removed by law from their family as well as the tens of thousands of survivors of specific abuses. In effect, these efforts directly aim at addressing the effects of trauma and physical/cultural displacement caused by a system designed to sever ties to parents, cultures, languages and spiritual practices.

The work of the SRSC, and many at the university, has been inspired and informed by Shingwauk's Vision as represented by the Shingwauk Alumni and Elders. Initiatives undertaken by the SRSC have been numerous and varied: research, many reunions, healing circles, publications, videos, displays, curriculum development, historical tours, archive, library, document and photo collections, art installations, student and staff directories, website and visitors' centre, among others. As the project has developed, the partners have worked to accomplish nationally for former Residential School students what the Shingwauk Project did regionally.

Collections and services were expanded to include research; the collection of photographs, documents and information; and the development and/or circulation of educational material, including displays, publications and presentations regarding Indian and Inuit Residential and Day Schools across Canada and their impacts on Indian, Inuit and Métis students and their families and communities (Shingwauk.org).

The aforementioned Remember the Children: National Residential School Photo Identification Project, is an especially good example of how a collections, archiving, digitization, and distribution initiative with relevant partners can perform an important national service. It continues to be one of the most welcomed and appreciated initiatives of the centre, with its resources regularly taken to Residential School gatherings and other functions. As Thomas noted in his work with photographs, Survivors had recollections of photographs being taken but no expectation that the photographs were to help them remember their time as students, as most of us have found with school yearbooks and other initiatives. The reclaimed and newly discovered photographs and other material records of their experiences (workbooks, art work, even administrative records) allow Survivors to form a link with other Survivors, family members and siblings they were purposefully separated from, and to literally retrace where they had come from.

Digitization and distribution, and the sharing and discussions that follow, have been essential to the project's success as a healing initiative. The more resources are shared and discussed, the more new information and resources are donated and collected. Several dozen different books, touching upon Schools in all the provinces and territories where they existed, have been produced and made available. This foundational work led Survivors across the country to develop other healing initiatives and to lobby for still more action, including apology and redress.

## Apology and Redress

During these years (culminating in 2005 with the Agreement in Principle that would become the Indian Residential Schools Settlement Agreement), advocates across the country began to demand that those responsible for Residential School legislation, policies, mission and administration tell truths as well. At roughly the same time, various health, healing and social movements began to grow within and across Aboriginal communities, as Emma LaRocque explores in *When the Other Is Me: Native Resistance Discourse 1850–1990* (2010). Communities also began to demand and receive apologies from churches that had run particular schools. The first to apologize was the United Church of Canada in 1986. Other apologies and statements followed: the Oblate Missionaries of Mary Immaculate (Roman Catholic) in 1991, the Anglican Church in 1993, and the Presbyterian Church in 1994. See the work by Younging, et al. (2009), entitled "Timeline."

In 1991, Phil Fontaine, then Grand Chief of the Assembly of Manitoba Chiefs, publicly shared his story of the abuse he had suffered in the residential schools he had attended. As McKegney (2010) notes, "Fontaine's early efforts to intervene in this chronology of violence, like that of many courageous survivors, took the form of 'disclosure.' To disclose is to open up to view what has been hidden, to give voice to what has been silenced" (Mckegney, 2010, p.5). Fontaine told his first-person truth and encouraged others to do the same, which they began to do in greater numbers over the following decades.

However, the issue came to then unprecedented national prominence in 1996 with the release of the *Report of the Royal Commission on Aboriginal Peoples (RCAP Report)*. The commission was organized in large part as a response to the 1990 armed standoff at the Oka reserve in Quebec that came to be known as the Oka crisis (RCAP, 1996) but it raised much broader questions about the past and present realties of Canada's Aboriginal peoples. The authors of the *Report* write: "This Royal Commission on Aboriginal Peoples was born in a time of ferment when the future of the Canadian federation was being debated passionately. It came to fruition in the troubled months following the demise of the Meech Lake Accord and the confrontation, in the summer of 1990, between Mohawks and the power of the Canadian state at Kanesatake (Oka), Quebec" (RCAP, 1996).

We must remember how surprising it was for both the commissioners and their researchers, as well as for the government and public that received the report, that Survivor accounts of their experiences dominated all aspects of the inquiry into the realities of Aboriginal peoples in Canada. The negative impacts of the Residential School experience for Survivors and their descendants loomed large throughout the *RCAP Report*. In fact, RCAP received in excess of 60,000 formal complaints of abuse suffered while attending one or more schools (Fournier and Crey, 1998, p. 49). The many shocking details led to the 1998 federal policy document entitled *Gathering Strength: Canada's Aboriginal Action Plan.*

RCAP paved the way for the creation, in March 1998, of the Aboriginal Healing Foundation (AHF), a national, Aboriginal-managed, not-for-profit corporation funded by a grant of $350 million. The AHF was given an eleven-year mandate to encourage and support community-based, Aboriginal-directed healing initiatives that would address the legacy of physical and sexual abuse suffered in the residential school system and its intergenerational impacts (Aboriginal Healing Foundation, 2012). In 2005, the government of Canada committed an additional

$40 million to the AHF for a further two-year period through March 31, 2007, enabling the AHF to extend 88 projects for 36 months. This funding augmented the initial $350 million but did not extend the timing of the AHF mandate and no new projects were funded.

These additional funds were intended to carry the AHF and its funded projects through to the implementation of the Indian Residential School Settlement Agreement, which would take place on September 19, 2007. During these years, individual lawsuits against government, churches, and perpetrators grew in number, as did class action lawsuits such as the one Johnston mentions. This wave of activity led to negotiations that culminated in 2005 with an agreement-in-principle for the multi-billion dollar Indian Residential Schools Settlement Agreement that was finalized on September 19, 2007. Two components of the IRSSA in particular received significant (and often negative) mainstream attention: compensation and the creation of a Truth and Reconciliation Commission (TRC).

There are two compensation elements: first, the Common Experience Payment (CEP), a process through which all former students who can prove their residency at a school on the government-approved list could apply for compensation based on a formula of $10,000 for the first year of attendance and $3,000 for each additional year; and second, the Independent Assessment Process for specific abuse claims. The media attention in 2007 was decidedly negative, focusing on speculation that Survivors would not or could not handle an influx of money responsibly, and that it would lead to drug and alcohol abuse, violence and financial predation. The AHF conducted two studies that explore these issues: *Lump Sum Compensation Payments Research Project: The Circle Rechecks Itself* (2007) and *The Indian Residential Schools Settlement Agreement's Common Experience Payment and Healing: A Qualitative Study Exploring Impacts on Recipients* (2010).

The TRC was meant to be an official, independent body with a five-year mandate to provide former students and anyone else affected by the Indian Residential School System with an opportunity to share, through statement-taking, their individual experiences in a safe and culturally appropriate manner.

The TRC finally got under way in September 2007 and the commissioners began their work on June 1, 2008. Despite all these developments, the legacy of Residential Schools only received true national prominence on June 11, 2008, when Prime Minister Stephen Harper delivered an official apology in the House of Commons. The full amount of needed funding, however, was not guaranteed. Survivor advocates and supporters, including Health Canada, responded to the absence of additional funding for healing in the federal budget of 2010, but recommendations to that end were ignored by the government of Canada.

As more and more Aboriginal artists engage Residential Schools in overtly thematic ways this will, by sheer necessity, grow to include the notion of apology. Take, for example, playwright Drew Hayden Taylor, never one to shy away from controversial topics. Taylor, a regular contributor to Canada's national and regional newspapers, wrote "Cry Me a River, White Boy." In typical Taylor fashion, this jokey but pointed personal essay attempts to contextualize the experience of hearing, viewing, *receiving* the Apology, from his personal and cultural perspective:

> *Aabwehyehnmigziwin* is the Anishnawbe word for apology. That is what Prime Minister Stephen Harper delivered in the House of Commons on the eleventh of June 2008 to the Survivors of Canada's residential school system. . . . I know a lot of people who were a little cynical about the sincerity of the apology. That is their right. If an abusive husband apologizes to his abused wife and kids, however sincere it might sound, some may doubt the authenticity of that apology. Same as in this situation, an admission of responsibility is as good a place as any to start. Ask any lawyer. But the healing must start somewhere (Taylor, 2009, p. 94).

And for many Survivors, that starting point is in creative work.

## Art and Truth and Reconciliation

The TRC has also made an open call for artist submissions, initially placing the call firmly on the testimony side of its mandate with a more refined and detailed description that followed, saying that the TRC:

> . . . believes that artists have a profound contribution to make in expressing both truth and reconciliation. The TRC invites all artists to submit works that relate to experiences at Indian Residential Schools or that relate to the legacy and impact of those experiences on former students, parents, future generations, communities, and on relationships within families and between communities. In addition, the TRC invites artists to submit works relating to apology, truth, cultural oppression, cultural genocide, resistance, resilience, spirituality, remembrance, reconciliation, rejuvenation and restoration of Aboriginal culture and pride. Why is the Truth and Reconciliation Commission of Canada gathering artistic works? The TRC believes that collecting artistic works is an important and meaningful way to express the truth, impact and legacy of the Residential School experience and to assist with reconciliation (*Open Call*).

Many Survivors and others impacted by the legacy have submitted artworks to the TRC. It goes without saying, of course, that Aboriginal artists have been exploring the above themes for decades, that a call by a TRC in 2009 was not *the* catalyst for Residential Schools-related art. It may prove to be *a* catalyst, however. The AHF's funding certainly was a catalyst for poet and playwright Armand Garnet Ruffo, who responded to an early call put out by the AHF to begin work on the screenplay that would eventually become *A Windigo Tale* (2010). He, too, notes the silence in relation to Residential Schools and the trauma experienced there: "[In the 1960s, '70s and '80s] nobody talked about it. . . . We played right by the residential school. When I'd ask my mother what's that building she'd say, don't worry about that and then eventually it was torn down" (Dewar, *Ruffo Interview*,

2010*)*. And with regard to themes of truth and reconciliation he says:

> [W]hen I'm writing . . . I don't say "This is a play, or this is a book about reconciliation." It doesn't work that way. The story itself has its own kind of integrity and its own impetus and I just go along with it. But because I'm thinking about those issues, they find their way into the story. . . .

But *A Windigo Tale* was very much about healing:

> [W]hat struck me is that [Armstrong and Highway] were dealing with [Residential Schools] in an oblique way, not hitting it dead on. But really talking about the impact of it more, and that's what I was interested in, as well, loss of culture . . . and language. So that became a big issue and of course residential schools did come up, because that's why most of us have lost it, either directly or indirectly. . . . So I wanted to talk about those issues as well, like we were all doing [at the Enowkin Centre in Penticton, B.C. in the 1980s and early 1990s]. . . . [Y]ou've been interviewing writers and painters and other artists and I bet they all talk about their work in terms of healing. I don't know any Native artist who doesn't. I mean we might say yes, it's really about the story, and yes it's about the color, it's about the visual impact of what I'm doing, but in a sense, by just creating voice, it's healing.

And the healing connection goes even deeper, with artists realizing the importance of creating a space for Indigenous voices to speak to these experiences, which builds on a tradition of addressing suppression of identity through arts and literatures. As Ruffo said:

> When I got the money from the [AHF] I knew that their mandate was healing, education, and so I started writing the screenplay and I wouldn't say that I tailored it to them because the story was already there, but I knew it was a good fit. . . . Was it opportunistic? No. That's what I wanted to do after coming from the Enowkin Centre. I left knowing I wanted to expose, show, tell a story that talked about this intergenerational impact.

In the closing decades of the twentieth century, many artists wrote back to the empire (Ashcroft et al., 1995). In fact, there was a proliferation of heralded Aboriginal literature that one could argue fits the postcolonial mould and, as such, much heralded scholarship developed alongside as well. There were also critiques of reading Aboriginal literatures as postcolonial, as LaRocque (2010) notes in her exploration of Native resistance discourse, writing that "Native Canadians hardly enjoy 'postcoloniality' since their colonial experience is imbricated with the past and present" (Larocque, 2010, p. 23). And Thomas King (1990) has written, "[T]he term itself assumes that the starting point for that discussion is the advent of Europeans in North America" ("Godzilla," p. 11) and that postcolonial theory cuts Indigenous North Americans off from their history and cultures, passed down through generations in spite of colonization. Another important point that LaRocque makes, which is extremely relevant to this context, is this cautionary note about an "aesthetic of healing":

> As constructive as [it may sound], we must be careful not to squeeze the life out of native literature by making it serve, yet again, another utilitarian function. Poets, playwrights, and novelists, among others, must also write for the love of words. Healing is fast becoming the new cultural marker by which we define or judge Aboriginal literature. (LaRocque, 2010, p. 168)

Some may see this as contradictory to many artists' and critics' assertions that, as Jo-Ann Episkenew writes, "Contemporary Indigenous writers manipulate the English language and its literary traditions to narrate Indigenous experiences under colonialism in an effort to heal themselves and their audiences from the colonial trauma" (2009, p. 12). Though this may seem contradictory, it is not; rather it speaks to the complexity of the role of art in healing. Simply ask First Nations, Inuit, and Métis writers. I realize that suggestion is anathema to many critics who, perhaps primarily in decades past, decry such a need or critical focus. But times have changed. I do, however, share LaRocque's concern. I also argue there is far more to say about *healing* than about *reconciliation*.

## Healing and Reconciliation: Discourse and Debates

Just as Aboriginal artists and scholars rejected post-colonialism, some also reject notions of reconciliation. Taiaiake Alfred and Jeff Corntassel (2005) argue that the reconciliation discourse is, in fact, flawed at its very roots:

> Far from reflecting any true history or honest reconciliation with the past or present agreements and treaties that form an authentic basis for Indigenous-state relations in the Canadian context, "aboriginalism" is a legal, political and cultural discourse designed to serve an agenda of silent surrender to an inherently unjust relation at the root of the colonial state itself (Alfred and Corntassel, 2005, p. 598).

The authors reject the term "aboriginal" outright in favour of "Indigenous," arguing that the former "identity is purely a state construction that is instrumental to the state's own attempt to gradually subsume Indigenous existences into its own constitutional system and body politic." Alfred further calls reconciliation an "emasculating concept" (2005, p. 152), saying that

> [r]econciliation as a concept or process is not as compelling, factually or logically speaking, as resurgence because, being so embedded in the supposedly progressive discourses on Onkwehonwe-Settler [Aboriginal-

non-Aboriginal] relations . . . it is almost unassailable from within established legal and political discourses, thus presenting a huge obstacle to justice and real peacemaking. . . . [Without] massive restitution . . . for past harms and continuing injustices committed against our peoples, reconciliation would permanently enshrine colonial injustices and is itself a further injustice (2005, p. 152).

Alfred further argues we must place the discourse within the broader colonial context of Canada's history and present, otherwise Indigenous-Settler relations will continue to be built on a foundation of "false decolonization" (2005, p. 112) which continues to be immoral. Alfred attacks the notion of Indigenous peoples being "victims of history" (2005, p. 130), arguing that the discourse has been too conciliatory on the Indigenous side, with Indigenous people seeking only to "*recover* from the past" (emphasis in original) and settling for White notions of reconciliation. This is not resistance or "survivance," Gerald Vizenor's (1999) concept of survival and resistance. Instead it is acquiescence to "a *resolution* that is acceptable to and non-disruptive for the state and society that we have come to embrace and identify with" (Vizenor, 1999). Others, like Thomas King in *The Inconvenient Indian (2012)*, argue less for rejection of reconciliation but rather for the same kind of caution called for by LaRocque. King's work looks to tell some of the truths about Aboriginal/non-Aboriginal relations, with this particular work attempting to do so quite comprehensively. Of Canada's prospects for reconciliation, King can be said to argue that ignorance is not the problem; rather, "[t]he problem was and continues to be unexamined confidence in western civilization and the unwarranted certainty of Christianity. And arrogance. Perhaps it is unfair to judge the past by the present, but it is also necessary" (King, 2012, p. 265).

Like King, who highlights loss of languages and culture, Jeannette Armstrong (2010) zeroes in on the specifics of reconciliation in practice:

My concern has been mostly about the broader effects to our Indigenous Nations (as opposed to the heinous effects on individuals which other experts are engaged in) in regard to the decline and extinctions of original languages and cultures as a result of the subtractive (to indigenous culture) and submersion (in colonial culture) education process that the schools were about. The loss of language is a loss of a way to see and experience the world from within an Indigenous perspective unique to each specific place each language and culture is indigenous to. The concept has been the subject at the centre of all of my arts, my writing, my activism in arts and culture as well as indigenous rights, and my work in culture and language revitalization, for living indigenous language renewal, for authentic indigenous arts practice recovery, for the revival in education pedagogy, of indigenous philosophy (I don't like to use the word "knowledge" since it has other connotations) and science perspectives. I believe that the role of reconciliation in a broader sense must provide ways and means to assist in the remedy of what has been destroyed. . . . Understanding the whole picture is the first step to reconciliation. It seems to me, only an artist might attempt to make these visible whether through formal or informal response as artist (interview with Armstrong, 2010).

And she has gone further in her writings with what we might call the theory of *En'owkin*: "[T]his idea of community, as understood by my ancestors, encompassed a holistic view of interconnectedness that demands our responsibility to everything we are connected to" (Armstrong, 1999. p. 3). This, too, is a note of caution. And how do we practice that — or the responsible, ethical, and indigenous-centred literary criticism of Indigenous writings (Sinclair and Eigenbrod, 2009)? First, we acknowledge that the jury is still out on the practice of reconciliation, particularly with regard to Canada's and individual Canadians' coming to terms with the history and living legacy of Residential Schools. And, in terms of reconciliation being a part of Indigenous literatures in the same way we may argue that these works tell *truths* and do or do not contribute to *healing*, we should, first and foremost, consider ensuring that said jury is comprised of the real experts — those engaged in ongoing survival despite the conditions wrought by centuries of legislation and policy meant to destabilize and eradicate Indigenous cultures.

## Conclusions

What has been presented above does not mean that only Survivors can speak of Residential Schools, or that only Aboriginal scholars can study and teach Aboriginal arts and literatures or issues generally. But these topics do require a careful and critical consideration of the Aboriginal/Settler/ally relationship. This chapter argued that such a topic is still nascent, and one that has itself been destabilized by the significant recent developments, many of which have left individual Survivors "reeling," as well as those who have been affected at an intergenerational level. Many others continue the work of supporting their fellow Survivors. As such, we owe them our support, primarily through the acceptance that they are leaders in the efforts to educate Canada and the world about our shared history. This is a key point of departure for those who work as allies in these efforts.

This chapter underscored the importance of photographs and records (and the archives and collections that hold those records) not simply as essential to enhancing the historical record but also to Survivors' individual and collective efforts to heal from and reconcile their experiences. Photographs and records also enhance others' capacities to empathize with these experiences and legacies and, as the Shingwauk project purports, to share, heal and learn in turn. Further to these ends, creative outputs, particularly the Survivor memoir and other narratives, whether literary, visual, textile or performative, continue to be extremely useful healing tools, for the author/artist him/herself, whether supported by the handful of formal funding opportunities and/or other supportive initiatives or endeavoured independently, and for the audiences who encounter these stories of trauma, dislocation, resilience and resistance, and survival. The Shingwauk Residential School Centre is one example of an initiative where these many elements come together under a Survivor-led partnership between former Residential School students, their families and communities, and a mainstream post-secondary institution.

## References

Aboriginal Healing Foundation (2012). FAQs. Retrieved from www.ahf.ca/faqs.

Aboriginal Healing Foundation (2007). *Lump Sum Compensation Payments Research Project: The Circle Rechecks Itself*. Ottawa: Aboriginal Healing Foundation.

Aboriginal Healing Foundation. (2010). *The Indian Residential Schools Settlement Agreement's Common Experience Payment and Healing: A Qualitative Study Exploring Impacts on Recipients* Ottawa: Aboriginal Healing Foundation.

Alfred, T. (2005). *Wasáse: Indigenous Pathways of action and Freedom*. Peterborough, ON: Broadview.

Alfred, T., & Corntassel, J. (2005) Being Indigenous: Resurgences against contemporary colonialism. *Government and Opposition 40*(4), 597–614.

Armstrong, J. (1999). Let us begin with courage. *Centre for Ecoliteracy*. Retrieved from http://www.ecoliteracy.org/publications/pdf/jarmstrong_letusbegin.pdf.

Ashcroft, B., Griffiths, G., & Tiffin, H. (1995). *The empire writes back: Theory and practice in post-colonial literature*. New York: Routledge.

Brant Castellano, M., Archibald, L., & DeGagné, M. (2008). Timeline. *From truth to reconciliation*. Ottawa: Aboriginal Healing Foundation.

*Canadian Journal of Native Studies* (2009), *29* (1 & 2).

Chartrand, L.N., Logan, T.E., & Daniels, J.D. (2006). *Métis history and experience and Residential Schools in Canada*. Ottawa: Aboriginal Healing Foundation.

Chrisjohn, R., & Young, S. (1997). *The circle game: Shadows and substance in the Indian Residential School experience in Canada*. Penticton, B.C.: Theytus Books.

Dewar, J. (2011). Interview with Armand Garnet Ruffo. Unpublished.

Dewar, J. (2010). Interview with Jeannette Armstrong. Unpublished.

Dickason, O., & McNab, D. T. (2009). *Canada's First Nations: A history of founding peoples from earliest times* (4th ed.). Toronto: Oxford University Press.

Episkenew, J. (2009). *Taking back our spirits: Indigenous literature, public policy, and healing*. Winnipeg: University of Manitoba Press.

Fournier, S., & Cray, E. (1998). *Stolen from our embrace: The abduction of Aboriginal children and the restoration of Aboriginal communities*. Toronto: Douglas & McIntyre.

Johnston, B. (1989). *Indian school days*. Norman, OK: University of Oklahoma Press.

King, T. (1990) Godzilla vs. postcolonial. *World literature written in English, 30*(2), 10–16.

King, T. (2012). *The inconvenient Indian: A curious account of Native people in North America*. Toronto: Random House.

LaRocque, E. (2010). *When the other is me: Native resistance discourse, 1850–1990*. Winnipeg: University of Manitoba Press.

Legacy of Hope Foundation (2012). Where are the children? Healing the legacy of Residential Schools website. Retrieved from http://www.legacyofhope.ca/projects/where-are-the-children/website.

Legacy of Hope Foundation (2013). The healing movement. Posted on Where are the children? Healing the legacy of Residential Schools website. Retrieved from http://www.wherearethechildren.ca/en/blackboard/page-18.html.

Lemkin, R. (1944). *Axis rule in occupied Europe: Laws of occupation, analysis of government, proposals for redress*. Washington: Carnegie Endowment for International Peace.

McCall, S. (2011). *First person plural: Aboriginal storytelling and the ethics of collaborative authorship*. Vancouver: University of British Columbia Press.

McKegney, S. (2007). *Magic weapons: Aboriginal writers remaking community after Residential School*. Winnipeg: University of Manitoba Press.

Miller, J. R. (1996). *Shingwauk's Vision: A history of Native Residential Schools*. Toronto: University of Toronto Press.

Milloy, J. S. (1999). *A national crime: The Canadian government and the Residential School system, 1879 to 1986*. Winnipeg: University of Manitoba Press.

Reder, D. (2009). Writing autobiographically: A neglected Indigenous intellectual tradition. In *Across cultures, across borders: Canadian Aboriginal and Native American literatures*. Peterborough, ON: Broadview Press.

Ruffo, A.G. (producer/writer/director). (2010). *A Windigo tale: the feature film*. Retrieved from http://www.awindigotale.com.

Shingwauk Residential Schools Centre (2013). *The Shingwauk Project*. Retrieved from http://www.shingwauk.org/srsc/node/7.

Taylor, D. H. (2009) Cry me a river, white boy. In Younging, G., Dewar, J. & DeGagné, M. (Eds.), *Response, responsibility, and renewal: Canada's truth and reconciliation journey*. Ottawa: Aboriginal Healing Foundation: Ottawa.

Truth and Reconciliation Commission of Canada (2013). *Open Call for Artistic Submissions*. Retrieved from http://www.trc.ca/websites/trcinstitution/index.php?p=194.

Truth and Reconciliation Commission of Canada (2012). *The Truth and Reconciliation Commission of Canada: Interim report*. Winnipeg: Truth and Reconciliation Commission.

Truth and Reconciliation Commission of Canada (2012). *They came for the children: Aboriginal peoples and Residential Schools*. Winnipeg: Truth and Reconciliation Commission.

Vizenor, G. (1999). *Manifest manners: Narratives on postindian survivance*. Lincoln, NE: University of Nebraska Press.

## CHAPTER SEVENTEEN

# Art as a Tool for Resistance and Recovery

## *Bethany Osborne*

In this chapter, I will explore alternative approaches to working with people who have experienced violence. I will focus on the impact of violence on the individual and on the broader community to which they belong. Drawing on work being done around the world, with a particular focus on Canada, this chapter will examine how we can use art to support people who have experienced violence, with the goal of recovery from trauma. Another important aspect of this chapter will be to examine various coping and healing strategies, including arts-based approaches to empowering individuals and communities who have been impacted by violence. This chapter concludes by providing practical resources needed to start your own creative empowerment support group.

### Introduction to the Trauma of Forced Migration

Elie Wiesel (1996) described the time that we are living in as "the age of the expatriate, the refugee, the stateless and the wanderer." He states that "[n]ever before have so many human beings fled from so many homes" (Wiesel,

> **Learning Activity**
>
> *Test yourself:* What do you know about working with immigrants and refugees who have experienced violence in their migration journey?
>
> 1. Name three different approaches that you have learned for working with individuals and families.
> 2. How would you approach working with a refugee family who has just arrived from a country affected by war or conflict? Why would you choose this approach?
> 3. What are some of the challenges that this family would face in trying to settle in Canada?
> 4. What kinds of resources would this family need? How do you think they could attain these things?
> 5. Do you think that art could be used in helping people recover from their experiences of violence? If you answered yes, think of some ways that you could use art in working with clients who have experienced violence. If you answered no, explain why you don't think that art could be used in this context.

1996, p. 19). The reasons for forced migration are many but you will find violence, in one of its many forms, at the root. There is no one state that is innocent of repressing or discriminating against one or more people or groups. Canada has its own history of violence and forced migration, beginning with the treatment of Indigenous people. We often think about colonization as happening in other countries but the current state and government in Canada is a result of British (and French) colonization of North America. White British and French settlers displaced the Aboriginal peoples of Canada, taking their land and their livelihoods through both direct violent action and then through the more subtle action of unfair land treaties. In an attempt to assimilate the first peoples, the church and state established a residential school system, forcing aboriginal children from their families into the schools. Within these schools, children were not permitted to speak their language and often faced many kinds of abuse (Chansonneuve, 2005).

The impacts of colonization are far-reaching and span generations. It is one of the forces that have shaped the world that we now live in, privileging some groups of people over others. Oppressive forces like imperialism, fascism, patriarchy and capitalism are other factors that contribute to forced migration globally. Francisca's case study, which is interwoven throughout this chapter, illustrates some of the different kinds of violence that immigrants and refugees face before they arrive in Canada. Like the Aboriginal people of Canada, their experiences of violence do not end when they have been relocated. They encounter systemic barriers to integration in their new country and must deal with the legacy of their experiences of violence.

## Case Study 17.1: Francisca, Part One[1]

Francisca Valdez grew up in a small town in South America. She dreamt about becoming a writer. At age 16, there was a military coup in her country followed by a curfew that was imposed to stop all resistance to the dictatorship. Francisca felt frustrated and powerless to do anything about it. Eventually, with the support of her brothers and friends, she published a small newspaper criticizing the new government. They used an old printing press in the basement of her uncle's house. Her uncle warned them to be careful, and to use the back door when entering the house. One day her uncle's home was raided, and Francisca's uncle and two team members were arrested. Fearful for their lives, Francisca and her brothers decided to leave the city for a few weeks. They went separately, arranging a rendezvous a short distance away. While on her way to the bus station, Francisca was arrested and taken to the police station, and from there, to prison. Her captors tortured her, but were unsuccessful in extracting information from her. She was sentenced to 10 years for treason. During one of their visits, her parents told her that two of her brothers had managed to escape into the mountains but that her oldest brother had been executed. Francisca spent many dark days in prison and at times felt like giving up. It was

---

[1] The subject of this case study, Francisca Valdez was created to illustrate the experiences of many different women and men living in countries that use violence to control those who resist their policies.

her fellow prisoners who supported her, becoming like family to her. After five years, Francisca's parents finally managed to bribe an official for her early release. The world seemed so big and so bright as they drove from the prison to her parent's home. Soon, Francisca understood that the political situation hadn't changed and that she would still be in great danger. Her parents helped her to obtain a fake passport and said their tearful good-byes. Two months later, her parents received a message — Francisca had arrived in Canada and had applied for refugee status. They were relieved that she was safe but wondered what kind of life their daughter would have in this new country.

## Reflective Questions

In the case study above, Francisca, her family and her friends experienced many kinds of violence.

1.  Can you name some of the different types of violence that they experienced?
2.  What kind of effects do you think these violent acts could have had on the different people involved (Francisca, her mother, her father, her brothers, their friends, the larger community)?
3.  If you were working in the field and you met someone with a story like Francisca's, how would you begin working with her?

John Paul and Angela Jill Lederach (2010) propose that healing done in the context of community is **social healing** — a place of healing that exists "between micro-individual healing and a wider collective reconciliation" (p. 6). They suggest that social healing requires that the community which has experienced violence locate both the individual and collective voice in order that the process of healing can begin (Lederach and Lederach, 2010, p. 7). When the community is included in the recovery process, the possibility for rebuilding the community and for resisting oppression emerges.

In the next sections, we will look at diverse creative approaches to working with people who have experienced violence and displacement. First, we will look at North American and, more broadly, western approaches to recovery — individual therapy and support groups. We will concentrate on the way that support groups function and can play an important role in the recovery process. We will then look at the function of art and creative expression as tools to help in the recovery process and to move people to a place of active resistance. We will also examine the importance of storytelling within the context of community and within public forums, for personal healing and to impact social and political change.

### The Road to Recovery: Individual Therapy and Mutual Support Groups

Because violence often has a negative impact on individuals, families and communities, and also creates distance, distrust and disconnection between people, healing and recovery need to be about reconnection, reconstruction and finding meaning (Swinomish Tribal Mental Health Project, 2002, p. 77). Within the North American and western contexts, the typical approach to working with people who have experienced trauma involves individual counselling or therapy as well as support groups or dynamic group therapy (Montgomery, 2002). Individual counselling or therapy is often partnered with dynamic group therapy. Both are held in a therapeutic setting and are dependent on feedback from the therapist who is facilitating the process. In the case of individual therapy, a client brings up an issue or issues, and the therapist listens and responds to the concerns. The feedback that the therapist gives the client can vary depending on the particular therapeutic approach that the therapist subscribes to. This kind of relationship takes time to build and so the therapeutic effect may take some time to emerge (Tomasulo, 2010). Dynamic group therapy often involves interaction with people outside of a client's social and familial network. The facilitator often has specialized training in group therapy. Dynamic group therapy is often used in conjunction with individual counselling or therapy (Tomasulo, 2010).

Mutual support groups (also called mutual aid and mutual help groups) are one type of dynamic group therapy. This approach to recovery is distinct because it encourages members to talk about different themes and insights that they have in relation to their own experiences. The facilitator is present to help guide the discussion, but does not position themselves as an expert. Individual therapeutic approaches are also very central to the North American and western context. In fact, all of the major systems or theories of counselling or therapy have emerged from the western world, and so there is a need to consider the structure and needs of people coming from other cultures (Patterson, 1978). Our identities are often closely tied to our communities and that is even more the case in non-western cultures, including those of Canada's Aboriginal peoples (Chansonneuve, 2005). It is in the context of our families and our communities that we establish who we are and that we can continue to be ourselves. When we focus predominantly on the individual in the recovery process, we miss a large part of the picture. Healing strategies that only target individuals are not enough to help someone who has experienced violence to recover. Over the last five decades, front-line practitioners have long seen the value of support groups because they foster community, allow people to share experiences, break isolation and help develop new friendships. In the process, a sense of hope and possibility is born. Mutual support groups provide a place where people can affirm that they have agency and can affect positive change, healing some of the things that are wrong with society.

Mutual support groups play an important role, either by themselves or in conjunction with individual or family counselling, by giving survivors an opportunity to share experiences and break their sense of isolation. Sometimes these groups stop at the point of both giving and receiving personal healing, but there are other groups that go one step further, to give group members a growing sense of their capacity to engage with and combat oppressive systemic societal forces.

There are important issues to take into consideration when establishing a support group, facilitating a support group and connecting clients to a mutual support group as part of their recovery process. Recruiting people for a support group is not something that will necessarily happen quickly or easily. For people to be willing to join a support group and talk about their experiences of violence, they need to trust that the process will be helpful for them. Either the organization that is hosting the mutual support group and/or the facilitator of the group must have a good reputation with the community. The organization or facilitator may also need to begin building relationships with possible participants before they even start attending a mutual support group. It is typical for clients from other programs offered by an organization to be referred to a mutual support group (CCVT, n.d.). For recovery to take place, participants need to feel a sense of both emotional and physical safety. As a result, it is also important to think about the space you will be using and to discuss with the participants as a group the kinds of boundaries that need to be in place for them to feel a sense of safety and security (Partners in Education and Outreach, 2007). Professional ethics should be followed and it is important to put an accountability structure in place through your organization (White, 2007). Working with people who have experienced violence can have a significant impact on you as the facilitator, and so it is important that you observe healthy self-care practices.

One of the most important things for you to remember as a practitioner working in the community and/or social service sector is the fact that you are not alone. You need to use available resources to support both yourself and your clients. Helping an individual like Francisca can be an important step in supporting them to move forward. It is important to provide clients with spaces where they can meet others who have had similar experiences, and where they are encouraged to use creative expression as a tool to express and to resist. Whether you are connecting to existing programming or working with staff and clients to create new spaces, you will be surprised at the positive changes that you will see in your clients as they begin to remember their capacity to function as agents of change in a world impacted by violence. As you work with clients and help them to process through the trauma that they have experienced, you are actively engaging in the fight against violence in all of its forms. This is an incredibly important role to play.

As people gain confidence in their capacity to engage with and effect positive change in their lives and in society, they can begin to move forward. This process happens as people "become aware of the power dynamics at work in their interpersonal and societal contexts" and as they "develop the skills and capacity for gaining more control over their lives [and] exercise this control without infringing upon the rights of others, and support others in the same process" (McWhirter, 1991, p. 224). As people begin this process and connect with others who are engaged in a similar process, larger scale change is possible. This will be discussed further in the sections on "Art as Recovery" and "Art as Resistance" with specific examples of groups formed of women and men who have participated in a process of recovery that moved them from a place of individual recovery to collective recovery through advocacy and activism.

## Case Study 17.2: Francisca, Part Two

By the time Francisca arrived in Canada, she was exhausted. Her journey had included many close brushes with border control, and at times she had feared for her safety and even her life. She found it hard to believe that she was finally safe. Her ESL teacher referred her to a community organization that supported people who had experienced state violence. She began individual counselling and her counsellor suggested that she join a support group. The first day that Francisca attended the group, she found a room full of people engaged in different art projects. Some people were sitting at tables writing, others were painting on easels and there were others listening to music and dancing in the far corner. It also looked like there were people in the room from around the world. Francisca wasn't sure what to do. The group facilitator, Shova, invited her to choose an art form to work with. Francisca had loved Plasticine and clay when she was a child and so she chose a table full of blocks of Plasticine. She created a picture of the ocean meeting the sky, the view from her family's home. Shova eventually asked people to share and some people showed pictures representing their homes, others pictures that represented the violence they had experienced. One group from Somalia performed a small dance performance, representing life in a refugee camp, and a woman from Iran read a poem she had written. Shova led a discussion about possible ways of sharing their creative work with others and they began to plan for an exhibit and performance. At the end of the session, Francisca felt more at home than she had in months. She walked to her apartment, thinking about possibilities for the first time in a long time.

## Art as Recovery

The purpose of art workshops such as the one described in the case study above is to provide a space for people who had experienced violence to express themselves. For many people, an art workshop or support group is the first opportunity they have to talk about their experiences of violence. Not everyone who attends a support group has had the same experience of violence, although there are always points of commonality. Violence causes people to lose things that are important to them — family or friends, their physical health, their social standing, a chance for an education, as well as loss of community and loss of home. These significant losses can cause people to lose a sense of who they are. Violence can also affect the way you perceive yourself or the world around you, as it calls into question basic human relationships, breaches attachments, shatters the construction of self and undermines belief systems (Herman, 1992, p. 51). People who have suffered the violence of incarceration, torture, loss of loved ones or loss of country have often been traumatized. The impacts of trauma on individual and community are complex and depend on many factors such as the capacity for resiliency, type and duration of trauma, and the personal and/or societal conditions that exist once the direct trauma has stopped. Part of the process of recovery requires the people who have experienced violence to remember it, because it is only as they remember that they are able to begin the process of healing. Jenna Wu (2011) suggests "remembering is a much-needed 'ethical act' and the healing process cannot begin if the truth of unjust suffering is forgotten even before it is uncovered, discussed, understood, and properly dealt with" (pp. 3–4). The kind of healing that I am referring to is the increased freedom that people experience through remembering and telling their stories. People who are in the recovery process often describe this as a process of untangling their emotions, removing barriers of fear or panic, feeling more able to be themselves (Osborne, 2014). Remembering with others provides people with support; it also provides the opportunity for those who have experienced violence to give testimony and those hearing the stories to bear witness to the atrocities that were committed. This is all part of the healing process.

In the case of traumatic events, the way people remember publicly can obscure meaning and leave the true nature of the event in question. There are particular memories that are acknowledged by the nation-state or society and others that are not. This makes it difficult for people who had different lived experiences than what the prevailing memories are at a societal level. Remembering is complicated because it is often partnered with forgetting. This may be because the events the individual or group experienced were so devastating or because to remember events differently than the "official version" endorsed by the state may put individuals or communities in danger. Forgetting can become a key element in the construction of collective memory when individuals censor themselves. Their thoughts, words and actions are censored to avoid the pain of remembering the horrors of the past. This can occur in an effort to protect their equilibrium or, in the case of people continuing to live in the nation-state or society that perpetrated the violence, it may be essential to protecting their physical well-being (Espinoza, 2004, p. 55).

Societies emerging from periods of violence often harbour competing and conflicting understandings of the past and intense struggles over memory (Espinoza, 2004, p. 55). Essentially, they allow the forgetting of past experiences of violence to govern the present, in order to maintain a sense of safety and security for themselves and their families (Lira, 1997). Sometimes breaking the silence about the experiences of violence creates a risk for the individuals. In breaking silence, often one has to confront "institutional amnesia and official denial by the state itself, as forms of social and ideological control" (Rogers, Leyersdorf and Dawson, 1999, p. 11). For some people who are living in the diaspora because they needed to flee an oppressive state, breaking silence also comes with a great personal risk to both self and family members.

One particular case of this occurred in Guatemalan history during a period known as *la Violencia* (1978–1985). Following this violent period, the government forbade public mention of the atrocities it had committed in order to promote their version of the past. Like many oppressive regimes, the Guatemalan government blamed the dead and their rebellious acts for the violence (Zur, 1999, p. 49). Despite the consequences of speaking about their experiences, war widows have refused to be silenced and have found ways to tell their stories. These women talk about their experiences with people they perceive to be *"de la misma cabeza"* (literally, "of the same head"). They transform religious rites into opportunities to share their stories and experiences, because men are forbidden to participate in rites that involve female shamans. In less secure settings, women have developed linguistic codes and gestures that cannot be understood outside their circles (Zur, 1999, p. 49). By telling their stories, these widows are able to reposition themselves in the past — a past that, according to the government, never happened. The result of this is the construction of a sense of continuity and the restoration of dignity (Zur, 1999, p. 45). Because the unofficial version is forbidden by the government, their private thoughts and the speaking of those memories functioned as political acts of resistance. This type of remembering can help to realign purpose and give the community a sense of shared history, in remembering their resistance and survival. As people remember together, their remembering becomes an act of resistance.

## Art as Resistance

One of the important expressions of memory, particularly traumatic memory, has been the arts. The arts can be broadly defined as creative expression through different forms, such as visual arts (i.e., painting, sculpture), creative movement (i.e., drama, dance) and words (i.e., poetry, memoirs). Art lends itself to remembering in a public forum, and is an effective form of public protest. This has been true in Aboriginal communities in Canada that have historically used art as part of their resistance to the violence that they have experienced and to the denial of the reality of those experiences. A recent (2013) exhibit, *Attesting Resistance*, is an online archive of artwork curated in cooperation with various Canadian artists that responds to an imbalance in the reporting by mainstream media of Aboriginal resistance. The organizers state that the "exhibition is dedicated to supporting the alternative perspectives and narratives, which may help locate and/or re-discover some of the strategies of resistance employed by Indigenous peoples (throughout history) that might otherwise go unnoticed if not documented or articulated through these symbolic artworks" (Aboriginal Curatorial Collective, 2013). Remembering through art is also important to refugees who have experienced violence. Satrapi, in the introduction to her graphic novel about a girl growing up in Iran, discusses the importance of the creation of art in telling a more complete version of the story and in remembering those who lost their lives through their acts of resisting violence. The artist plays an important role in repressive regimes — telling the stories that need to be told. Ying Ruocheng's memoir describes art as a form of protest in Communist China, with artists often finding themselves in prison or work camps as punishment for their active resistance (Ruocheng and Conceison, 1999). Hedrick Smith (1976) details the importance of artists in active resistance against the Soviet regime. Many artists found themselves in internment camps because of their unwillingness to conform. The regime prevented publication of their poetry and exhibition of art. The poetry of Osip Mandelstom, who perished in a Soviet death camp in 1938, was preserved by his wife Nadezhda Mandelstom, who parcelled pieces of his poetry out to friends to commit to memory when the risk of having paper copies of his poetry was too great. They would gather together and recite his poetry to each other (Smith, 1976, p. 538). Art therefore brings people together and encourages further action and resistance.

Art can also act as resistance in the face of oppression. Ezat Mossallanejed, a trauma counsellor and policy analyst who works with the Canadian Centre for Victims of Torture (CCVT) and is also a former political prisoner, discusses the importance of the creation of art as affirming life and ensuring survival while in prison. Though he would not consider himself an artist, during his time in prison, he found great joy in creating beautiful pieces of art from simple objects (Mossallanejed, 2006, pp. 139–140). Soudabeh Ardavan, a former political prisoner, describes the function of art-making in the documentary *From Scream to Scream*. In her story, she also reflects the creativity and resourcefulness of the human spirit in the face of adversity. She says:

> I drew [pictures] with tea in a one-person cell. This was my last period in prison. I hid the razor from a pencil sharpener in my Chador. I cut some of my hair. Coincidentally I found a toothpick on the floor of a one-person cell. I pulled a plastic thread from my sock. I put the hairs on this toothpick and closed it tightly. I sharpened the toothpick with the razor and made a brush. Most of my paintings were portraits. It made me calm. I felt like I was not alone. It was interesting that, unintentionally, all of the portraits were of the same people that I lived with during these years . . . (Bahrami, 2004).

Espinoza (2004) talks about the importance for refugees to move past a sense of helplessness to engage in advocacy work for social and political change as they are integrating in their country of exile (p. 56). The Chilean community and their supporters in Canada faced this challenge and formed a group to resist the effects of the political violence. "The Memory and Justice in the Americas Working Group" is a community-based civic education project with two central objectives: the organization of an international tribunal to denounce the human rights violations that continue to take place in Latin America, and the implementation of what the group has theorized as a pedagogical and collective healing process, through education workshops and activities aimed at recovering collective memory in exile and also finding creative ways to take political action (Espinoza, 2004, p. 57). The international tribunal gave the group a sense that they had experienced justice, an acknowledgment that what they had experienced was wrong. With that acknowledgement came a sense of freedom to both remember and forgive, to move on and to learn new ways of engaging with the world.

What happens as people come together and form a common purpose is what Judith Herman calls a **survivor mission** (1992, p. 207). Herman talks about the importance of the survivor mission and the role it can play in the recovery process. It is when survivors recognize either a political or religious dimension to their experience that their survivor mission is formed. She discusses how most survivors seek the resolution of their traumatic experiences through engaging with their personal lives. It is a significant minority who move beyond their own traumatic experience to engage a wider world through acts of resistance. When they choose to do this, they see the possibility of transforming their own experience by using it as the basis for social action. They recognize that, although there is no way to compensate for the atrocity that they experienced, it can be transformed by making it a gift to others (Herman, 1992, p. 207).

This is the kind of work referred to in the case study, when the facilitator invites the support group participants to think about how they want to use the art work that they have created.

In my own experience, working with groups of people who have experienced different forms of violence, it has been important to challenge people to make connections between their individual efforts at remembering and recovery and a greater purpose. Over the last seven years, I have been working in solidarity with a group of former political prisoners from Iran at the University of Toronto. This memory project, named Words, Colour, Movement, brought together people with similar experiences within the prison system of the Islamic Republic of Iran. Participants have met together on a regular basis over the last seven years to remember together using creative methods. This has involved storytelling, art and creating different forms of expression.

When I first started working with these women and men, and heard their stories of both resistance and the resulting torture and imprisonment, I was struck by the fact that art was a common theme in their stories. Within the Iranian prison system, art was used as a tool of resistance; it affirmed life (Mossallanejed, 2005). The whole state mechanism of prison functioned to cause people to forget who they were. Creating art reminded people of the most important essence of who they were and are. In this case, remembering was an important form of resistance. In her memoir, Shahla Talebi also discusses the important function of art and creation. It was a sustaining force — sustaining their autonomy as the prison system sought to control all aspects of their bodies and minds. They became linked to life outside of themselves as they used their hands and fingers to "transform worthless objects such as the bones from [their] food or pebbles from [their] yard" (Talebi, 2011, p. 193). She links the purpose of art to the sustaining of life and consciousness, and writes: "This is how so many prisoners became artists in prison. In prison, art comes into existence, not so much for its aesthetic quality but for its existential purpose" (Talebi, 2011, p. 194). She suggests that those who were able to create were able to challenge destructive forces, restoring love and resilience. In the process, people begin to feel like themselves again (Talebi, 2011, p. 195).

Over the course of the Words, Colour, Movement project, I have seen a transformation in many of the participants. They moved from places of frustration at the continued oppression of the Islamic Republic of Iran, from places of fear of what might happen to them as they remembered the violence that they had experienced in the prison system, to a place where they recognized that change was possible, in themselves and in the world.

## Case Study 17.3: Francisca, Part Three

As Francisca continued to attend the support group at the community organization, she started to notice changes in herself. She hadn't felt like herself in such a long time and she had felt so alone since leaving her home. As she worked covering matte board with Plasticine, she created images of the world that she had left behind. She took the pictures home and hung them in her apartment. She was also beginning to develop friendships with some of the other women in the group. Most days after the group was finished, she and her friend, Hawa, from North Africa went out to drink tea at a local shop. In the beginning, they talked about their families, their homes, and eventually they began to talk about some of the violence that they had experienced. Hawa was a poet and wrote about her experiences in both her own language and in English. When it came time to present their work at the exhibit, Hawa prepared some of her poems and Francisca brought her Plasticine pictures from home so they could be added to the exhibit. It was a night full of expression. Francisca really felt like she was part of a community for the first time in many years.

### Acts of Testimony and the Witness

The process of creating art and then presenting artwork to others is an important step. It can also be a challenging one. Presenting in a public way means identifying yourself as someone who has experienced violence. However, Elizabeth Jelin suggests that, at the level of remembering violent events, particularly those inflicted by the state, members of the group must collectively overcome the challenges of silence, must be able to simultaneously distance themselves from the past and promote active debate, "rethinking the relationship between memory and politics and memory and justice" (Jelin, 2003, p. 12). She discusses the importance of both the testimony given by the survivors who witnessed the violence and also the testimony of those on whose behalf the survivor is narrating the stories of violence and survival (Jelin, 2003, p. 78).

For people like Hawa, described in Part 3 of the case study, talking about the violence that they have experienced is important. The poem that is included in this chapter is an example of an expression of the violence of the immigration process. Sharing a poem like this with others opens up the possibility of them becoming aware of the experience of isolation that immigrants and refugees often face.

Literature on **memorialization**, representation of a person or an event for the purpose of remembering, discusses the importance of an audience in bearing witness to experiences of atrocities. The performance of public remembering can have a transformative effect on both those sharing their stories and those bearing witness to the acts of atrocity. Sharing the experience of violence in a public setting connects those experiences to the continuum of violence as well as to the continuum of resistance (Caruth 1995, p. 117). Exhibits like the one held by the community organization in the case study provide an opportunity for experiences that had previously been invisible to be made visible.

As people find outlets like the art workshop or a support group to tell their stories, they bear witness to each other's stories. Facilitators support the process and stand as witnesses to those experiences. When this happens, the strength of the story can grow, as stories need to be told and heard in order to gain strength and power. When the art is displayed or performed, the strength and power of the story continues to grow. Taylor discusses this process as an *acción*, a Spanish word that refers to "an act, an avant-garde happening and rally or political intervention such as street theatre protests" (2003, p. 14). The *acción* brings together "both the aesthetic and the political dimensions" of performance, making the stories "alive and compelling" to those who are participating in the performance as the audience (Taylor, 2003, pp. 13–14).

---

*The following is a poem that was written by Hawa Jibril and translated by Faduma A. Alim. It discusses the way that many refugees feel once they have arrived in Canada. What kinds of experiences and feelings does this poem reflect on?*

**Refugees in Canada**

Indeed Canadians welcome refugees
And do not let them starve
Yet one is always unsatisfied and broke
For the little we get
Hardly suffices our food and shelter.
They are strange people coming from everywhere
Never notice you or even greet you
Each one keeps to himself
Always hastily locking his door.
I feel isolated and sick with loneliness
Deprived from my beautiful Africa
And the land of my inspirations and songs.
I must be contented with the fate
That my God has reserved for me.
(quoted in Israelite et al., 1999)

---

## Conclusion

Violence in its many forms can make us forget who we are. As people working in the social service sector and community sector, we are uniquely positioned to work closely with people who have experienced violence. We need to remember that people have survived their experiences and are reaching out for help, evidence of incredible resourcefulness and resilience. As you work with immigrants and refugees and hear their stories, keep your eyes open for evidence of the tenacity of the human spirit and of what kinds of things allowed people to resist and gave them hope. As we have seen throughout this chapter, art can function as a tool to both engage people and to help them in their process of recovery. Art can give people an outlet to tangibly remember their experiences and also think about possibilities as they move forward. Art can also invite witnesses into the process, as people share their experiences through different forms. When this happens, the community of the people who have experienced violence expands, as does the number of people who are working to make positive change. Arts-informed approaches to working with people who have experienced violence have the potential to transform individuals, communities and, in the process, to transform our world.

# References

Aboriginal Curatorial Collective (2013). *Attesting Resistance.* Retrieved from http://www.aboriginal cu-ratorialcollective.org/.

ArtBridges (2014). ArtBridges website. Retrieved from www.artbridges.ca.

Bahrami, PanteA. (2008). *And in love I live* [DVD]. Germany: Anahita Productions. Available from http://www.panteabahrami.com/index.html.

Canadian Centre for Victims of Torture (n.d.). *Mental health.* Retrieved from http://ccvt.org/index.php/programs/mental-health.

Caruth, C. (1995). *Trauma: Explorations in memory.* Baltimore, MD: Johns Hopkins University Press.

Chansonneuve, D. (2005). *Reclaiming connections: Understanding residential school trauma among Aboriginal people.* Ottawa: Aboriginal Healing Foundation. Retrieved from www.ahf.ca/down-loads/healing-trauma-web-eng.pdf.

Espinoza, A. E. (2004). Trials and tribulations for social justice. In Meiners, E. (Ed.), *Public acts and desires: Curriculum and social change* (pp. 55–67). Florence, KY: Routledge.

Herman, J. (1997). *Trauma and recovery: The aftermath of violence — From domestic abuse to political terror.* New York: Basic Books.

Israelite, N. K., Herman, A., Alim, F. A., Mohamed, H. A., & Khan, Y. (1999, July 10). Settlement experiences of Somali women in Toronto. Presentation for the 7th International Congress of Somali Studies, York University, Toronto. Retrieved from http://ceris.metropolis.net/virtual%20library/other/is raelite2/israelite2.html.

Jelin, E. (2003). *State repression and the labors of memory.* Minneapolis, MN: University of Minnesota Press.

Kreisberg, S. (1992). *Transforming power: Domination, empowerment, and education.* Albany, NY: State University of New York Press.

Lederach, J. P., & Lederach, A. J. (2010). *When blood and bones cry out: Journeys through the sound-scape of healing and reconciliation.* New York: Oxford University Press.

Lira, E. (1997). Remembering: Passing back through the heart. In Pennebaker, J., Paez, D., & Rimé, B. (Eds.), *Collective memory of political events: Social psychological perspectives* (pp. 223–236). Mahwah, NJ: Lawrence Erlbaum.

Lopez, C.C. (2011). The struggle for wholeness: Addressing individual and collective trauma in violence-ridden societies. *EXPLORE: The Journal of Science and Healing, 7*(5), 300–313.

Malchiodi, C. (2014). Trauma-informed art therapy (TI-AT) and trauma-informed expressive arts therapy. Retrieved from http://www.cathymalchiodi.com/Trauma Informed Art Therapy.html.

McWhirter, E.H. (1991). Empowerment in counseling. *Journal of Counseling and Development, 69*(3), 222–227.

Montgomery, C. (2002). Role of dynamic group therapy in psychiatry. *Advances in Psychiatric Treatment, 8,* 34–41.

Mossallanejad, E. (2005). *Torture in the age of fear.* Hamilton, ON: Seraphim Editions.

Osborne, B. (2014). State violence, learning and the art of memory: A journey towards understanding resistance and community building in the Iranian diaspora. In Plumb, D. (Ed.), *Proceedings of the 33rd annual conference of the Canadian Association for the Study of Adult Education (CASAE),* pp. 181–184.

Partners in Education and Outreach (2007). *Peer support guidebook.* Retrieved from https://1in6.org/w p-content/uploads/2011/12/Peer-Support-Guidebook.pdf.

Patterson, C.H. (1978). Cross-cultural or intercultural psychotherapy. *International Journal for the Advancement of Counselling, 1*(3), 231–247.

Pearlman, L. A., & McKay, L. (2008). *Understanding and addressing vicarious trauma.* Pasadena, CA: Headington Institute.

Rogers, K. L., Leydesdorff, S., & Dawson, G. (Eds.). (1999). *Trauma and life stories: International perspectives.* New York: Routledge.

Ruocheng, Y., & Conceison, C. (2009). *Voices carry: Behind bars and backstage during China's revolution and reform.* Lanham, MD: Rowman & Littlefield.

Smith, H. (1976). *The Russians.* New York: Ballantine Books.

Satrapi, M. (2003). *The Complete Persepolis.* New York: Pantheon.

Swinomish Tribal Mental Health Project (2002). *A gathering of wisdoms: Tribal mental health: A cultural perspective* (2nd ed.). LaConner, WA: Swinomish Tribal Mental Health.

Talebi, S. (2011). *Ghosts of revolution: Rekindled memories of imprisonment in Iran.* Palo Alto, CA: Stanford University Press.

Taylor, D. (2003). *The archive and the repertoire: Performing cultural memory in the Americas.* Durham, NC: Duke University Press.

Tomasulo, D. J. (2010, December 12). What is the difference between individual and group therapy? *The Healing Crowd: Psychology Today.* Retrieved from http://www.psychologytoday.com/blog/the-healing-crowd/201012/what-is-the-difference-between-individual-and-group-therapy.

White, W. I. (2007). Ethical guidelines for the delivery of peer-based recovery groups. *Counselling 4*(1), 231–272.

Wiesel, E. (1996). Longing for home. In Rouner, L. S. (Ed.), *The longing for home.* Notre Dame, IN: University of Notre Dame Press.

Wu, J., & Livescu, S. (2011). Introduction. In Wu, J. & Livescu, S. (Eds.). *Human rights, suffering, and aesthetics in political prison literature* (pp. 1–16). Toronto: Lexington Books.

Zur, J. (1999). Remembering and forgetting: Guatemalan war-widows' forbidden memories. In Rogers, K. L., Leyersdorf, S., & Dawson, G. (Eds.), *Trauma and life stories: International perspectives* (pp. 45–59). New York: Routledge.

# Contributors

**Angie Arora**, M.S.W., R.S.W., is an activist and educator in the areas of violence against women, issues affecting immigrant and refugee communities, and pet loss bereavement. She has worked with organizations including Springtide Resources, Woman Abuse Council of Toronto, the Ontario Ministry of the Attorney General, the Council of Agencies Serving South Asians, Herizon House and Humber College. She is currently a professor with Seneca College's Social Service Worker — Immigrants and Refugees Program, and operates her private practice, New Wave Consulting, which provides a range of services to the non-profit sector. Angie practices from anti-oppressive and critical approaches to social work. She holds a Masters of Social Work, and also completed the Bereavement Education certificate program, an advanced program dealing with issues of bereavement, trauma and loss. Angie is a Certified Compassion Fatigue Specialist, trained through the Traumatology Institute. She is the author of chapters in *Out of the Shadows: Woman Abuse in Ethnic, Aboriginal and Refugee Communities* and in *Unsettled Settlers: Barriers to Integration.*

**Annette Bailey** is an assistant professor with the Daphne Cockwell School of Nursing at Ryerson University in Toronto. Her research interests are in trauma, resilience, grief and violent loss. Much of her current work is focused on understanding the grief and trauma experiences of adults and youth survivors of gun violence. She has published and disseminated work in this area locally and internationally. Annette recently collaborated with several practitioners and experts from diverse disciplines across 20 countries to contribute to the development of the book, *Gun Violence, Disability and Recovery,* which explores trauma, rehabilitation, and economic challenges faced by survivors of gun violence across diverse countries.

**Rebecca Beaulne-Stuebing** (Naawakwe giizhigookwe) is a Métis Anishinabe woman of the eagle clan. She currently works with Shingwauk Kinoomaage Gamig, an Anishinabe culture-based institute operating in partnership with Algoma University in Sault Ste. Marie. Rebecca is a First Degree Midewiwin woman of the Three Fires Society. She holds a Masters of Education in Language, Culture and Teaching from York University.

**Jennifer Clarke** is an assistant professor in the School of Social Work at Ryerson University. She teaches courses in advanced social work practice and transformative social work at both the graduate and undergraduate levels. Her most recent research focuses on the organizational framework for safety in Ontario public schools and the impact on marginalized students, particularly Black males. Her research interests also include anti-racism and anti-oppression practices in social service agencies. Jennifer's interest in these areas is informed by her years of work with marginalized youth, families and communities in the areas of school exclusion, child welfare, immigration and settlement and grief and bereavement. She has presented her research in these areas at local and international conferences and has authored several journal articles and book chapters. Jennifer is a Ph.D. candidate in the Faculty of Education at York University.

**Janet Cleveland,** Ph.D., is a psychologist, anthropologist and legal scholar. Since 2003, she has conducted research on the impact of Canada's policies towards refugee claimants on their health and human rights. In particular, she has studied the role of psychological reports in the context of refugee status determination procedures; the impact of administrative detention on refugee claimants' psychological health; and, most recently, the impact of changes to the Interim Federal Health Program on refugee claimants' access to health care.

**Neil Cruickshank** is assistant professor of Political Science at Algoma University, and faculty associate, Centre for European Studies, Carleton University. He earned his Ph.D. in International Relations from St Andrews University, Scotland, and has published on European Roma, the European Court of Human Rights, secessionist movements and discourse, and Europeanization. Recent articles appear in the *British Journal of Canadian Studies* (with Nadia Verrelli) and *L'Europe en Formation: Journal of Studies on European Integration and Federalism.* He has contributed chapters to the edited volumes *From Mediation to Nation-Building: Third Parties and the Management of Communal Conflict* (Lexington Press) and *The Democratic Dilemma: Reforming Canada's Supreme Court* (McGill-Queen's University Press).

**Tania Das Gupta** is full professor in the Department of Equity Studies at York University. She teaches, researches and publishes about race, gender and class issues in the workplace and in the labour market; migrant and immigrant women; "twice-migrated" South Asians in Canada and their transnational living; and community development, labour movements and activism in racialized communities. Her publications include *Real Nurses and Others, Racism and Paid Work* and numerous book chapters and journal articles.

**Laïla Demirdache** has been working since 2002 as a staff lawyer with Community Legal Services (CLS) in Ottawa. She has taught immigration and refugee law at the Faculty of Common Law, University of Ottawa. Prior to her work at CLS,

Laïla worked as a protection delegate in Ethiopia with the International Committee of the Red Cross, where she was in charge of visiting persons in detention as well as monitoring their judicial guarantees. Laïla is a member of the following committees: the RPD/RAD Working Group of the Canadian Association of Refugee Lawyers; the Canadian Council for Refugees' Legal Affairs Committee; the Ottawa Legal Aid Area Committee; and the Ottawa Immigration Conference Organizing Committee. She is also part of a legal team representing Amnesty International Canada (English) before the Supreme Court of Canada. In recent years, Laïla has been acting as a designated representative for minors and persons with mental disabilities.

**Jonathan Dewar** is the director of the Shingwauk Residential Schools Centre and special advisor to the president at Algoma University. From 2007 to 2012 he served as director of research and evaluation at the Aboriginal Healing Foundation and he is a past director of the Métis Centre at the National Aboriginal Health Organization. Jonathan is of mixed heritage, descended from Huron-Wendat, Scottish and French-Canadian grandparents with an academic background in Aboriginal literatures and drama (M.A. in Literature and Creative Writing) and Canadian and Indigenous Studies, with focuses on identity, (re)connection to culture and community, Indian Residential Schools and healing, and truth and reconciliation. A former SSHRC doctoral fellow, Jonathan is completing a doctorate in Canadian Studies at Carleton University. His research explores the role of art and artist in truth, healing, and reconciliation. Jonathan also served as the founding executive director of the Iqaluit, Nunavut-based Qaggiq Theatre Company from its inception in 2002 to 2006. While in Nunavut, Jonathan also served in senior roles with the Office of the Languages Commissioner of Nunavut and the Intergovernmental Affairs and Inuit Relations unit of Indian and Northern Affairs Canada.

**Rubaiyat Karim** holds a B.Sc. in Business Administration and Psychology. She commenced her career at NOW Legal Defense and Education Fund in Washington, D.C., as a policy intern, where she tracked and lobbied congressional staff on immigration legislation. Rubaiyat has conducted extensive research and advocacy on violence directed towards the South Asian, Muslim and Arab communities in the post 9-11 era and contributed a chapter to *Voices of Pain, Voices of Hope*. She is currently working as a program manager for South Asian Network, York Region Violence against Women Coordinating Committee and Sandgate Women's Shelter of York Region, Inc. to prevent and intervene in the areas of domestic violence, child abuse, sexual assault and human trafficking. She is currently responsible for facilitating the development, implementation and evaluation of a Family Justice Centre in partnership with over 25 partner agencies. Rubaiyat is a certified solution-focused counsellor, trained through the Faculty of Social Work, University of Toronto.

**Doug Gruner** is an assistant professor in the Department of Family Medicine at the University of Ottawa and practices both emergency and family medicine. He worked with refugees in East Timor in 2000 as a member of the ICRC (International Committee of the Red Cross). He teaches family medicine at the Bruyere Family Health team as well as doing research in refugee health. Most recently he has helped to create an innovative e-learning tool — now being used at several Canadian universities — to introduce medical students to the basic concepts of global and refugee health. He was instrumental in 2006 in creating the Champlain Immigrant Health Network, whose main goal is to reduce access barriers for the most vulnerable refugees through a provider network, and he was the medical coordinator of the network until 2010. He is one of the founding members of CDRC (Canadian Doctors for Refugee Care).

**Sheila Gruner** has worked for a number of years with Indigenous, ethno-territorial, labour, gender and human rights movements and organizations in Canada and Latin America. She has produced academic and audio-visual work on development, conflict, displacement and social movements, including a chapter for a book of the Ethics of Development Induced Displacement Project (Centre for Refugee Studies, York University) called *Development's Displacements: Ecologies, Economies and Cultures at Risk* (2007). She has (co)authored reports and journal articles for the *Paquataskamik Project* (2005–2012), a community-based research initiative of Fort Albany First Nation. Her recent institutional ethnography analysis of land use planning, environmental protection and development policy centered on examining institutional "text processes" related to displacement and dispossession in the Treaty 9 region of Northern Ontario. Sheila is an associate professor in Community Economic and Social Development (CESD), Algoma University, holding a Masters in Environmental Studies with a Certificate in Refugee Studies (York University), and a Ph.D. in Adult Education and Community Development (OISE/University of Toronto).

**Ezat Mossallanejad** holds a Ph.D. in Political Economy. A survivor of torture in Iran, he escaped to Canada in 1985. In Montreal, he was a founding member of the Iranian Cultural and Community Centre, Institut Éducatif pour les Jeunes Iraniens, and the Montreal Democratic Forum. In Toronto, he worked as a youth counsellor with St. Christopher House and as a refugee policy analyst and, later, as the director of the Jesuit Refugee Service – Canada. At present, he serves as counsellor and policy analyst with the Canadian Centre for Victims of Torture. He has served as a board member of Inter-Church Committee for Refugees, Refugee Update, Culturelink, and the Canadian Centre for International Justice. He has presented as a guest lecturer in various universities and has taught at Seneca College. He is the author of four books in Persian and three in English. In his mission for protection of survivors, he has travelled to the United States, Mexico, Rwanda, Switzerland, Austria, Australia, Nigeria, Thailand, Uganda, India and Cyprus.

**Bethany J. Osborne** holds a Ph.D. in Adult Education and Community Development from the Ontario Institute for Studies in Education of the University of Toronto. Her research focuses on violence and learning; memory, trauma and resistance and the arts and resistance with a particular focus on working with refugees. Her background is in community development using arts-based approaches to community engagement. She facilitates art workshops and performances for and with diverse communities. Bethany has taught at Seneca College in the Social Service Worker — Immigrant and Refugee Program since 2009.

**Sepehr Pashang** is a Ph.D. candidate at the University of Waterloo. His research interests lie in cross-sector innovations and strategic alliances between NGOs, government, corporations, and academic institutions. Sepehr's interest in environmentally induced migration stems from field visits in North America, northwestern Africa, the Middle East, and Central America. During these visits he worked with local community members facing drought, floods, mudslides, deforestation, food insecurity, and various health risks. It became evident to him that vulnerability and insecurity among marginalized communities was increasing, making way for forced displacement and migration. In addition to this, Sepehr founded a social enterprise (sustaidability.org) in 2004. His interdisciplinary experience positions him to work towards bridging the gaps between fields such as community development, business sustainability, social enterprise, and innovation. On a professional level, Sepehr held leadership positions in several consulting firms and financial institutions. He has received numerous awards for his work in sustainability, social entrepreneurship, and photography.

**Soheila Pashang** is an academic coordinator and a professor in Seneca College's Social Service Worker – Immigrants and Refugees program. In 2011, she edited *Unsettled Settlers: Barriers to Integration*, and has published poetry on social justice issues in various international anthologies. Soheila has worked as a social worker and therapist for over 20 years with immigrants, refugees and non-status persons at various community-based organizations. She has been highly involved in social justice and advocacy roles, and has initiated a number of networks and programs in Toronto. Her expertise is in the area of displacement and forced migration, trauma, refugee mental health, gender violence, poverty and anti-racist and anti-oppressive education. Her Ph.D. research focuses on the lived conditions of non-status women in Canada. In the past four years Soheila has engaged in national and international work as a subject matter expert (SME) on issues of violence against women, mental health and trauma.

**Donald E. Payne** graduated from the University of Toronto Medical School in 1963. He was certified as a specialist in psychiatry by the Royal College of Physicians and Surgeons of Canada in 1971. He is presently in private practice of psychiatry in Toronto. Since 1979, he has performed psychiatric assessments and treatment on more than 1,500 victims of torture and/or war. He has testified at refugee determination hearings, at the Ontario Supreme Court and the Canada Federal Court. He has provided in-service training to members of the Immigration and Refugee Board, and has made presentations and written articles regarding torture and treatment of torture victims. He provided testimony on torture at the Commission of Inquiry into the Actions of Canadian Officials in Relation to Mahar Arar. He has been a member of the board of directors of the Canadian Centre for Victims of Torture in Toronto. He was one of two elected North American members on the Council of the International Rehabilitation Council for Torture Victims (IRCT) based in Denmark, from 2003 through 2006.

**Kevin Pottie** is an associate professor and practicing physician at the Departments of Family Medicine and Epidemiology and Community Medicine and principal scientist at the Institute of Population Health, University of Ottawa. He is a member of the Canadian Task Force on Preventive Health Care and the GRADE Methods Working Group. He published the Canadian Immigrant Health Guidelines (CMAJ 2011), an internationally unique evidence-based series covering intestinal parasites, malaria, TB, post-traumatic stress disorder, child maltreatment, and other topics relevant for primary care. He has published over 100 peer-reviewed articles and chapters, including "Migrant Health" in Oxford Bibliographies Online.

**Bukola Salami** is an assistant professor at the Faculty of Nursing, University of Alberta. She holds a Ph.D. in nursing from the University of Toronto. Bukola's program of research seeks to support the integration of internationally educated nurses in Canada. Her main area of research focuses on the links between immigration policies and health policies and practices. Bukola's doctoral research explored the migration of nurses to Canada through the Live-in Caregiver Program. It revealed issues of abuse and exploitation of migrant live-in caregivers, as well as the pain experienced by these mothers because of prolonged separation from their children. Findings in this area of research will inform immigration policies and health policies and services for permanent and temporary immigrants in Canada.

**Sharifa Sharif** teaches with Seneca College's Social Service Worker – Immigrants and Refugees program and as an ESL teacher with Centennial College. She obtained her doctorate in education policy at the University of Illinois. She is an independent consultant/expert on Afghanistan culture and society, mainly in the area of women, culture and development, as well as on adult education, journalism and politics in Kabul, Canada, India and Prague. She has worked with President Karzai as his advisor on international affairs and media advisor to his chief of staff in Kabul. Her published work includes her memoir, *On The Edge of Being: An Afghan Woman's Journey*, and two collections of short stories, one in Dari, *The Guilty Judges of Stoning*, and another in Pashto, *Window*. In the second collection, she relied on feminist narrative through an inner conscious monologue of a woman pulled between past and future. Her recent academic contributions include a book chapter on child marriage.

**Sajedeh Zahrai** holds a Ph.D. from the Factor-Inwentash Faculty of Social Work, University of Toronto. Her passion and research interests revolve around social determinants of immigrant and refugee mental health and health equity for racialized populations. Sajadeh's dissertation research focused on the impact of the "war on terror" on Arab Iraqi refugee women in Toronto. She has 15 years of experience working as a social worker in the mental health field. Since 1999, she has been working in various capacities at the Centre for Addiction and Mental Health (CAMH). For the past 10 years, her work at CAMH has involved research, partnership, program, and community development focused on addressing gaps in services for diverse individuals with mental health and addictions issues.

# Index